Metal

by

Tutorials

By Caroline Begbie & Marius Horga

Metal by Tutorials

By Caroline Begbie & Marius Horga

Copyright ©2019 Razeware LLC.

Notice of Rights

Notice of Liability

Trademarks

ISBN: 978-1-942878-98-8

Table of Contents

About the Cover

The comb jellyfish — or Ctenophora — has been swimming in both shallow and deep waters for nearly 500 million years.

While just as seemingly alien as other jelly species, comb jellies are especially unusual, boasting a completely transparent body with groups of cilia — or "combs" — arranged in rows along the axis of the jelly's body. While appearing to be a bioluminescent species, these jellies only *appear* to glow as their moving cilia scatter the light, causing a glowing rainbow-like effect.

Perhaps most incredibly — and much like Metal's own low-level, low-overhead features — these jellies' bodies use only what they need to live and produce their amazing shading effects: They have no stomach, intestines or lungs, and they are known to have one of the most basic nervous systems of any multicellular animal on the planet.

You can learn more about comb jellies and see them in action in this video clip: https://www.youtube.com/watch?v=sTFskdKVNs4

Dedications

"To Warren Moore, who first made it possible for me to learn Metal, to my wonderful children Robin and Kayla, and to my best friends who patiently waited for me to indulge my dream."

— *Caroline Begbie*

"To my wife, Adina, and my son, Victor Nicholas, without whose patience, support and understanding I could not have made it. To Warren Moore who first whet my appetite for Metal, offered his advice when needed and motivated me to get involved with Metal too. To Chris Wood who taught me that most of the times all you need to render is a ray, a camera and a few distance fields. To Simon Gladman whose amazing work with compute kernels inspired me to write more about particles and fluid dynamics. To Jeff Biggus who keeps the GPU programming community in Chicago alive. Our daily conversations motivate me to stay hungry for more. To everyone else who believes in me. A huge Thanks to all of you!"

— *Marius Horga*

About the Authors

Caroline Begbie is a co-author of this book. Caroline is an indie iOS developer. When she's not developing, she's playing around with 2D and 3D animation software, or learning Arduino and electronics. She has previously taught the elderly how to use their computers, done marionette shows for pre-schools, and created accounting and stock control systems for mining companies.

Marius Horga is a co-author of this book. Marius is an iOS developer and Metal API blogger. He is also a computer scientist. He has more than a decade of experience with systems, support, integration and development. You can often see him on Twitter talking about Metal, GPGPU, games and 3D graphics. When he's away from computers, he enjoys music, biking or stargazing.

About the Editors

Adrian Strahan is the technical editor of this book. Adrian is a freelance iOS developer and Project Manager living in the South West of England. He's worked on iPhone and iPad apps since 2010 (iOS3) and specializes in mobile- and web-based application development.

Tammy Coron is the final pass editor of this book. Tammy is an independent creative professional and the host of Roundabout: Creative Chaos. She's also the founder of Just Write Code. Find out more at tammycoron.com.

About the Artist

 **Vicki Wenderlich** is the designer and artist of the cover of this book. She is Ray's wife and business partner. She is a digital artist who creates illustrations, game art and a lot of other art or design work for the tutorials and books on raywenderlich.com. When she's not making art, she loves hiking, a good glass of wine and attempting to create the perfect cheese plate.

What You Need

To follow along with the tutorials in this book, you need the following:

- A Metal-capable Mac running macOS Catalina 10.15 or later. All Macs built since 2012 should run Metal, although not all of them will be able to run the most recent features in Metal 2. Nvidia GPUs will have issues, in some cases serious, as drivers have not been updated since macOS High Sierra.

- Xcode 11.0 or later.

- [optional] A Metal-capable iPhone or iPad running iOS 13 or later. Any iOS device running the A7 chip or later will run Metal. The latest features, such as tile shading and imageblocks, will only run on the A11 (or later) chipset. The projects will build and run on macOS, and most of them will run on the iOS Simulator, so using an iOS device is optional. If you wish to make an iOS game, the game engine you build while reading this book will have an iOS target as well. The Metal API, with a few exceptions, works the same on macOS as it does on iOS so it won't be difficult to add an iOS target to your project later on.

Book License

By purchasing *Metal by Tutorials*, you have the following license:

- You are allowed to use and/or modify the source code in *Metal by Tutorials* in as many apps as you want, with no attribution required.

- You are allowed to use and/or modify all art, images and designs that are included in *Metal by Tutorials* in as many apps as you want, but must include this attribution line somewhere inside your app: "Artwork/images/designs: from *Metal by Tutorials*, available at www.raywenderlich.com".

- The source code included in *Metal by Tutorials* is for your personal use only. You are NOT allowed to distribute or sell the source code in *Metal by Tutorials* without prior authorization.

- This book is for your personal use only. You are NOT allowed to sell this book without prior authorization, or distribute it to friends, coworkers or students; they would need to purchase their own copies.

Book Source Code & Forums

If you bought the digital edition

The digital edition of this book comes with the source code for the starter and completed projects for each chapter. These resources are included with the digital edition you downloaded from https://store.raywenderlich.com.

If you bought the print version

You can get the source code for the print edition of the book here:

- https://store.raywenderlich.com/products/metal-by-tutorials-source-code

Forums

We've also set up an official forum for the book at forums.raywenderlich.com.This is a great place to ask questions about the book or to submit any errors you may find.

Digital book editions

We have a digital edition of this book available in both ePUB and PDF, which can be handy if you want a soft copy to take with you, or you want to quickly search for a specific term within the book.

Buying the digital edition version of the book also has a few extra benefits: free updates each time we update the book, access to older versions of the book, and you can download the digital editions from anywhere, at anytime.

Visit our book store page here:

- https://store.raywenderlich.com/products/metal-by-tutorials.

And if you purchased the print version of this book, you're eligible to upgrade to the digital editions at a significant discount! Simply email support@razeware.com with your receipt for the physical copy and we'll get you set up with the discounted digital edition version of the book.

Introduction

Welcome to *Metal by Tutorials*!

Metal is a unified, low-level, low-overhead application programming interface (API) for the graphics processing unit, or GPU. It's unified because it applies to both 3D graphics and data-parallel computation paradigms. Metal is a low-level API because it provides programmers near-direct access to the GPU. Finally, Metal is a low-overhead API because it reduces the runtime cost by multi-threading and pre-compiling of resources.

But beyond the technical definition, Metal is the most appropriate way to use the GPU's parallel processing power to visualize data or solve numerical challenges. It's also tailored to be used for machine learning, image/video processing or, as this book describes, graphics rendering.

About this book

This book introduces you to low-level graphics programming in Metal — Apple's framework for programming on the graphics processing unit (GPU). As you progress through this book, you'll learn many of the fundamentals that go into making a game engine and gradually put together your own engine. Once your game engine is complete, you'll be able to put together 3D scenes and program your own simple 3D games. Because you'll have built your 3D game engine from scratch, you'll be able to customize every aspect of what you see on your screen.

How did Metal come to life?

Historically, you had two choices to take advantage of the power of the GPU: OpenGL and the Windows-only DirectX. In 2013, the GPU vendor AMD announced the Mantle project in an effort to revamp GPU APIs and come up with an alternative to Direct3D (which is part of DirectX) and OpenGL. AMD were the first to create a true low-overhead API for low-level access to the GPU. Mantle promised to be able to generate up to 9 times more draw calls (the number of objects drawn to the screen) than similar APIs and also introduced asynchronous command queues so that graphics and compute workloads could be run in parallel. Unfortunately, the project was terminated before it could become a mainstream API.

Metal was announced at the Worldwide Developers Conference (WWDC) on June 2, 2014 and was initially made available only on A7 or newer GPUs. Apple created a new language to program the GPU directly via shader functions. This is the **Metal Shading Language** (MSL) based on the C++11 specification. A year later at WWDC 2015, Apple announced two Metal sub-frameworks: **MetalKit** and **Metal Performance Shaders** (MPS). In 2018, MPS made a spectacular debut as a Ray Tracing accelerator.

The API has continued to evolve, and WWDC 2017 introduced an exciting new version of the API: **Metal 2**. Metal 2 adds support for Virtual Reality (VR), Augmented Reality (AR) and accelerated machine learning (ML), among many new features. Fall 2017 brought new updates to Metal including image blocks, tile shading and threadgroup sharing, which are available on iOS devices powered by the A11 Bionic chip, which comes with the first GPU ever designed in-house by Apple. MSL was also updated to version 2.0 in Fall 2017 and is now based on the C++14 specification.

Why would you use Metal?

Metal is a top-notch graphics API. That means Metal can empower graphics pipelines and, more specifically, game engines such as the following:

- **Unity and Unreal Engine**: The two leading cross-platform game engines today are ideal for game programmers who target a range of console, desktop and mobile devices. However, these engines haven't always kept pace with new features in Metal. For example, Unity announced that tessellation on iOS was to be released in 2018, despite it being demonstrated live at WWDC 2016. If you to use cutting-edge Metal developments, you can't always depend on third-party engines.

- **The Witness**: This award-winning puzzle game has a custom engine that runs on top of Metal. By taking advantage of Metal, the iPad version is every bit as stunning as the desktop version and is highly recommended for puzzle game fans.

- **Many Others**: From notable game titles such as *Hitman*, *BioShock*, *Deus Ex*, *Mafia*, *Starcraft*, *World of Warcraft*, *Fortnite*, *Unreal Tournament*, *Batman* and even the beloved *Minecraft*.

But Metal isn't limited to the world of gaming. There are many apps that benefit from GPU acceleration for image and video processing:

- **Procreate**: An app for sketching, painting and illustrating. Since converting to Metal, it runs four times faster than it did before.

- **Astropad**: An app for drawing using Apple Pencil. The most notable improvements since adding Metal show a 30% increase over wifi and two times faster overall performance on most Macs.

- **Pixelmator**: A Metal-based app that provides image distortion tools. In fact, they were able to implement a new painting engine and dynamic paint blending technology powered by Metal 2.

- **Affinity Photo**: A recent release, available on the iPad. According to the developer Serif, "Using Metal allows users to work easily on large, super high-resolution photographs, or complex compositions with potentially thousands of layers."

Metal, and in particular, the MPS sub-framework, is incredibly useful in the realm of machine and deep learning on convolutional neural networks. Apple presented a practical machine learning application at WWDC 2016 that demonstrated the power of CNNs in high-precision image recognition.

When should you use Metal?

GPUs belong to a special class of computation that Flynn's taxonomy terms Single Instruction Multiple Data (SIMD). Simply, GPUs are processors that are optimized for throughput (how much data can be processed in one unit of time), while CPUs are optimized for latency (how much time it takes a single unit of data to be processed). Most programs execute serially: they receive input, process it, provide output and then the cycle repeats.

Those cycles sometimes perform computationally-intensive tasks, such as large matrix multiplication, which would take CPUs a lot of time process serially, even in a multithreaded manner on a handful of cores.

In contrast, GPUs have hundreds or even thousands of cores which are smaller and have less memory than CPU cores, but perform fast parallel mathematical calculations.

Choose Metal when:

• You want to render 3D models as efficiently as possible.

• You want your game to have its own unique style, perhaps with custom lighting and shading.

• You will be performing intensive data processes, such as calculating and changing the color of each pixel on the screen every frame, as you would when processing images and video.

• You have large numerical problems, such as scientific simulations, that you can partition into independent sub-problems to be processed in parallel.

• You need to process multiple large datasets in parallel, such as when you train models for deep learning.

Who this book is for

This book is for intermediate Swift developers interested in learning 3D graphics or gaining a deeper understanding of how game engines work. If you don't know Swift, you can still follow along, as all the code instructions are included in the book. You'll gain general graphics knowledge, but it would be less confusing if you cover Swift basics first. We recommend the *Swift Apprentice* book, available from our store:

https://store.raywenderlich.com/products/swift-apprentice

A smattering of C++ knowledge would be useful too. The Metal Shader Language that you'll use when writing GPU shader functions is based on C++. But, again, all the code you'll need is included in the book.

How to read this book

If you're a beginner to iOS/macOS development or Metal, you should read this book from cover to cover.

If you're an advanced developer, or already have experience with Metal, you can skip from chapter to chapter or use this book as a reference.

Section I: The Player

It takes a wealth of knowledge to render a simple triangle on the screen or animate game characters. This section will guide you through the necessary basics of vertex wrangling, lighting, textures and character animation; and if you're worried about the math, don't be! Although computer graphics is highly math-intensive, each chapter explains everything you need, and you'll get experience creating and rendering models.

Specifically, you'll learn:

- **Chapter 1: Hello Metal!**: This is a quick start overview to Metal. Create a render of a red ball in a playground that touches on almost everything you need to render a model. Metal is a complex API, so don't worry if everything isn't immediately crystal clear. Later chapters will expand on each concept introduced here.

- **Chapter 2: 3D Models**: 3D assets are what makes your game stand out from all the others. Whether your game style is simple cuboids or detailed animated zombies, you should understand how 3D models are put together. Explore Blender and see how to reshape models by moving vertices, and recolor them by adding materials.

- **Chapter 3: The Rendering Pipeline**: Find out how the GPU works and discover all the stages in the graphics pipeline. You'll find out what parts of the pipeline are hard-wired and what parts you can control with shader functions.

- **Chapter 4: Coordinate Spaces**: An understanding of vectors and matrices is critical to positioning all scenery and characters in your game. Take your game into the third dimension with projection matrices.

- **Chapter 5: Lighting Fundamentals**: The Phong lighting model is an easy entry into understanding how you can add artistic lighting effects. Color each individual pixel of your rendered models by exploring light and shade.

- **Chapter 6: Textures**: Make your models more detailed by wrapping them in a texture. These textures can be realistic using photo imagery, or hand-painted in a paint program. Once you have a few hundred models in your game with thousands of textures, you'll appreciate what the asset catalog can do for you.

- **Chapter 7: Maps and Materials**: Games use low-poly models, but that doesn't mean they can't have fine detail. You can scratch and dent your models with texture maps, or give them shiny surfaces with material settings.

- **Chapter 8: Character Animation**: Find out how to animate your player and import animations from Blender and other 3D apps.

Chapter 1: Hello, Metal!

By Caroline Begbie & Marius Horga

You've been formally introduced to Metal and discovered its history and why you should use it. Now you're going to to try it out for yourself in a Swift playground. To get started, you're going to render this sphere on the screen:

It may not look exciting, but this is a great starting point because it lets you touch on almost every part of the rendering process. But before you get started, it's important to understand the terms **rendering** and **frames**.

What is rendering?

The Oxford Dictionary describes computer rendering as:

> The processing of an outline image using color and shading to make it appear solid and three-dimensional.

There are many ways to render a 3D image, but most start with a model built in a modeling app such as Blender or Maya. Take, for example, this train model that was built in Blender:

This model, like all other models, is made up of **vertices**. A vertex refers to a point in three dimensional space where two or more lines, curves or edges of a geometrical shape meet, such as the corners of a cube. The number of vertices in a model may vary from a handful, as in a cube, to thousands or even millions in more complex models. A 3D renderer will read in these vertices using *model loader code*, which parses the list of vertices. The renderer then passes the vertices to the GPU, where shader functions process the vertices to create the final image or texture to be sent back to the CPU and displayed on the screen.

The following render uses the 3D train model and some different shading techniques to make it appear as if the train were made of shiny copper:

The entire process from importing a model's vertices to generating the final image on your screen, is commonly known as a *rendering pipeline*. The rendering pipeline is a list of commands sent to the GPU, along with resources (vertices, materials and lights) that make up the final image.

The pipeline includes programmable and non-programmable functions; the former, known as **vertex functions** and **fragment functions**, are where you can manually influence the final look of your rendered models. You will learn more about each later in the book.

What is a frame?

A game wouldn't be much fun if it simply rendered a single still image. Moving a character around the screen in a fluid manner requires the GPU to render a still image roughly 60 times a second.

Each still image is known as a **frame** and the speed at which the images appear is called the **frame rate**.

When your favorite game appears to stutter, it's usually because of a decrease in the frame rate, especially if there's an excessive amount of background processing eating away at the GPU.

When designing a game, it's important to balance the result you want with what the hardware can deliver.

While it might be cool to add real-time shadows, water reflections and millions of blades of animated grass — all of which you'll learn how to do in this book — finding the right balance between what is possible and what the GPU can process in 1/60th of a second can be tough.

Your first Metal app

In your first Metal app, the shape you'll be rendering will look more like a flat circle than a 3D sphere. That's because your first model will not include any perspective or shading; however, its vertex mesh contains the full three-dimensional information.

The process of Metal rendering is much the same no matter the size and complexity of your app, and you'll become very familiar with the following sequence of drawing your models on the screen:

You may initially feel a little overwhelmed by the number of steps Metal requires, but rest assured that you'll always perform these steps in the same sequence, and they'll gradually become second nature.

This chapter won't go into detail on every step, but as you progress through the book, you'll get more information as you need it. For now, concentrate on getting your first Metal app running.

Getting started

Start Xcode and create a new playground by selecting **File ▸ New ▸ Playground...** from the main menu. When prompted for a template, choose **macOS Blank**.

Name the playground **Chapter1** and click **Create**. Next, delete everything in the playground.

The view

Now that you have a playground, you'll create a view to render into. Import the two main frameworks that you'll be using:

```
import PlaygroundSupport
import MetalKit
```

PlaygroundSupport lets you see live views in the assistant editor, and MetalKit is a framework that makes using Metal easier. MetalKit has a customized view named MTKView and many convenience methods for loading textures, working with Metal buffers and interfacing with another useful framework: **Model I/O**, which you'll learn about later.

Check for a suitable GPU by creating a device:

```
guard let device = MTLCreateSystemDefaultDevice() else {
  fatalError("GPU is not supported")
}
```

> **Note**: Are you getting an error? If you accidentally created an iOS playground instead of a macOS playground, you'll get a fatal error, as the iOS simulator is not supported.

Set up the view:

```
let frame = CGRect(x: 0, y: 0, width: 600, height: 600)
let view = MTKView(frame: frame, device: device)
view.clearColor = MTLClearColor(red: 1, green: 1, blue: 0.8,
alpha: 1)
```

This configures an MTKView for the Metal renderer. MTKView is a subclass of NSView on macOS and of UIView on iOS.

MTLClearColor represents an RGBA value — in this case, cream. The color value is stored in clearColor and is used to set the color of the view.

The model

Model I/O is a framework that integrates with Metal and SceneKit. Its main purpose is to load 3D models that were created in apps like Blender or Maya, and to set up data buffers for easier rendering.

Instead of loading a 3D model, you're going to load a Model I/O basic 3D shape, also called a **primitive**. A primitive is typically considered a cube, a sphere, a cylinder or a torus.

Add this code to the end of the playground:

```
// 1
let allocator = MTKMeshBufferAllocator(device: device)
// 2
let mdlMesh = MDLMesh(sphereWithExtent: [0.75, 0.75, 0.75],
                      segments: [100, 100],
                      inwardNormals: false,
                      geometryType: .triangles,
                      allocator: allocator)
// 3
let mesh = try MTKMesh(mesh: mdlMesh, device: device)
```

Going through this code:

1. The `allocator` manages the memory for the mesh data.

2. Model I/O creates a sphere with the specified size and returns an `MDLMesh` with all the vertex information in data buffers.

3. For Metal to be able to use the mesh, you convert it from a Model I/O mesh to a MetalKit mesh.

Queues, buffers and encoders

Each frame consists of commands that you send to the GPU. You wrap up these commands in a **render command encoder**. Command buffers organize these command encoders and a command queue organizes the command buffers.

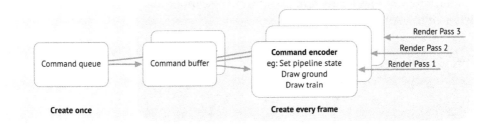

Add this code to create a command queue:

```
guard let commandQueue = device.makeCommandQueue() else {
  fatalError("Could not create a command queue")
}
```

You should set up and the device and the command queue at the start of your app, and generally you should use the same device and command queue throughout.

On each frame, you'll create a command buffer and at least one render command encoder. These are lightweight objects that point to other objects, such as shader functions and pipeline states, that you set up only once at the start of the app.

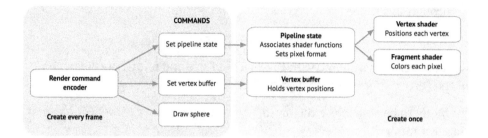

Shader functions

Shader functions are small programs that run on the GPU; you write them in the Metal Shading Language which is a subset of C++.

Normally, you'd create a separate file with a `.metal` extension specifically for shader functions but for now, create a multi-line string containing the shader function code and add it to your playground:

```
let shader = """
#include <metal_stdlib>
using namespace metal;

struct VertexIn {
  float4 position [[ attribute(0) ]];
};

vertex float4 vertex_main(const VertexIn vertex_in
[[ stage_in ]]) {
  return vertex_in.position;
}

fragment float4 fragment_main() {
  return float4(1, 0, 0, 1);
}
"""
```

There are two shader functions in here: a vertex function named `vertex_main` and a fragment function named `fragment_main`. The vertex function is where you usually manipulate vertex positions and the fragment function is where you specify the pixel color.

Set up a Metal library containing these two functions:

```
let library = try device.makeLibrary(source: shader, options:
nil)
let vertexFunction = library.makeFunction(name: "vertex_main")
```

```
let fragmentFunction = library.makeFunction(name:
"fragment_main")
```

The compiler will check that these functions exist and make them available to a
pipeline descriptor.

The pipeline state

In Metal, you set up a **pipeline state** for the GPU. By setting up this state, you're
telling the GPU that nothing will change until the state changes. With the GPU in a
fixed state, it can run more efficiently. The pipeline state contains all sorts of
information that the GPU needs, such as which pixel format it should use and
whether it should render with depth. The pipeline state also holds the vertex and
fragment functions that you just created.

However, you don't create a pipeline state directly, rather you create it through a
descriptor. This descriptor holds everything the pipeline needs to know, and you only
change the necessary properties for your particular rendering situation.

Add this code:

```
let pipelineDescriptor = MTLRenderPipelineDescriptor()
pipelineDescriptor.colorAttachments[0].pixelFormat = .bgra8Unorm
pipelineDescriptor.vertexFunction = vertexFunction
pipelineDescriptor.fragmentFunction = fragmentFunction
```

Here you've specified the pixel format to be 32 bits with color pixel order of blue/
green/red/alpha. You also set the two shader functions.

You'll also describe to the GPU how the vertices are laid out in memory using a
vertex descriptor. Model I/O automatically created a vertex descriptor when it
loaded the sphere mesh, so you can just use that one.

Add this code:

```
pipelineDescriptor.vertexDescriptor =
    MTKMetalVertexDescriptorFromModelIO(mesh.vertexDescriptor)
```

You've now set up the pipeline descriptor with the necessary information.
`MTLRenderPipelineDescriptor` has many other properties, but for now you'll just
use the defaults.

Create the pipeline state from the descriptor:

```
let pipelineState =
```

```
     try device.makeRenderPipelineState(descriptor:
  pipelineDescriptor)
```

Creating a pipeline state takes valuable processing time, so all of the above should be a one-time setup. In a real app, you might create several pipeline states to call different shading functions or use different vertex layouts.

Rendering

From now on, the code should be performed every frame. MTKView has a delegate method that runs every frame, but as you're doing a simple render which will simply fill out a static view, you don't need to keep refreshing the screen every frame.

When performing graphics rendering, the GPU's ultimate job is to output a single texture from a 3d scene. This texture is similar to the digital image created by a physical camera. The texture will be displayed on the device's screen each frame.

Render passes

If you're trying to achieve a realistic render, you'll want to take into account shadows, lighting and reflections. Each of these takes a lot of calculation and is generally done in separate **render passes**. For example, a shadow render pass will render the entire scene of 3D models, but only retain grayscale shadow information. A second render pass would render the models in full color. You can then combine the shadow and color textures to produce the final output texture that will go to the screen.

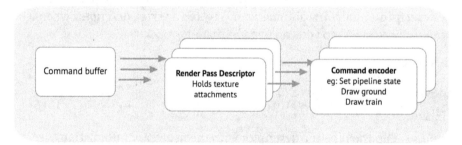

You'll learn about multipass rendering later; for the first part of this book you'll use a single render pass.

Conveniently, `MTKView` provides a render pass descriptor that will hold a texture called the **drawable**.

Add this code to the end of the playground:

```
// 1
guard let commandBuffer = commandQueue.makeCommandBuffer(),
// 2
  let renderPassDescriptor = view.currentRenderPassDescriptor,
// 3
  let renderEncoder =
commandBuffer.makeRenderCommandEncoder(descriptor:
    renderPassDescriptor)
else { fatalError() }
```

Here's what's happening:

1. You create a command buffer. This stores all the commands that you'll ask the GPU to run.

2. You obtain a reference to the view's render pass descriptor. The descriptor holds data for the render destinations, called **attachments**. Each attachment will need information such as a texture to store to, and whether to keep the texture throughout the render pass. The render pass descriptor is used to create the render command encoder.

3. From the command buffer, you get a render command encoder using the render pass descriptor. The render command encoder holds all the information necessary to send to the GPU so that it can draw the vertices.

If the system fails to create a metal object, such as the command buffer or render encoder, that's a fatal error. The view's `currentRenderPassDescriptor` may not be available in a particular frame, and usually you'll just return from the rendering delegate method. As you're only asking for it once in this playground, it's a fatal error here.

Now add the following code:

```
renderEncoder.setRenderPipelineState(pipelineState)
```

This gives the render encoder the pipeline state that you set up earlier.

The sphere mesh that you loaded earlier holds a buffer containing a simple list of vertices. Give this buffer to the render encoder:

```
renderEncoder.setVertexBuffer(mesh.vertexBuffers[0].buffer,
                              offset: 0, index: 0)
```

The `offset` is the position in the buffer where the vertex information starts. The `index` is how the GPU vertex shader function will locate this buffer.

Submeshes

The mesh is made up of submeshes. When the artist creates a 3D model, they design it with different material groups. These translate to submeshes. For example, if you were rendering a car object, you might have a shiny car body and rubber tires. One material is a `shiny paint` and another material `rubber`. On import, Model I/O will create two different submeshes that index to the correct vertices for that group. One vertex can be rendered multiple times by different submeshes. This sphere only has one submesh, so you'll just use one.

Add this code:

```
guard let submesh = mesh.submeshes.first else {
  fatalError()
}
```

Now for the exciting part: drawing! You draw in Metal with a *draw call*.

Add this code:

```
renderEncoder.drawIndexedPrimitives(type: .triangle,
                        indexCount: submesh.indexCount,
                        indexType: submesh.indexType,
                        indexBuffer:
submesh.indexBuffer.buffer,
                        indexBufferOffset: 0)
```

Here, you're instructing the GPU to render a vertex buffer consisting of triangles with the vertices placed in the correct order by the submesh index information. This code does not do the actual render — that doesn't happen until the GPU has received all the command buffer's commands.

To complete sending commands to the render command encoder and finalize the frame, add this code:

```
// 1
renderEncoder.endEncoding()
// 2
guard let drawable = view.currentDrawable else {
  fatalError()
}
// 3
commandBuffer.present(drawable)
commandBuffer.commit()
```

Going through the code:

1. You tell the render encoder that there are no more draw calls.

2. You get the `drawable` from the `MTKView`. The `MTKView` is backed by a Core Animation `CAMetalLayer` and the layer owns a drawable texture which Metal can read and write to.

3. Ask the command buffer to present the `MTKView`'s drawable and commit to the GPU.

Finally, add this code to the end of the playground:

```
PlaygroundPage.current.liveView = view
```

With that line of code, you'll be able to see the Metal view in the assistant editor.

Run the playground and in the playground's live view, you will see a red sphere on a cream background.

> **Note**: Sometimes playgrounds don't compile or run when they should. If you're sure you've written the code correctly, then restart Xcode and reload the playground. Wait for a second or two before running.

Congratulations! You've written your first Metal app, and you've also used many of the Metal API commands that you will use in every single Metal app you write.

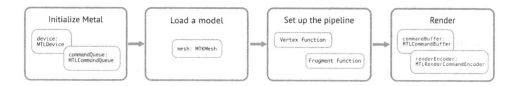

Challenge

Where you created the initial sphere mesh, experiment with setting the sphere to different sizes. What happens if you change the size from:

```
[0.75, 0.75, 0.75]
```

To:

```
[0.2, 0.75, 0.2]
```

Change the color of the sphere. In the shader function string, you'll see

```
return float4(1, 0, 0, 1);
```

This returns red=1, green=0, blue=0, alpha=1, which results in the red color. Try changing the numbers (from zero to 1) for a different color. Stay on brand with Ray Wenderlich green :]

```
float4(0, 0.4, 0.21, 1)
```

In the next chapter, you'll examine 3D models up close in Blender. Then continuing in your Swift Playground, you'll import and render a train model.

Chapter 2: 3D Models

By Caroline Begbie

What makes a good game even better? Gorgeous graphics! Creating amazing graphics like those in The Witcher 3, Doom and Uncharted 4, requires a team of programmers and 3D artists working closely together. What you see on the screen are 3D models rendered with custom renderers, much like the one you wrote in the previous chapter, only more advanced. Nonetheless, the principle of rendering 3D models is the same.

In this chapter, you'll examine 3D models. You'll learn how to create them, what they're made of and how to render them with different colors and styles.

What are 3D models?

3D Models are made up of vertices. Each vertex refers to a point in 3D space, made up of **x**, **y** and **z** values.

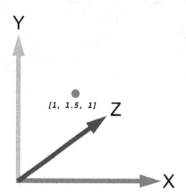

As you saw in the previous chapter, you send these vertex points to the GPU for rendering.

Open the starter playground for this chapter. This playground contains **two pages**, **Render and Export 3D Model** and **Import Train**. It also contains the train **.obj model**. If you don't see these things, you may need to show the Project navigator using the icon at the top-right.

From the Project navigator, select **Render and Export 3D Model**. This contains the code from Chapter 1, "Hello, Metal!". Examine the rendered sphere in the playground's live view; at the moment, the sphere renders as a solid red shape. To view the sphere as vertices instead, switch the render mode from triangles to points. Near the end of the playground, change the draw call from using type: `.triangle` to type: `.point`:

```
renderEncoder.drawIndexedPrimitives(type: .point,
                  indexCount: submesh.indexCount,
                  indexType: submesh.indexType,
                  indexBuffer: submesh.indexBuffer.buffer,
                  indexBufferOffset: 0)
```

Run the playground and you'll see this result:

You can really see the 3D nature of the sphere now! The vertices are evenly spaced horizontally, but because you're viewing on a two dimensional screen, the points at the edges of the sphere appear closer to each other than the points in the middle.

Undo that last change and revert back to rendering solid triangles.

Rendering a model in **wireframe** allows you to see the edges of each individual triangle. To render in wireframe, add the following line of code just before the draw call:

```
renderEncoder.setTriangleFillMode(.lines)
```

This tells the GPU to render lines instead of solid triangles. Run the playground:

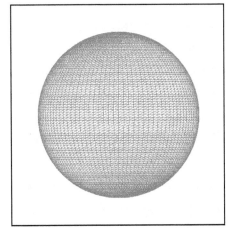

The sphere edges look curved because of the number of triangles being rendered - the GPU is only rendering straight lines here. If you render fewer triangles, curved models can look "blocky".

In 3D apps such as Blender or Maya, you generally manipulate points, lines and faces. Points are the vertices. Lines, also called edges, are the lines between the vertices. Faces are the triangular flat areas.

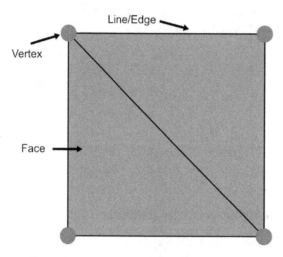

The vertices are generally ordered into triangles because GPU hardware is specialized to process them. The GPU's core instructions are expecting to see a triangle.

Of all possible shapes, why a triangle?

- A triangle has the least number of points of any polygon that can be drawn in two dimensions.

- No matter which way you move the points of a triangle, the three points will always be on the same plane.

- When you divide a triangle starting from any vertex, it always becomes two triangles.

When you're modeling in a 3D app, you generally work with quads (four point polygons). Quads work well with subdivision or smoothing algorithms.

Creating models with Blender

To create 3D models, you need a good 3D modeling app. These range from free to hugely expensive. The best of the free apps — and the one used throughout this book — is Blender (v. 2.8). Blender is used by many professionals, but if you're more familiar with another 3D app, such as Cheetah3D or Maya, then feel free to use it — the concepts are the same.

Download and install Blender from https://www.blender.org. Run Blender, click outside the splash screen to close it, and you'll see an interface similar to this one:

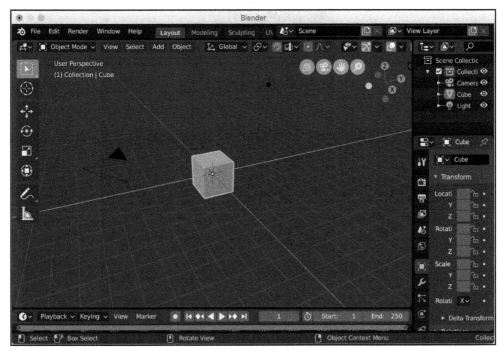

Your interface may look different. To get Blender to look the same as the one shown here, choose **Edit Menu ▸ Preferences**. Click the hamburger menu at the bottom left, choose **Load Factory Settings**, and then click **Load Factory Preferences** which will appear under the cursor.

> **Note**: If you want to create your own models, the best place to start is with our Blender tutorial at https://www.raywenderlich.com/49955/blender-tutorial-for-beginners-how-to-make-a-mushroom.

That tutorial teaches you how to make a mushroom. You can then render that mushroom in your playground at the end of this chapter.

3D file formats

There are a number of standard 3D file formats. In this book, you'll use **Wavefront OBJ (.obj)** for single non-animated models, **USDZ** for animated and non-animated models and **Blender format (.blend)** for Blender files.

Here's an overview of what each offers:

- **.obj**: This format, developed by Wavefront Technologies, has been around for awhile; almost every 3D app supports importing and exporting .obj files. You can specify materials (textures and surface properties) using an accompanying .mtl file, but the format does not support animation.

- **.glTF**: Developed by Khronos — who oversee Vulkan and OpenGL — this format is relatively new and is still under active development. It has strong community support because of its flexibility. It supports animated models.

- **.blend**: This is the native Blender file format.

- **.dae**: This is the COLLADA open standard format. This format supports animation. At the time of this writing, SceneKit can import .dae but Model I/O cannot.

- **.fbx**: A proprietary format owned by Autodesk. This is a commonly used format that supports animation but is losing favor because it's proprietary and doesn't have a single standard.

- **.usd**: A scalable open source format introduced by Pixar. USD can reference many models and files, which is not ideal for sharing assets. .usdz is a USD archive file that contains everything needed for the model or scene. Apple have adopted the USDZ format for their AR models.

> **Note**: Apple have provided tools for converting and inspecting USDZ files. These are available for download at https://developer.apple.com/augmented-reality/quick-look/.

An .obj file contains only a single model, whereas .glTF and .usd files are containers for entire scenes, complete with models, animation, cameras and lights.

Exporting to Blender

Now that you have Blender all set up, it's time to export a model from your playground into Blender.

Still in **Render and Export 3D Model**, toward the top of the playground, where you create the mesh, change:

```
let mdlMesh = MDLMesh(sphereWithExtent: [0.75, 0.75, 0.75],
                      segments: [100, 100],
                      inwardNormals: false,
                      geometryType: .triangles,
                      allocator: allocator)
```

To:

```
let mdlMesh = MDLMesh(coneWithExtent: [1,1,1],
                      segments: [10, 10],
                      inwardNormals: false,
                      cap: true,
                      geometryType: .triangles,
                      allocator: allocator)
```

This will generate a primitive cone mesh in place of the sphere. Run the playground and you'll see the wireframe cone.

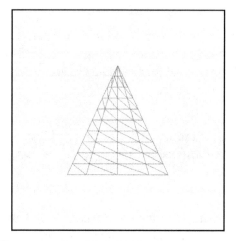

This is the model you'll export using Model I/O.

In Finder, in the **Documents** folder, create a new directory named **Shared Playground Data**. This is where saved files from Playgrounds will end up, so make sure you name it correctly.

> **Note**: The global constant `playgroundSharedDataDirectory` holds this folder name.

To export the cone, add this code just after creating the mesh:

```
// begin export code
// 1
let asset = MDLAsset()
asset.add(mdlMesh)
// 2
let fileExtension = "obj"
guard MDLAsset.canExportFileExtension(fileExtension) else {
  fatalError("Can't export a .\(fileExtension) format")
}
// 3
do {
  let url =
playgroundSharedDataDirectory.appendingPathComponent(
    "primitive.\(fileExtension)")
  try asset.export(to: url)
} catch {
  fatalError("Error \(error.localizedDescription)")
```

```
}
// end export code
```

Take a look at what's happening:

1. The top level of a scene in Model I/O is an `MDLAsset`. You can add child objects such as meshes, cameras and lights to the asset and build up a complete scene hierarchy.

2. Check that Model I/O can export a .obj file type.

3. Export the cone to the directory stored in Shared Playground Data.

Run the playground to export the cone object.

The .obj file format

In Finder, navigate to **Documents ▸ Shared Playground Data**. The playground export created two files: **primitive.obj** and **primitive.mtl**.

Using a plain text editor, open **primitive.obj**.

The following is an example .obj file. It describes a plane primitive with four corner vertices; the cone .obj file is laid out in a similar way, except it will have more data.

```
# Apple ModelIO OBJ File: plane
mtllib plane.mtl
g submesh
v 0 0.5 -0.5
v 0 -0.5 -0.5
v 0 -0.5 0.5
v 0 0.5 0.5
vn -1 0 0
vt 1 0
vt 0 0
vt 0 1
vt 1 1
usemtl material_1
f 1/1/1 2/2/1 3/3/1
f 1/1/1 3/3/1 4/4/1
s off
```

Here's the breakdown:

- `mtllib`: This is the name of the accompanying .mtl file. It holds the material and texture file names for the model.

- **g**: Starts a group of vertices.

- **v**: Vertex. For the cone, you'll have 102 of these.

- **vn**: Surface normal. This is a vector that points orthogonally — that's directly outwards. You'll read more about normals later.

- **vt**: uv coordinate. Textures use uv coordinates rather than xy coordinates.

- **usemtl**: The name of a material providing the surface information, such as color, for the following faces. This material is defined in the accompanying .mtl file.

- **f**: Defines faces. In this plane example, there are two faces. Each face has three elements consisting of a vertex/texture/normal index. For example, the last face listed: 4/4/1 would be the fourth vertex element / the fourth texture element / the first normal element: 0 0.5 0.5 / 1 1 / −1 0 0.

- **s**: Smoothing, currently off, means there are no groups that will form a smooth surface.

The .mtl file format

The second file you exported contains the model's materials. Materials describe how the 3D renderer should color the vertex. Should the vertex be smooth and shiny? Pink? Reflective? The .mtl file contains values for these properties.

Using a plain text editor, open **primitive.mtl**:

```
# Apple ModelI/O MTL File: primitive.mtl

newmtl material_1
    Kd 1 1 1
    Ka 0 0 0
    Ks 0
    ao 0
    subsurface 0
    metallic 0
    specularTint 0
    roughness 0.9
    anisotropicRotation 0
    sheen 0.05
    sheenTint 0
    clearCoat 0
    clearCoatGloss 0
```

- **newmtl material_1**: This is the group that contains all of the cone's vertices.

- **Kd**: The diffuse color of the surface. In this case, 1 1 1 will color the object white.

- **Ka**: The ambient color. This models the ambient lighting in the room.

- **Ks**: The specular color. The specular color is the color reflected from a highlight.

You'll read more about these and the other material properties later.

Because Blender can not import the .obj file as-is, you need modify it. In **primitive.mtl**, change the specular value:

```
Ks 0
```

To:

```
Ks 0 0 0
```

Then, save the file.

You'll now import the cone into Blender. To start with a clean and empty Blender file, do the following:

1. Open Blender.

2. Choose **File ▸ New ▸ General**.

3. Left-click the cube that appears in the start-up file to select it.

4. Press **X** to delete the cube.

5. Left-click **Delete** in the menu under the cursor to confirm the deletion.

Your Blender file is now clear and ready for import.

Choose **File ▸ Import ▸ Wavefront (.obj)** and select **primitive.obj** from the Playground directory **Documents ▸ Shared Playground Data**.

The cone imports into Blender.

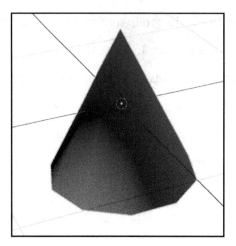

Left-click the cone to select it and press **Tab** to put Blender into Edit Mode allowing you to see the vertices and triangles that make up the cone.

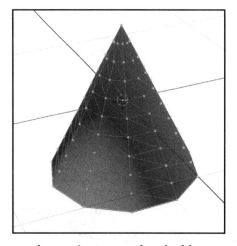

In Edit Mode you can move the vertices around and add new vertices to create any 3D model you can imagine.

> **Note**: In the Resources directory for this chapter, there's a file with links to some excellent Blender tutorials.

Using only a playground, you now have the ability to create, render and export a primitive. In the next part of this chapter, you'll review and render a more complex model with separate material groups.

Material groups

In Blender, open **train.blend**, which is located in the Resources directory for this chapter. This is the Blender original of the .obj train in your playground. **Left-click the model** to select it and press **Tab** to go into edit mode.

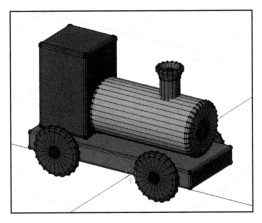

Unlike the cone, this train has several material groups — one for each color. On the right-hand side of the Blender screen is the Properties panel. The **Material context** should already be selected — that's the icon at the bottom of the vertical list of icons.

The list of materials making up the train shows at the top of this context. Select **Body** and then click **Select** underneath the material list. The vertices assigned to this material are now colored orange.

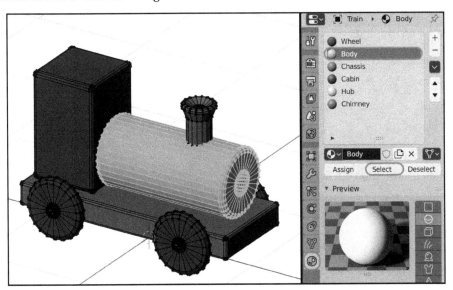

Notice how all the vertices are separated into different groups or materials; this lets you assign different colors but also allows easy selection within Blender.

> **Note**: When you first import this model into your playground, the renderer will render each of the material groups but won't pick up the correct color. Loading a model into Blender and reviewing the material groups is a good way of confirming what the model should look like, versus how your app renders it.

Back in Xcode, from the Project navigator, open the **Import Train** playground page.

In the playground's Resources folder, are two files named **train.obj** and **train.mtl**.

> **Note**: Files in the Playground Resources folder are available to all playground pages. Files in each page's Resources folder are only available to that page.

In **Import Train**, remove the line where you create the MDLMesh cone:

```
let mdlMesh = MDLMesh(coneWithExtent: [1, 1, 1],
                      segments: [10, 10],
                      inwardNormals: false,
                      cap: true,
                      geometryType: .triangles,
                      allocator: allocator)
```

Don't worry! Your code won't compile until you've finished this section and recreated mdlMesh using the train mesh.

In its place, add this code:

```
guard let assetURL = Bundle.main.url(forResource: "train",
                                     withExtension: "obj") else
{
  fatalError()
}
```

This sets up the file URL for the model.

Vertex descriptors

Metal uses descriptors as a common pattern to create objects. You saw this in the previous chapter when you set up a pipeline descriptor to describe a pipeline state. Before loading the model, you'll tell Metal how to lay out the vertices and other data by creating a vertex descriptor.

The following diagram describes an incoming buffer of data. It has two vertices with position, normal and texture coordinate **attributes**. The vertex descriptor informs Metal as to how you want to view this data.

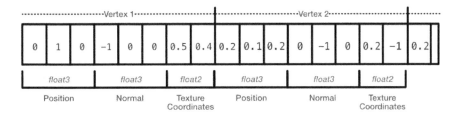

Add this code below the previous code:

```
// 1
let vertexDescriptor = MTLVertexDescriptor()
// 2
vertexDescriptor.attributes[0].format = .float3
// 3
vertexDescriptor.attributes[0].offset = 0
// 4
vertexDescriptor.attributes[0].bufferIndex = 0
```

Going through the code:

1. You create a vertex descriptor that you'll use to configure all the properties that an object will need to know about.

> **Note:** You can reuse this vertex descriptor with either the same values or reconfigured values to instantiate a different object.

2. The .obj file holds normal and texture coordinate data as well as vertex position data. For the moment, you don't need the surface normals or texture coordinates, just the position. You tell the descriptor that the xyz position data should load as a `float3`, which is a simd data type consisting of three `Float` values. An `MTLVertexDescriptor` has an array of 31 attributes where you can configure the

data format, and in future chapters you'll load up the normal and texture coordinate attributes.

3. The offset specifies where in the buffer this particular data will start.

4. When you send your vertex data to the GPU via the render encoder, you send it in an MTLBuffer and identify the buffer by an index. There are 31 buffers available and Metal keeps track of them in a **buffer argument table**. Use buffer 0 here so that the vertex shader function will be able to match the incoming vertex data in buffer 0 with this vertex layout.

Continue with this code:

```
// 1
vertexDescriptor.layouts[0].stride =
MemoryLayout<SIMD3<Float>>.stride
// 2
let meshDescriptor =
        MTKModelIOVertexDescriptorFromMetal(vertexDescriptor)
// 3
(meshDescriptor.attributes[0] as! MDLVertexAttribute).name =
        MDLVertexAttributePosition
```

Going through this code:

1. Here, you specify the stride for buffer 0. The stride is the number of bytes between each set of vertex information. Referring back to the previous diagram which described position, normal and texture coordinate information, the stride between each vertex would be float3 + float3 + float2. However, here you're only loading position data, so to get to the next position, you jump by a stride of float3. Using this buffer layout index and stride format, you can set up complex vertex descriptors referencing multiple MTLBuffers with different layouts. You have the option of interleaving position, normal and texture coordinates, or you can lay out a buffer containing all position data first, followed by other data.

> **Note**: The SIMD3<Float> type is Swift's equivalent to float3. Later you'll set up a typealias for float3.

2. Model I/O needs a slightly different format vertex descriptor, so you create a new Model I/O descriptor from the Metal vertex descriptor.

3. Assign a string name "position" to the attribute. This tells Model I/O that this is positional data. The normal and texture coordinate data is also available, but with this vertex descriptor, you told Model I/O that you're not interested in those attributes.

Continue with this code:

```
let asset = MDLAsset(url: assetURL,
                     vertexDescriptor: meshDescriptor,
                     bufferAllocator: allocator)
let mdlMesh = asset.childObjects(of: MDLMesh.self).first as!
MDLMesh
```

This reads the asset using the URL, vertex descriptor and memory allocator. You then read in the first Model I/O mesh buffer in the asset. Some more complex objects will have multiple meshes, but you'll deal with that later.

Now that you've loaded the model vertex information, the rest of the code will be the same. Your playground will load mesh from the new mdlMesh variable.

Run the playground to see your train in wireframe.

Uh-oh! This train isn't going anywhere. It only has two wheels, which are way too high off the ground, and the rest of the train is missing.

Time to fix that, starting with its position.

Metal coordinate system

All models have an **origin**. The origin is the location of the mesh. The train's origin is at [0, 0, 0]. In Blender, this places the train right at the center of the scene.

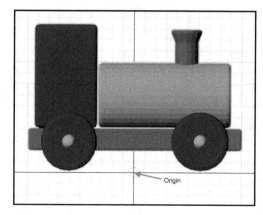

The Metal NDC (Normalized Device Coordinate) system is a 2-unit wide by 2-unit high by 1-unit deep box where **X** is right / left, **Y** is up / down and **Z** is in / out of the screen.

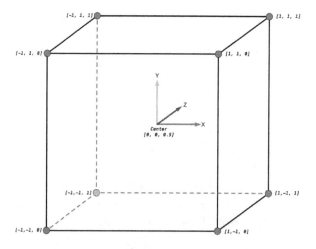

To normalize means *to adjust to a standard scale*. On a screen, you might address a location in screen coordinates of width 0 to 375, whereas the Metal normalized coordinate system doesn't care what the physical width of a screen is — its coordinates along the X axis are -1.0 to 1.0. In Chapter 4, "3D Transforms," you'll learn about various coordinate systems and spaces. Because the origin of the train is at [0,0,0], the train appears halfway up the screen which is where [0,0,0] is in the Metal coordinate system.

Select **train.obj** in the Project navigator; this will show you the train model in the SceneKit editor. Now, click on the train to select it. Open the **Node inspector** on the right and change **y Position** to **-1**.

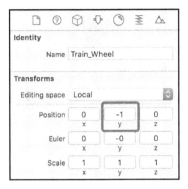

> **Note**: Typically, you'll change the position of the model in code; this example is only to illustrate how you can affect the model.

Go back to **Import Train** and run the playground. The wheels now appear at the bottom of the screen.

Of course, no one can board an invisible train so it's time to fix that next.

Submeshes

Up to now, your primitive models included only one material group, and thus one submesh. Take a look at the following image. It's a plane with four vertices and two material groups.

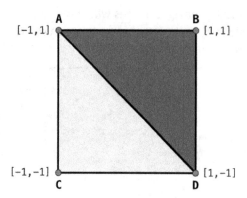

When Model I/O loads the plane, it places the four vertices in an MTLBuffer. The following image shows only the vertex position data, however, it also shows how the two submesh buffers index into the vertex data.

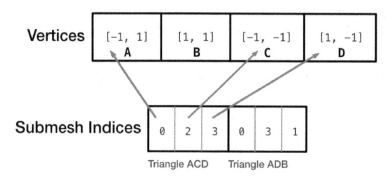

The first submesh buffer holds the vertex indices of the light-colored triangle ACD. These indices point to vertices 0, 2 and 3. The second submesh buffer holds the indices of the dark triangle ADB.

The submesh also has an **offset** where the submesh buffer starts. The index can be held in either a uint16 or a uint32. The offset of this second submesh buffer would be three times the size of the uint type.

Winding order

The vertex order, also called **winding order**, is important here. The vertex order of this plane is counter-clockwise, as is the default .obj winding order. With a counter-clockwise winding order, triangles that are defined in counter-clockwise order are facing towards you. Any triangles that are in clockwise order are therefore facing away from you.

In the next chapter, you'll go down the graphics pipeline and you'll see that the GPU can cull triangles that are not facing towards you, thus saving valuable processing time.

Render submeshes

Currently, you're only rendering the first submesh, but because the train has several material groups, you'll need to loop through the submeshes to render them all.

At the end of the playground, change:

```
guard let submesh = mesh.submeshes.first else {
  fatalError()
}
renderEncoder.drawIndexedPrimitives(
                      type: .triangle,
                      indexCount: submesh.indexCount,
                      indexType: submesh.indexType,
                      indexBuffer:
submesh.indexBuffer.buffer,
                      indexBufferOffset: 0
  )
```

To:

```
for submesh in mesh.submeshes {
  renderEncoder.drawIndexedPrimitives(
                      type: .triangle,
                      indexCount: submesh.indexCount,
                      indexType: submesh.indexType,
                      indexBuffer:
submesh.indexBuffer.buffer,
                      indexBufferOffset:
submesh.indexBuffer.offset
    )
}
```

This loops through the submeshes and issues a draw call for each one. The mesh and submeshes are in `MTLBuffers`, and the submesh holds the index listing of the vertices in the mesh.

Run the playground and your train renders completely, minus the material colors, which you'll take care of in Chapter 7, "Maps and Materials."

Congratulations! You're now rendering 3D models — for now, don't worry that you're only rendering them in two dimensions and the colors aren't correct. After the next chapter, you'll know more about the internals of rendering, and following on from that, you'll learn how to move those vertices into the third dimension.

Challenge

If you're in for a fun challenge, complete the Blender tutorial to make a mushroom at https://www.raywenderlich.com/49955/blender-tutorial-for-beginners-how-to-make-a-mushroom and then export what you make in Blender to an .obj file. If you want to skip the modeling, you'll find the **mushroom.obj** file in the Resources directory for this chapter.

Import **mushroom.obj** into the playground and render it.

If you used the mushroom from the Resources directory, you'll first have to rotate, scale and reposition the mushroom in the SceneKit editor to view it correctly.

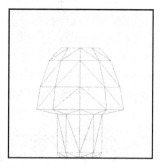

If you have difficulty, the completed playground is in the Projects ▸ Challenge directory for this chapter.

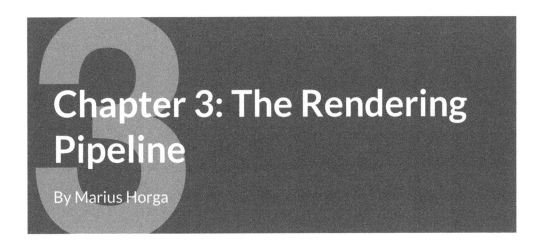

Chapter 3: The Rendering Pipeline

By Marius Horga

In this chapter, you'll take a deep dive through the rendering pipeline and create a Metal app that renders a red cube. Along the way, you'll discover all of the hardware chips responsible for taking the 3D objects and turning them into the gorgeous pixels that you see on the screen.

The GPU and the CPU

All computers have a **Central Processing Unit (CPU)** that drives the operations and manages the resources on a computer. They also have a **Graphics Processing Unit (GPU)**.

A GPU is a specialized hardware component that can process images, videos and massive amounts of data *really* fast. This is called **throughput**. The throughput is measured by the amount of data processed in a specific unit of time.

A CPU, on the other hand, can't handle massive amounts of data really fast, but it can process many sequential tasks (one after another) *really* fast. The time necessary to process a task is called **latency**.

The ideal setup includes low latency and high throughput. Low latency allows for the serial execution of queued tasks so the CPU can execute the commands without the system becoming slow or unresponsive; and high throughput lets the GPU render videos and games asynchronously without stalling the CPU. Because the GPU has a highly parallelized architecture, specialized in doing the same task repeatedly, and with little or no data transfers, it's able to process larger amounts of data.

The following diagram shows the major differences between the CPU and the GPU.

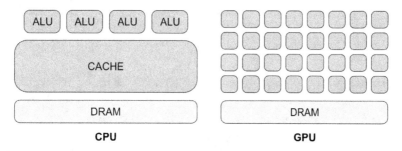

The CPU has a large cache memory and a few **Arithmetic Logic Unit (ALU)** cores. The low latency cache memory on the CPU is used for fast access to temporary resources. The GPU does not have much cache memory and there's room for more ALU cores which only do calculations without saving partial results to memory.

Also, the CPU typically only has a handful of cores while the GPU has hundreds — even thousands of cores. With more cores, the GPU can split the problem into many smaller parts, each running on a separate core in parallel, thus hiding latency. At the end of processing, the partial results are combined and the final result returned to the CPU. But cores aren't the only thing that matters!

Besides being slimmed down, GPU cores also have special circuitry for processing geometry and are often called **shader cores**. These shader cores are responsible for the beautiful colors you see on the screen. The GPU writes a whole frame at a time to fit the entire rendering window. It will then proceed to rendering the next frame as quickly as possible to maintain a good frame rate.

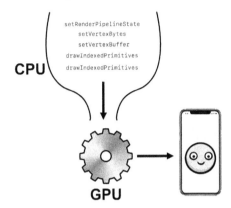

The CPU continues to issue commands to the GPU to keep it busy, but at some point, either the CPU will finish sending commands or the GPU will finish processing the commands it received. To avoid stalling, Metal on the CPU queues up multiple commands in command buffers and will issue new commands, sequentially, for the next frame without having to wait for the GPU to finish the first frame. This way, no matter who finishes the work first, there will be more work available to do.

The GPU part of the graphics pipeline starts once it's received all of the commands and resources.

The Metal project

You've been using Playgrounds to learn about Metal. Playgrounds are great for testing and learning new concepts. In fact, you'll use Playgrounds occasionally throughout this book, however, it's important to understand how to set up a full Metal project. Since the Metal framework is almost identical on macOS and iOS, you'll create a macOS app.

> **Note**: The project files for this chapter's challenge project also include an iOS target, so you can see the few differences between iOS and macOS. The Metal files will all be shared between the two targets.

Create a new macOS project using the **macOS App** template.

Name your project **Pipeline** and ensure the **User Interface** dropdown is set to **Storyboard**. Leave all the checkbox options unchecked.

Open **Main.storyboard** and select View under the **View Controller Scene**.

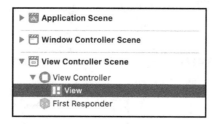

In the Identity inspector, change the view from NSView to MTKView.

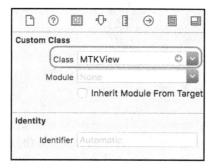

This sets up the main view as a MetalKit View.

If **ViewController.swift** doesn't exist in your project, create a new Cocoa Class file and name the class ViewController. Make it a subclass of NSViewController. Uncheck the XIB file option. An NSViewController is the macOS equivalent to iOS's UIViewController.

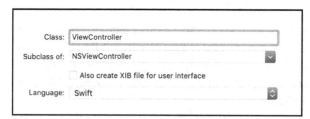

In **ViewController.swift**, at the top of the file, import the MetalKit framework:

```
import MetalKit
```

Then, add this code to `viewDidLoad()`:

```
guard let metalView = view as? MTKView else {
  fatalError("metal view not set up in storyboard")
}
```

You now have a choice. You can subclass `MTKView` and use this view in the storyboard. In that case, the subclass's `draw(_:)` will be called every frame and you'd put your drawing code in that method. However, in this book, you'll set up a `Renderer` class that conforms to `MTKViewDelegate` and sets `Renderer` as a delegate of `MTKView`. `MTKView` calls a delegate method every frame, and this is where you'll place the necessary drawing code.

> **Note**: If you're coming from a different API world, you might be looking for a game loop construct. You do have the option of extending `CAMetalLayer` instead of creating the `MTKView`. You can then use `CADisplayLink` for the timing; but Apple introduced `MetalKit` with its protocols to manage the game loop more easily.

The Renderer class

Create a new Swift file named **Renderer.swift** and replace its contents with the following code:

```
import MetalKit

class Renderer: NSObject {
  init(metalView: MTKView) {
    super.init()
  }
}

extension Renderer: MTKViewDelegate {
  func mtkView(_ view: MTKView, drawableSizeWillChange size:
CGSize) {
  }

  func draw(in view: MTKView) {
    print("draw")
  }
}
```

Here, you create an initializer and make `Renderer` conform to `MTKViewDelegate` with the two `MTKView` delegate methods:

- **mtkView(_:drawableSizeWillChange:)**: Gets called every time the size of the window changes. This allows you to update the render coordinate system.

- **draw(in:)**: Gets called every frame.

In **ViewController.swift**, add a property to hold the renderer:

```
var renderer: Renderer?
```

At the end of `viewDidLoad()`, initialize the renderer:

```
renderer = Renderer(metalView: metalView)
```

Initialization

Just as you did in the first chapter, you need to set up the Metal environment.

Metal has a major advantage over OpenGL in that you're able to instantiate some objects up-front rather than create them during each frame. The following diagram indicates some of the objects you can create at the start of the app.

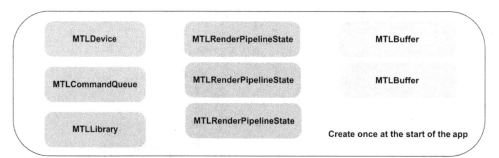

- **MTLDevice**: The software reference to the GPU hardware device.

- **MTLCommandQueue**: Responsible for creating and organizing `MTLCommandBuffers` each frame.

- **MTLLibrary**: Contains the source code from your vertex and fragment shader functions.

- **MTLRenderPipelineState**: Sets the information for the draw, such as which shader functions to use, what depth and color settings to use and how to read the vertex data.

- **MTLBuffer**: Holds data, such as vertex information, in a form that you can send to the GPU.

Typically, you'll have one MTLDevice, one MTLCommandQueue and one MTLLibrary object in your app. You'll also have several MTLRenderPipelineState objects that will define the various pipeline states, as well as several MTLBuffers to hold the data.

Before you can use these objects, however, you need to initialize them. Add these properties to the Renderer class:

```
static var device: MTLDevice!
static var commandQueue: MTLCommandQueue!
var mesh: MTKMesh!
var vertexBuffer: MTLBuffer!
var pipelineState: MTLRenderPipelineState!
```

These are the properties you need to keep references to the different objects. They are currently all implicitly unwrapped optionals for convenience, but you can change this after you've completed the initialization. Also, you won't need to keep a reference to the MTLLibrary, so there's no need to create it.

You're using class properties for the device and the command queue to ensure that only one of each exists. In rare cases, you may require more than one — but in most apps, one will be plenty.

Still in **Renderer.swift**, add this code to init(metalView:), before super.init():

```
guard
  let device = MTLCreateSystemDefaultDevice(),
  let commandQueue = device.makeCommandQueue() else {
    fatalError("GPU not available")
}
Renderer.device = device
Renderer.commandQueue = commandQueue
metalView.device = device
```

This initializes the GPU and creates the command queue.

Finally, after super.init(), add this:

```
metalView.clearColor = MTLClearColor(red: 1.0, green: 1.0,
                                     blue: 0.8, alpha: 1.0)
metalView.delegate = self
```

This sets metalView.clearColor to a cream color. It also sets Renderer as the delegate for metalView so that the view will call the MTKViewDelegate drawing methods.

Build and run the app to make sure everything's set up and working. If all's well, you should see a plain gray window. In the debug console, you'll see the word "draw" repeatedly. Use this to verify that your app is calling `draw(in:)` for every frame.

> **Note**: You won't see `metalView`'s cream color because you're not asking the GPU to do any drawing yet.

Set up the data

A class to build 3D primitive meshes is always useful. In the previous chapter, you created a sphere and a cone. In this chapter, you'll set up a class for creating 3D shape primitives, and you'll add a cube to it.

Create a new Swift file named **Primitive.swift** and replace the default code with this:

```swift
import MetalKit

class Primitive {
  static func makeCube(device: MTLDevice, size: Float) ->
MDLMesh {
    let allocator = MTKMeshBufferAllocator(device: device)
    let mesh = MDLMesh(boxWithExtent: [size, size, size],
                       segments: [1, 1, 1],
                       inwardNormals: false,
                       geometryType: .triangles,
                       allocator: allocator)
    return mesh
  }
}
```

This method returns a cube and is similar to the code used to draw a sphere and a cone from the previous chapter.

In **Renderer.swift**, in `init(metalView:)`, before calling `super.init()`, set up the mesh:

```swift
let mdlMesh = Primitive.makeCube(device: device, size: 1)
do {
  mesh = try MTKMesh(mesh: mdlMesh, device: device)
} catch let error {
  print(error.localizedDescription)
}
```

Then, set up the `MTLBuffer` that contains the vertex data you'll send to the GPU.

```
vertexBuffer = mesh.vertexBuffers[0].buffer
```

This puts the mesh data in an `MTLBuffer`. Now, you need to set up the pipeline state so that the GPU will know how to render the data.

First, set up the `MTLLibrary` and ensure that the vertex and fragment shader functions are present.

Continue adding code before `super.init()`:

```
let library = device.makeDefaultLibrary()
let vertexFunction = library?.makeFunction(name: "vertex_main")
let fragmentFunction =
    library?.makeFunction(name: "fragment_main")
```

You'll create these shader functions later in this chapter. Unlike OpenGL shaders, these are compiled when you compile your project which is more efficient than compiling on the fly. The result is stored in the library.

Now, create the pipeline state:

```
let pipelineDescriptor = MTLRenderPipelineDescriptor()
pipelineDescriptor.vertexFunction = vertexFunction
pipelineDescriptor.fragmentFunction = fragmentFunction
pipelineDescriptor.vertexDescriptor =

MTKMetalVertexDescriptorFromModelIO(mdlMesh.vertexDescriptor)
pipelineDescriptor.colorAttachments[0].pixelFormat =
metalView.colorPixelFormat
do {
  pipelineState =
    try device.makeRenderPipelineState(descriptor:
pipelineDescriptor)
} catch let error {
  fatalError(error.localizedDescription)
}
```

This sets up a potential state for the GPU. The GPU needs to know its complete state before it can start managing vertices. You set the two shader functions the GPU will call, and you also set the pixel format for the texture to which the GPU will write.

You also set the pipeline's vertex descriptor. This is how the GPU will know how to interpret the vertex data that you'll present in the mesh data `MTLBuffer`.

If you need to call different vertex or fragment functions, or use a different data layout, then you'll need more pipeline states. Creating pipeline states is relatively time-consuming which is why you do it up-front, but switching pipeline states during frames is fast and efficient.

The initialization is complete and your project will compile. However, if you try to run it, you'll get an error because you haven't yet set up the shader functions.

Render frames

In **Renderer.swift**, using the same commands as in Chapter 1, "Hello Metal!" replace the `print` statement in `draw(in:)` with this code:

```
guard
  let descriptor = view.currentRenderPassDescriptor,
  let commandBuffer = Renderer.commandQueue.makeCommandBuffer(),
  let renderEncoder =
    commandBuffer.makeRenderCommandEncoder(
        descriptor: descriptor) else {
    return
}

// drawing code goes here

renderEncoder.endEncoding()
guard let drawable = view.currentDrawable else {
  return
}
commandBuffer.present(drawable)
commandBuffer.commit()
```

This sets up the render command encoder and presents the view's drawable texture to the GPU.

Drawing

On the CPU side, to prepare the GPU, you need to give it the data and the pipeline state. Then, you will issue the draw call.

Still in `draw(in:)`, replace the comment:

```
// drawing code goes here
```

With:

```
renderEncoder.setRenderPipelineState(pipelineState)
renderEncoder.setVertexBuffer(vertexBuffer, offset: 0, index: 0)
for submesh in mesh.submeshes {
  renderEncoder.drawIndexedPrimitives(type: .triangle,
```

```
                        indexCount: submesh.indexCount,
                        indexType: submesh.indexType,
                        indexBuffer: submesh.indexBuffer.buffer,
                        indexBufferOffset: submesh.indexBuffer.offset)
    }
```

You've now set up the GPU commands to set the pipeline state, the vertex buffer, and perform the draw calls on the mesh's submeshes. When you commit the command buffer at the end of `draw(in:)`, this indicates to the GPU that all the data and the pipeline are ready and the GPU can take over.

The rendering pipeline

You finally get to investigate the GPU pipeline! In the following diagram, you can see the stages of the pipeline.

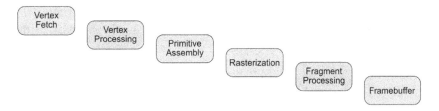

The graphics pipeline takes the vertices through multiple stages during which the vertices have their coordinates transformed between various spaces. You'll read more about coordinate spaces in Chapter 4, "Coordinate Spaces."

As a Metal programmer, you're only concerned about the Vertex and Fragment Processing stages since they're the only two programmable stages. Later in the chapter, you'll write both a vertex shader and a fragment shader. For all the non-programmable pipeline stages, such as Vertex Fetch, Primitive Assembly and Rasterization, the GPU has specially designed hardware units to serve those stages.

1 - Vertex Fetch

The name of this stage varies among various graphics **Application Programming Interfaces (APIs)**. For example, **DirectX** calls it **Input Assembler**.

To start rendering 3D content, you first need a scene. A scene consists of models that have meshes of vertices. One of the simplest models is the cube which has 6 faces (12 triangles).

As you saw in the previous chapter, you use a vertex descriptor to define the way vertices will be read in along with their attributes such as position, texture coordinates, normal and color.

You do have the option **not** to use a vertex descriptor and just send an array of vertices in an `MTLBuffer`, however, if you decide not to use one, you'll need to know how the vertex buffer is organized ahead of time.

When the GPU fetches the vertex buffer, the `MTLRenderCommandEncoder` draw call tells the GPU whether the buffer is indexed.

If the buffer is not indexed, the GPU assumes the buffer is an array and reads in one element at a time in order.

In the previous chapter, you saw how Model I/O imports .obj files and sets up their buffers indexed by submesh. This indexing is important because vertices are cached for reuse.

For example, a cube has twelve triangles and eight vertices (at the corners). If you don't index, you'll have to specify the vertices for each triangle and send thirty-six vertices to the GPU.

This may not sound like a lot, but in a model that has several thousand vertices, vertex caching is important!

There is also a second cache for shaded vertices so that vertices that are accessed multiple times are only shaded once. A shaded vertex is one to which color was already applied. But that happens in the next stage.

A special hardware unit called the **Scheduler** sends the vertices and their attributes on to the **Vertex Processing** stage.

2 - Vertex Processing

In this stage, vertices are processed individually. You write code to calculate per-vertex lighting and color. More importantly, you send vertex coordinates through various coordinate spaces to reach their position in the final framebuffer.

You learned briefly about shader functions and about the **Metal Shading Language (MSL)** in Chapter 1, "Hello Metal!" Now it's time to see what happens under the hood at the hardware level.

Take a look at this modern architecture of an AMD GPU:

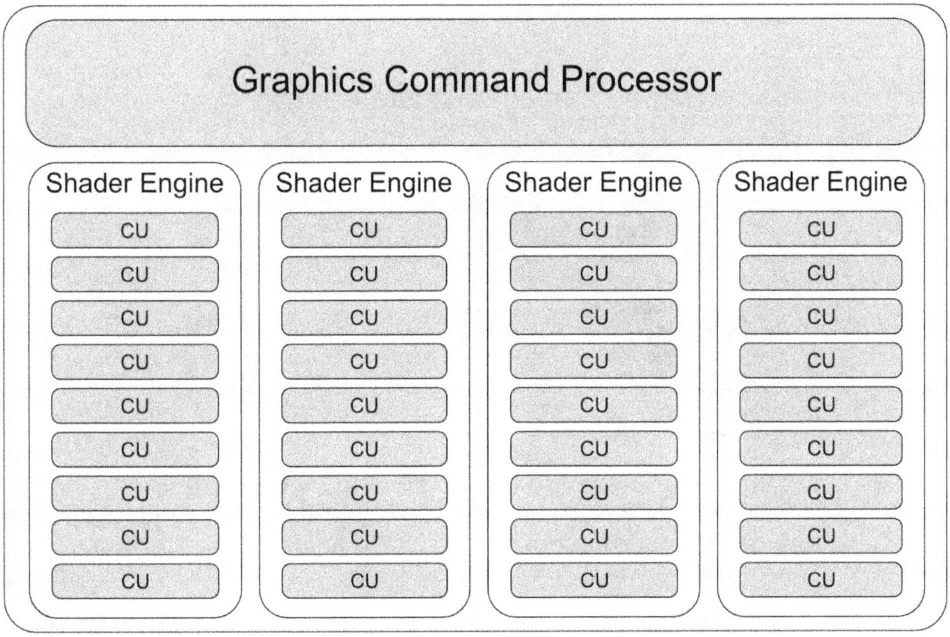

Going top-down, the GPU has:

- 1 **Graphics Command Processor**: This coordinates the work processes.

- 4 **Shader Engines (SE)**: An **SE** is an organizational unit on the GPU that can serve an entire pipeline. Each **SE** has a geometry processor, a rasterizer and Compute Units.

- 9 **Compute Units (CU)**: A **CU** is nothing more than a group of shader cores.

- 64 **shader cores**: A **shader core** is the basic building block of the GPU where all of the shading work is done.

In total, the 36 **CUs** have 2304 **shader cores**. Compare that to the number of cores in your quad-core CPU. Not fair, I know! :]

For mobile devices, the story is a little different. For comparison, take a look at the following image showing a GPU similar to those in recent iOS devices. Instead of having **SEs** and **CUs**, the PowerVR GPU has **Unified Shading Clusters (USC)**.

This particular GPU model has 6 **USCs** and 32 **cores** per **USC** for a total of only 192 **cores**.

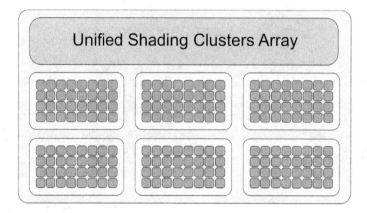

> **Note**: The iPhone X had the first mobile GPU entirely designed in-house by Apple. Unfortunately, Apple has not made the GPU hardware specifications public.

So what can you do with that many cores? Since these cores are specialized in both vertex and fragment shading, one obvious thing to do is give all the cores work to do in parallel so that the processing of vertices or fragments is done faster. There are a few rules, though.

Inside a CU, you can only process either vertices or fragments at one time. Good thing there's thirty-six of those! Another rule is that you can only process one shader function per SE. Having four SE's lets you combine work in interesting and useful ways. For example, you can run one fragment shader on one SE and a second fragment shader on a second SE at one time. Or you can separate your vertex shader from your fragment shader and have them run in parallel but on different SEs.

It's now time to see vertex processing in action! The **vertex shader** you're about to write is minimal but encapsulates most of the necessary vertex shader syntax you'll need in this and subsequent chapters.

Create a new file using the **Metal File** template and name it **Shaders.metal**. Then, add this code at the end of the file:

```
// 1
struct VertexIn {
  float4 position [[attribute(0)]];
```

```
};

// 2
vertex float4 vertex_main(const VertexIn vertexIn [[stage_in]])
{
  return vertexIn.position;
}
```

Going through this code:

1. Create a struct `VertexIn` to describe the vertex attributes that match the vertex descriptor you set up earlier. In this case, just `position`.

2. Implement a vertex shader, `vertex_main`, that takes in `VertexIn` structs and returns vertex positions as `float4` types.

Remember that vertices are indexed in the vertex buffer. The vertex shader gets the current index via the `[[stage_in]]` attribute and unpacks the `VertexIn` struct cached for the vertex at the current index.

Compute Units can process (at one time) batches of vertices up to their maximum number of shader cores. This batch can fit entirely in the CU cache and vertices can thus be reused as needed. The batch will keep the CU busy until the processing is done but other CUs should become available to process the next batch.

As soon as the vertex processing is done, the cache is cleared for the next batches of vertices. At this point, vertices are now ordered and grouped, ready to be sent to the primitive assembly stage.

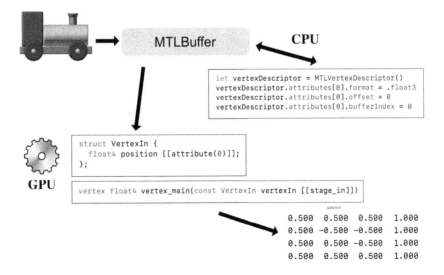

To recap, the CPU sent the GPU a vertex buffer that you created from the model's mesh. You configured the vertex buffer using a vertex descriptor that tells the GPU how the vertex data is structured. On the GPU, you created a struct to encapsulate the vertex attributes. The vertex shader takes in this struct, as a function argument, and through the `[[stage_in]]` qualifier, acknowledges that `position` comes from the CPU via the `[[attribute(0)]]` position in the vertex buffer. The vertex shader then processes all the vertices and returns their positions as a `float4`.

Note that when you use a vertex descriptor with attributes, you don't have to match types. The `MTLBuffer` position is a `float3`, whereas `VertexIn` struct can read the position as a `float4`.

A special hardware unit called **Distributer** sends the grouped blocks of vertices on to the **Primitive Assembly** stage.

3 - Primitive Assembly

The previous stage sent processed vertices grouped into blocks of data to this stage. The important thing to keep in mind is that vertices belonging to the same geometrical shape (primitive) are always in the same block. That means that the one vertex of a point, or the two vertices of a line, or the three vertices of a triangle, will always be in the same block, hence a second block fetch will never be necessary.

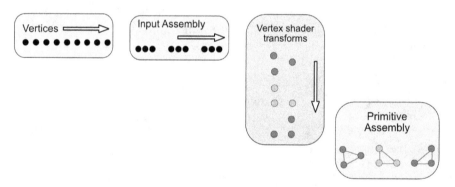

Along with vertices, the CPU also sends vertex connectivity information when it issues the **draw call** command, like this:

```
renderEncoder.drawIndexedPrimitives(type: .triangle,
                indexCount: submesh.indexCount,
                indexType: submesh.indexType,
                indexBuffer: submesh.indexBuffer.buffer,
                indexBufferOffset: 0)
```

The first argument of the draw function contains the most important information about vertex connectivity. In this case, it tells the GPU that it should draw triangles from the vertex buffer it sent.

The Metal API provides five primitive types:

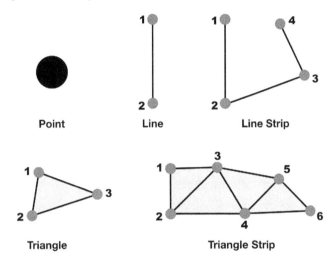

- **point**: For each vertex, rasterize a point. You can specify the size of a point that has the attribute `[[point_size]]` in the vertex shader.

- **line**: For each pair of vertices, rasterize a line between them. If a vertex was already included in a line, it cannot be included again in other lines. The last vertex is ignored if there are an odd number of vertices.

- **lineStrip**: Same as a simple line, except that the line strip connects all adjacent vertices and forms a poly-line. Each vertex (except the first) is connected to the previous vertex.

- **triangle**: For every sequence of three vertices, rasterize a triangle. The last vertices are ignored if they cannot form another triangle.

- **triangleStrip**: Same as a simple triangle, except adjacent vertices can be connected to other triangles as well.

There is one more primitive type called a **patch** but this needs special treatment. You will read more about patches in Chapter 11, "Tessellation and Terrains."

As you read in the previous chapter, the pipeline specifies the winding order of the vertices. If the winding order is counter-clockwise, and the triangle vertex order is counter-clockwise, it means they are front-faced. Otherwise, they are back-faced and can be culled since we cannot see their color and lighting.

Primitives will be culled when they are totally occluded by other primitives; however, when they are only partially off-screen, they'll be clipped.

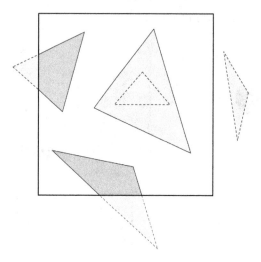

For efficiency, you should set winding order and enable back-face culling in the pipeline state.

At this point, primitives are fully assembled from connected vertices and they move on to the rasterizer.

4 - Rasterization

There are two modern rendering techniques currently evolving on separate paths but sometimes used together: **ray tracing** and **rasterization**. They are quite different; both have pros and cons.

Ray tracing — which you'll read more about in Chapter 18, "Rendering with Rays" — is preferred when rendering content that is static and far away, while rasterization is preferred when the content is closer to the camera and more dynamic.

With ray tracing, for each pixel on the screen, it sends a ray into the scene to see if there's an intersection with an object. If yes, change the pixel color to that object's color, but only if the object is closer to the screen than the previously saved object for the current pixel.

Rasterization works the other way around: for each object in the scene, send rays back into the screen and check which pixels are covered by the object. Depth information is kept the same way as for ray tracing, so it will update the pixel color if the current object is closer than the previously saved one.

At this point, all connected vertices sent from the previous stage need to be represented on a two-dimensional grid using their X and Y coordinates. This step is known as the **triangle setup**.

Here is where the rasterizer needs to calculate the slope or steepness of the line segments between any two vertices. When the three slopes for the three vertices are known, the triangle can be formed from these three edges.

Next, a process called **scan conversion** runs on each line of the screen to look for intersections and to determine what is visible and what is not. To draw on the screen at this point, only the vertices and the slopes they determine are needed.

The scan algorithm determines if all the points on a line segment, or all the points inside of a triangle are visible, in which case the triangle is filled with color entirely.

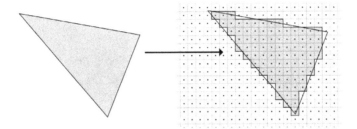

For mobile devices, the rasterization takes advantage of the tiled architecture of PowerVR GPUs by rasterizing the primitives on a 32x32 tile grid in parallel. In this case, 32 is the number of screen pixels assigned to a tile but this size perfectly fits the number of cores in a **USC**.

What if one object is behind another object? How can the rasterizer determine which object to render? This hidden surface removal problem can be solved by using stored depth information (early-Z testing) to determine whether each point is in front of other points in the scene.

After rasterization is finished, three more specialized hardware units take the stage:

- A buffer called **Hierarchical-Z** is responsible for removing fragments that were marked for culling by the rasterizer.

- The **Z and Stencil Test** unit then removes non-visible fragments by comparing them against the depth and stencil buffer.

- Finally, the **Interpolator** unit takes the remaining visible fragments and generates fragment attributes from the assembled triangle attributes.

At this point, the **Scheduler** unit again dispatches work to the shader cores, but this time it's the rasterized fragments sent for **Fragment Processing**.

5 - Fragment Processing

Time for a quick review of the pipeline.

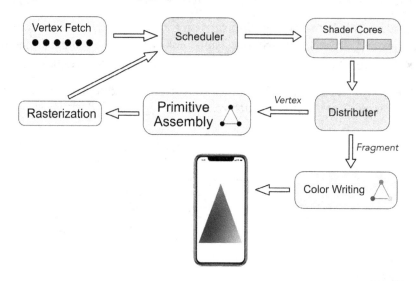

- The **Vertex Fetch** unit grabs vertices from the memory and passes them to the **Scheduler** unit.

- The **Scheduler** unit knows which shader cores are available so it dispatches work on them.

- After work is done, the **Distributer** unit knows if this work was **Vertex or Fragment Processing**.

- If it was **Vertex Processing** work, it sends the result to the **Primitive Assembly** unit. This path continues to the **Rasterization** unit and then back to the **Scheduler** unit.

- If it was **Fragment Processing** work, it sends the result to the **Color Writing** unit.

- Finally, the colored pixels are sent back to the memory.

The primitive processing in the previous stages was sequential because there is only one **Primitive Assembly** unit and one **Rasterization** unit. However, as soon as fragments reach the **Scheduler** unit, work can be *forked* (divided) into many tiny parts, and each part is given to an available shader core.

Hundreds or even thousands of cores are now doing parallel processing. When the work is finished, the results will be *joined* (merged) and sent to the memory, again sequentially.

The fragment processing stage is another programmable stage. You create a fragment shader function that will receive the lighting, texture coordinate, depth and color information that the vertex function outputs.

The fragment shader output is a single color for that fragment. Each of these fragments will contribute to the color of the final pixel in the framebuffer. All the attributes are interpolated for each fragment.

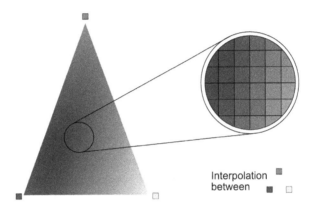

Interpolation between

For example, to render this triangle, the vertex function would process three vertices with the colors red, green and blue. As the diagram shows, each fragment that makes up this triangle is interpolated from these three colors. Linear interpolation simply averages the color at each point on the line between two endpoints. If one endpoint has red color, and the other has green color, the midpoint on the line between them will be yellow. And so on.

The interpolation equation is parametric and has this form, where parameter **p** is the percentage (or a range from 0 to 1) of a color's presence:

```
newColor = p * oldColor1 + (1 - p) * oldColor2
```

Color is easy to visualize, but all the other vertex function outputs are also similarly interpolated for each fragment.

> **Note:** If you don't want a vertex output to be interpolated, add the attribute [[flat]] to its definition.

In **Shaders.Metal**, add the fragment function to the end of the file:

```
fragment float4 fragment_main() {
  return float4(1, 0, 0, 1);
}
```

This is the simplest fragment function possible. You return the interpolated color red in the form of a `float4`. All the fragments that make up the cube will be red. The GPU takes the fragments and does a series of post-processing tests:

- **alpha-testing** determines which opaque objects are drawn and which are not based on depth testing.

- In the case of translucent objects, **alpha-blending** will combine the color of the new object with that already saved in the color buffer previously.

- **scissor testing** checks whether a fragment is inside of a specified rectangle; this test is useful for masked rendering.

- **stencil testing** checks how the stencil value in the framebuffer where the fragment is stored, compares to a specified value we choose.

- In the previous stage **early-Z testing** ran; now a **late-Z testing** is done to solve more visibility issues; stencil and depth tests are also useful for ambient occlusion and shadows.

- Finally, **antialiasing** is also calculated here so that final images that get to the screen do not look jagged.

You will learn more about post-processing tests in Chapter 10, "Fragment Post-Processing."

6 - Framebuffer

As soon as fragments have been processed into pixels the **Distributer** unit sends them to the **Color Writing** unit. This unit is responsible for writing the final color in a special memory location called the **framebuffer**. From here, the view gets its colored pixels refreshed every frame. But does that mean the color is written to the framebuffer while being displayed on the screen?

A technique called **double-buffering** is used to solve this situation. While the first buffer is being displayed on the screen, the second one is updated in the background. Then, the two buffers are swapped, and the second one is displayed on the screen while the first one is updated, and the cycle continues.

Whew! That was a lot of hardware information to take in. However, the code you've written is what every Metal renderer uses, and despite just starting out, you should begin to recognize the rendering process when you look at Apple's sample code.

Build and run the app, and your app will render this red cube:

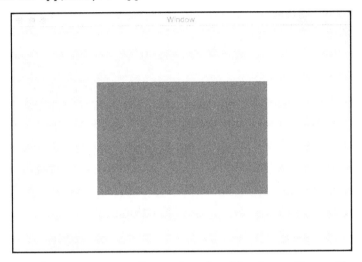

Notice how the cube is not square. Remember that Metal uses **Normalized Device Coordinates (NDC)** that is -1 to 1 on the X axis. Resize your window, and the cube will maintain a size relative to the size of the window. In the next chapter, you'll be able to position objects precisely on the screen.

Send data to the GPU

Metal is all about gorgeous graphics and fast and smooth animation. As a next step, you'll make your cube move up and down the screen. To do this, you'll have a timer that updates every frame and the cube's position will depend on this timer. The vertex function is where you update vertex positions so you'll send the timer data to the GPU.

At the top of `Renderer`, add the timer property:

```
var timer: Float = 0
```

In `draw(in:)`, just before:

```
renderEncoder.setRenderPipelineState(pipelineState)
```

add:

```
// 1
timer += 0.05
var currentTime = sin(timer)
// 2
renderEncoder.setVertexBytes(&currentTime,
                                  length:
MemoryLayout<Float>.stride,
                                  index: 1)
```

1. Every frame you update the timer. You want your cube to move up and down the screen, so you'll use a value between -1 and 1. Using `sin()` is a great way to achieve this as sine values are always -1 to 1.

2. If you're only sending a small amount of data (less than 4kb) to the GPU, `setVertexBytes(_:length:index:)` is an alternative to setting up a `MTLBuffer`. Here, you set `currentTime` to be at index 1 in the buffer argument table.

In **Shaders.metal**, replace the `vertex_main` function with:

```
vertex float4 vertex_main(const VertexIn vertexIn
[[ stage_in ]],
                            constant float &timer [[ buffer(1) ]])
{
  float4 position = vertexIn.position;
  position.y += timer;
  return position;
}
```

Here, the function receives the timer as a float in buffer 1. You add the timer value to the y position and return the new position from the function.

Build and run the app, and you now have an animated cube!

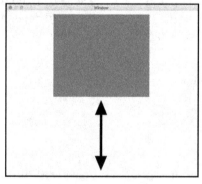

What an incredible journey. You learned how pipelines work and you even added a little animation. In the next chapter, you'll move to another dimension and render models in 3D rather than 2D.

Challenge

Using the `train.obj` model in **resources ▸ Models**, replace the cube with this train. When importing the model, make sure **Create Groups** is selected. Refer back to the previous chapter for the vertex descriptor code.

Once you've done this, animate the train from side-to-side, instead of up and down.

Finally, color your train blue.

The challenge sample code project for this chapter contains both macOS and iOS targets. Take a look at this project to see how it's constructed.

Pipeline-macOS contains files for only the macOS target; **Pipeline-iOS** contains files for only the iOS target.

Pipeline contains files common to both targets. The Metal and shader code will all go in this folder. To select which target to run, choose the scheme at the top left of the Xcode window.

> **Note:** Most of the sample code from now on will contain both macOS and iOS targets. Be sure when you create new files that you add the new file to both targets. You choose the target for a file in the File inspector.

If you have any difficulties, the full code is in the project challenge directory for this chapter.

Chapter 4: Coordinate Spaces

By Caroline Begbie

Everything you see on your device's screen, from the characters you type to the digital art you admire, is all math under the surface.

We'd all love to be math geniuses, but some of us lost the opportunity early in life. Fortunately, to use math, you don't always have to know what's under the hood. In this chapter, you're going to become a matrix master, and you'll learn what matrices can do for you and how to manipulate them painlessly.

You'll start by learning how to move, scale and rotate a triangle using matrices. Once you've mastered one triangle, it's a cinch to rotate thousands of triangles at once. Then, you'll upgrade your train project from the previous chapter and understand why you use matrices and what coordinate spaces are.

Transformations

In this picture, the vector image editor, Affinity Designer, was used to translate, scale and rotate a cat through a series of affine transformations.

Instead of individually working out each position, Affinity Designer creates a transformation matrix that holds the combination of the transformations. It then applies the transformation to each element.

> **Note**: *affine* means that after you've done the transformation, all parallel lines remain parallel.

Scaling cats is difficult because they can bite, so instead, you'll try out translating, scaling and rotating vertices in a Playground.

Translation

Open the starter project playground located in the starter folder for this chapter. Run the playground, and you'll get a blank cream screen. The starter playground is set up ready for drawing but has nothing to draw yet.

In this playground, you won't be importing models like you've been doing — you'll be sending vertices to the GPU as a simple array rather than having to set up vertex descriptors. You'll start by setting up the vertex and fragment functions to draw these single vertices.

Vertex function

Inside the Resources folder for the playground, open **Shaders.metal**.

Before the existing vertex function, add the struct that will contain the values you'll return from the vertex function:

```
struct VertexOut {
  float4 position [[position]];
  float point_size [[point_size]];
};
```

Here, you set the [[position]] attribute which tells the rasterizer which value contains the position. You also create a property with the [[point_size]] attribute. Points are tiny; the size of a pixel. On a retina screen, you wouldn't see the point, so you'll make it larger. The value of this property tells the GPU the size of the point that it will draw.

Replace the vertex function with:

```
// 1
vertex VertexOut
      vertex_main(constant float3 *vertices [[buffer(0)]],
// 2
  uint id [[vertex_id]])
{
  // 3
  VertexOut vertex_out {
    .position = float4(vertices[id], 1),
    // 4
    .point_size = 20.0
  };
  return vertex_out;
}
```

Going through this code:

1. Initially you'll just draw a single point, but shortly you'll be sending to the GPU the three vertices of a triangle. These will be an array of float3s containing the xyz position of the vertex. On the Swift side, you'll set the vertices up in buffer index 0.

    constant tells the GPU to use **constant address space**. This is optimized for accessing the same variable over several vertex functions in parallel. **Device address space**, keyword device, is best for when you access different parts of a buffer over the parallel functions. You would use device when using a buffer with points and color data interleaved, for example.

2. The attribute [[vertex_id]] informs the vertex function of the current id of the vertex. It's the index into the array.

3. Extract out the vertex position from the array and turn it into a float4.

4. Set the point size. You can make this larger or smaller as you prefer.

Fragment function

Now replace the fragment function with this code:

```
fragment float4
        fragment_main(constant float4 &color [[buffer(0)]])
{
  return color;
}
```

You'll send the fragment function the color that it should draw. You'll put this color value in buffer index 0 on the Swift side.

Set up the data

Back in the main playground page, you'll draw two vertices. You'll hold one vertex point in an array and create two buffers: one containing the original point, and one containing the translated point.

In the playground page, under:

```
// drawing code here
```

Add this code:

```
var vertices: [float3] = [[0, 0, 0.5]]
```

This is the vertex position which is at the center of the screen (in Normalized Device Coordinates). You load it into an array so you can create a triangle with two more vertices later.

> **Note:** float3 is a typealias of type SIMD3<Float>. This is defined for you in Utility.swift as a convenience to match the MSL float3 type.

Create the Metal buffer:

```
let originalBuffer = device.makeBuffer(bytes: &vertices,
    length: MemoryLayout<float3>.stride * vertices.count,
    options: [])
```

Here, you create an MTLBuffer containing vertices. The length is the number of vertices multiplied by the size of a float3.

Set up the buffers for the vertex and fragment functions:

```
renderEncoder.setVertexBuffer(originalBuffer,
                    offset: 0, index: 0)
renderEncoder.setFragmentBytes(&lightGrayColor,
            length: MemoryLayout<float4>.stride,
            index: 0)
```

Here, you assign the MTLBuffer containing vertices to index 0 and then assign the color, light gray, to index 0 for the fragment function. lightGrayColor is defined in Utility.swift.

Draw

Do the draw call using the primitive type .point:

```
renderEncoder.drawPrimitives(type: .point, vertexStart: 0,
                    vertexCount: vertices.count)
```

Because you're not using submesh indices, you use drawPrimitives instead of drawIndexedPrimitives to handle the draw.

Run the playground, and the GPU renders the vertex point at the center of NDC (Normalized Device Coordinates). You will see a gray square at the center of the playground's live view.

You'll now move the vertex right and down and create a second buffer with the new values. Add this code under the previous code:

```
vertices[0] += [0.3, -0.4, 0]
var transformedBuffer = device.makeBuffer(bytes: &vertices,
        length: MemoryLayout<float3>.stride * vertices.count,
        options: [])
```

Here, you added a displacement value to the original vertex and created a new `MTLBuffer` that holds these new values.

Set up the vertex function with the new buffer, color the point red and draw.

```
renderEncoder.setVertexBuffer(transformedBuffer,
                          offset: 0, index: 0)
renderEncoder.setFragmentBytes(&redColor,
                   length: MemoryLayout<float4>.stride,
                   index: 0)
renderEncoder.drawPrimitives(type: .point, vertexStart: 0,
                   vertexCount: vertices.count)
```

This is the same code as with the original buffer.

> **Note**: Why do you need two buffers to draw the same point? Logically, it might seem that you've created and drawn the first point, so you can change the vertex and assign it to the same `originalBuffer` for the second draw call. However, the GPU does not do the draw immediately when `drawPrimitives(type:vertexStart:vertexCount:)` is called. It does the draw some time after the command buffer presents the drawable. If you want to overwrite the vertex array before drawing it, you need to have two separate data buffers.

The translation code here is straightforward: aside from all the Metal code, you changed the vertex value, just as if you were moving a view's frame around using `CGPoints`. Run the playground and see the two points - the gray one in the original position, and the red one in the translated position.

Generally, as well as translation, you'll need to turn your model around or make it larger or smaller, and this involves rotation and scaling. A transformation encapsulates translation, scaling and rotation all in one, and you can represent a transformation in a **matrix**.

Vectors and matrices

You can describe your previous translation as a displacement **vector** of [0.3, -0.4, 0]. You moved the vertex 0.3 units in the x-direction, and -0.4 in the y-direction from its starting position.

In this image, the blue arrows are vectors.

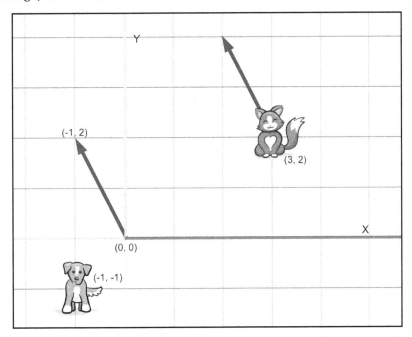

The left blue arrow is a vector with a value [-1, 2]. Coincidentally, the right blue arrow, partially behind the cat, is a vector, also with a value [-1, 2].

Positions (points) are locations in space, whereas vectors are displacements in space; in other words, a vector contains the amount and direction to move.

If you were to displace the cat by the blue vector, it would end up at point (2, 4). That's the cat's position (3, 2) plus the vector [-1, 2].

This 2D vector is a **1x2** matrix. It has one column and two rows.

> **Note:** Matrices can be ordered by rows or by columns. Metal matrices are constructed in **column-major** order, which means that columns are contiguous in memory.

A matrix is a two-dimensional array. Even the single number **1** is a 1×1 matrix. In fact, the number 1 is unique in that when you multiply a number by 1, the answer is always that number. All square matrices — where the array width is the same as the array height — have a matrix with this same property. It's called the **identity matrix**. Any vector or matrix multiplied by an identity matrix returns the same value.

A 4×4 identity matrix looks like this (all zeros, except for the diagonal 1s):

1	0	0	0
0	1	0	0
0	0	1	0
0	0	0	1

A 3D **transformation matrix** has four rows and four columns. It holds scaling and rotation information in the upper left 3×3 matrix, with the translation information in the last column. When you multiply vectors and matrices, the number of columns of the left side matrix or vector must equal the number of rows of the right side. For example, you can't multiply a float3 by a float4×4. Shortly, you'll see that you have to add an extra **w** dimension to your 3D points.

Included in this chapter's Resources folder is a matrix calculator app named **MatrixCalculator**. This calculator app will help you visualize the mathematics of how matrices work. Open up the project and run the app.

On the right-hand side, change Matrix to Vector. The matrix on the left will hold the transformation information and is currently an identity matrix. The vector on the right represents your point in 3D space. The left matrix multiplies the right vector (or matrix) to produce a Result.

Column 3 of the transformation matrix holds a vector that will displace a point.

Compute the cat displacement example from above using a matrix. Change the vector on the right to the cat's position [3, 2, 0, 1]. In the transformation matrix, change column 3 to [-1, 2, 0, 1]. That's the two-dimensional vector with an extra z and w value.

The app multiplies the vector by the matrix, and the result is [2, 4, 0, 1], which is the same result as above.

As you go through the following examples, experiment with the matrix calculator to see how your original point changes with the various matrices.

Now you'll translate your vertex in your playground in the same way. To set up a transformation matrix, add this line of code after declaring the `vertices` array:

```
var matrix = matrix_identity_float4x4
```

Here, you set up a 4×4 identity matrix.

Set the last column of the matrix to be your displacement vector. Replace:

```
vertices[0] += [0.3, -0.4, 0]
```

With:

```
matrix.columns.3 = [0.3, -0.4, 0, 1]
```

Following on from that code, process each vertex and multiply by the transformation matrix.

```
vertices = vertices.map {
  let vertex = matrix * float4($0, 1)
  return [vertex.x, vertex.y, vertex.z]
}
```

Remember that you can only multiply similar matrices, where the number of columns of the left matrix or vector is equal to the number of rows of the one on the right. Here, you convert the `float3` from the `vertices` array into a `float4`, adding the extra w component to your vertex so that you can then multiply the vertex by the 4×4 matrix.

Run the playground, and you get the same result as you did before using the matrix.

Matrices on the GPU

You may have noticed that this vertex processing code is taking place on the CPU. This is serial processing, which is much more inefficient compared to parallel processing. There's another place where each vertex is being processed — the GPU. You can pass the GPU your transformation matrix and multiply every vertex in the vertices array by the matrix in the vertex shader. The GPU is optimized for matrix calculation.

Replace the code:

```
vertices = vertices.map {
  let vertex = matrix * float4($0, 1)
  return [vertex.x, vertex.y, vertex.z]
}
```

With:

```
renderEncoder.setVertexBytes(&matrix,
      length: MemoryLayout<float4x4>.stride, index: 1)
```

Here, you're sending the matrix to the GPU.

In **Shaders.metal**, change the vertex function definition to:

```
vertex VertexOut
        vertex_main(constant float3 *vertices [[buffer(0)]],
                    constant float4x4 &matrix [[buffer(1)]],
                    uint id [[vertex_id]])
```

This will receive your matrix into your vertex function via buffer index 1.

Replace:

```
.position = float4(vertices[id], 1),
```

With:

```
.position = matrix * float4(vertices[id], 1),
```

This is where you multiply each vertex by the transformation matrix.

Because you've changed the vertex function, you'll also need to send the matrix for drawing the first point. In the playground page, add this before the first draw call:

```
renderEncoder.setVertexBytes(&matrix,
          length: MemoryLayout<float4x4>.stride, index: 1)
```

Run the playground, and you should still get the same result. This time though, the multiplication is happening on the GPU in parallel and is more efficient.

Scaling

Translating a single vertex is useful, but you'll want to scale and rotate your models to fit inside your scene.

Instead of a single vertex, you'll now draw and manipulate a triangle with three vertices.

Change:

```
var vertices: [float3] = [[0, 0, 0.5]]
```

To:

```
var vertices: [float3] = [
   [-0.7,  0.8,   1],
   [-0.7, -0.4,   1],
   [ 0.4,  0.2,   1]
]
```

You're now sending three vertices at a time to the GPU, and when you run your playground, it should display three gray points and the three points transformed by the matrix. To display a solid triangle, change the two draw calls to render triangles instead of points. Change both draw calls from:

```
renderEncoder.drawPrimitives(type: .point, vertexStart: 0,
                        vertexCount: vertices.count)
```

To:

```
renderEncoder.drawPrimitives(type: .triangle, vertexStart: 0,
                        vertexCount: vertices.count)
```

The original untranslated triangle displays in light gray, and the translated triangle displays in red.

You'll now scale the red triangle. Later, you'll use pre-made functions to create these transformation matrices, but just so that you can get a feel for what's happening under the hood, you'll set up the matrices manually here.

Remove this line of code:

```
matrix.columns.3 = [0.3, -0.4, 0, 1]
```

And replace it with:

```
let scaleX: Float = 1.2
let scaleY: Float = 0.5
matrix = float4x4(
    [scaleX, 0, 0, 0],
    [0, scaleY, 0, 0],
    [0,      0, 1, 0],
    [0,      0, 0, 1]
)
```

Without going into the mathematics too much, this is how you set up a scale matrix.

The vertex function will process all vertices. The following result for the top-left vertex shows that you'll scale the x vector value by 1.2 and the y vector value by 0.5.

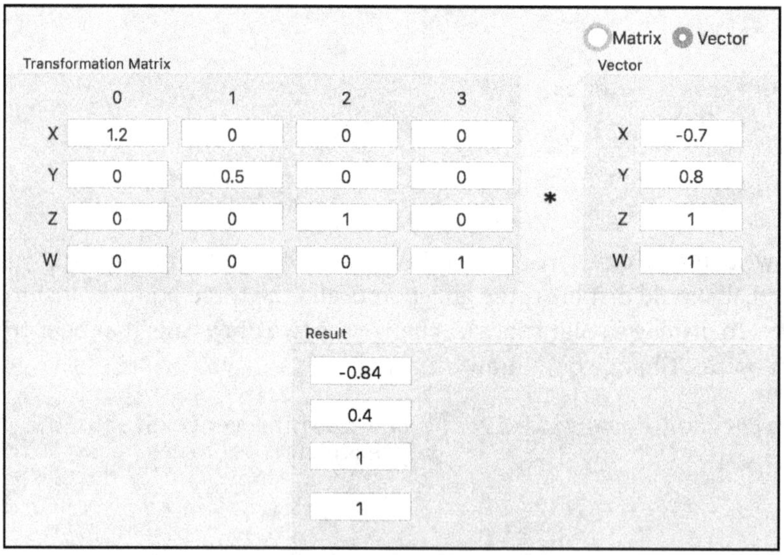

Run the playground. You've set up the matrix maths already on the GPU, so the scale transformation happens to the red triangle just by sending the correct scale matrix.

The following screen capture demonstrates a scaled x coordinate.

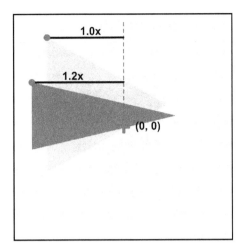

Rotation

You perform rotation in a similar way to scaling. Replace:

```
let scaleX: Float = 1.2
let scaleY: Float = 0.5
matrix = float4x4(
  [scaleX, 0, 0, 0],
  [0, scaleY, 0, 0],
  [0,      0, 1, 0],
  [0,      0, 0, 1]
)
```

With:

```
let angle = Float.pi / 2.0
matrix.columns.0 = [cos(angle), -sin(angle), 0, 0]
matrix.columns.1 = [sin(angle), cos(angle), 0, 0]
```

Instead of setting up the entire matrix, you have the option of only setting the changed matrix columns. Here you set a rotation around the z axis of the angle in radians.

> **Note**: `Float.pi / 2.0` is the same as 90°. If you're not sure how to convert between radians and degrees, the project for this chapter includes an extension on `Float` that will convert degrees to radians in MathLibrary.swift. Radians is the standard unit in computer graphics.

Run the playground, and the red triangle is rotated.

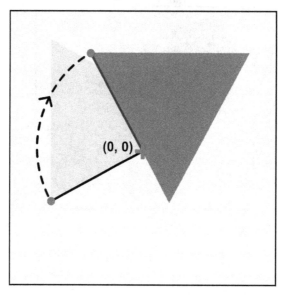

Notice that the rotation takes place around the center of the screen. The center of the screen is the world's origin. Each vertex rotates around the world origin.

Matrix concatenation

You may want the rotation to take place around a point other than the world origin. You'll now rotate the triangle around its right-most point.

To do this, you'll work out the distance between the world origin and the right-most point. You'll translate all the vertices by this distance, rotate, and then translate back again.

Change your previous rotation code:

```
matrix.columns.0 = [cos(angle), -sin(angle), 0, 0]
matrix.columns.1 = [sin(angle), cos(angle), 0, 0]
```

To:

```
var distanceVector = float4(vertices.last!.x,
                            vertices.last!.y,
                            vertices.last!.z, 1)
var translate = matrix_identity_float4x4
translate.columns.3 = distanceVector
var rotate = matrix_identity_float4x4
rotate.columns.0 = [cos(angle), -sin(angle), 0, 0]
```

```
rotate.columns.1 = [sin(angle), cos(angle), 0, 0]
```

Here, you set up two separate matrices: one for translation and one for rotation. The translation matrix is using the right-most point of the triangle.

Now for the magic! You can multiply several matrices together to get one final matrix that holds all of the transformations.

Remember the steps. Step 1 was to translate all the other vertices by the distance from the world origin. You can achieve this by setting a matrix to the vertex's vector value and using the translate matrix's **inverse**.

Run the playground after each of the following steps to follow what the matrix multiplication does. Add this after the previous code:

```
matrix = translate.inverse
```

You moved the triangle so that the right-most point is at the world origin.

Change the code you just entered to:

```
matrix = rotate * translate.inverse
```

The triangle rotates by 90° around the world origin.

> **Note**: Matrix multiplication order is important. Try changing the previous code to:
>
> ```
> matrix = translate.inverse * rotate
> ```
>
> You get a completely different (and incorrect in this instance) result. Generally, the order of multiplication is TRS or `translate * rotate * scale * point`. The matrix operations work backward — you first scale the point, then rotate the result, then finally translate that result.

Change the code you just entered to:

```
matrix = translate * rotate * translate.inverse
```

Now you're doing all the steps of translating each vertex by the distance of the right-most vertex from the world origin; then rotating it; then translating it back again.

Run the playground, and you'll see the final 90° rotation around the right-most triangle point.

You now know how to translate, rotate and scale points and triangles using transformation matrices.

Coordinate spaces

Now that you know about matrices, you'll be able to convert models and entire scenes between different coordinate spaces. Coordinate spaces map different coordinate systems, and just by multiplying a vertex by a particular matrix, you convert the vertex to a different space.

A vertex on its trip through the pipeline will pass through (usually) six spaces:

- Object space

- World space

- Camera space

- Clip space

- NDC (Normalized Device Coordinate) space

- Screen space

This is starting to sound like a description of Voyager leaving our solar system, so take a closer conceptual look at each space.

Object space

You may be familiar with Cartesian coordinates from your graphing days. This image is a 2D grid showing possible vertices mapped out in Cartesian coordinates.

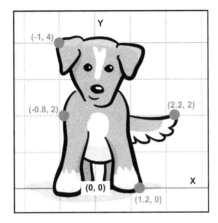

The positions of these vertices are in relation to the **origin** of the dog, which is at (0, 0). They are in what's called **object space** (or **local** or **model** space).

World space

In the following picture, the direction arrows mark the origin. This is the center of world space at (0, 0, 0). In world space, the dog is at (1, 0, 1) and the cat is at (-1, 0, -2).

However, cats are always the center of their universe, so in cat space, the cat thinks that he is at (0, 0, 0). This would make the dog's position relative to the cat (2, 0, 3). When the cat moves, in his universe he is always at (0, 0, 0) and the position of everything else in the world changes relative to the cat.

> **Note**: Cat space is not recognized as a traditional 3D coordinate space, but mathematically, you can create your own space and use any position in the universe as the origin. Every other point in the universe is now relative to that origin. In a later chapter, you'll discover other spaces besides the ones described here.

Camera space

For the dog, the center of his universe is the person holding the camera behind the picture. In camera space, the camera is at (0, 0, 0), and the dog is approximately at (−3, −2, 7). When the camera moves, it stays at (0, 0, 0), but the positions of the dog and cat move relative to the camera.

Clip space

The main reason for doing all this math is to turn a three-dimensional scene with perspective into a two-dimensional scene. Clip space is a cube that is ready for flattening.

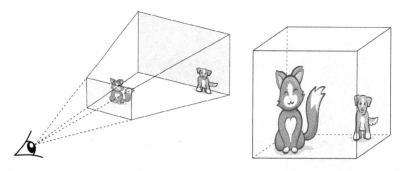

> **Note**: If you want to render engineering drawings, for example, you might use orthographic or isometric projection instead of perspective projection.

NDC space

Projection into clip space creates a half cube of w size. During rasterization, the GPU will convert the w into normalized coordinate points between -1 and 1 for the x-axis and y-axis and 0 and 1 for the z-axis.

Screen space

Now that the GPU has a normalized cube, it will flatten clip space and convert into screen coordinates ready to display on the device's screen.

In this image, the dog is the same size as the cat, but it's further away from the camera.

Converting between spaces

You may have already guessed it: you use transformation matrices to convert from one space to another.

For example, in the following image, the vertex on the dog's ear, which was (−1, 4, 0) in object space, is now, looking at the picture, at about (0.75, 1.5, 1) in world space.

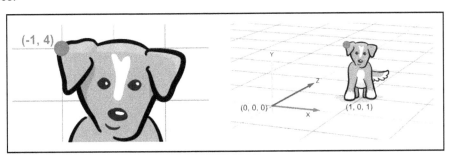

To move the dog vertices from object space to world space, using a transformation matrix, you'd translate (move) them, and also scale them down.

There are four spaces that you control, so there are three corresponding matrices that you'll shortly construct:

- model matrix: between object and world space

- view matrix: between world and camera space

- projection matrix: between camera and clip space

Coordinate systems

Different graphics APIs use different systems. You already found out that Metal's NDC (Normalized Device Coordinates) use 0 to 1 on the z-axis. You may already be familiar with OpenGL, which uses 1 to -1 on the z-axis.

In addition to being a different size, OpenGL's z-axis points in the opposite direction from Metal's z-axis. OpenGL's system is called a **right-handed** coordinate system, and Metal's is a **left-handed** coordinate system.

Both systems use x to the right and y as up. Blender uses a different coordinate system again, where z is up, and y is into the screen.

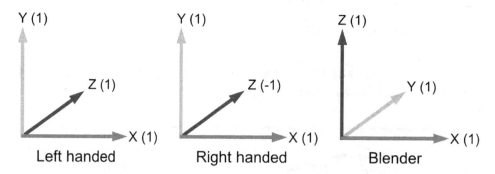

If you are consistent with your coordinate system and create matrices accordingly, it doesn't matter what coordinate system you use. In this book, we chose to use Metal's left-handed coordinate system, but we could equally have decided to use a right-handed coordinate system with different matrix creation methods.

Upgrade the engine

Open the starter app for this chapter, named **Matrices**. This app is the same as at the end of the previous chapter, with the addition of **MathLibrary.swift**. This utility file contains methods that are extensions on float4x4 for creating the translation, scale and rotation matrices that you created in your 3DTransforms playground.

Currently, your train takes up the whole screen, is stretched to fill the window, resizes when you resize the window and has no depth perspective.

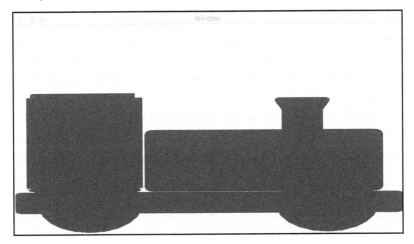

You can decouple the train's vertex positions from the window size by taking the train into other coordinate spaces. It's the vertex function that is responsible for converting the model vertices through these various coordinate spaces, and that's where you will perform the matrix multiplications that do the conversions between different spaces.

Uniforms

Constant values that are the same across all vertices or fragments are generally referred to as **uniforms**. You'll create a uniform struct to hold the conversion matrices and then apply them to every vertex.

Both the shaders and the code on the Swift side will access these uniform values. If you were to create a struct in Renderer and a matching struct in **Shaders.metal**, it's effortless to forget to keep them synchronized. The easiest method is to create a bridging header that both C++ and Swift can access.

Create a new file in the **Matrices** group, using the macOS **Header File** template. Name it **Common.h**.

In the Project navigator, click the main **Matrices** project folder.

Select the **Project Build Settings**. In the search bar, type **bridg** to narrow down the settings. Double click the **Objective-C Bridging Header** value and enter **Matrices/Common.h**.

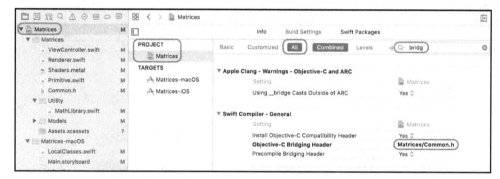

This tells Xcode to use this file for both the Metal Shading Language and Swift.

In **Common.h**, before the final #endif, import the **simd** framework. This framework provides types and functions for working with vectors and matrices. Add this code:

```
#import <simd/simd.h>
```

Model matrix

Add the uniforms struct to **Common.h**:

```
typedef struct {
  matrix_float4x4 modelMatrix;
  matrix_float4x4 viewMatrix;
  matrix_float4x4 projectionMatrix;
} Uniforms;
```

These three matrices with four rows and four columns, will hold the necessary conversion between spaces as mentioned earlier.

Your train vertices are currently in object space. You'll now use modelMatrix to convert them to world space. Simply by changing modelMatrix you'll easily be able to translate, scale and rotate your train.

In **Renderer.swift**, add the new struct to `Renderer`:

```
var uniforms = Uniforms()
```

Common.h is the bridging header file, so Swift is able to pick up the `Uniforms` type.

At the bottom of `init(metalView:)` add:

```
let translation = float4x4(translation: [0, 0.3, 0])
let rotation =
    float4x4(rotation: [0, 0, Float(45).degreesToRadians])
uniforms.modelMatrix = translation * rotation
```

Here, you set `modelMatrix` to have a translation of 0.3 units up and a counterclockwise rotation of 45 degrees.

In `draw(in:)`, replace:

```
timer += 0.05
var currentTime: Float = sin(timer)
renderEncoder.setVertexBytes(&currentTime,
            length: MemoryLayout<Float>.stride, index: 1)
```

With:

```
renderEncoder.setVertexBytes(&uniforms,
            length: MemoryLayout<Uniforms>.stride, index: 1)
```

That's set up the uniform matrix values on the Swift side. In **Shaders.metal**, import the bridging header file below setting the namespace:

```
#import "Common.h"
```

Change the vertex function to:

```
vertex float4 vertex_main(const VertexIn vertexIn [[stage_in]],
                  constant Uniforms &uniforms [[buffer(1)]])
{
  float4 position = uniforms.modelMatrix * vertexIn.position;
  return position;
}
```

Here, you receive the `Uniforms` struct as a parameter and multiply all the vertices by the model matrix. Build and run the app.

You should see the following:

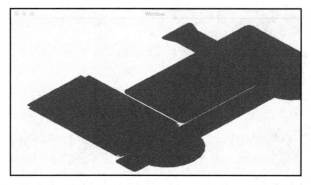

All the vertices are translated by 0.3 units in the y-direction and then rotated. Notice how the train is skewed. Make your window square to see the train rotated correctly.

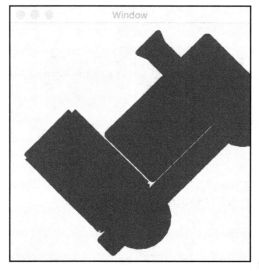

You'll fix this skewing shortly.

View matrix

To convert between world space and camera space, you'll set a view matrix. Depending on how you want to move the camera in your app, you can construct the view matrix appropriately. The view matrix you'll create here is a simple one that is best for FPS (First Person Shooter) style games.

In **Renderer.swift**, at the end of init(metalView:), add this code:

```
uniforms.viewMatrix = float4x4(translation: [0.8, 0, 0]).inverse
```

Remember that all the objects in the scene should move in the opposite direction to the camera. inverse does an opposite transformation. For example, as the camera moves to the right, everything in the world will move 0.8 units to the left. You set the camera as you want it in world space, and then add .inverse on the end so that all objects will react relatively to the camera.

In **Shaders.metal**, change:

```
float4 position = uniforms.modelMatrix * vertexIn.position;
```

To:

```
float4 position = uniforms.viewMatrix * uniforms.modelMatrix
                      * vertexIn.position;
```

Build and run the app, and the train moves to the left. Later, you'll navigate through a scene using the keyboard and just changing the view matrix will update all the objects in the scene around the camera.

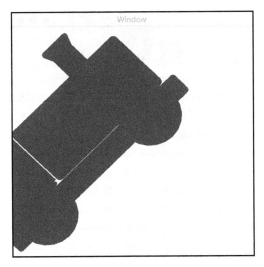

The last matrix you'll set will prepare the vertices to move from camera space to clip space. It will also allow you to use unit values instead of the -1 to 1 NDC (Normalized Device Coordinates) that you've been using up to now.

Rotate the train on the y-axis to demonstrate why this is necessary. In **Renderer.swift**, in draw(in:), just above:

```
renderEncoder.setVertexBytes(&uniforms,
        length: MemoryLayout<Uniforms>.stride, index: 1)
```

Add this code:

```
timer += 0.05
uniforms.viewMatrix = float4x4.identity()
uniforms.modelMatrix = float4x4(rotationY: sin(timer))
```

Here, you reset the camera and replace the translation matrix with a rotation around the y-axis.

Build and run the app.

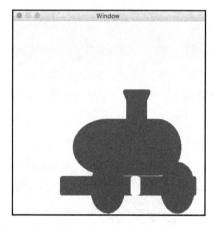

You can see that when the train rotates, any vertices that are greater than 1.0 on the z-axis are being clipped. Remember that any vertex outside Metal's NDC will be clipped.

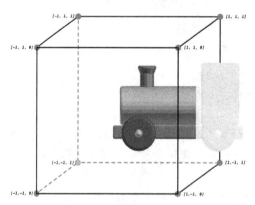

Projection

So far you haven't applied any perspective to your render. Perspective is where close objects appear bigger than objects that are farther away.

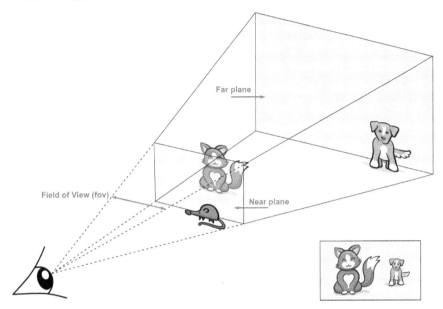

When you render a scene, you'll have to take into account:

- How much of that scene will fit on the screen. Your eyes have a **field of view** of about 200°, and within that field of view, your computer screen takes up about 70°.

- How far you can see by having a **far plane**. Computers can't see to infinity.

- How close you can see by having a **near plane**.

- The **aspect ratio** of the screen. Currently, your train changes size when the screen size changes. When you take into account the width and height ratio, this won't happen.

The image above shows all these. The shape created from the near to the far plane is a cut-off pyramid called a **frustum**. Anything in your scene that is located outside the frustum will not render.

Compare the rendered image again to the scene setup. The rat in the scene does not render because he is in front of the near plane.

MathLibrary.swift provides a projection method that returns the matrix to project objects within this frustum into clip space ready for conversion to NDC coordinates.

Projection Matrix

Open **Renderer.swift**, and at the end of init(metalView:) set up the projection matrix:

```
let aspect = Float(metalView.bounds.width) /
Float(metalView.bounds.height)
let projectionMatrix =
  float4x4(projectionFov: Float(45).degreesToRadians,
           near: 0.1,
           far: 100,
           aspect: aspect)
uniforms.projectionMatrix = projectionMatrix
```

You're using a field of view of 45°; a near plane of 0.1, and a far plane of 100 units.

In **Shaders.metal**, in the vertex function, change the position matrix calculation to:

```
float4 position =
    uniforms.projectionMatrix * uniforms.viewMatrix
    * uniforms.modelMatrix * vertexIn.position;
```

Build and run the app. The z-coordinates measure differently now, so you're zoomed in on the train.

In **Renderer.swift**, in draw(in), replace:

```
timer += 0.05
uniforms.viewMatrix = float4x4.identity()
uniforms.modelMatrix = float4x4(rotationY: sin(timer))
```

With:

```
uniforms.viewMatrix = float4x4(translation: [0, 0, -3]).inverse
```

This moves the camera back into the scene by three units.

In init(metalView:), change:

```
let rotation =
    float4x4(rotation: [0, 0, Float(45).degreesToRadians])
```

To:

```
let rotation =
    float4x4(rotation: [0, Float(45).degreesToRadians, 0])
```

This changes the model's rotation from around the z axis to around the y axis.

In `init(metalView:)`, change the projection matrix's `projectionFOV` parameter to **70°**: the train appears smaller because the field of view is wider, and more objects horizontally will fit into the rendered scene.

 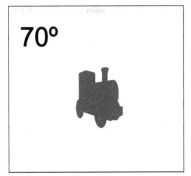

Note: Experiment with the projection values in `init(metalView:)`. Set `translation`'s z value to a distance of 97: the front of the train is just visible. At z = 98, the train is no longer visible. (The projection far value is 100 units, and the camera is back 3 units.) If you change the projection's far parameter to 1000, the train is visible again.

Perspective divide

Now that you've converted your vertices from object space through world space through camera space to clip space, the GPU takes over to convert to NDC coordinates (that's -1 to 1 in the x and y directions and 0 to 1 in the z direction). The ultimate aim is to scale all the vertices from clip space into NDC space, and by using the fourth **w** component, this becomes easy.

To scale a point such as (1, 2, 3), you can have a fourth component: (1, 2, 3, 3). Divide by that last w component to get (1/3, 2/3, 3/3, 1). The xyz values are now scaled down. These coordinates are called **homogeneous**. (Homogeneous means *of the same kind*.)

The projection matrix projected the vertices from a frustum to a cube in the range -w to w. After the vertex leaves the vertex function along the pipeline, the GPU will perform a **perspective divide** and divide the x, y and z values by their w value. The higher the w value, the further back the coordinate is. The result of this is that all visible vertices will now be within NDC.

> **Note**: To avoid a divide by zero, the projection near plane should always be a value slightly more than zero.

In the following picture, the dog and the cat are the same height — perhaps a y value of 2 for example. With projection, as the dog is further back, it should appear smaller in the final render.

After projection, the cat might have a w value of ~1 and the dog a w value of ~8. Dividing by w would give the cat a height of 2 and the dog a height of 1/4 which will make the dog appear smaller.

NDC to screen

Lastly, the GPU converts from normalized coordinates to whatever the device screen size is. You may already have done something like this at some time in your career when converting between normalized coordinates and screen coordinates.

To convert Metal NDC (Normalized Device Coordinates) which are between -1 and 1 to a device, you could use code something like this:

```
converted.x = point.x * screenWidth/2  + screenWidth/2
converted.y = point.y * screenHeight/2 + screenHeight/2
```

However, you can also do this with a matrix by scaling half the screen size and translating by half the screen size. The clear advantage of this is that you can set up a transformation matrix once and multiply any normalized point by the matrix to convert it into the correct screen space using code like this:

```
converted = matrix * point
```

As you can see in **MatrixCalculator**, this transformation matrix transforms a normalized point to iPhone XS (375×812) space:

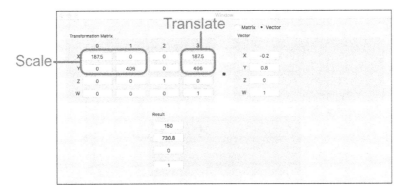

The rasterizer on the GPU takes care of this matrix calculation for you.

Update screen dimensions

Currently, when you rotate your iOS device or rescale the macOS window, the train stretches with the size of the window. You'll need to update the aspect ratio for the projection matrix whenever this happens. Fortunately MTKViewDelegate gives you a method whenever the view's drawable size changes.

In **Renderer.swift**, add the following to mtkView(_:drawableSizeWillChange:):

```
let aspect = Float(view.bounds.width) /
Float(view.bounds.height)
let projectionMatrix =
  float4x4(projectionFov: Float(70).degreesToRadians,
           near: 0.001,
           far: 100,
           aspect: aspect)
uniforms.projectionMatrix = projectionMatrix
```

In `init(metalView:)`, replace the projection code similar to the above with:

```
mtkView(metalView,
        drawableSizeWillChange: metalView.bounds.size)
```

Build and run the app; now the projection matrix updates every time you resize the window.

Where to go from here?

You've covered a lot of mathematical concepts without diving too far into the underlying mathematical principles. To get started in computer graphics, you can fill your transform matrices and continue multiplying them at the usual times, but to be sufficiently creative, you will need to understand some linear algebra.

A great place to start is Grant Sanderson's Essence of Linear Algebra at https://www.youtube.com/playlist?list=PLZHQObOWTQDPD3MizzM2xVFitgF8hE_ab. This treats vectors and matrices visually.

You'll also find some further references in **references.markdown** in the Resources for this chapter.

Even though your train is rendering in three dimensions, it still *looks* two dimensional. Some lighting and fake shadows will help improve the render in the next chapter.

Chapter 5: Lighting Fundamentals

By Caroline Begbie

In this chapter, you'll learn basic lighting. However, more importantly, you'll learn how to manipulate data in shaders and be on the path to mastering shader artistry. Lighting, shadows, non-photorealistic rendering — these are all techniques that start with the methods you'll learn in this chapter.

One of the simplest methods of lighting is the **Phong reflection model**. It's named after Bui Tong Phong who published a paper in 1975 extending older lighting models. The idea is not to attempt duplication of light and reflection physics but to generate pictures that look realistic.

This model has been popular for over 40 years and is a great place to start learning how to fake lighting using a few lines of code. All computer images are fake, but there are more modern real-time rendering methods that model the physics of light.

In Chapter 7, "Maps & Materials," you'll briefly look at Physically Based Rendering (PBR), the lighting technique that your renderer will eventually use.

The starter project

Open the starter project for this chapter. There's substantial refactoring, but no new Metal code. The resulting render is the same as from the end of the previous chapter, but the refactored code makes it easier to render more than one model.

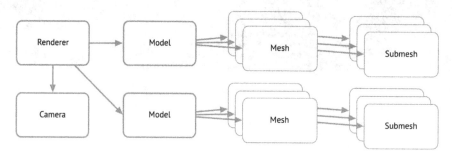

- **Node.swift**: This defines the base class for everything that needs a transform matrix. Models, camera and lights will all need position information, so they will all eventually be subclasses of Node. The transform information in Node abstracts away the matrices. So you just set the position, rotation and scale of a Node, and Node will automatically update its model matrix.

- **Camera.swift**: All the code dealing with the view matrix and the projection matrix is now abstracted into a Camera class. By having Camera as a subclass of Node, you can give the camera a position which will automatically update the view matrix. This will make it easier, later on, to move about the scene or have a First or Third Person camera. In Camera, you can also update field of view and aspect ratio properties which will affect the projection matrix. A new Camera subclass, ArcballCamera, with some fancy matrix calculation, allows you to rotate the scene and zoom into it, so that you'll be able to fully appreciate your new lighting.

- **Model.swift**: Most of the code from Renderer's init(metalView:) that set up the train model is now in the Model class. You can simply set up a Model instance with a name and Model will load up the model file into a mesh with submeshes. You're not restricted to .obj files now either. Model I/O will also read in .usdz files. Try importing the wheelbarrow from Apple's AR samples at https://developer.apple.com/augmented-reality/quick-look/. You'll need to change the model's scale to about 0.01. Not all USDZ files will work - you'll be able to import animated models after Chapter 8, "Character Animation".

- **Mesh.swift**: So far, you have been taking the first `MDLMesh` and converting it to the `MTKMesh` that goes into the Metal vertex buffer. Some models will have more than one `MDLMesh`, so `Mesh` uses `zip()` to combine all the `MDLMeshes` and `MTKMeshes` to create a `Mesh` array held by `Model`.

- **Submesh.swift**: Submeshes are in a class of their own. `Submesh` will later hold surface material and texture information.

- **VertexDescriptor.swift**: Vertex descriptor creation is now an extension on `MDLVertexDescriptor`.

Take some time to review the above changes, as these will persist throughout the book.

`Renderer` now has a `models` property which is an array of `Models`. You're no longer limited to just one train. To render a second model, you create a new instance of `Model`, specifying the filename. You can then append the model to Renderer's `models` array and change the new model's position, rotation and scale at any time.

You now can rotate the camera using your mouse or trackpad. **ViewControllerExtension.swift** is two files: one for the macOS target and one for iOS. It adds the appropriate gestures to the view. **ViewControllerExtension.swift** contains the handler functions to do the zooming and rotating. These update the camera's position and rotation, which in turn updates the scene's view matrix. On macOS, you can scroll to zoom, and click and drag to rotate the scene. On iOS, you can pinch to zoom and pan to rotate.

The project also contains an extra model: a tree. You'll add this to your scene during the chapter.

DebugLights.swift contains some code that you'll use later for debugging where lights are located. Point lights will draw as dots and the direction of the sun will draw as a line.

Familiarize yourself with the code and build and run the project and rotate and zoom the train with your mouse or trackpad.

> **Note**: Experiment with projection too. When you run the app and rotate the train, you'll see that the distant pair of wheels is much smaller than the front ones. In Renderer, in `mtkView(_:drawableSizeWillChange:)`, change the projection field of view from 70° to 40° and rerun the app. You'll see that the size difference is a lot less due to the narrower field of view. Remember to change the field of view back to 70°.

Representing color

The physics of light is a vast, fascinating topic with many books and a large part of the internet dedicated to it. However, in this book, you'll learn the necessary basics to get you rendering light, color and simple shading. You can find further reading in **references.markdown** in the resources directory for this chapter.

In the real world, the reflection of different wavelengths of light is what gives an object its color. A surface that absorbs all light is black. Inside the computer world, pixels display color. The more pixels, the better the resolution and this makes the resulting image clearer. Each pixel is made up of subpixels. These are a predetermined single color, either red, green or blue. By turning on and off these subpixels, depending on the color depth, the screen can display most of the colors visible to the human eye.

In Swift, you can represent a color using the RGB values for that pixel. For example, `float3(1, 0, 0)` is a red pixel, `float3(0, 0, 0)` is black and `float3(1, 1, 1)` is white.

From a shading point of view, you can combine a red surface with a gray light by multiplying the two values together:

```
let result = float3(1.0, 0.0, 0.0) * float3(0.5, 0.5, 0.5)
```

The result is `(0.5, 0, 0)`, which is a darker shade of red.

For simple Phong lighting, you can use the slope of the surface. The more the surface slopes away from a light source, the darker the surface becomes.

Normals

The slope of a surface can determine how much a surface reflects light.

In the following diagram, **point A** is facing straight toward the sun and will receive the most amount of light; **point B** is facing slightly away but will still receive some light; **point C** is facing entirely away from the sun and shouldn't receive any of the light.

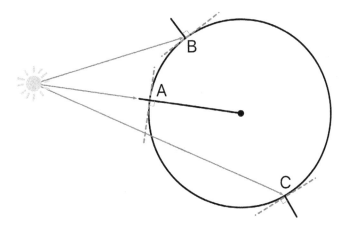

> **Note**: In the real world, light bounces from surface to surface; if there's any light in the room, there will be some reflection from objects that gently lights the back surfaces of all the other objects. This is **global illumination**. The Phong lighting model lights each object individually and is called **local illumination**.

The dotted lines in the diagram are **tangent** to the surface. A tangent line is a straight line that best describes the slope of the curve at a point.

The lines coming out of the circle are at right angles to the tangent lines. These are called **surface normals**, or usually just **normals**. In Chapter 2, "3D Models." you took a look at an .obj file. This file generally contains surface normal values which you can use for finding out the slope of a surface at any given point.

> **Note**: If the .obj file does not contain surface normals, Model I/O can generate them on import using `MDLMesh`'s
> `addNormals(withAttributeNamed:creaseThreshold:)`.

Add normals to vertex descriptor

To be able to assess the slope of the surface in the fragment function, you'll need to send the vertex normal to the fragment function via the vertex function. You'll add the normals to the vertex descriptor so that the vertex function can process them.

In **VertexDescriptor.swift**, when initializing `defaultVertexDescriptor`, you currently create the vertex descriptor with one attribute: the position.

The normal will be the second attribute.

In `defaultVertexDescriptor`, locate the comment `// add the normal attribute here`. After the comment, add this code:

```
vertexDescriptor.attributes[1] =
    MDLVertexAttribute(name: MDLVertexAttributeNormal,
                       format: .float3,
                       offset: offset,
                       bufferIndex: 0)
offset += MemoryLayout<float3>.stride
```

This tells the vertex descriptor to add the normal attribute as a `float3` at an offset of 12 (the stride of a `float3`). That offset is the length of the `position` attribute.

The layout's stride changes by the second `float3`. The vertex buffer now has its data laid out as:

```
[0:position, 0:normal, 1:position, 1:normal, ...]
```

Update the shader functions

Remember that the pipeline state uses this vertex descriptor so that the vertex function can process the attributes. You added another attribute to the vertex descriptor, so in **Shaders.metal**, add this to the struct `VertexIn`:

```
float3 normal [[attribute(1)]];
```

You've now matched the struct attribute 1 with the vertex descriptor attribute 1, and you will be able to access the normal attribute in the vertex function.

Currently, you're only returning the position from the vertex function, but now you'll need to send the repositioned normal to the fragment function. Instead of returning a float4 from the vertex function, you'll return a struct.

Still in **Shaders.metal**, before the vertex function, add this struct:

```
struct VertexOut {
  float4 position [[position]];
  float3 normal;
};
```

The GPU still needs to know which of these properties is the position, so you mark position with the position attribute.

In **Shaders.metal**, change the vertex function to this:

```
vertex VertexOut
      vertex_main(const VertexIn vertexIn [[stage_in]],
                  constant Uniforms &uniforms [[buffer(1)]])
{
  VertexOut out {
    .position = uniforms.projectionMatrix * uniforms.viewMatrix
                * uniforms.modelMatrix * vertexIn.position,
    .normal = vertexIn.normal
  };
  return out;
}
```

You're now returning both the position and the normal from the vertex function inside a struct, instead of just the position.

Now for the fragment function. Change the fragment function to:

```
fragment float4 fragment_main(VertexOut in [[stage_in]]) {
  return float4(in.normal, 1);
}
```

Here, you use the attribute [[stage_in]] to receive the VertexOut information from the vertex function. Just for fun, so that you can visualize the normal values, you return the normal value as a color, converting it to a float4.

Build and run.

That looks messed up!

As you rotate the train, parts of it seem almost transparent. The rasterizer is jumbling up the depth order of the vertices. When you look at a train from the front, you expect the back of the train to be hidden behind the front of the train so you can't see it. However, the rasterizer does not process depth order by default, so you need to give the rasterizer the information it needs with a **depth stencil state**.

Depth

You may remember from Chapter 3, "The Rendering Pipeline," that during the rendering pipeline, the Stencil Test unit checks whether fragments are visible after the fragment function. If a fragment is determined to be behind another fragment, then it's discarded. You'll give the render encoder an `MTLDepthStencilState` property that will describe how this testing should be done.

Back to **Renderer.swift**. First tell the view what sort of depth information to hold:

Toward the top of `init(metalView:)`, but after setting `metalView.device`, add:

```
metalView.depthStencilPixelFormat = .depth32Float
```

The pipeline state that's used by the render encoder has to have the same depth pixel format. The pipeline state is now held by `Model`.

So in **Model.swift**, in buildPipelineState(), before creating the pipeline state, add the depth information to the descriptor:

```
pipelineDescriptor.depthAttachmentPixelFormat = .depth32Float
```

In **Renderer.swift**, add a property for the depth stencil state:

```
let depthStencilState: MTLDepthStencilState
```

Your code won't compile until you have completed the initialization.

Create this method to instantiate the depth stencil state:

```
static func buildDepthStencilState() -> MTLDepthStencilState? {
// 1
  let descriptor = MTLDepthStencilDescriptor()
// 2
  descriptor.depthCompareFunction = .less
// 3
  descriptor.isDepthWriteEnabled = true
  return
      Renderer.device.makeDepthStencilState(
          descriptor: descriptor)
}
```

Going through this code:

1. You create a descriptor that you'll use to initialize the depth stencil state, just as you did the pipeline state.

2. You specify how to compare between the current fragment and fragments already processed. In this case, if the current fragment depth is less than the depth of the previous fragment in the framebuffer, the current fragment replaces that previous fragment.

3. You state whether to write depth values or not. If you have multiple passes (see Chapter 14, "Multipass Rendering"), sometimes you will want to read the already drawn fragments, in which case set it to false. However, this is always true if you are drawing objects and you need them to have depth.

Call the method from init(metalView:) before super.init():

```
depthStencilState = Renderer.buildDepthStencilState()!
```

Your code should now compile.

In draw(in:), add this to the top of the method after guard:

```
renderEncoder.setDepthStencilState(depthStencilState)
```

Build and run to see your train in glorious 3D. As you rotate the train, it will appear in shades of red, green, blue and black.

Consider what you see in this render. The train is no longer a single color blue because you're returning the normal value as a color. The normals are currently in object space, so even though the train is rotated 45° in world space, and you are updating the camera/view space as you rotate the train, the colors/normals don't change.

When a normal points along the model's x-axis (to the right) the value is [1, 0, 0]. That's the same as red in RGB values. Thus the fragment is colored red for those normals pointing to the right. The normals pointing upwards are 1 on the y-axis, so the color is green. The normals pointing towards the camera are negative. When a color is [0, 0, 0] or less, it's black. If you rotate the train, you'll see that the normals pointing in the z direction are blue [0, 0, 1].

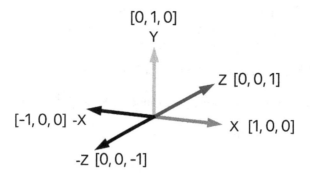

Although this is not a final render, returning values as colors from the fragment function is an excellent way of debugging and determining what a value is.

Now that you have normals in the fragment function, you can start manipulating colors depending on the direction they're facing.

Hemispheric lighting

Hemispheric lighting is where half of a scene is lit in one color, and the other half in another. In the following image, the sky lights the top of the sphere and the ground lights the bottom of the sphere.

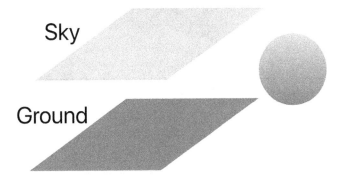

You'll change the fragment function to light the train with this hemispheric lighting. If the normals face up, they'll be blue; if they face down, they'll be green; for the interim values, they'll blend.

In **Shaders.metal**, replace `fragment_main()` with:

```
fragment float4 fragment_main(VertexOut in [[stage_in]]) {
  float4 sky = float4(0.34, 0.9, 1.0, 1.0);
  float4 earth = float4(0.29, 0.58, 0.2, 1.0);
  float intensity = in.normal.y * 0.5 + 0.5;
  return mix(earth, sky, intensity);
}
```

The function `mix` interpolates between the first two values depending on the third value which needs to be between 0 and 1. Your normal values are between -1 and 1, so you convert the intensity to be between 0 and 1.

Build and run to see your lit train. The top of the train is blue, and its underside is green.

You should now be starting to understand the power of the fragment shader. You can color any object precisely the way you want. In Chapter 11, "Tessellation and Terrains," you'll be doing a similar effect: placing snow on a terrain depending on the slope.

Hemispheric lighting isn't very realistic, so now you'll move on to better lighting effects.

Light types

There are several standard light options in computer graphics, each of which has their origin in the real world.

- **Directional Light**: Sends light rays in a single direction. The sun is a directional light.

- **Point Light**: Sends light rays in all directions like a light bulb.

- **Spotlight**: Sends light rays in limited directions defined by a cone. A flashlight or a desk lamp would be a spotlight.

Directional light

A scene can have many lights. In fact, in studio photography, it would be highly unusual to have just a single light. By putting lights into a scene, you control where shadows fall and the level of darkness. You'll add several lights to your scene through the chapter.

The first light you'll create is the sun. The sun is a point light that puts out light in all directions, but for computer modeling, you can consider it a **directional** light. It's a powerful light source a long way away. By the time the light rays reach the earth, the rays appear to be parallel. Check this outside on a sunny day — everything you can see has its shadow going in the same direction.

To define the light types, you'll create a `Light` struct that both the GPU and the CPU can read, and you'll hold an array of `Lights` in `Renderer`.

At the end of **Common.h**, before `#endif`, create an enum of the light types you'll be using:

```
typedef enum {
  unused = 0,
  Sunlight = 1,
  Spotlight = 2,
  Pointlight = 3,
  Ambientlight = 4
} LightType;
```

Under this, add the struct that defines a light:

```
typedef struct {
  vector_float3 position;
  vector_float3 color;
  vector_float3 specularColor;
```

```
    float intensity;
    vector_float3 attenuation;
    LightType type;
} Light;
```

You'll learn about these properties later in the chapter.

Because you'll have several lights, in **Renderer.swift**, create a method for a default light:

```
func buildDefaultLight() -> Light {
    var light = Light()
    light.position = [0, 0, 0]
    light.color = [1, 1, 1]
    light.specularColor = [0.6, 0.6, 0.6]
    light.intensity = 1
    light.attenuation = float3(1, 0, 0)
    light.type = Sunlight
    return light
}
```

Still in **Renderer.swift**, create a property for a sun directional light:

```
lazy var sunlight: Light = {
    var light = buildDefaultLight()
    light.position = [1, 2, -2]
    return light
}()
```

`position` is in world space. This will place a light to the right of the scene, and forward of the train. The train is currently placed at the world's origin.

Under that property, create an array to hold the various lights you'll be creating shortly:

```
var lights: [Light] = []
```

At the end of `init(metalView:)`, add the sun to the array of lights:

```
lights.append(sunlight)
```

You'll do all the light shading in the fragment function so you'll need to pass the array of lights to that function. There is no way to find out the number of items in an array in Metal Shading Language, so you'll pass this in a uniform struct. In **Common.h**, before #endif, add this:

```
typedef struct {
```

Chapter 5: Lighting Fundamentals   137

```
    uint lightCount;
    vector_float3 cameraPosition;
} FragmentUniforms;
```

You'll need the camera position property later.

Set up a new property in Renderer:

```
var fragmentUniforms = FragmentUniforms()
```

At the end of init(metalView:), add this:

```
fragmentUniforms.lightCount = UInt32(lights.count)
```

In Renderer in draw(in:), just before // render all the models in the array, add this:

```
renderEncoder.setFragmentBytes(&lights,
        length: MemoryLayout<Light>.stride * lights.count,
        index: 2)
renderEncoder.setFragmentBytes(&fragmentUniforms,
        length: MemoryLayout<FragmentUniforms>.stride,
        index: 3)
```

Here, you send the array of lights to the fragment function in buffer index 2 and the total count of all the lights in index 3. With all the buffer indexes floating around, the hard-coded index numbers are starting to be difficult to remember; you'll organize this in the challenge at the end of this chapter.

You've now set up a sun light on the Swift side. You'll do all the actual light calculations in the fragment function, and go into more depth about light properties.

The Phong reflection model

In the Phong reflection model, there are three types of light reflection. You'll calculate each of these, and then add them up to produce a final color.

- **Diffuse**: In theory, light coming at a surface bounces off at an angle reflected about the surface normal at that point. However, surfaces are microscopically rough, so light bounces off in all directions as the picture above indicates. This produces a diffuse color where the light intensity is proportional to the angle between the incoming light and the surface normal. In computer graphics, this model is called **Lambertian reflectance** named after Johann Heinrich Lambert who died in 1777. In the real-world, this diffuse reflection is generally true of dull, rough surfaces, but the surface with the most Lambertian property is human-made: Spectralon (https://en.wikipedia.org/wiki/Spectralon), which is used for optical components.

- **Specular**: The smoother the surface, the shinier it is, and the light bounces off the surface in fewer directions. A mirror completely reflects off the surface normal without deflection. Shiny objects produce a visible specular highlight, and rendering specular lighting can give your viewers hints about what sort of surface an object is — whether a car is an old wreck or fresh off the sales lot.

- **Ambient**: In the real-world, light bounces around all over the place, so a shadowed object is rarely entirely black. This is the ambient reflection.

A surface color is made up of an emissive surface color plus contributions from ambient, diffuse and specular. For diffuse and specular, to find out how much light the surface should receive at a particular point, all you have to do is find out the angle between the incoming light direction and the surface normal.

The dot product

Fortunately, there's a straightforward mathematical operation to discover the angle between two vectors called the dot product.

$$A \cdot B = a_1 b_1 + a_2 b_2 + a_3 b_3$$

And:

$$A \cdot B = \|A\| \, \|B\| \, cos(\Theta)$$

Where $\|A\|$ means the length (or magnitude) of vector A.

Even more fortunately, both simd and Metal Shading Language have a function dot() to get the dot product, so you don't have to remember the formulas.

As well as finding out the angle between two vectors, you can use the dot product for checking whether two vectors are pointing in the same direction.

Resize the two vectors into unit vectors — that's vectors with a length of 1. You can do this using the normalize() function. If the unit vectors are parallel with the same direction, the dot product result will be 1. If they are parallel but opposite directions, the result will be -1. If they are at right angles (orthogonal), the result will be 0.

Looking at the previous diagram, if the yellow (sun) vector is pointing straight down, and the blue (normal) vector is pointing straight up, the dot product will be -1. This value is the cosine angle between the two vectors. The great thing about cosines is that they are always values between -1 and 1 so you can use this range to determine how bright the light should be at a certain point.

Take the following example:

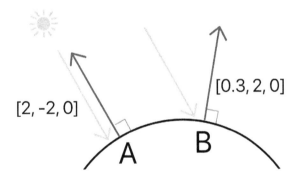

The sun is pouring down from the sky with a direction vector of [2, -2, 0]. Vector A is a normal vector of [-2, 2, 0]. The two vectors are pointing in opposite directions, so when you turn the vectors into unit vectors (normalize them), the dot product of them will be -1.

Vector B is a normal vector of [0.3, 2, 0]. Sunlight is a directional light, so uses the same direction vector. Sunlight and B when normalized have a dot product of -0.59.

This playground code demonstrates the calculations.

```
88  <  >    MyPlayground
1  import simd
2  func degrees(fromRadians radians: Float) -> Float {
3    return (radians / Float.pi) * 180                    (3 times)
4  }
5
   let sun = normalize(float3(2, -2, 0))                  float3(0.707107, -0.707107, 0.0)
   let pointA = normalize(float3(-2, 2, 0))               float3(-0.707107, 0.707107, 0.0)
8
   var result = dot(sun, pointA)                          -0.9999998
   degrees(fromRadians: acos(result))                     179.9657
11
   let pointB = normalize(float3(0.3, 2, 0))              float3(0.14834, 0.988936, 0.0)
   result = dot(sun, pointB)                              -0.5943909
   degrees(fromRadians: acos(result))                     126.4692
15
```

Note: The result after line 8 shows that you should always be careful when
using floating points, as results are never exact. Never use an expression such
as if (x == 1.0) - always check <= or >=.

In the fragment shader, you'll be able to take these values and multiply the fragment
color by the dot product to get the brightness of the fragment.

Diffuse reflection

In this app, shading from the sun does not depend on where the camera is. When you
rotate the scene, you're rotating the world, including the sun. The sun's position will
be in world space, and you'll put the model's normals into the same world space to be
able to calculate the dot product against the sunlight direction. You can choose any
space, as long as you are consistent and are sure to calculate with vectors and
positions in the same space.

To be able to assess the slope of the surface in the fragment function, you'll
reposition the normals in the vertex function in much the same way as you
repositioned the vertex position earlier. You'll add the normals to the vertex
descriptor so that the vertex function can process them.

In **Shaders.metal**, change VertexOut to:

```
struct VertexOut {
  float4 position [[position]];
  float3 worldPosition;
  float3 worldNormal;
};
```

The last two properties, `worldPosition` and `worldNormal`, will hold the vertex position and normal in world space.

In `vertex_main()` remove:

```
.normal = vertexIn.normal
```

You'll replace the fragment function in a moment, so don't worry about the compiler error there.

Calculating the new position of normals is a bit different from the vertex position calculation. **MathLibrary.swift** contains a matrix method to create a normal matrix from another matrix. This normal matrix is a 3×3 matrix, because firstly, you'll do lighting in world space which doesn't need projection, and secondly, translating an object does not affect the slope of the normals. Therefore, you don't need the fourth W dimension. However, if you scale an object in one direction (non-linearly), then the normals of the object are no longer orthogonal and this approach won't work. As long as you decide that your engine does not allow non-linear scaling, then you can use the upper-left 3×3 portion of the model matrix, and that's what you'll do here.

In **Common.h**, add this matrix property to `Uniforms`:

```
matrix_float3x3 normalMatrix;
```

This will hold the normal matrix in world space.

In **Renderer.swift**, in `draw(in:)`, near the top of the `for model in models` loop, after you've set `uniforms.modelMatrix`, add this:

```
uniforms.normalMatrix = uniforms.modelMatrix.upperLeft
```

This creates the normal matrix from the model matrix.

In **Shaders.metal**, in `vertex_main`, when defining `out`, populate the `VertexOut` properties:

```
.worldPosition = (uniforms.modelMatrix * vertexIn.position).xyz,
.worldNormal = uniforms.normalMatrix * vertexIn.normal
```

Here, you convert the vertex position and normal to world space.

Earlier in the chapter, you sent `Renderer`'s `lights` array to the fragment function in index 2, but you haven't changed the fragment function to receive the array.

Change the fragment function to the following:

```
fragment float4 fragment_main(VertexOut in [[stage_in]],
// 1
    constant Light *lights [[buffer(2)]],
    constant FragmentUniforms &fragmentUniforms [[buffer(3)]]) {
  float3 baseColor = float3(0, 0, 1);
  float3 diffuseColor = 0;
// 2
  float3 normalDirection = normalize(in.worldNormal);
  for (uint i = 0; i < fragmentUniforms.lightCount; i++) {
    Light light = lights[i];
    if (light.type == Sunlight) {
      float3 lightDirection = normalize(-light.position);
      // 3
      float diffuseIntensity =
              saturate(-dot(lightDirection, normalDirection));
      // 4
      diffuseColor += light.color
                        * baseColor * diffuseIntensity;
    }
  }
// 5
  float3 color = diffuseColor;
  return float4(color, 1);
}
```

Going through this code:

1. You accept the lights into constant space. You also make the base color of the train blue again.

2. You get the light's direction vector from the light's position and turn the direction vectors into unit vectors so that both the normal and light vectors have a length of 1.

3. You get the dot product of the two vectors. When the fragment fully points toward the light, the dot product will be -1. It's easier for further calculation to make this value positive, so you negate the dot product. `saturate()` makes sure the value is between 0 and 1 by clamping the negative numbers. This gives you the slope of the surface, and therefore the intensity of the diffuse factor.

4. Multiply the blue color by the diffuse intensity to get the diffuse shading.

5. Set the final color to the diffuse color. Shortly this value will include ambient, specular and other lights too.

DebugLights.swift has some debugging methods. You'll find **DebugLights.swift** in the **Utility** group. Remove /* and */ around debugLights(renderEncoder:lightType:), but leave the other comment marks there so as not to get a compile error.

To visualize the direction of the sun light using this debugging method, in **Renderer.swift**, toward the end of draw(in:), before renderEncoder.endEncoding(), add this:

```
debugLights(renderEncoder: renderEncoder, lightType: Sunlight)
```

Build and run.

The red lines show the parallel sun light direction vector. As you rotate the train, you can see that the brightest parts are the ones facing towards the sun.

> **Note:** the debug method uses .line as the rendering type. Unfortunately line width is not configurable, so the lines may disappear at certain angles when they are too thin to render.

This shading is pleasing, but not accurate. Take a look at the back of the train. The back of the cabin is black; however, you can see that the top of the chassis is bright blue because it's facing up. In the real-world, the chassis would be blocked by the cabin and so be in the shade. However, you're currently not taking occlusion into account, and you won't be until you master shadows in Chapter 14, "Multipass and Deferred Rendering".

Ambient reflection

In the real-world, colors are rarely pure black. There's light bouncing about all over the place. To simulate this, you can use ambient lighting. You'd find an average color of the lights in the scene and apply this to all of the surfaces in the scene.

In **Renderer.swift**, add an ambient light property:

```
lazy var ambientLight: Light = {
  var light = buildDefaultLight()
  light.color = [0.5, 1, 0]
  light.intensity = 0.1
  light.type = Ambientlight
  return light
}()
```

This light is a bright green color, but it's toned down so it will be only 10% of the intensity.

Add this bright green light to `lights`. In `init(metalView:)`, after `lights.append(sunlight)`, add this:

```
lights.append(ambientLight)
```

In **Shaders.metal**, in `fragment_main()`, add a variable to hold ambience from all the ambient lights at the top of the function:

```
float3 ambientColor = 0;
```

Inside the `for` loop after the end of the `if (light.type == Sunlight)` conditional, add this:

```
else if (light.type == Ambientlight) {
  ambientColor += light.color * light.intensity;
}
```

Change:

```
float3 color = diffuseColor;
```

To:

```
float3 color = diffuseColor + ambientColor;
```

Build and run. If you look closely, the black shadows are now tinged green as if there is a green light being bounced around the scene. Change `light.intensity` if you want more pronounced ambient light.

Specular reflection

Last, but not least, is the specular reflection. Your train is starting to look great, but now you have a chance to put a coat of shiny varnish on it and make it spec(-tac-)ular. The specular highlight depends upon the position of the observer. If you pass a shiny car, you'll only see the highlight at certain angles.

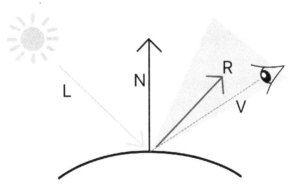

The light comes in (L) and is reflected (R) about the normal (N). If the viewer (V) is within a particular cone around the reflection (R), then the viewer will see the specular highlight. That cone is an exponential shininess parameter. The shinier the surface is, the smaller and more intense the specular highlight.

In your case, the viewer is your camera so you'll need to pass the camera coordinates, again in world position, to the fragment function. Earlier, you set up a `cameraPosition` property in `fragmentUniforms`, and this is what you'll use to pass the camera position.

In **Renderer.swift**, in draw(in:), just after uniforms.viewMatrix = camera.viewMatrix, add this:

```
fragmentUniforms.cameraPosition = camera.position
```

camera.position is already in world space, and you're already passing fragmentUniforms to the fragment function, so you don't need to take further action here.

In **Shaders.metal**, in fragment_main(), add the following variables:

```
float3 specularColor = 0;
float materialShininess = 32;
float3 materialSpecularColor = float3(1, 1, 1);
```

These hold the specular value for all the lights, the surface material properties of a shininess factor and the specular color. These variables are temporary as you'll later take the values from the model's material properties in a subsequent chapter.

Inside the for loop and inside the if (light.type == Sunlight) conditional, after calculating diffuseColor, add this:

```
if (diffuseIntensity > 0) {
  // 1 (R)
  float3 reflection =
      reflect(lightDirection, normalDirection);
  // 2 (V)
  float3 cameraDirection =
      normalize(in.worldPosition
        - fragmentUniforms.cameraPosition);
  // 3
  float specularIntensity =
      pow(saturate(-dot(reflection, cameraDirection)),
          materialShininess);
  specularColor +=
      light.specularColor * materialSpecularColor
        * specularIntensity;
}
```

Going through this code:

1. Looking at the image above, for the calculation, you'll need (L)ight, (R)eflection, (N)ormal and (V)iew. You already have (L) and (N), so here you use the Metal Shading Language function `reflect()` to get (R).

2. You need the view vector between the fragment and the camera for (V).

3. Now you calculate the specular intensity. You find the angle between the reflection and the view using the dot product, clamp the result between 0 and 1 using `saturate()`, and raise the result to a shininess power using `pow()`. You then use this intensity to work out the specular color for the fragment.

At the end of the function, change:

```
float3 color = diffuseColor + ambientColor;
```

To:

```
float3 color = diffuseColor + ambientColor + specularColor;
```

You can build and run now, but to get a more exciting render, add a second model to the scene.

In **Renderer.swift**, in `init(metalView:)`, after `models.append(train)`, add this code:

```
let fir = Model(name: "treefir.obj")
fir.position = [1.4, 0, 0]
models.append(fir)
```

With the new `Model` class, that's how easy it is to add models to your scene!

At the top of `Renderer`, change the camera properties to show the scene better:

```
lazy var camera: Camera = {
  let camera = ArcballCamera()
  camera.distance = 2.5
  camera.target = [0.5, 0.5, 0]
  camera.rotation.x = Float(-10).degreesToRadians
  return camera
}()
```

Build and run to see your completed lighting.

Your tree is a bit too blue and shiny. In Chapter 7, "Maps and Materials" you'll find out how to read in material and texture properties from the model to change its color and lighting.

You've created a realistic enough lighting situation for a sun. You can add more variety and realism to your scene with point and spot lights.

Point lights

As opposed to the sun light, where we converted the position into parallel direction vectors, point lights shoot out light rays in all directions.

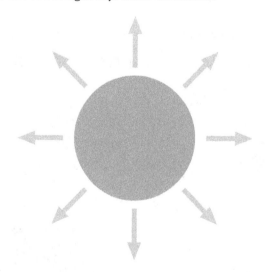

A light bulb will only light an area of a certain radius, beyond which everything is dark. So you'll also specify **attenuation** where a ray of light doesn't travel infinitely far.

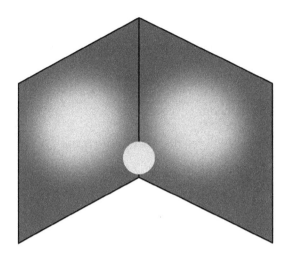

Light attenuation can occur abruptly or gradually. The formula for attenuation is:

$$\frac{1.0}{x + y * distance + z * distance^2}$$

This formula gives the curved fall-off. You'll represent xyz with a float3. No attenuation at all will be float3(1, 0, 0) — substituting x, y and z into the formula results in a value of 1.

In **Renderer.swift**, add a point light property to Renderer:

```
lazy var redLight: Light = {
  var light = buildDefaultLight()
  light.position = [-0, 0.5, -0.5]
  light.color = [1, 0, 0]
  light.attenuation = float3(1, 3, 4)
  light.type = Pointlight
  return light
}()
```

Here, you created a red point light with a position and attenuation. You can experiment with the attenuation values to change radius and fall-off.

Toward the end of `init(metalView)`, add the light to the `lights` array:

```
lights.append(redLight)
```

Toward the end of `draw(in:)`, to debug the point light instead of the sun, change:

```
debugLights(renderEncoder: renderEncoder, lightType: Sunlight)
```

To:

```
debugLights(renderEncoder: renderEncoder, lightType: Pointlight)
```

Build and run. You'll see a small red dot next to the train. This is the position of the point light.

> **Note**: The shader for the point light debug dot is worth looking at. In **DebugLights.metal**, in `fragment_light()`, the square point is turned into a circle by discarding fragments greater than a certain radius from the center of the point.

The debug lights function shows you where the point light is, but it does not produce any light yet. You'll do this in the fragment shader.

In **Shaders.metal**, in the fragment function, add a third part to the conditional testing of the light type:

```
else if (light.type == Pointlight) {
  // 1
```

```
    float d = distance(light.position, in.worldPosition);
    // 2
    float3 lightDirection = normalize(in.worldPosition
                                  - light.position);
    // 3
    float attenuation = 1.0 / (light.attenuation.x +
        light.attenuation.y * d + light.attenuation.z * d * d);

    float diffuseIntensity =
        saturate(-dot(lightDirection, normalDirection));
    float3 color = light.color * baseColor * diffuseIntensity;
    // 4
    color *= attenuation;
    diffuseColor += color;
}
```

Going through this code:

1. You find out the distance between the light and the fragment position.

2. With the directional sun light, you used the position as a direction. Here, you calculate the direction from the fragment position to the light position.

3. Calculate the attenuation using the attenuation formula and the distance to see how bright the fragment will be.

4. After calculating the diffuse color as you did for the sun light, multiply this color by the attenuation.

Build and run, and — no change!

This is because the base color is $(0, 0, 1)$ and the light color is $(1, 0, 0)$. When multiplying the light color by the base color, the result will be $(0, 0, 0)$, and so the light will have no contribution towards the fragment color.

In **Shaders.metal**, at the top of the fragment function, change the base color to:

```
    float3 baseColor = float3(1, 1, 1);
```

Build and run, and you see the full effect of the red point light.

As well as on the side of the train, the red light shines on the back of the wheel and on the top of the chassis.

The models are shaded slightly green because of the ambient light.

Spotlights

The last type of light you'll create in this chapter is the spotlight. This sends light rays in limited directions. Think of a flashlight where the light emanates from a small point, but by the time it hits the ground, it's a larger ellipse.

You define a cone angle to contain the light rays with a cone direction. You also define a cone power to control the attenuation at the edge of the ellipse.

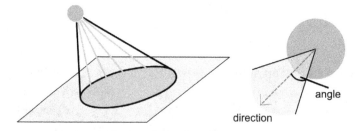

In **Common.h**, add the cone properties to the Light struct:

```
float coneAngle;
vector_float3 coneDirection;
float coneAttenuation;
```

In **Renderer.swift**, add a new light to `Renderer`:

```
lazy var spotlight: Light = {
  var light = buildDefaultLight()
  light.position = [0.4, 0.8, 1]
  light.color = [1, 0, 1]
  light.attenuation = float3(1, 0.5, 0)
  light.type = Spotlight
  light.coneAngle = Float(40).degreesToRadians
  light.coneDirection = [-2, 0, -1.5]
  light.coneAttenuation = 12
  return light
}()
```

This light is similar to the point light with the added cone angle, direction and cone attenuation. Add the light to the array of lights in `init(metalView)`:

```
lights.append(spotlight)
```

At the end of `draw(in:)`, change the debug light render to `Spotlight`:

```
debugLights(renderEncoder: renderEncoder, lightType: Spotlight)
```

Additionally, in **DebugLights.swift**, un-comment out the two lines of code from `debugLights(renderEncoder: lightType:)`. This will render the spotlight position and direction for debugging.

In **Shaders.metal**, in the fragment function, add another part to the conditional testing of the light type:

```
else if (light.type == Spotlight) {
  // 1
  float d = distance(light.position, in.worldPosition);
  float3 lightDirection = normalize(in.worldPosition
                                    - light.position);
  // 2
  float3 coneDirection = normalize(light.coneDirection);
  float spotResult = dot(lightDirection, coneDirection);
  // 3
  if (spotResult > cos(light.coneAngle)) {
    float attenuation = 1.0 / (light.attenuation.x +
        light.attenuation.y * d + light.attenuation.z * d * d);
    // 4
    attenuation *= pow(spotResult, light.coneAttenuation);
    float diffuseIntensity =
            saturate(dot(-lightDirection, normalDirection));
    float3 color = light.color * baseColor * diffuseIntensity;
    color *= attenuation;
    diffuseColor += color;
```

```
    }
  }
}
```

This is very similar to the point light code. Going through the comments:

1. Calculate the distance and direction as you did for the point light. This ray of light may be outside of the spot cone.

2. Calculate the cosine angle (that's the dot product) between that ray direction and the direction the spot light is pointing.

3. If that result is outside of the cone angle, then ignore the ray. Otherwise, calculate the attenuation as for the point light. Vectors pointing in the same direction have a dot product of 1.0.

4. Calculate the attenuation at the edge of the spot light using `coneAttenuation` as the power.

Build and run, and rotate the scene.

The spotlight is behind the train and tree.

Experiment with changing the various attenuations. A cone angle of 5° with attenuation of (1, 0, 0) and a cone attenuation of 1000 will produce a very small targeted soft light; whereas a cone angle of 20° with a cone attenuation of 1 will produce a sharp-edged round light.

Challenge

You're currently using hard-coded magic numbers for all the buffer indices and attributes. As your app grows, these indices and attributes will be much harder to keep track of. Your challenge for this chapter is to hunt down all of the magic numbers and give them names. Just as you did for `LightType`, you'll create an enum in **Common.h**.

This code should get you started:

```
typedef enum {
  BufferIndexVertices = 0,
  BufferIndexUniforms = 1
} BufferIndices;
```

You can now use these constants in both Swift and C++ shader functions:

```
//Swift
renderEncoder.setVertexBytes(&uniforms,
                length: MemoryLayout<Uniforms>.stride,
                index: Int(BufferIndexUniforms.rawValue))

// Shader Function
vertex VertexOut
    vertex_main(const VertexIn vertexIn [[stage_in]],
                constant Uniforms &uniforms
                          [[buffer(BufferIndexUniforms)]])
```

The completed code is in the challenge folder for this chapter.

Where to go from here?

You've covered a lot of lighting information in this chapter. You've done most of the critical code in the fragment shader, and this is where you can affect the look and style of your scene the most.

You've done some weird and wonderful calculations by passing values through the vertex function to the fragment function and working out dot products between surface normals and various light directions. The formulas you used in this chapter are a small cross-section of computer graphics research that various brilliant mathematicians have come up with over the years. If you want to read more about lighting, you'll find some interesting internet sites listed in **references.markdown** in the Resources folder for this chapter.

In the next chapter, you'll learn another important method of changing how a surface looks: Texturing.

Chapter 6: Textures

By Caroline Begbie

Now that you have light in your scene, the next step is to add color. The easiest way to add fine details to a model is to use an image texture. Using textures, you can make your models come to life!

In this chapter, you'll learn about:

- **UV coordinates**: How to unwrap a mesh so that you can apply a texture to it.

- **Texturing a model**: How to read the texture in a fragment shader.

- **Samplers**: Different ways you can read (sample) a texture.

- **Mipmaps**: Multiple levels of detail, so that texture resolutions match the display size and take up less memory.

- **The asset catalog**: How to organize your textures.

Textures and UV maps

The following image shows a simple house model with twelve vertices. So you can experiment, the Blender and .obj files are included in the Resources ▸ LowPolyHouse folder for this chapter. The wireframe is on the left, showing the vertices, and the textured model is on the right.

The house started as a cube but has four extra vertices, two of which raise the roof.

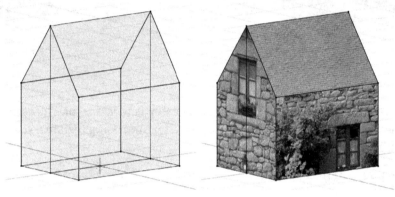

To texture the model, you first have to flatten it using a process called **UV unwrapping**. With UV unwrapping, you create a **UV map** by unfolding the model; this unfolding can be done by marking and cutting seams using your modeling app. The following image is the result of UV unwrapping the house in Blender and exporting the UV map:

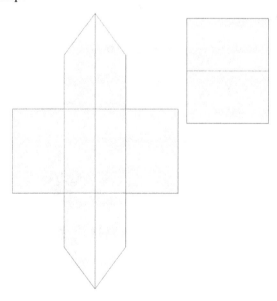

The walls of the house have been marked as seams so they can lie flat; the roof has also been separated out by marking seams as well. If you print this UV map on paper and cut it out, you can fold it back into the house model. In Blender, you have complete control of where the seams are, and how to cut up your mesh. Blender automatically unwraps the model by cutting the mesh at these seams, but if necessary, you can also move every vertex in the UV Unwrap window to suit your texture.

Now that you have a flattened map, you can paint on it by using the UV map exported from Blender as a guide. This is the house texture made in Photoshop. It was created by cutting up a photo of a real house.

Note how the edges of the texture aren't perfect, and there's a copyright message. In the spaces where there are no vertices in the map, you can put whatever you want, as it won't show up on the model. It's a good idea not to match the UV edges exactly, but to let the color bleed, as sometimes computers don't accurately compute floating point numbers.

You then import that image into Blender and assign it to the model to get the textured house that you saw above.

When you export a UV mapped model to an .obj file, Blender adds the UV coordinates to the file. Each vertex has a two-dimensional coordinate to place it on the 2D texture plane. The top-left is (0, 1) and the bottom-right is (1, 0).

The following diagram indicates some of the house vertices, with the matching coordinates from the .obj file. You can look at the contents of the .obj file using TextEdit.

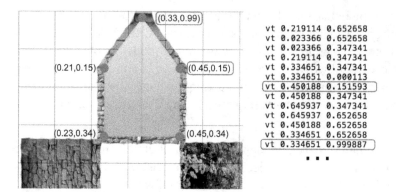

One of the advantages of mapping from 0 to 1 is that you can swap in lower or higher resolution textures. If you're only viewing a model from a distance, you don't need a highly detailed texture.

The house is easy to unwrap, but imagine how complex unwrapping curved surfaces might be. This is the UV map of the train (which is still a simple model):

Photoshop, naturally, is not the only solution for texturing a model. You can use any image editor for painting on a flat texture. In the last few years, several other apps that allow painting directly on the model have become mainstream:

- **Blender** (free)

- **Substance Designer** and **Substance Painter** by Adobe ($$): In Designer, you can create complex materials procedurally. Using Painter, you can paint these materials on the model. The yellow house you'll encounter in the next chapter was textured in Substance Painter.

- **3DCoat** by 3Dcoat.com ($$)

- **Mudbox** by Autodesk ($$)

- **Mari** by Foundry ($$$)

In addition to texturing, using Blender, 3DCoat or Mudbox, you can sculpt models in a similar fashion to ZBrush and create low poly models from the high poly sculpt.

As you'll find out in the next chapter, color is not the only texture you can paint using these apps, so having a specialized texturing app is invaluable.

Texture the model

Open up the starter project for this chapter. The code is almost the same as the challenge project from the previous chapter, except that the scene lighting is refactored to a new `Lighting` struct, and the light debugging code is gone. The initial scene contains the house model that you've already been introduced to with a background color more appropriate to a pastoral scene.

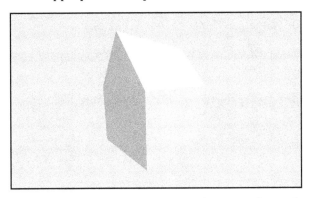

Take a look at `fragment_main()` in **Shaders.metal**. Currently, you're defining the color of the model using `baseColor` with a constant `float3(1, 1, 1)` (white). In this chapter, you'll replace that constant with color from a texture. Initially, you'll use `lowpoly-house-color.png` located in the group **Models ▸ LowPolyHouse**.

To read the image in the fragment function, these are the steps you'll take:

1. Add texture UV coordinates to the model's vertex descriptor.

2. Add a matching UV coordinates attribute to the shader's `VertexIn` struct.

3. Load the image using a protocol extension method.

4. Pass the loaded texture to the fragment function before drawing the model.

5. Change the fragment function to read the appropriate pixel from the texture.

1. Add UV coordinates to the vertex descriptor

As you learned previously, when you unwrap a model in Blender (or the modeling app of your choice), it saves the UV coordinates with the model. To load these into your app, Model I/O needs to have a texture coordinate attribute set up in the vertex descriptor.

First, set up the index number for the texture coordinate attribute in **Common.h**.

Find the `Attributes` enum created for the Challenge sample in the previous chapter, and change it to:

```
typedef enum {
  Position = 0,
  Normal = 1,
  UV = 2
} Attributes;
```

Saving on typing, UV references `TextureCoordinates`.

In **VertexDescriptor.swift**, add a new attribute to `MDLVertexDescriptor`'s `defaultVertexDescriptor`:

```
vertexDescriptor.attributes[Int(UV.rawValue)] =
    MDLVertexAttribute(name:
  MDLVertexAttributeTextureCoordinate,
                       format: .float2,
                       offset: offset,
                       bufferIndex:
  Int(BufferIndexVertices.rawValue))
offset += MemoryLayout<float2>.stride
```

This specifies that you want to read in a `float2` for the texture coordinates at an offset of 24 bytes (the position and normal attributes, being `float3`s, take up 12 bytes each).

The stride of the vertex descriptor layout will now include the size of the `float2` UV attributes.

2. Update the shader attributes

In **Shaders.metal**, the vertex function `vertexIn` parameter uses the `stage_in` attribute which relies on the vertex descriptor layout. By simply updating the `VertexIn` struct with the new texture coordinate attribute, the vertex function will read in the texture coordinate data.

Add this to `struct VertexIn`:

```
float2 uv [[attribute(UV)]];
```

This matches your previous entry in the vertex descriptor attributes.

You'll also need to pass along these coordinates to the fragment function. Add this to `struct VertexOut`:

```
float2 uv;
```

In `vertex_main()`, include setting this property when defining `out`:

```
.uv = vertexIn.uv
```

(Don't forget to add a comma to the end of the line above this.)

As with all of the other values in `VertexOut`, the rasterizer will interpolate the correct UV coordinate for each fragment so the shader will read the appropriate value from the texture — that's why you're sending the UVs through the vertex shader and not straight to the fragment shader.

3. Load the image

Each submesh of a model's mesh has a different material characteristic. In the next chapter, you'll use a model that has a submesh for each unique color. For textured models, each submesh will contain a reference to a unique texture.

> **Note**: For the sake of simplicity, this is a restriction in your app where you don't hold the same texture over multiple submesh materials. To get around this, you could set up a texture controller and hold a list of textures, and point several submeshes to the one texture.

Create a new Swift file named **Texturable.swift**, and include it in both the macOS and iOS targets. Replace the code with:

```
import MetalKit

protocol Texturable {}

extension Texturable {
}
```

Inside the protocol extension, add a default method:

```
static func loadTexture(imageName: String) throws -> MTLTexture?
{
  // 1
  let textureLoader = MTKTextureLoader(device: Renderer.device)

  // 2
  let textureLoaderOptions: [MTKTextureLoader.Option: Any] =
            [.origin: MTKTextureLoader.Origin.bottomLeft]
  // 3
  let fileExtension =
    URL(fileURLWithPath: imageName).pathExtension.isEmpty ?
      "png" : nil
  // 4
  guard let url = Bundle.main.url(forResource: imageName,
                                  withExtension: fileExtension)
    else {
      print("Failed to load \(imageName)")
      return nil
  }

  let texture =
    try textureLoader.newTexture(URL: url,
                                 options: textureLoaderOptions)
  print("loaded texture: \(url.lastPathComponent)")
  return texture
}
```

Going through the code:

1. Loading textures can get complicated. When Metal was first released, you had to specify everything about the image — including pixel format, dimensions and usage — using `MTLTextureDescriptor`. MetalKit introduced `MTKTextureLoader` which provides defaults you can optionally change using loading options.

2. Here, you change a loading option to ensure that the texture loads with the origin at the bottom-left. If you don't specify this option, the texture will be flipped. Try it later: `lowpoly-house-color.png` is almost vertically symmetrical, but with

the texture flipped, the model's roof will be a plain color and show the copyright text.

3. Provide a default extension for the image name.

4. Finally, create a new `MTLTexture` using the provided image name and loader options, and return the newly created texture. Then, for debugging purposes, print the name of the loaded texture.

Now, conform `Submesh` to `Texturable`. In **Submesh.swift**, add this to the bottom of the file:

```
extension Submesh: Texturable {}
```

`Submesh` now has access to the texture loading method.

Conveniently, Model I/O loads a model complete with all the materials. Find **lowpoly-house.mtl** in the group **Models ▸ LowPolyHouse**. The Kd value holds the diffuse material color, in this case, a light gray. At the very bottom of the file, you'll see `map_Kd lowpoly-house-color.png`. This gives Model I/O the diffuse color map file name.

You'll have various textures, so, back in **Submesh.swift**, inside `Submesh`, create a struct and a property to hold the textures:

```
struct Textures {
  let baseColor: MTLTexture?
}

let textures: Textures
```

Your project won't compile until you've initialized `textures`.

`MDLSubmesh` holds each submesh's material in an `MDLMaterial` property. You provide the material with a **semantic** to retrieve the value for the relevant material. For example, the semantic for base color is `MDLMaterialSemantic.baseColor`.

At the end of **Submesh.swift**, add an initializer for `Textures`:

```
private extension Submesh.Textures {
  init(material: MDLMaterial?) {
    func property(with semantic: MDLMaterialSemantic)
        -> MTLTexture? {
      guard let property = material?.property(with: semantic),
        property.type == .string,
        let filename = property.stringValue,
        let texture =
```

```
            try? Submesh.loadTexture(imageName: filename)
        else { return nil }
        return texture
    }
    baseColor = property(with: MDLMaterialSemantic.baseColor)
  }
}
```

`property(with:)` looks up the provided property in the submesh's material, finds the filename string value of the property and returns a texture if there is one. You may remember that there was another material property in the file marked Kd. That was the base color using floats. As you'll see in the next chapter, material properties can also be float values where there is no texture available for the submesh.

This loads the base color texture with the submesh's material. Here, **Base color** means the same as **diffuse**. In the next chapter, you'll load other textures for the submesh in the same way.

At the bottom of `init(submesh:mdlSubmesh:)` add:

```
textures = Textures(material: mdlSubmesh.material)
```

This completes the initialization and removes the compiler warning.

Build and run your app to check that everything's working. Your model should look the same as in the initial screenshot, however, you should get a message in the console:

loaded texture: lowpoly-house-color.png

4. Pass the loaded texture to the fragment function

In the next chapter, you'll learn about several other texture types and how to send them to the fragment function using different indices. So in **Common.h**, set up a new enum to keep track of these texture buffer index numbers:

```
typedef enum {
  BaseColorTexture = 0
} Textures;
```

In **Renderer.swift**, in `draw(in:)`, where you're processing the submeshes, add the following below the comment `// set the fragment texture here`:

```
renderEncoder.setFragmentTexture(submesh.textures.baseColor,
                    index: Int(BaseColorTexture.rawValue))
```

You're now passing the texture to the fragment function in texture buffer 0.

> **Note**: Buffers, textures and sampler states are held in argument tables and, as you've seen, you access them by index numbers. On iOS, you can hold up to 31 buffers and textures and 16 sampler states in the argument table; the number of textures on macOS increases to 128. You can find out features for your device at https://developer.apple.com/metal/Metal-Feature-Set-Tables.pdf

5. Update the fragment function

You'll now change the fragment function to accept the texture and read from it.

In **Shaders.metal**, add the following new argument to `fragment_main()`, immediately after `VertexOut in [[stage_in]],`:

```
texture2d<float> baseColorTexture [[texture(BaseColorTexture)]],
```

When you read in, or **sample** the texture, you may not land precisely on a particular pixel. In texture space, the units that you sample are called **texels**, and you can decide how each texel is processed using a **sampler**. You'll learn more about samplers shortly. Add the following to the start of `fragment_main()`:

```
constexpr sampler textureSampler;
```

This will be used as a default sampler. Next, replace:

```
float3 baseColor = float3(1, 1, 1);
```

With:

```
float3 baseColor = baseColorTexture.sample(textureSampler,
                                    in.uv).rgb;
```

Here, you're sampling the texture using the interpolated UV coordinates sent from the vertex function and retrieving the RGB values. In Metal Shading Language, you can use rgb to address the float elements as an equivalent of xyz.

Temporarily, add this on the next line so that you can see the texture color before you process it with lighting code:

```
return float4(baseColor, 1);
```

Build and run the app to see your textured house!

sRGB color space

You'll notice that the rendered texture looks much darker than the original image.

This is because lowpoly-house-color.png is a sRGB texture. sRGB is a standard color format that compromises between how cathode ray tube monitors worked and what colors the human eye sees. As you can see in the following example of grayscale values from 0 to 1, sRGB colors are not linear. Humans are more able to discern between lighter values than darker ones.

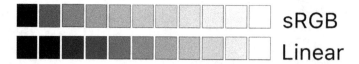

Unfortunately, it's not easy to do the math on colors in a non-linear space. If you multiply a color by 0.5 to darken it, the difference in sRGB will vary along the scale.

You're currently loading the texture as sRGB pixel data and rendering into a linear color space. So when you're sampling a value of, say 0.2 which in sRGB space is mid-gray, the linear space will read that as dark-gray.

To *approximately* convert the color, you can use the inverse of **gamma 2.2**:

```
sRGBcolor = pow(linearColor, 1.0/2.2);
```

If you use this formula on baseColor before returning from the fragment function, your house texture will look about the same as the original sRGB texture. However, a better way of dealing with this is not to load the texture as sRGB at all. In **Texturable.swift**, find:

```
let textureLoaderOptions: [MTKTextureLoader.Option: Any] =
    [.origin: MTKTextureLoader.Origin.bottomLeft]
```

And change it to:

```
let textureLoaderOptions: [MTKTextureLoader.Option: Any] =
    [.origin: MTKTextureLoader.Origin.bottomLeft, .SRGB: false]
```

Build and run, and the texture will now load with the linear color pixel format bgra8Unorm.

Note: You'll find further reading on chromaticity and color in references.markdown in the Resources directory for this chapter.

GPU frame capture

There's an easy way to find out what format your texture is in on the GPU, and also to look at all the other Metal buffers currently residing there: the **GPU frame capture tool** (also called the **GPU Debugger**).

Run your app, and at the bottom of the Xcode window (or above the debug console if you have it open), click the camera icon:

This button captures the current GPU frame. On the left, in the Debug navigator, you'll see the GPU trace:

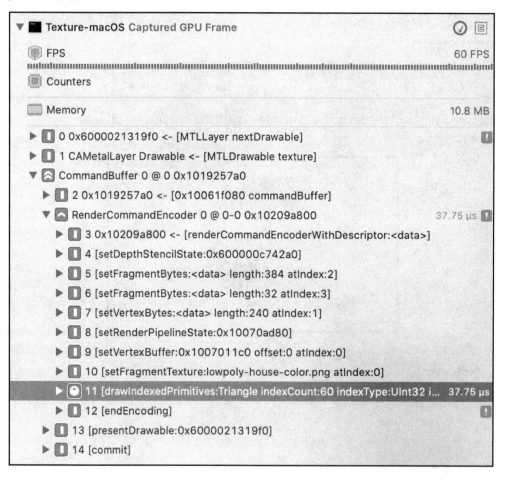

You can see all the commands that you've given to the render command encoder in draw(in:), such as setFragmentBytes and setRenderPipelineState.

Later, when you have several command encoders, you'll see each one of them listed, and you can select them to see what actions or textures they have produced from their encoding.

When you select drawIndexedPrimitives, the Vertex and Fragment resources show.

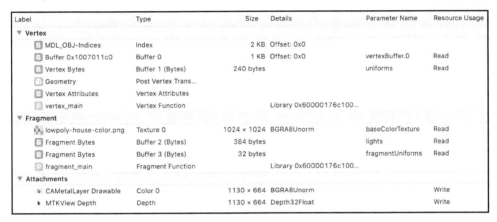

Double-click on each vertex resource to see what's in the buffer:

• **MDL_OBJ-Indices**: The vertex indices.

• **Buffer 0x000000**: The vertex position, normal and texture coordinate data, matching the attributes of your VertexIn struct.

• **Vertex Bytes**: The uniform matrices.

• **Vertex Attributes**: The incoming data from VertexIn, and the VertexOut return data from the vertex function.

• **vertex_main**: The vertex function. When you have multiple vertex functions, this is very useful to make sure that you've got the correct pipeline state set.

Going through the fragment resources:

• **lowpoly-house-color.png**: The house texture in texture slot 0.

• **Fragment Bytes**: You have two of them: one holds the lights array, and the other holds the fragment uniforms light count.

• **fragment_main**: The fragment function.

- **CAMetalLayer Drawable**: The result of the encoding in color attachment 0. In this case, this is the view's current drawable. Later, you'll use multiple color attachments.

- **MTKView Depth**: The depth buffer. Black is closer and white is farther. The rasterizer uses the depth map.

You can see from this list that the GPU is holding the texture as BGRA8Unorm.

If you reverse the previous section's texture loading options and comment out .SRGB: false, you will be able to see that the texture is now BGRA8Unorm_sRGB. (Make sure you restore the option .SRGB: false before continuing.)

If you're ever uncertain as to what is happening in your app, capturing the GPU frame might give you the heads-up because you can examine every render encoder command and every buffer. It's a good idea to use it throughout this book to examine what's happening on the GPU. Chapter 23, "Debugging and Profiling" will give you a more thorough grounding in the GPU Frame Capture tool.

Samplers

When sampling your texture just now, you used a default sampler. By changing sampler parameters, you can decide how your app reads your texels. You'll now add a ground plane to your scene to see how you can control the appearance of the ground texture.

In **Renderer.swift**, in init(metalView:), find where you add the house to the models array. After that, add:

```
let ground = Model(name: "plane.obj")
ground.scale = [40, 40, 40]
models.append(ground)
```

This adds a ground plane and scales it up to be huge.

The ground plane texture will stretch to fit. Build and run:

You can see every individual pixel of the ground texture, which doesn't look good in this particular scene. By changing one of the sampler parameters, you can tell Metal how to process the texel where it's smaller than the assigned fragments.

In **Shaders.metal**, in fragment_main(), change:

```
constexpr sampler textureSampler;
```

To:

```
constexpr sampler textureSampler(filter::linear);
```

This instructs the sampler to smooth the texture. Build and run, and see that the ground texture — although still stretched — is now smooth.

There will be times, such as when you make a retro game of Frogger, that you'll want to keep the pixelation. In that case, use **nearest** filtering.

Linear   Nearest

In this particular case, however, you want to tile the texture. That's easy with sampling!

Change the sampler definition and the baseColor assignment to:

```
constexpr sampler textureSampler(filter::linear,
                                 address::repeat);
float3 baseColor = baseColorTexture.sample(textureSampler,
                                           in.uv * 16).rgb;
```

This multiples the UV coordinates by 16 and accesses the texture outside of the allowable limits of 0 to 1. address::repeat changes the sampler's addressing mode, so here it will repeat the texture 16 times across the plane.

The following image illustrates the other address sampling options shown with a tiling value of 3. You can use s_address or t_address to change only the width or height coordinates respectively.

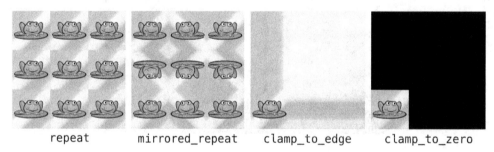

repeat   mirrored_repeat   clamp_to_edge   clamp_to_zero

Build and run your app.

The ground looks great! The house… not so much. The shader has tiled the house texture as well. To overcome this, you'll create a `tiling` property on the model and send it to the fragment function with `fragmentUnforms`.

In **Model.swift**, create a new property on `Model`:

```
var tiling: UInt32 = 1
```

In **Common.h** add this to struct `FragmentUniforms`:

```
uint tiling;
```

In **Renderer.swift**, where you set up the ground in `init(metalView:)`, just before you append the ground to `models`, define the required tiling:

```
ground.tiling = 16
```

In `draw(in:)`, just inside the `for` loop where you process the models, add this:

```
fragmentUniforms.tiling = model.tiling
```

Your assignment of `fragmentUniforms` to an `MTLBuffer` currently takes place before the `for` loop, so move:

```
renderEncoder.setFragmentBytes(&fragmentUniforms,
        length: MemoryLayout<FragmentUniforms>.stride,
        index: Int(BufferIndexFragmentUniforms.rawValue))
```

Inside the `for` loop, after your assignment of the tiling variable.

In **Shaders.metal**, you're already receiving `fragmentUniforms` as a parameter into `fragment_main()`, so replace the constant tiling value with the variable:

```
float3 baseColor = baseColorTexture.sample(textureSampler,
                        in.uv * fragmentUniforms.tiling).rgb;
```

Build and run. Both your ground and the house now tile correctly! :]

Metal API sampler states

Creating a sampler in the shader is not the only option. Instead, you're going to create an `MTLSamplerState` in the Metal API and hold it with the model. You'll then send the sampler state to the fragment function.

In **Model.swift**, add a new property to `Model`:

```
let samplerState: MTLSamplerState?
```

The compile error will go away after you've initialized `samplerState`.

Now add the following method:

```
private static func buildSamplerState() -> MTLSamplerState? {
  let descriptor = MTLSamplerDescriptor()
  descriptor.sAddressMode = .repeat
  descriptor.tAddressMode = .repeat
  let samplerState =
      Renderer.device.makeSamplerState(descriptor: descriptor)
  return samplerState
}
```

This creates the sampler state and you set the sampler to repeat mode, just as you did in the fragment function.

In `init(name:)`, call your new method before `super.init()`:

```
samplerState = Model.buildSamplerState()
```

The compile error should now go away.

In **Renderer.swift**, in `draw(in:)`, locate the `for` loop where you process the models. Inside the `for` loop, just after where you assigned the tiling variable, add this:

```
renderEncoder.setFragmentSamplerState(model.samplerState,
                                      index: 0)
```

You're now sending the sampler state to the fragment function using sampler state slot 0 in the argument table.

In **Shaders.metal**, add a new parameter to `fragment_main`, immediately after `texture2d<float> baseColorTexture [[texture(BaseColorTexture)]],`:

```
sampler textureSampler [[sampler(0)]],
```

Now that you're receiving the sampler into the function, remove:

```
constexpr sampler textureSampler(filter::linear,
                                 address::repeat);
```

Build and run, and the output should be the same as when you were creating the sampler within the fragment function. The main advantage is that it's now easier to set individual parameters per model on the sampler state.

Zoom out of the scene quite a long way, and as you do, notice a moiré pattern is happening on the roof of the house.

Moiré is a rendering artifact that happens when you're undersampling a texture.

As you rotate the scene, there's also distracting noise on the grass toward the horizon, almost as if it's sparkling. You can solve these artifact issues by sampling correctly using resized textures called mipmaps.

Mipmaps

Check out the relative sizes of the roof texture and how it appears on the screen:

The pattern occurs because you're sampling more texels than you have pixels. The ideal would be to have the same number of texels to pixels, meaning that you'd require smaller and smaller textures the further away an object is. The solution is to use **mipmaps** which will let the GPU sample the texture at a suitable size.

MIP stands for *multum in parvo* — a Latin phrase meaning "*much in small.*"

Mipmaps are texture maps resized down by a power of 2 for each level, all the way down to 1 pixel in size. If you have a texture of 64 pixels by 64 pixels, then a complete mipmap set would consist of:

Level 0: 64 x 64, **1**: 32 x 32, **2**: 16 x 16, **3**: 8 x 8, **4**: 4 x 4, **5**: 2 x 2, **6**: 1 x 1.

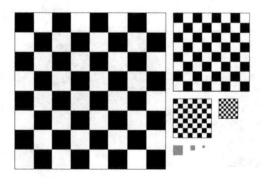

In the following image, the top checkered texture has no mipmaps; but in the bottom image, every fragment is sampled from the appropriate MIP level. As the checkers recede, there's much less noise, and the image is cleaner. At the horizon, you can see the solid color smaller gray mipmaps.

No mipmap

Mipmap

You can easily and automatically generate these mipmaps when first loading the texture.

In **Texturable.swift**, change the texture loading options to:

```
let textureLoaderOptions: [MTKTextureLoader.Option: Any] =
    [.origin: MTKTextureLoader.Origin.bottomLeft,
     .SRGB: false,
     .generateMipmaps: NSNumber(booleanLiteral: true)]
```

This will create mipmaps all the way down to the smallest pixel.

There's one more thing to change: the sampler state. In **Model.swift**, in `buildSamplerState()`, add this before creating the sampler state:

```
descriptor.mipFilter = .linear
```

The default for `mipFilter` is `.notMipmapped`; however, if you provide either `.linear` or `.nearest`, then the GPU will sample the correct mipmap.

Build and run. The noise from both the building and the ground should be gone when you zoom and rotate.

Using the GPU Frame Capture tool, you can inspect the mipmaps. Double-click a texture, and at the bottom-left, you can choose the MIP level. This is MIP level 4 on the house texture:

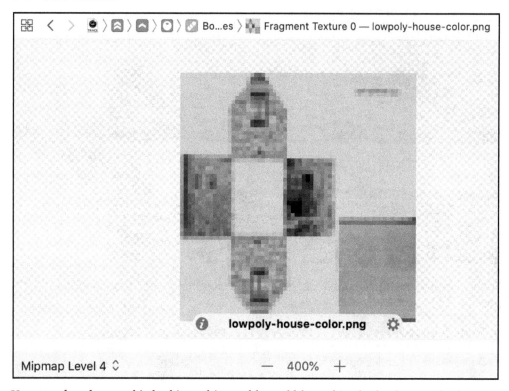

Your rendered ground is looking a bit muddy and blurred in the background. This is due to **anisotropy**. Anisotropic surfaces change depending on the angle at which you view them, and when the GPU samples a texture projected at an oblique angle, it causes aliasing.

In **Model.swift**, in `buildSamplerState()`, add this before creating the sampler state:

```
descriptor.maxAnisotropy = 8
```

Metal will now take 8 samples from the texel to construct the fragment. You can specify up to 16 samples to improve quality. Use as few as you can to obtain the quality you need because the sampling can slow down rendering.

Build and run, and your render should be artifact-free.

When you write your full game, you're likely to have many textures for the different models. Some models are likely to have several textures. Organizing all these textures and working out which ones need mipmaps can become labor intensive. Plus, you'll also want to compress images where you can and send textures of varying sizes and color gamut to different devices. The asset catalog is where you'll turn.

The asset catalog

As its name suggests, the asset catalog can hold all of your assets, whether they be data, images, textures or even colors. You've probably used the catalog for app icons and images. Textures differ from images in that the GPU uses them, and thus they have different attributes in the catalog. To create textures, you add a new texture set to the asset catalog.

You'll now replace the textures for the low poly house and ground and use textures from a catalog. Create a new file using the **Asset Catalog** template under **Resource**, and name it **Textures**. Remember to check both the iOS and macOS targets. With **Textures.xcassets** open, choose **Editor ▸ Add Assets ▸ New Texture Set** (or click the + at the bottom of the panel and choose **New Texture Set**). Double-click the **Texture** name and rename it to **grass**.

Open the **Models ▸ Textures** group and drag **barn-ground.png** to the **Universal** slot in your catalog. With the **Attributes inspector** open, click on the grass to see all of the texture options.

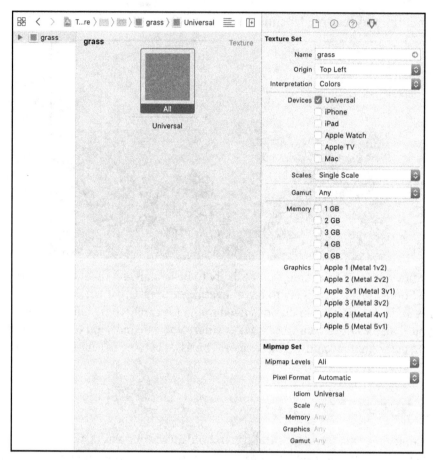

Here, you can see that by default, all mipmaps are created automatically. If you change **Mipmap Levels** to **Fixed**, you can choose how many levels to make. If you don't like the automatic mipmaps, you can replace them with your own custom mipmaps by dragging them to the correct slot. Asset catalogs give you complete control of your textures without having to write cumbersome code; although you can still write the code using the `MTLTextureDescriptor` API if you want.

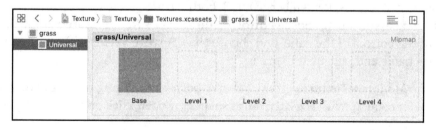

Open **Texturable.swift**, and replace:

```
print("Failed to load \(imageName)")
return nil
```

With:

```
print(
  "Failed to load \(imageName)\n - loading from Assets Catalog")
return try textureLoader.newTexture(name: imageName,
                                    scaleFactor: 1.0,
                                    bundle: Bundle.main,
                                    options: nil)
```

This now searches the bundle for the named image. When loading from the asset catalog, the options that you set in the attributes inspector take the place of most of the texture loading options, so these options are now nil. However, `.textureUsage` and `.textureStorageMode` options still have effect.

> **Note**: You can reverse the read order of the textures to make the asset catalog the default.

The last thing to do is to make sure the model points to the new texture. Open **plane.mtl** located in **Models ▸ Ground**.

Replace:

```
map_Kd ground.png
```

With:

```
#map_Kd ground.png
map_Kd grass
```

Here, you commented out the old texture and added the new one. Build and run, and you now have a new grass texture loading.

Repeat this for the low poly house to change it in to a barn:

1. Create a new texture set in the asset catalog and rename it **barn**.

2. Drag **lowpoly-barn-color.png** into the texture set from the **Models ▸ Textures** group.

3. Change the name of the diffuse texture in **Models ▸ LowPolyHouse ▸ lowpoly-house.mtl** to barn.

> **Note:** Be careful to drop the images on the texture's Universal slot. If you drag the images into the asset catalog, they are, by default, **images** and not **textures**. And you won't be able to make mipmaps on images or change the pixel format.

Build and run and your app to see your new textures.

You can see that the textures have reverted to the sRGB space because you're now loading them in their original format. You can confirm this using the GPU debugger. If you want to avoid converting sRGB to linear in your shader, you can instead set up the texture to be **data**. In **Textures.xcassets**, click on the barn texture, and in the **Attributes inspector**, change the **Interpretation** to **Data**:

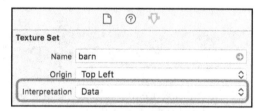

When your app loads the sRGB texture to a non-sRGB buffer, it automatically converts from sRGB space to linear space. (See Apple's Metal Shading Language document for the conversion rule.) By accessing as data instead of colors, your shader can treat the color data as linear.

You'll also notice in the above image that the origin, unlike loading the .png texture manually, is **Top Left**. The asset catalog loads textures differently.

Repeat for the grass texture.

Build and run, and your colors should now be correct.

The right texture for the right job

Using asset catalogs gives you complete control over how to deliver your textures. Currently, you only have two color textures. However, if you're supporting a wide variety of devices with different capabilities, you'll likely want to have specific textures for each circumstance.

For example, here is a list of individual textures you can assign by checking the different options in the Attributes inspector, for the Apple watch, 1x, 2x and 3x sizes, and sRGB and P3 displays.

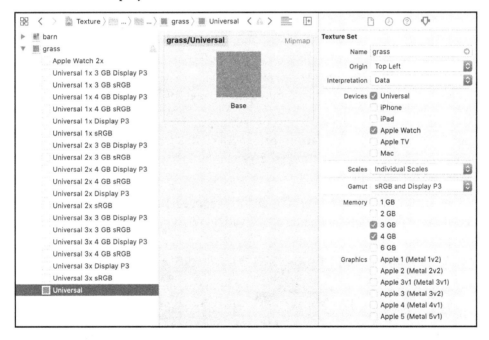

Texture compression

In recent years, people have put in much effort towards compressing textures to save both CPU and GPU memory. There are various formats you can use, such as ETC and PVRTC. Apple has embraced ASTC as being the most high-quality compressed format. ASTC is available on the A8 chip and newer.

Using texture sets within the asset catalog allows your app to determine for itself which is the best format to use.

With your app running on macOS, take a look at how much memory it's consuming. Click on the **Debug navigator** and select Memory. This is the usage after 30 seconds — your app's memory consumption will increase for about five minutes and then stabilize:

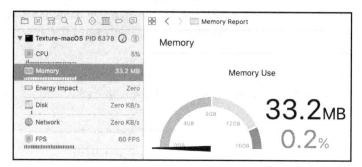

If you capture the frame with the GPU Capture button, you'll see that the texture format on the GPU is **BC7_RGBAUnorm**. When you use asset catalogs, Apple will automatically determine the most appropriate format for your texture.

In **Textures.xcassets**, select each of your textures and in the **Attributes inspector**, change the Pixel Format from **Automatic** to **ASTC 8×8 Compressed - Red Green Blue Alpha**. This is a highly compressed format. Build and run your app, and check the memory usage again.

You'll see that the memory footprint is slightly reduced. However, so is the quality of the render. For distant textures, this quality might be fine, but you have to balance memory usage with render quality.

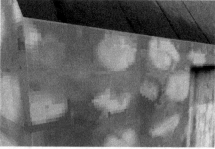

Automatic   ASTC 8x8

> **Note:** You may have to test the app on an iOS device to see the change in texture format in the GPU Debugger. On iOS, the automatic format will be ASTC 4×4, which is indistinguishable from the png render.

Where to go from here?

In this chapter, you found out how to wrap a model in a texture, how to sample that texture in a shader and how to enhance your renders using mipmaps. You also learned how to use the invaluable GPU Frame Capture tool. The GPU Frame Capture tool is great for looking at what's happening on the GPU and analyzing whether or not the shaders are performing the proper steps.

Topics such as color and compression are huge. In the Resources folder for this chapter, in **references.markdown**, you'll find some recommended articles to read further.

But you're not done with textures just yet. In fact, the barn stone wall texture looks a little flat. In the next chapter, you'll find out how to make those stones pop out and appear to have dimension using a *normal* texture. You'll also find out some of the other uses for textures, and you'll examine material properties and how they react to physically based lighting.

Chapter 7: Maps & Materials

By Caroline Begbie

In the previous chapter, using Model I/O, you imported and rendered a simple house with a flat color texture. But if you look at the objects around you, you'll notice how their basic color changes according to how light falls on them. Some objects have a smooth surface, and some have a rough surface. Heck, some might even be shiny metal!

In this chapter, you'll find out how to use material groups to describe a surface, and how to design textures for micro detail. This is also the final chapter on how to render still models.

Normal maps

The following example best describes normal maps:

On the left, there's a lit cube with a color texture. On the right, there's the same low poly cube with the same color texture and lighting, however, it also has a second texture applied to it, called a **normal map**.

With the normal map, it looks as if the cube is a high poly cube with all of the nooks and crannies modeled into the object. But this is just an illusion!

For this illusion to work, it needs a texture, like this:

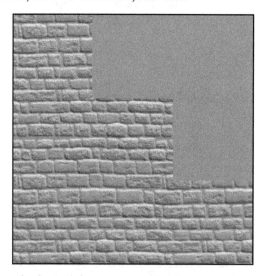

All models have normals that stick out perpendicular to each face. A cube has six faces, and each face's normal points in a different direction. Also, each face is flat. If you wanted to create the illusion of bumpiness, you need to change a normal in the fragment shader.

In the following image, on the left is a flat surface with normals in the fragment shader. On the right, you see perturbed normals. The texels in a normal map supply the direction vectors of these normals through the RGB channels.

Take a look at this single brick split out into the red, green and blue channels that make up an RGB image.

Each channel has a value between 0 and 1, and you generally visualize them in grayscale as it's easier to read color values. For example, in the red channel, a value of 0 is no red at all, while a value of 1 is full red. When you convert 0 to an RGB color (0, 0, 0), that results in black. On the opposite spectrum, (1, 1, 1) is white, and in the middle you have (0.5, 0.5, 0.5) which is mid-gray. In grayscale, all three RGB values are the same, so you only need refer to a grayscale value by a single float.

Take a closer look at the edges of the red channel's brick. Look at the left and right edges in the grayscale image. The red channel has the darkest color where the normal values of that fragment should point left (-X, 0, 0), and the lightest color where it should point right (+X, 0, 0).

Now look at the green channel. The left and right edges have equal value but are different for the top and bottom edges of the brick. The green channel in the grayscale image has darkest for pointing down (0, -Y, 0) and lightest for pointing up (0, +Y, 0).

Finally, the blue channel is mostly white in the grayscale image because the brick — except for a few irregularities in the texture — points outward. The edges of the brick are the only places where the normals should point away.

Note: Normal maps can be either right-handed or left-handed. Your renderer will expect positive y to be up, but some apps will generate normal maps with positive y down. To fix this, you can take the normal map into Photoshop and invert the green channel.

The base color of a normal map — where all normals are "normal" (orthogonal to the face) — is (`0.5, 0.5, 1`).

This is an attractive color but was not chosen arbitrarily. RGB colors have values between 0 and 1, whereas a model's normal values are between -1 and 1. A color value of 0.5 in a normal map translates to a model normal of 0.

The result of reading a flat texel from a normal map should be a z value of 1 and the x and y values as 0. Converting these values (0, 0, 1) into the colorspace of a normal map results in the color (0.5, 0.5, 1). This is why most normal maps appear bluish.

Creating normal maps

To create successful normal maps, you need a specialized app. In the previous chapter, you learned about texturing apps, such as Substance Designer and Mari. Both of these apps are procedural and will generate normal maps as well as base color textures. In fact, the brick texture in the image at the start of the chapter was created in Substance Designer.

Sculpting programs, such as ZBrush, 3D-Coat, Mudbox and Blender will also generate normal maps from your sculpts. You sculpt a detailed high poly mesh; then, the app looks at the cavities and curvatures of your sculpt, and **bakes** a normal map. Because high poly meshes with tons of vertices aren't resource-efficient in games, you should create a low poly mesh and then apply the normal map to this mesh.

Photoshop CC (from 2015), CrazyBump and Bitmap2Material can generate a normal map from a photograph or diffuse texture. Because these apps look at the shading and calculate the values, they aren't as good as the sculpting or procedural apps, but it can be quite amazing to take a photograph of a real-life, personal object, run it through one of these apps, and render out a shaded model.

Here's a normal map that was created using Allegorithmic's Bitmap2Material:

Tangent space

You send the normal map to the fragment function in the same way as a color texture, and you extract the normal values using the same UVs. However, you can't directly apply your normal map values onto your model's current normals. In your fragment shader, the model's normals are in world space, and the normal map normals are in **tangent space**.

Tangent space is a little hard to wrap your head around. Think of the brick cube with all its six faces pointing in different directions. Now think of the normal map with all the bricks the same color on all the six faces.

If a cube face is pointing toward negative x, how does the normal map know to point in that direction?

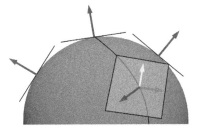

Using a sphere as an example, every fragment has a tangent — that's the line that touches the sphere at that point. The normal vector in this tangent space is thus relative to the surface. You can see that all of the arrows are at right angles to the tangent. So if you took all of the tangents and laid them out on a flat surface, the blue arrows would point upward in the same direction. That's tangent space!

The following image shows a cube's normals in world space.

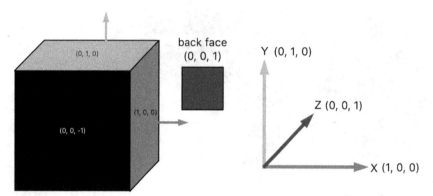

To convert the cube's normals to tangent space, you create a **TBN matrix** - that's a **Tangent Bitangent Normal matrix** that's calculated from the tangent, bitangent and normal value for each vertex.

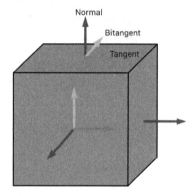

In the TBN matrix, the normal is the perpendicular vector as usual; the tangent is the vector that points along the horizontal surface; and the bitangent is the vector — as calculated by the **cross product** — that is perpendicular to both the tangent and the normal.

> **Note**: the cross product is an operation that gives you a vector perpendicular to two other vectors.

The tangent can be at right angles to the normal in any direction; however, to share normal maps across different parts of models, and even entirely different models, there are two standards:

1. The tangent and bitangent will represent the directions that u and v point, respectively, defined in model space.

2. The red channel will represent curvature along u, and the green channel, along v.

You could calculate these values when you load the model; however, with Model I/O, as long as you have data for both the position and texture coordinate attributes, Model I/O can calculate and store these tangent and bitangent values at each vertex for you.

Finally some code! :]

Using normal maps

Open up the starter project for this chapter. Note there are a few changes from the previous chapter's final code:

- `pipelineState` moved to `Submesh` from `Model`. Materials may need different rendering requirements, so each material needs its own pipeline state.

> **Note:** if you are in control of the asset pipeline and know that all models are textured consistently across all models, then you can centralize your pipeline state object (PSO) more. Holding the PSO on the submesh allows for the times when part of the model is textured and part of it isn't.

- The model is now a textured cottage, and the textures are in **Textures.xcassets**.

- There is additional code in **Submesh.swift** and **Shaders.metal** to read the normal texture in the same way as you read the diffuse color texture in the previous chapter.

Open up **Submesh.swift**. You'll find a new property, `normal`, in `Textures`, with the corresponding loading of the texture file in `Submesh.Textures`, in `init(material:)` using the Model I/O material property, `.tangentSpaceNormal`.

Open `cottage1.mtl` located in the **Models** folder. The `map_tangentSpaceNormal` property is what Model I/O is expecting for the normal texture. **cottage-normal** is a texture in **Textures.xcassets**.

You'll deal with multiple textures that hold data instead of color. Looking at these textures in a photo editor, you'd think they are color, but the trick is to regard the RGB (`0, 0, 0`) values as numerical data instead of color data.

In **Renderer.swift**, in `draw(in:)`, you're sending `submesh.textures.normal` in the same way as you did the base color texture in the previous chapter. Similarly, in **Shaders.metal**, the fragment function receives the normal texture in texture index 1; but aside from normalizing the value, the fragment function doesn't do anything with the texture value.

Build and run, and you'll see a quaint cartoon cottage.

It's a bit plain, but you're going to add a normal map to help give it some surface details.

The first step is to apply the normal texture to the cottage as if it were a color texture.

Open **Shaders.metal**. In `fragment_main`, after reading `normalValue` from `normalTexture`, add this:

```
return float4(normalValue, 1);
```

This is only temporary to make sure the app is loading the normal map correctly, and that the normal map and UVs match.

Build and run to verify the normal map is providing the fragment color.

You can see all the surface details the normal map will provide. There are scattered bricks on the wall, wood grain on the door and windows and a shingle-looking roof.

Excellent! You tested that the normal map loads, so it's time to remove the previous line of code. Remove this from the fragment function:

```
return float4(normalValue, 1);
```

You may have noticed that in the normal map's bricks, along the main surface of the house, the red seems to point along negative y, and the green seems to map to positive x. You might expect that red (1, 0, 0) maps to x and green (0, 1, 0) maps to y. This is because the UV island for the main part of the house is rotated 90 degrees counterclockwise.

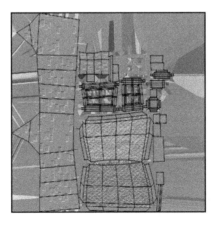

Not to worry; the mesh's stored tangents will map everything correctly! They take UV rotation into account.

Don't celebrate just yet! You have several tasks ahead of you. You still need to:

1. Load tangent and bitangent values using Model I/O.

2. Tell the render command encoder to send the newly created `MTLBuffer`s containing the values to the GPU.

3. In the vertex shader, change the values to world space — just as you did normals — and pass the new values to the fragment shader.

4. Calculate the new normal based on these values.

1. Load tangents and bitangents

Open **VertexDescriptor.swift** and look at `defaultVertexDescriptor`. Model I/O is currently reading into the vertex buffer the normal values from the .obj file. And you can see that you're telling the vertex descriptor that there are normal values in the attribute named `MDLVertexAttributeNormal`.

So far, your models have normal values included with them, but you may come across odd files where you have to generate normals. You can also override how the modeler **smoothed** the model. For example, the house model has smoothing applied in Blender so that the roof, which has very few faces, does not appear too blocky.

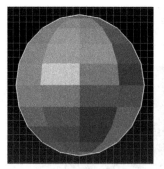 

Flat shaded   Smooth shaded

Smoothing recalculates vertex normals so that they interpolate smoothly over a surface. Blender stores smoothing groups in the .obj file, which Model I/O reads in and understands. Notice how the edges of the above sphere are unchanged. Smoothing only changes the way the renderer evaluates the surface. Smoothing does not change the geometry.

Try reloading vertex normals and overriding the smoothing. Open **Model.swift** and in init(name:), replace:

```
let (mdlMeshes, mtkMeshes) =
    try! MTKMesh.newMeshes(asset: asset,
                             device: Renderer.device)
```

With:

```
var mtkMeshes: [MTKMesh] = []
let mdlMeshes =
    asset.childObjects(of: MDLMesh.self) as! [MDLMesh]
_ = mdlMeshes.map { mdlMesh in
  mdlMesh.addNormals(withAttributeNamed:
                       MDLVertexAttributeNormal,
                     creaseThreshold: 1.0)
  mtkMeshes.append(try! MTKMesh(mesh: mdlMesh,
                               device: Renderer.device))
}
```

You're now loading the MDLMeshes first and changing them before initializing the MTKMeshes. You ask Model I/O to recalculate normals with a crease threshold of 1. This crease threshold, between 0 and 1, determines the smoothness, where 1.0 is unsmoothed.

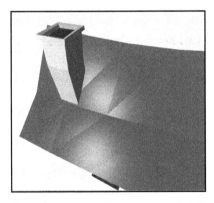

Build and run, and notice that the cottage is now completely unsmoothed, and you can see all of its separate faces. If you were to try a creaseThreshold of zero, where everything is smoothed, you'd get a lot of rendering artifacts because of the surfaces rounding too far. When dealing with smoothness remember this: Smoothness is good, but use it with caution. The artist needs to set up the model with smoothing in mind.

Remove the line you just added that said:

```
mdlMesh.addNormals(withAttributeNamed: MDLVertexAttributeNormal,
                   creaseThreshold: 1.0)
```

and replace it with this:

```
mdlMesh.addTangentBasis(forTextureCoordinateAttributeNamed:
          MDLVertexAttributeTextureCoordinate,
       tangentAttributeNamed: MDLVertexAttributeTangent,
       bitangentAttributeNamed: MDLVertexAttributeBitangent)
```

All of the models have normals provided by Blender, so this new code loads the vertex tangent and bitangent values directly. Model I/O does a few things behind the scenes:

- Add two named attributes to `mdlMesh`'s vertex descriptor: `MDLVertexAttributeTangent` and `MDLVertexAttributeBitangent`.

- Calculate the tangent and bitangent values.

- Create two new `MTLBuffer`'s to contain them.

- Update the layout strides on `mdlMesh`'s vertex descriptor to match the two new buffers.

With the addition of these two new attributes, you should change the vertex descriptor. Each `mdlMesh` provides a vertex descriptor, so for convenience, you'll hold this as a class property. Add this new property to `Model`:

```
static var vertexDescriptor: MDLVertexDescriptor =
  MDLVertexDescriptor.defaultVertexDescriptor
```

Inside the `map` closure just after where you added the tangent and bitangent attributes, update the `Model` vertex descriptor:

```
Model.vertexDescriptor = mdlMesh.vertexDescriptor
```

In **Submesh.swift**, in `makePipelineState(textures:)`, change `vertexDescriptor` to use this new vertex descriptor:

```
let vertexDescriptor = Model.vertexDescriptor
```

You've completed the necessary updates to the model's vertex layouts, and now you'll update the rendering code to match.

2. Send tangent and bitangent values to the GPU

In **Renderer.swift**, in draw(in:), locate // render multiple buffers and these lines of code:

```
let vertexBuffer = mesh.mtkMesh.vertexBuffers[0].buffer
renderEncoder.setVertexBuffer(vertexBuffer, offset: 0,
                    index: Int(BufferIndexVertices.rawValue))
```

This only sends one MTLBuffer to the GPU per mesh. The buffer contains the position, normal and UV data — all interleaved and unpacked by the vertex function according to the vertex descriptor attributes.

However, you now have two more buffers added by Model I/O for the tangent and bitangent values, with two more attributes to deal with, so you need to update the code.

Replace the two lines of code that follow // replace the following two lines with:

```
for (index, vertexBuffer) in
      mesh.mtkMesh.vertexBuffers.enumerated() {
  renderEncoder.setVertexBuffer(vertexBuffer.buffer,
                      offset: 0, index: index)
}
```

Now, you're enumerating all of the mesh's vertex buffers and sending them all to the GPU.

Build and run, and you'll get the dreaded clear screen!

In the code you just added, you're sending three MTLBuffers, with three different argument table indices. With the earlier code, you specified that you would send uniforms in argument table index 1. With the new code, you're overwriting the table with the new MTLBuffers and the vertex function. Since it's expecting uniforms in index 1, it thinks it has incorrect values.

You can easily fix this by changing the index numbers in **Common.h**.

In **Common.h**, change:

```
typedef enum {
  BufferIndexVertices = 0,
  BufferIndexUniforms = 1,
```

```
    BufferIndexLights = 2,
    BufferIndexFragmentUniforms = 3
} BufferIndices;
```

To:

```
typedef enum {
    BufferIndexVertices = 0,
    BufferIndexUniforms = 11,
    BufferIndexLights = 12,
    BufferIndexFragmentUniforms = 13
} BufferIndices;
```

Here, you're leaving a gap so that you can assign indices 0 to 10 for various `MTLBuffers`. Build and run, and your cottage should be back.

Click the Capture GPU Frame button to see the buffers on the GPU.

The tangent and bitangent values are in argument table indices 1 and 2, and `uniforms` is now in argument table index 11.

3. Convert tangent and bitangent values to world space

Just as you converted the model's normals to world space, you need to convert the tangents and bitangents to world space in the vertex function.

In **Common.h**, add this to enum `Attributes`:

```
Tangent = 3,
Bitangent = 4
```

In **Shaders.metal**, add these new attributes to struct `VertexIn`:

```
float3 tangent [[attribute(Tangent)]];
float3 bitangent [[attribute(Bitangent)]];
```

Add new properties to struct `VertexOut` so that you can send the values to the fragment function:

```
float3 worldTangent;
float3 worldBitangent;
```

In `vertex_main`, after calculating `out.worldNormal`, add this:

```
.worldTangent = uniforms.normalMatrix * vertexIn.tangent,
.worldBitangent = uniforms.normalMatrix * vertexIn.bitangent,
```

This moves the tangent and bitangent values into world space.

4. Calculate the new normal

Now that you have everything in place, it'll be a simple matter to calculate the new normal.

Before doing the normal calculation, consider the normal color value that you're reading. Colors are between 0 and 1, and normal values range from -1 to 1.

Still in **Shaders.metal**, in `fragment_main`, after reading the normal from the texture, but before normalizing it, add:

```
normalValue = normalValue * 2 - 1;
```

This redistributes the normal value to be within the range -1 to 1.

Further down in the function, replace:

```
float3 normalDirection = normalize(in.worldNormal);
```

With:

```
float3 normalDirection = float3x3(in.worldTangent,
                                  in.worldBitangent,
                                  in.worldNormal) * normalValue;
normalDirection = normalize(normalDirection);
```

Build and run to see the normal map applied to the cottage.

As you rotate the cottage, notice how the lighting affects the small cavities on the model, especially on the door and roof where the specular light falls — it's almost like you created new geometry but didn't! :]

Normal maps are almost like magic, and great artists can add amazing detail to simple low poly models.

Other texture map types

Normal maps are not the only way of changing a model's surface. There are other texture maps:

- **Roughness**: Describes the smoothness or roughness of a surface. You'll add a roughness map shortly.

- **Metallic**: White for metal and black for dielectric. Metal is a conductor of electricity, whereas a dielectric material is a non-conductor.

- **Ambient Occlusion**: Describes areas that are occluded; in other words, areas that are hidden from light.

- **Reflection**: Identifies which part of the surface is reflective.

- **Opacity**: Describes the location of the transparent parts of the surface.

In fact, any value (thickness, curvature, etc.) that you can think of to describe a surface, can be stored in a texture. You just look up the relevant fragment in the texture using the UV coordinates and use the value recovered. That's one of the bonuses of writing your own renderer. You can choose what maps to use and how to apply them.

You can use all of these textures in the fragment shader, and the geometry doesn't change.

> **Note**: A displacement or height map can change geometry. You'll read about displacement in Chapter 11, "Tessellation and Terrains."

Materials

Not all models have textures. For example, the train you rendered earlier in the book has different material groups that specify a color instead of using a texture.

Take a look at **cottage1.mtl** in the **Models** folder. This is the file that describes the visual aspects of the cottage model. In the previous chapter, you loaded the diffuse texture using map_Kd from **LowPolyHouse.mtl**, and you experimented with material groups in Blender in Chapter 2, "3D Models."

Each of the groups here has values associated with a property. You'll be extracting these properties from the file and using them in the fragment shader.

- Ns: Specular exponent (shininess)

- Kd: Diffuse color

- Ks: Specular color

> **Note**: You can find a full list of the definitions at http://paulbourke.net/dataformats/mtl/.

The current .mtl file loads the color using map_Kd, but for experimentation, you'll switch the rendered cottage file to one that gets its color from the material group and not a texture. Open **cottage2.mtl** and see that none of the groups, except the glass group, has a map_Kd property. This map_Kd on the glass group is an error by the texture artist that you'll highlight later in the chapter.

In **Renderer.swift**, in init(metalView:), change the model from "cottage1.obj" to "cottage2.obj".

The diffuse color won't be the only material property you'll be reading. Add a new struct in **Common.h** to hold the material values:

```
typedef struct {
    vector_float3 baseColor;
    vector_float3 specularColor;
```

```
    float roughness;
    float metallic;
    vector_float3 ambientOcclusion;
    float shininess;
} Material;
```

There are more material properties available, but these are the most common. For now, you'll read in `baseColor`, `specularColor` and `shininess`.

Open up **Submesh.swift** and create a new property to hold the materials:

```
let material: Material
```

> **Note**: Your project won't compile until you've initialized `material`.

At the bottom of **Submesh.swift**, create a new `Material` initializer:

```
private extension Material {
  init(material: MDLMaterial?) {
    self.init()
    if let baseColor = material?.property(with: .baseColor),
      baseColor.type == .float3 {
      self.baseColor = baseColor.float3Value
    }
  }
}
```

In `Submesh.Textures`, you read in string values for the textures' file names from the submesh's material properties. If there's no texture available for a particular property, you want to check whether there is a single float value instead. For example, if an object is solid red, you don't have to go to the trouble of making a texture, you can just use `float3(1, 0, 0)` to describe the color. You're reading in the material's base color.

Add the specular and shininess values to the end of `Material`'s `init(material:)`:

```
if let specular = material?.property(with: .specular),
  specular.type == .float3 {
  self.specularColor = specular.float3Value
}
if let shininess = material?.property(with: .specularExponent),
  shininess.type == .float {
  self.shininess = shininess.floatValue
}
```

In Submesh, in init(mdlSubmesh:mtkSubmesh:), initialize material:

```
material = Material(material: mdlSubmesh.material)
```

You'll now send this material to the shader. This sequence of coding should be familiar to you by now.

In **Common.h**, add another index to BufferIndices:

```
BufferIndexMaterials = 14
```

In **Renderer.swift**, in draw(in:), add the following below // set the materials here:

```
var material = submesh.material
renderEncoder.setFragmentBytes(&material,
            length: MemoryLayout<Material>.stride,
            index: Int(BufferIndexMaterials.rawValue))
```

This sends the materials struct to the fragment shader.

In **Shaders.metal**, add the following as the second parameter of fragment_main:

```
constant Material &material [[buffer(BufferIndexMaterials)]],
```

You've now passed the model's material properties to the fragment shader.

In fragment_main, temporarily comment out the baseColor assignment from the texture file, and add the following:

```
float3 baseColor = material.baseColor;
```

Finally, replace the assignments of materialShininess and materialSpecularColor with:

```
float3 materialSpecularColor = material.specularColor;
float materialShininess = material.shininess;
```

Build and run, and you're now loading **cottage2** with the colors coming from the Kd values instead of a texture.

As you rotate the cottage, you can see the roof, door and window frames are shiny with strong specular highlights. Open **cottage2.mtl**, and in both the roof and wood groups, change:

- **Ns:** 1.0

- **Ks:** 0.2 0.2 0.2

These changes eliminate the specular highlights for those two groups.

You can now render either a cottage *with* a color texture, or a cottage *without* a color texture simply by changing the baseColor assignment in the fragment shader.

As you can see, models have various requirements. Some models need a color texture; some models need a roughness texture; and some models need normal maps. It's up to you to check conditionally in the fragment function whether there are textures or constant values. You also don't want to be sending spurious textures to the fragment function if your models don't use textures. You can fix this dilemma with **function constants**.

Function specialization

Over the years there has been much discussion about how to render different materials. Should you create separate short fragment shaders for the differences? Or should you have one long "uber" shader with all of the possibilities listed conditionally? Function specialization deals with this problem, and allows you to create one shader that the compiler turns into separate shaders.

When you create the model's pipeline state, you set the Metal functions in the Metal Shading library, and the compiler packages them up. At this stage, you can create booleans to indicate whether your model's submesh material requires particular textures.

You can then pass these booleans to the Metal library when you create the shader functions. The compiler will then examine the functions and generate specialized versions of them.

In the shader file, you reference the set of booleans by their index numbers.

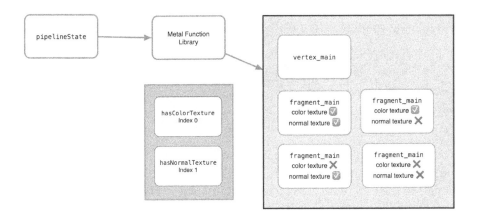

Open **Submesh.swift** and locate the extension where you create the pipeline state.

You'll first create a set of function constant values that will indicate whether the textures exist for the current submesh material. Create a new method in the extension where you create the pipeline state:

```
static func makeFunctionConstants(textures: Textures)
                                -> MTLFunctionConstantValues {
    let functionConstants = MTLFunctionConstantValues()
    var property = textures.baseColor != nil
    functionConstants.setConstantValue(&property,
                                type: .bool, index: 0)
    property = textures.normal != nil
    functionConstants.setConstantValue(&property,
                                type: .bool, index: 1)
    return functionConstants
}
```

MTLFunctionConstantValues is a set that contains two boolean values depending on whether the two textures exist. You defined boolean values here, but the values can be any type specified by MTLDataType. On the GPU side, you'll soon create boolean constants using the same index values; and in the functions that use these constants, you can conditionally perform tasks.

You'll use this set when creating the fragment function. At the top of
makePipelineState(textures:), add this:

```
let functionConstants =
      makeFunctionConstants(textures: textures)
```

Change the assignment to fragmentFunction to:

```
let fragmentFunction: MTLFunction?
do {
  fragmentFunction =
        try library?.makeFunction(name: "fragment_main",
                          constantValues: functionConstants)
} catch {
  fatalError("No Metal function exists")
}
```

Here, you tell the compiler to create a library of functions using the function
constants set. The compiler creates multiple shader functions and optimizes any
conditionals in the functions. This makeFunction method throws an exception, so
you check to see if the function exists in the project.

Now for the GPU side! Open **Shaders.metal**. After the import statement, add these
constants:

```
constant bool hasColorTexture [[function_constant(0)]];
constant bool hasNormalTexture [[function_constant(1)]];
```

These match the constants you just created in the MTLFunctionConstantValues set.

In fragment_main, replace:

```
float3 baseColor = material.baseColor;
```

With:

```
float3 baseColor;
if (hasColorTexture) {
  baseColor = baseColorTexture.sample(textureSampler,
                      in.uv * fragmentUniforms.tiling).rgb;
} else {
  baseColor = material.baseColor;
}
```

Similarly, change the `normalValue` assignment to:

```
float3 normalValue;
if (hasNormalTexture) {
  normalValue = normalTexture.sample(textureSampler,
                          in.uv * fragmentUniforms.tiling).rgb;
  normalValue = normalValue * 2 - 1;
} else {
  normalValue = in.worldNormal;
}
normalValue = normalize(normalValue);
```

Depending on the constant value, you either read the texture value or the base value. Generally, you should try to avoid conditional branching in GPU functions, but the compiler removes these conditionals when it creates the specialized functions.

One more thing: you don't want to receive a texture into the function if it doesn't exist.

Change the function parameters for `baseColorTexture` and `normalTexture` to:

```
texture2d<float> baseColorTexture [[texture(BaseColorTexture),
                        function_constant(hasColorTexture)]],
texture2d<float> normalTexture [[texture(NormalTexture),
                        function_constant(hasNormalTexture)]],
```

Here, you're telling the shader to check the function constant value and only load the texture if the constant value is `true`.

Build and run, and you'll see that your green cottage still renders as it used to using the base material colors.

In **Renderer.swift**, render **cottage1** again and notice that the textures render now. You can use this for error checking too. Render **cottage2**, and place this at the top of the fragment function:

```
if (hasColorTexture) {
  return float4(1, 0, 0, 1);
}
return float4(0, 1, 0, 1);
```

This highlights that *cottage2* erroneously has a texture map in the glass group.

Remove that error checking code before continuing.

Physically based rendering

To achieve spectacular scenes, you need to have good textures, but lighting plays an even more significant role. In recent years, the concept of physically based rendering (PBR) has become much more popular than the simplistic Phong shading model. As its name suggests, PBR attempts physically realistic interaction of light with surfaces. Now that Augmented Reality has become part of our lives, it's even more important to render your models to match their physical surroundings.

The general principles of PBR are:

• Surfaces should not reflect more light than they receive.

• Surfaces can be described with known, measured physical properties.

The Bidirectional Reflectance Distribution Function (BRDF) defines how a surface responds to light. There are various highly mathematical BRDF models for both diffuse and specular, but the most common are Lambertian diffuse; and for the specular, variations on the Cook-Torrance model (presented at SIGGRAPH 1981). This takes into account:

• **microfacet slope distribution**: You learned about microfacets and how light bounces off surfaces in many directions in Chapter 5, "Lighting Fundamentals."

• **Fresnel**: If you look straight down into a clear lake, you can see through it to the bottom, however, if you look across the surface of the water, you only see a reflection like a mirror. This is the Fresnel effect, where the reflectivity of the surface depends upon the viewing angle.

• **geometric attenuation**: Self-shadowing of the microfacets.

Each of these components have different approximations, or models written by many clever people. It's a vast and complex topic! In the Resources folder for this chapter, **references.markdown** contains a few places where you can learn more about physically based rendering and the calculations involved. You'll also learn some more about BRDF and Fresnel in Chapter 20, "Advanced Lighting."

Artists generally provide some textures with their models that supply the BRDF values. These are the most common:

- **Albedo**: You already met the albedo map in the form of the base color map. Albedo is originally an astronomical term describing the measurement of diffuse reflection of solar radiation, but it has come to mean in computer graphics the surface color without any shading applied to it.

- **Metallic**: A surface is either a conductor of electricity — in which case it's a metal; or it isn't a conductor — in which case it's a **dielectric**. Most metal textures consist of 0 (black) and 1 (white) values only: 0 for dielectric and 1 for metal.

- **Roughness**: A grayscale texture that indicates the shininess of a surface. White is rough, and black is smooth. If you have a scratched shiny surface, the texture might consist of mostly black or dark gray with light gray scratch marks.

- **Ambient Occlusion**: A grayscale texture that defines how much light reaches a surface. For example, less light will reach nooks and crannies.

Included in the starter project is a fragment function that uses a Cook-Torrance model for specular lighting. It takes as input the above textures, as well as the color and normal textures.

> **Note:** The PBR fragment function is an abbreviated version of a function from Apple's sample code `LODwithFunctionSpecialization`. This is a fantastic piece of sample code to examine, complete with a gorgeous fire truck model. It uses function constants for creating different levels of detail depending on distance from the camera. As a challenge, you can import the sample's fire truck into your renderer to see how it looks. Remember, though, that you haven't yet implemented great lighting and reflection.

PBR workflow

First, change the fragment function to use the PBR calculations. In **Submesh.swift**, in `makePipelineState(textures:)`, change the name of the referenced fragment function from `"fragment_main"` to `"fragment_mainPBR"`.

Open **PBR.metal**. In the File inspector, add the file to the macOS and iOS targets.

Examine `fragment_mainPBR`. It starts off similar to your previous `fragment_main` but with a few more texture parameters in the function header. The function extracts values from the textures and calculates the normals the same as previously. For simplicity, it only processes the first light in the lights array.

`fragment_mainPBR` calls `render(Lighting)` that works through a Cook-Torrance shading model to calculate the specular highlight. The end of `fragment_mainPBR` adds the diffuse color — which is the same calculation as your previous shader — to the specular value to produce the final color.

To add all of the PBR textures to your project is quite long-winded, so you'll only add roughness, however, you can choose to add the others as a challenge, if you'd like.

Open **Submesh.swift** and create a new property for roughness in `Textures`:

```
let roughness: MTLTexture?
```

In the `Submesh.Textures` extension, add this to the end of `init(material:)`:

```
roughness = property(with: .roughness)
```

In addition to reading in a possible roughness texture, you need to read in the material value too. At the bottom of Material's init(material:), add:

```
if let roughness = material?.property(with: .roughness),
   roughness.type == .float3 {
   self.roughness = roughness.floatValue
}
```

Now you need to change makeFunctionConstants() so that it sets up all the texture function constants. Add this code to the end of the function, before return functionConstants:

```
property = textures.roughness != nil
functionConstants.setConstantValue(&property,
                         type: .bool, index: 2)
property = false
functionConstants.setConstantValue(&property,
                         type: .bool, index: 3)
functionConstants.setConstantValue(&property,
                         type: .bool, index: 4)
```

Here, you tell the function constants set whether there is a roughness texture, and you set two constants for metallic and ambient occlusion to false since you're not reading in either of those textures. On the GPU-side, the function constants are already set up for you in **PBR.metal**.

In **Renderer.swift**, in draw(in:), locate where you send the base color and normal textures to the fragment function, then add this afterward:

```
renderEncoder.setFragmentTexture(submesh.textures.roughness,
                         index: 2)
```

Still in **Renderer.swift**, this time in init(metalView:), change the rendered model to **"cube.obj"**. Also, remove the rotation from the model.

Find where you set up the camera property, and change the camera distance and target to:

```
camera.distance = 3
camera.target = [0, 0, 0]
```

Build and run to see a cube with only an albedo texture applied. This texture has no lighting information baked into it. Textures altering the surface will change the lighting appropriately. Open **cube.mtl** in the **Models** group, and remove the # in front of map_tangentSpaceNormal cube-normal. The # is a comment, so the texture won't load.

Build and run to see the difference when the normal texture is applied.

Again, open **cube.mtl**, and remove the # in front of map_roughness cube-roughness. Previously, the roughness value in the .mtl file was 1.0, which is completely rough. Open **Textures.xcassets** and select **cube-roughness**. Select the image and press the spacebar to preview it. The dark gray values will be smooth and shiny (exaggerated here for effect), and the white mortar between the bricks will be completely rough (not shiny).

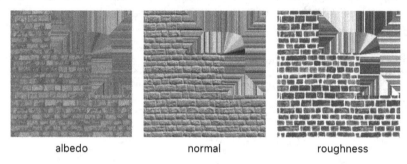

albedo   normal   roughness

Compare the roughness map to the cube's color and normal maps to see how the model's UV layout is used for all the textures.

Build and run to see the PBR function in action. Admire how much you can affect how a model looks just by a few textures and a bit of fragment shading.

Channel packing

Later on, you'll again be using the PBR fragment function for rendering. Even if you don't understand the mathematics, understand the layout of the function and the concepts used.

When loading models built by various artists, you're likely going to come up against a variety of standards. Textures may be a different way up; normals might point in a different direction; sometimes you may even find three textures *magically* contained in a single file, a technique called **channel packing**. Channel packing is an efficient way of managing external textures.

To understand how it works, open **PBR.metal** and look at the code where the fragment function reads single floats: roughness, metallic and ambient occlusion. When the function reads the texture for each of these values, it's only reading the red channel. For example:

```
roughness = roughnessTexture.sample(textureSampler, in.uv).r;
```

Available within the roughness file are green and blue channels that are currently unused. As an example, you could use the green channel for metallic and the blue channel for ambient occlusion.

Included in the **Resources** folder for this chapter is an image named **channel-packed.png**.

If you have Photoshop or some other graphics application capable of reading individual channels, open this file and inspect the channels.

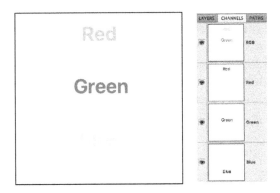

A different color channel contains each of the words. Similarly, you can load your different grayscale maps to each color channel. If you receive a file like this, you can split out each channel into a different file by hiding channels and saving the new file.

If you're organizing your maps through an asset catalog, channel packing won't impact the memory consumption and you won't gain much advantage. However, some artists *do use it* for easy texture management.

Challenge

In the **Resources** folder for this chapter is a fabulous treasure chest model from Demeter Dzadik at Sketchfab.com. Your challenge is to render this model! There are three textures that you'll load into the asset catalog. Don't forget to change Interpretation from Color to Data, so the textures don't load as sRGB.

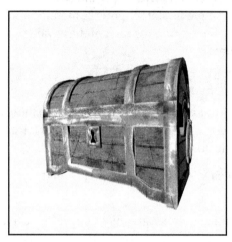

If you get stuck, you'll find the finished project in the challenge folder.

The challenge project can also render USDZ files with textures. When Model I/O loads USDZ files, the textures are loaded as `MDLTexture`s instead of string filenames. In the challenge project there is an additional method in `Texturable` to cope with this. To load these textures, you also have to preload the asset textures when you load the asset in `Model`, by using `asset.loadTextures()`.

You can download USDZ samples from https://developer.apple.com/augmented-reality/quick-look/ to try. The animated models, such as the toy robot, still won't work until after you've completed the next chapter, but the static models, such as the car, should render well once you scale the model down to `[0.1, 0.1, 0.1]`.

Where to go from here?

The sky's the limit! Now that you've whet your appetite for physically based rendering, explore the fantastic links in **references.markdown** which you'll find in the **Resources** folder. Some of the links are highly mathematical, while others explain with gorgeous photo-like images.

Since you now know how to render almost any model that you can export to .obj or .usd, try downloading models from http://www.sketchfab.com in the glTF format and convert them from glTF to .obj using Blender 2.8.

In Chapter 12, "Environment", you'll explore Image Based Lighting with reflection from a skycube texture. You'll revisit rendering metals with metallic textures at that point.

In good games you generally interact with interesting characters, so in the next chapter, you'll level up your skills by making your models come to life with animation!

Chapter 8: Character Animation

By Caroline Begbie

Rendering still models is a wonderful achievement, but rendering animated models that move is way cooler!

To animate means to *bring to life*. So what better way to play with animation than to render characters with personality and body movement. In this chapter, you'll start off by bouncing a ball. Then, you'll move on to rendering a friendly-looking skeleton.

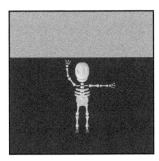

In earlier chapters, you focused on shading in the fragment function. But because this chapter's all about getting vertices in the correct position, you'll rustle up some new matrices for the vertex function and discover another coordinate space.

The starter project

Open the starter project for this chapter, and review the changes from the previous chapter's completed project:

- To keep your attention on vertex shading, **Shaders.metal** contains only the vertex shader function. You won't be dealing with materials or textures so **PBR.metal** holds the fragment shading.

- Look at Renderer's draw(in:). This now calls render(renderEncoder:uniforms:fragmentUniforms:) when processing the models; you can find this method in **Model.swift**. Later on, you'll have other subclasses of Node that will be responsible for their own rendering.

- Two debugging statements: renderEncoder.pushDebugGroup(model.name) and renderEncoder.popDebugGroup() surround the new render method. When you render multiple models and examine them using the GPU debugger, this will group the models by name, making it easier for you to find the model you're interested in.

- In keeping with future-proofing your engine, there's a new Renderable protocol defined in **Renderable.swift**. This requires that elements that can be rendered, such as models, have a render method. Model conforms to this protocol using the code that used to be in draw(in:).

- There's a new group called **"Animation Support"**. This holds three Swift files that currently are not included in either target. You'll add these later when you come to animating a jointed skeleton.

Run the starter project, and you'll see a beach ball. Notice how unnatural it looks just sitting there. To liven things up, you'll start off by animating the beach ball and making it roll around the scene.

Procedural animation

Earlier, in Chapter 3, "The Rendering Pipeline," you animated a cube and a train using sine. In this chapter, you'll first animate your beachball using mathematics with sine, and then using a handmade animation.

Open **Renderer.swift** and create a new property in Renderer:

```
var currentTime: Float = 0
```

Add a new method to update objects every frame:

```
func update(deltaTime: Float) {
  currentTime += deltaTime * 4
  let ball = models[0]
  ball.position.x = sin(currentTime)
}
```

This updates the ball's x position every frame by the sine of the accumulated current time. Sine is great for procedural animation; by changing the amplitude, period and frequency, you can create waves of motion, although, for a beach ball, that's not too realistic. However, with some physics, you can add a little bounce to help.

Now, call this method at the top of draw(in:), after the guard statement:

```
let deltaTime = 1 / Float(view.preferredFramesPerSecond)
update(deltaTime: deltaTime)
```

The property view.preferredFramesPerSecond defaults to 60 frames per second (that's 16.6 milliseconds per frame). Your app needs to ensure that your entire render for each frame fits within this time; otherwise, you should choose a lower frame rate. You'll use deltaTime to update your animations for each frame.

Build and run, and the beach ball now moves from side-to-side.

Animation using physics

Instead of creating animation by hand using an animation app, using physics-based animation means that your models can simulate the real world. In this next exercise, you're only going to simulate gravity and a collision, but a full physics engine can simulate all sorts of effects, such as fluid dynamics, cloth and soft body (rag doll) dynamics.

Create a new property in `Renderer` to track the ball's velocity:

```
var ballVelocity: Float = 0
```

Remove this code from `update(deltaTime:)`:

```
ball.position.x = sin(currentTime)
```

In `update(deltaTime:)`, set some constants for the individual physics you'll need for the simulation:

```
let gravity: Float = 9.8 // meter / sec2
let mass: Float = 0.05
let acceleration = gravity / mass
let airFriction: Float = 0.2
let bounciness: Float = 0.9
let timeStep: Float = 1 / 600
```

`gravity` represents the acceleration of an object falling to Earth. If you're simulating gravity elsewhere in the universe, for example, Mars, this value would be different.

Newton's Second Law of Motion is **F = ma** or `force = mass * acceleration`. Rearranging the equation gives `acceleration = force (gravity) / mass`.

The other constants describe the surroundings and the properties of the beach ball. If this were a bowling ball, it would have a higher mass and less bounce.

Add this code at the end of `update(deltaTime:)`:

```
ballVelocity += (acceleration * timeStep) / airFriction
ball.position.y -= ballVelocity * timeStep
if ball.position.y <= 0.35 {       // collision with ground
  ball.position.y = 0.35
  ballVelocity = ballVelocity * -1 * bounciness
}
```

Here, you calculate the position of the ball based on the ball's current velocity; you can read more about this in Chapter 16, "Particle Systems." The ball's origin is at its center, and it's approximately 0.7 units in diameter, so when the ball's center is 0.35 units above the ground, that's when you reverse the velocity and travel upward.

In `init(metalView:)`, change the ball's initial position to be up in the air:

```
ball.position = [0, 3, 0]
```

Build and run, and watch the beach ball bounce around.

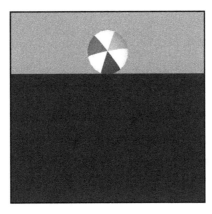

This is a simple physics animation, but it demonstrates the possibilities if you choose to take it further.

Axis-aligned bounding box

You hard-coded the ball's radius so that it collides with the ground, but collision systems generally require some kind of bounding box to test whether an object is impacted.

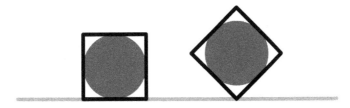

Obviously, the ball would benefit from a spherical bounding volume, and you can investigate physics engines, such as the open source **Bullet** physics engine. However, as your ball is simply using the y-axis, you can determine the ball's height using an **axis-aligned bounding box** that Model I/O calculates.

Open **Node.swift**, and add a bounding box property and a computed size property to Node:

```
var boundingBox = MDLAxisAlignedBoundingBox()
var size: float3 {
  return boundingBox.maxBounds - boundingBox.minBounds
}
```

In **Model.swift**, in init(name:), after calling super.init(), add the following line of code:

```
self.boundingBox = asset.boundingBox
```

This extracts the bounding box information from Model I/O.

In **Renderer.swift**, in update(deltaTime:), update the collision code with the correct size calculated from the bounding box value:

```
if ball.position.y <= ball.size.y / 2 { // collision with ground
    ball.position.y = ball.size.y / 2
    ballVelocity = ballVelocity * -1 * bounciness
}
```

Build and run, and your ball will collide with the ground, precisely at the edge of the ball.

Keyframes

If you want to animate the ball being tossed around, you'll need to input information about its position over time. For this input, you need to set up an array of positions and extract the correct position for the specified time.

In **BallAnimations.swift**, in the **Utility** group, there's already an array set up named ballPositionXArray. This array consists of 60 values ranging from -1 to 1, then back to -1. By calculating the current frame, you can grab the correct x position from the array.

In **Renderer.swift**, change update(deltaTime:) to:

```
func update(deltaTime: Float) {
    currentTime += deltaTime
    let ball = models[0]
    ball.position.y = ball.size.y

    let fps: Float = 60
    let currentFrame =
        Int(currentTime * fps) % (ballPositionXArray.count)
    ball.position.x = ballPositionXArray[currentFrame]
}
```

Here, you calculate the current frame working on a 60 fps (frames per seconds) basis, and you extract the correct value from the array.

Build and run. Watch as the ball moves around in a mechanical, backward and forward motion over 60 frames. This is almost the same result as the sine animation, but it's now animated by an array of values that you can control and re-use.

Interpolation

It's a lot of work inputting a value for each frame. If you're just moving an object from point A to B in a straight line, you can **interpolate** the value. Interpolation is where you can calculate a value given a range of values and a current location within the range. When animating, the current location is the current time as a percentage of the animation duration.

To work out the time percentage, use this formula:

$$time = \frac{(currentTime - min)}{(max - min)}$$

This results in a time value between 0 and 1.

For example, if you have a start value of 5, an end value of 10 and a duration of 2 seconds, after 1 second has passed, the interpolated value is 7.5.

$$time = \frac{(1.0 - 0)}{(2.0 - 0)}$$

$$value = (10 - 5) * time + 5$$

That's a linear interpolation. However, there are other ways of interpolating using different formulas.

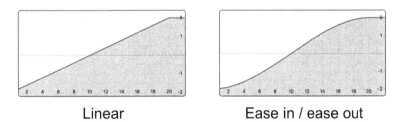

Linear   Ease in / ease out

In the above image, linear interpolation is on the left. The x-axis is time, and the y-axis is value. You sample the value at the appropriate time. The previous ball example was mechanical and can be improved using the ease in and out interpolation on the right.

With ease in and out, the ball gains speed slowly at the start and then slows down toward the end of the animation.

Instead of creating one value for every frame to animate your ball, you'll hold only key positions. These will be the **extreme** of a pose. In the ball example, the extreme pose positions are -1 and 1. You'll also hold key times that match the time of that key value. For example, if your animation is 2 seconds long, your extremes will be at 0 seconds for the starting pose on the left, 1 second for the ball to be on the right, and 2 seconds to take the ball back to the left again. All of the frames in between these times are interpolated.

Create a new Swift file named **Animation.swift**. Remember to add the file to both macOS and iOS targets. Here, you'll hold your animation data, and create methods to return the interpolated value at a given time.

Add the following:

```
struct Keyframe {
  var time: Float = 0
  var value: float3 = [0, 0, 0]
}
```

This creates a struct to hold the animation key values and times. Now add this:

```
struct Animation {
  var translations: [Keyframe] = []
  var repeatAnimation = true
}
```

This struct holds an array of keyframes; `repeatAnimation` will be used to choose to repeat the animation clip forever or play it just once.

Within `Animation`, add this:

```
func getTranslation(at time: Float) -> float3? {
  guard let lastKeyframe = translations.last else {
    return nil
  }
}
```

This will return the interpolated keyframe. First, you ensure that there are translation keys in the array, otherwise, return a `nil` float value.

Continue adding to this method with the following:

```
//1
var currentTime = time
if let first = translations.first, first.time >= currentTime {
  return first.value
}
```

```
//2
if currentTime >= lastKeyframe.time, !repeatAnimation {
  return lastKeyframe.value
}
```

Here's the breakdown:

1. If the first keyframe occurs on or after the time given, then return the first key value. The first frame of an animation clip *should* be at keyframe 0 to give a starting pose.

2. If the time given is greater than the last key time in the array, then check whether you should repeat the animation. If not, then return the last value.

Now add this after the previous code:

```
// 1
currentTime = fmod(currentTime, lastKeyframe.time)
// 2
let keyFramePairs = translations.indices.dropFirst().map {
  (previous: translations[$0 - 1], next: translations[$0])
}
// 3
guard let (previousKey, nextKey) = ( keyFramePairs.first {
  currentTime < $0.next.time
})
else { return nil }
// 4
let interpolant = (currentTime - previousKey.time) /
                  (nextKey.time - previousKey.time)
// 5
return simd_mix(previousKey.value,
                nextKey.value,
                float3(repeating: interpolant))
```

Going through this code:

1. Use the modulo operation to get the current time within the clip.

2. Create a new array of tuples containing the previous and next keys for all keyframes, except the first one.

3. Find the first tuple of previous and next keyframes where the current time is less than the next keyframe time. The current time will, therefore, be between the previous and next keyframe times.

4. Use the interpolation formula to get a value between 0 and 1 for the progress percentage between the previous and next keyframe times.

5. Use the simd_mix function to interpolate between the two keyframes. (interpolant must be a value between 0 and 1.)

In **BallAnimations.swift** in the **Utility** group, uncomment generateBallTranslations(). This method creates an array of Keyframes with seven keys. The length of the clip is 2 seconds. You can see this by looking at the key time of the last keyframe.

In the x-axis, the ball will start off at position -1 and then move to position 1 at 0.35 seconds. It will hold its position until 1 second has passed, then return to -1 at 1.35 seconds. It will then hold its position until the end of the clip.

By changing the values in the array, you can speed up the throw and hold the ball for longer at either end. In **Renderer.swift**, change update(deltaTime:) to:

```
func update(deltaTime: Float) {
  currentTime += deltaTime
  let ball = models[0]
  var animation = Animation()
  animation.translations = generateBallTranslations()
  ball.position = animation.getTranslation(at: currentTime)
                  ?? [0, 0, 0]
  ball.position.y += ball.size.y
}
```

Here, you load the animation clip with the generated keyframe translations. Generally, you'll want to load the animation clip outside of the update, but for the sake of simplicity, in this example, handling things within update(deltaTime:) is fine. You also extract the ball's position from the animation clip for the current time.

Build and run, and watch as creepy invisible hands toss your ball around.

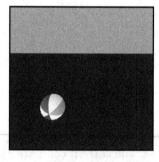

> **Note**: Notice the trajectory of the ball on the y-axis. It currently goes up and down in diagonal straight lines. Better keyframing can fix this.

Euler angle rotations

Now that you have the ball *translating* through the air, you probably want to *rotate* it as well. To express rotation of an object, you currently hold a float3 with rotation angles on x, y and z axes. These are called **Euler angles** after the mathematician Leonhard Euler. Euler is the one behind Euler's rotation theorem, a theorem which states that any rotation can be described using three rotation angles. This is OK for a single rotation, but interpolating between these three values doesn't work in a way that you may think.

To create a rotation matrix, you've been calling this function, hidden in the math library in **MathLibrary.swift**:

```
init(rotation angle: float3) {
  let rotationX = float4x4(rotationX: angle.x)
  let rotationY = float4x4(rotationY: angle.y)
  let rotationZ = float4x4(rotationZ: angle.z)
  self = rotationX * rotationY * rotationZ
}
```

Here, the final rotation matrix is made up of three rotation matrices multiplied in a particular order. This order is not set in stone and is one of six possible orders. Depending on the multiplication order, you'll get a different rotation.

> **Note**: Sometimes, for example in flight simulators, these rotations are referred to as Yaw-Pitch-Roll. Depending on your frame of reference, if you're using the y-axis as up and down (remember that's not universal), then Yawing is about the y-axis, Pitching is about the x-axis and Rolling is about the z-axis.

For static objects within one rendering engine, this is fine. The main problem comes with animation and interpolating these angles.

As you proceed through a rotation interpolation if two axes become aligned you get the terrifyingly named **gimbal lock**.

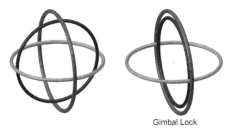

Gimbal Lock

This means that you've lost one axis of rotation. Because the inner axis rotations build on the outer axis rotation, the two rotations overlap. This causes odd interpolation.

Quaternions

Multiplying x, y and z rotations without compelling a sequence on them is impossible unless you involve the fourth dimension. In 1843, Sir William Rowan Hamilton did just that! He inscribed his fundamental formula for quaternion multiplication on to a stone on a bridge in Dublin:

$$i^2 = j^2 = k^2 = ijk = -1$$

The formula uses four-dimensional vectors and complex numbers to describe rotations. The mathematics is complicated, but fortunately, you don't have to understand how quaternions work to use them. The main benefit of quaternions are:

- They interpolate correctly when using spherical linear interpolation (or **slerp**).

- They never lose any axes of control.

- They always take the shortest path between two rotations unless you specifically ask for the longest path.

> **Note**: If you're interested in studying the internals of quaternions, **references.markdown** contains further reading.

You don't have to write any complicated interpolation code, as `simd` has quaternion classes and methods that handle it all for you using `simd_slerp()`. The quaternions perform a spherical interpolation along the shortest path as described here:

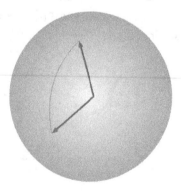

Internally in simd, quaternions are vectors of four elements, but Apple suggests that you treat them as abstract mathematical objects rather than delving into internal storage. That lets you off the hook for learning that the last element of the quaternion is the **real** part, and the first three elements are the **imaginary** part.

You'll switch from using Euler rotations to using quaternions for your rotations. Taking advantage of simd conversion of quaternions to and from rotation matrices, this switch is effortless. In **Node.swift**, add this property:

```
var quaternion = simd_quatf()
```

Where you define modelMatrix, change the definition of rotateMatrix to:

```
let rotateMatrix = float4x4(quaternion)
```

Now your Nodes will support quaternions instead of Euler angles. You should also change rotation so that it updates the quaternion. Change the definition of rotation to:

```
var rotation: float3 = [0, 0, 0] {
  didSet {
    let rotationMatrix = float4x4(rotation: rotation)
    quaternion = simd_quatf(rotationMatrix)
  }
}
```

This keeps the quaternion value in sync when you set a model's rotation.

To animate using quaternion rotation, you'll duplicate what you did for translations. In **Animation.swift**, add this struct (at top level) to hold the keyframe:

```
struct KeyQuaternion {
  var time: Float = 0
  var value = simd_quatf()
}
```

Add a new property to Animation:

```
var rotations: [KeyQuaternion] = []
```

Duplicate getTranslation(at:), but replace all translations and floats with rotations and quaternions:

```
func getRotation(at time: Float) -> simd_quatf? {
  guard let lastKeyframe = rotations.last else {
    return nil
```

```
    }
    var currentTime = time
    if let first = rotations.first, first.time >= currentTime {
      return first.value
    }
    if currentTime >= lastKeyframe.time, !repeatAnimation {
      return lastKeyframe.value
    }
    currentTime = fmod(currentTime, lastKeyframe.time)
    let keyFramePairs = rotations.indices.dropFirst().map {
      (previous: rotations[$0 - 1], next: rotations[$0])
    }
    guard let (previousKey, nextKey) = ( keyFramePairs.first {
      currentTime < $0.next.time
    })
    else { return nil }
    let interpolant = (currentTime - previousKey.time) /
                      (nextKey.time - previousKey.time)
    return simd_slerp(previousKey.value,
                      nextKey.value,
                      interpolant)
  }
```

Note that here you change the interpolation function to use `simd_slerp` instead of `simd_mix`. This does the necessary spherical interpolation.

In **BallAnimations.swift**, uncomment the method `generateBallRotations()`. This holds an array of rotation keyframes. The rotation starts out at 0, then rotates by 90° on the z-axis over several keyframes to a rotation of 0 at 0.35 seconds.

The reason for rotating several times by 90° is because if you rotate from 0° to 360°, the shortest distance between those is 0° so that the ball won't rotate at all.

For final rotation of the ball, in **Renderer.swift**, change `update(deltaTime:)` to this:

```
func update(deltaTime: Float) {
  currentTime += deltaTime
  let ball = models[0]

  var animation = Animation()
  animation.translations = generateBallTranslations()
  animation.rotations = generateBallRotations()
  ball.position = animation.getTranslation(at: currentTime)
                  ?? float3(repeating: 0)
  ball.position.y += ball.size.y / 2
  ball.quaternion = animation.getRotation(at: currentTime)
                  ?? simd_quatf()
}
```

Build and run, and your ball moves back and forth with rotation.

If you're doing more complex animating, you'll probably want to do it in a 3D app. The beach ball actually holds some hidden transformation animation in its USD file.

USD and USDZ files

One major problem to overcome is how to import animation from 3D apps. Model I/O can import .obj files, but they only hold static information, not animation. USD is a format devised by Pixar, which can hold massive scenes with textures, animation and lighting information. There are various file extensions:

- **.usd**: A Universal Scene Description (USD) file consists of assets or links to assets which allows multiple artists to work on the same scene. The file can contain mesh geometry, shading information, models, cameras and lighting.

- **.usdz**: A single archive file that contains all the files - not just links - necessary for rendering a model.

- **.usda**: This file is the USD file in text format. The models included in this chapter's project are in .usda format so that you can open them with TextEdit and inspect the contents.

- **.usdc**: This file is the USD file in binary format.

Apple has adopted USDZ, the archive derivation of the USD format, as their preferred augmented reality 3D format. However, as yet, there aren't many 3D apps that export to the USD format. Maya and Houdini do, but Blender doesn't.

Apple have provided a set of USD Python tools, including an app named usdconvert that will convert to USD from supported formats. Currently the supported formats are .obj, .fbx, .abc and .glTF.

Note: You can download the tools from the bottom of the AR Quick Look Gallery page: https://developer.apple.com/augmented-reality/quick-look/. This is a set of USDZ tools that will convert, generate, validate and inspect .usdz files.

glTF was developed by the Khronos Group and they have open sourced the format so that anyone can use it in their engines. http://sketchfab.com is a major provider and showcase of 3D models; all of their downloadable models are available in the glTF format, many of which you can convert to USD using Apple's usdconvert.

Animating meshes

The file **beachball.usda** holds translation and rotation animation, and Model I/O can extract this animation. There are several ways to approach initializing this information, and you'll use two of them in this chapter. Model I/O transform components don't allow you to access the rotation and translation values directly, but provides you with a method that returns a transform matrix at a particular time. So for mesh transform animation you'll extract the animation data for every frame of the animation during the model loading process.

Later, when you come to define skeletal animation, you'll have access to joint rotation and translation, so you'll load data only where there are keyframes, and use your interpolation methods to interpolate each frame.

Note: When writing your own engine, you will have the choice to load this animation data up front for every frame, to match the transfomation animation. You should consider the requirements of your game and what information your models hold. Generally it is more efficient to extract the loading code to a separate app which loads models and saves materials, textures and animation data into a more efficient format that matches your game engine. A good example of this asset pipeline is Apple's video and sample code *From Art to Engine with Model I/O* at https://developer.apple.com/videos/play/wwdc2017/610/.

You'll be running your game at a fixed fps - generally 60, and you'll hold a transform matrix for every frame of animation.

In **Renderer.swift**, add a new static variable to Renderer to hold this fps centrally:

```
static var fps: Int!
```

In init(metalView:), update fps with the other static variables:

```
Renderer.fps = metalView.preferredFramesPerSecond
```

In draw(in:), replace:

```
let deltaTime = 1 / Float(view.preferredFramesPerSecond)
update(deltaTime: deltaTime)
```

with:

```
let deltaTime = 1 / Float(Renderer.fps)
for model in models {
  model.update(deltaTime: deltaTime)
}
```

Currently update(deltaTime:) is a method in Node. You'll override this in Model to set the correct pose for the frame. You can remove Renderer's update method now if you wish.

Model I/O can hold transform information on all objects within the MDLAsset. For simplicity, you'll hold a transform component on each Mesh, and just animate the transforms for the duration given by the asset.

Create a new file called **TransformComponent.swift** to hold this transformation information, remembering to add the file to both the macOS and iOS targets.

Replace the code with:

```
import ModelIO

class TransformComponent {
  let keyTransforms: [float4x4]
  let duration: Float
  var currentTransform: float4x4 = .identity()
}
```

You'll hold all the transform matrices for each frame for the duration of the animation. For example, if the animation has a duration of 2.5 seconds at 60 frames per second, keyTransforms will have 150 elements. You'll later update all the Meshs' currentTransform every frame with the transform for the current frame taken from keyTransforms.

Now add the following to the class:

```
init(transform: MDLTransformComponent,
     object: MDLObject,
     startTime: TimeInterval,
     endTime: TimeInterval) {
  duration = Float(endTime - startTime)
  let timeStride = stride(from: startTime,
                          to: endTime,
                          by: 1 / TimeInterval(Renderer.fps))
  keyTransforms = Array(timeStride).map { time in
    return MDLTransform.globalTransform(with: object,
                                        atTime: time)
  }
}
```

This initializer will receive an MDLTransformComponent from either an asset or a mesh and then creates all the transform matrices for every frame for the duration of the animation.

Now add the following:

```
func setCurrentTransform(at time: Float) {
  guard duration > 0 else {
    currentTransform = .identity()
    return
  }
  let frame = Int(fmod(time, duration) * Float(Renderer.fps))
  if frame < keyTransforms.count {
    currentTransform = keyTransforms[frame]
  } else {
    currentTransform = keyTransforms.last ?? .identity()
  }
}
```

This retrieves a transform matrix at a particular, given, time. You calculate the current frame of the animation from the time. Using the floating point modulo operation fmod function, you can loop the animation. For example, if the animation is 2.5 seconds long, at 60 frames per second, that would mean there are 150 frames in the animation. If the current time is 5 seconds, that will be the last frame of the animation looped for a second time, and the current frame will be 150.

You save the current transform on the transform component. You'll use this to update the position of the mesh vertices shortly.

You'll need the start and end time from the asset, so, in **Mesh.swift**, change the init parameters to:

```
init(mdlMesh: MDLMesh, mtkMesh: MTKMesh,
     startTime: TimeInterval,
     endTime: TimeInterval)
```

Open **Model.swift** and, where you initialize meshes, you should have a compile error. Change the Mesh initialization to:

```
Mesh(mdlMesh: $0.0, mtkMesh: $0.1,
     startTime: asset.startTime,
     endTime: asset.endTime)
```

The compile error should now go away.

Back in **Mesh.swift**, add a new transform component property to Mesh:

```
let transform: TransformComponent?
```

Add this at the end of init(mdlMesh:mtkMesh:startTime:endTime:):

```
if let mdlMeshTransform = mdlMesh.transform {
  transform = TransformComponent(transform: mdlMeshTransform,
                                 object: mdlMesh,
                                 startTime: startTime,
                                 endTime: endTime)
} else {
  transform = nil
}
```

Now that you've set up the transform component with animation, you'll be able to use it when rendering each frame.

In **Model.swift**, add a new property to keep track of elapsed game time:

```
var currentTime: Float = 0
```

Create a new override method update(deltaTime:) with this code:

```
override func update(deltaTime: Float) {
  currentTime += deltaTime
  for mesh in meshes {
    mesh.transform?.setCurrentTransform(at: currentTime)
  }
}
```

Here you update all the transforms in the model ready for rendering.

In render(renderEncoder:uniforms:fragmentUniforms:), at the top of the for mesh in meshes loop, replace the assignment to uniforms.modelMatrix with:

```
let currentLocalTransform =
  mesh.transform?.currentTransform ?? .identity()
uniforms.modelMatrix = modelMatrix * currentLocalTransform
```

Here you combine the model's world transform with the mesh's transform.

Build and run and the beachball is huge and mostly out of frame. This is because of the ball's initial scale. When you weren't using the transform information from the file, you needed to set the initial scale and position in Renderer, but now you can remove this. In **Renderer.swift**, in init(metalView:) remove:

```
ball.position = [0, 3, 0]
ball.scale = [100, 100, 100]
```

Build and run and see a wild beachball animation.

> **Note:** Try downloading and rendering some of Apple's animated USDZ samples from https://developer.apple.com/augmented-reality/quick-look. The objects with animation currently are the robot, the drummer and the biplane. The scale is too big for your scene, so you'll need to set the scale to [0.1, 0.1, 0.1].

Now that you've learned about simple mesh animation, you're ready to move on to animating a jointed figure.

Blender for animating

Imagine creating a walk cycle for a human figure by typing out keyframes! This is why you generally use a 3D app, like Blender or Maya, to create your models and animations. You then export those to your game or rendering engine of choice.

In the Resources folder for this chapter, you'll find **skeleton.blend**. Open this file in Blender.

You'll see something like this:

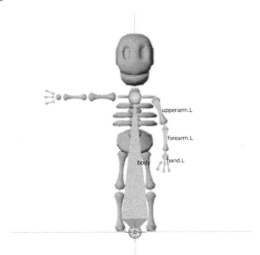

Before examining the bones further, left-click on the skeleton's head to select the skeleton object, and press the **Tab** key to go into **Edit Mode**:

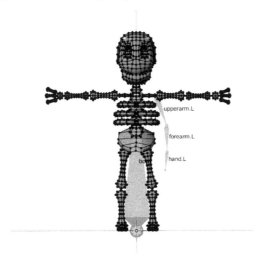

Note: If you are using a version of Blender earlier than 2.8, your interface will be different, and you should right-click instead of left-click to select.

Here, you can see all of the skeleton's vertices. This is the original model which you can export as a static .obj file. It's in what's called **the bind pose** with the arms stretched out. This is a standard pose for figures as it makes it easy to add animation bones to the figure.

Press the **Tab** key to go back to **Object Mode**. To animate the figure, you need to have control of groups of vertices. For example, to rotate the head, you'd need to rotate all of the head's vertices. **Rigging** a figure means creating an **Armature** with a hierarchy of **Joints**. Joints and bones are generally used synonymously, but a bone is just a visual cue to see which joint affects which vertices.

The general process of creating a figure for animation goes like this:

1.   Create the model.

2.   Create an armature with a hierarchy of joints.

3.   Apply the armature to the model with automatic weights.

4.   Use weight painting to change which vertices go with each joint.

Just as in the song *Dem Bones*: "the toe bone's connected to the foot bone," this is how a typical rigged figure's joint hierarchy might look:

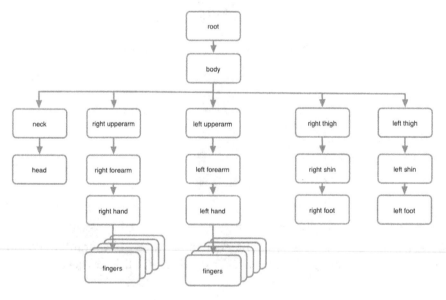

In character animation, it's (usually) all about rotation — your bones don't translate unless you have some kind of disjointing skeleton. With this hierarchy of joints, when you rotate one joint, all the child joints follow.

Try bending your elbow without moving your wrist. Because your wrist is lower in the hierarchy, even though you haven't actively changed the wrist's position and rotation, it still follows the movement of your elbow.

This movement is called **forward kinematics** and is what you'll be using in this chapter. It's a fancy name for making all child joints follow.

> **Note**: Inverse kinematics allows the animator to make actions, such as walk cycles, more easily. Place your hand on a table or in a fixed position. Now, rotate your elbow and shoulder joint with your hand fixed. The hierarchical chain no longer moves your hand as in forward kinematics. As opposed to forward kinematics, the mathematics of inverse kinematics is quite complicated.

This Blender skeleton has a limited rig for simplicity. It only has four bones: the body, left upper arm, left forearm and left hand. Each of these joints controls a group of vertices.

Weight painting in Blender

Left-click the skeleton's head. At the bottom of the Blender window, click on the drop-down that currently reads **Object Mode**, and change it to **Weight Paint**.

This shows you how each bone affects the vertices. Currently the body vertex group is selected, which is attached to the body bone. All vertices affected by the body bone are shown in red.

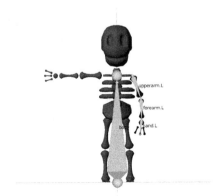

The process of weight painting and binding each bone to the vertices is called **skinning**. Unlike human arms, the skeleton's arm bones here have space between them, so all mesh is assigned to only one bone. However, if you're rigging a human arm, you would typically weight the vertices to multiple bones.

Here's a typically weighted arm with the forearm selected to show gradual blending of weights at the elbow and the wrist.

This is a side-by-side example of blended and non-blended weights at the elbow joint with the forearm selected:

The blue area indicates no weighting; the red area indicates total weighting. You can see in the right image, the forearm vertices dig uncomfortably into the upper arm vertices, whereas in the left image, the vertices move more evenly around the elbow joint.

At the elbow, where the vertices are green, the vertex weighting would be 50% to the upper arm, and 50% to the forearm; when the forearm rotates, the green vertices will rotate at 50% of the forearm's rotation. By blending the weights gradually, you can achieve an even deformation of vertices over the joint.

Animation in Blender

Select the drop-down at the bottom of the window that currently reads **Weight Paint**, and go back into **Object Mode**. Press the **space bar** to start an animation. Your skeleton should now get friendly and wave at you. This wave animation is a 60 frame looping animation clip.

At the top of Blender's window, click the **Animation** tab to show the Animation workspace.

You can now see the animation keys at the top left in the **Dope Sheet**. This is a summary of the keyframes in the scene. The joints are listed on the left, and each circle in the dope sheet means there's a keyframe at that frame.

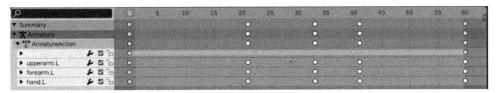

> **Note**: Although animated transformations are generally rotations, the keyframe can be a translation or a scale; you can click the arrow on the left of the joint name to see the specific channel the key is set on.

Press **space bar** to stop the animation if it's still going. **Scrub** through the animation by dragging the playhead at the top of the pane (the blue rectangle with 0 in it in the above image). Pause the playhead at each set of keyframes. Notice the position of the arm; at each keyframe, it's in an extreme position. Blender interpolates all the frames between the extremes.

Now that you've had a whirlwind tour of how to create a rigged figure and animate it in Blender, you'll move on to learning how to render it in your rendering engine.

> **Note**: You've only skimmed the surface of creating animated models. If you're interested in creating your own, you'll find some additional resources in **references.markdown**.

Skeletal Animation

Importing a skeletal animation into your app is a bit more difficult than importing a simple .obj file or a USDZ file with transform animation, because you have to deal with the joint hierarchy and joint weighting. You'll read in the data from the USD file and restructure it to fit your rendering code. This is how the objects will fit together in your app:

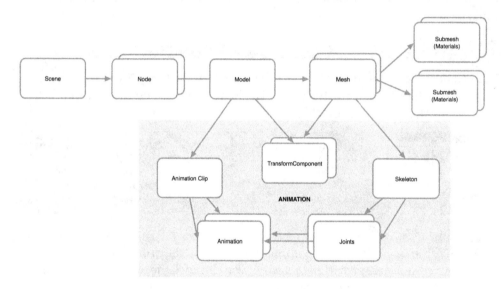

Each model can have a number of animation clips, such as **walk** and **wave**. Each animation clip has a list of animations for a particular joint. Each mesh can have a skeleton that holds a list of joint names, and, using the joint name as a key, you'll be able to access the correct animation for that joint.

The starter project has several classes to aid with importing the animation.

To create the Mesh's skeleton, in **Skeleton.swift**, you'll use the MDLAnimationBindComponent from the mdlMesh, if there is one. Skeleton holds the joint names in an array, and also the joints' parent indices in another array.

To load the animations for the asset, in **AnimationComponent.swift**, load(animation:) iterates through the joints and loads up Animations for each joint. These are all combined into an AnimationClip. Model will hold a dictionary of these AnimationClips keyed on the animation's name.

In the **File inspector**, add these three files to both macOS and iOS targets:

- AnimationClip.swift

- AnimationComponent.swift

- Skeleton.swift

Build the project to ensure that it compiles.

In **Renderer.swift**, change the model that you'll render. Replace:

```
let ball = Model(name: "beachball.usda")
models.append(ball)
```

...with:

```
let skeleton = Model(name: "skeletonWave.usda")
skeleton.rotation = [0, .pi, 0]
models.append(skeleton)
```

This is the skeleton model that you examined in Blender converted to USD format, so that you can load it in your app. You rotate him to look at the camera.

In **Model.swift**, add a new property to `Model` to hold the animation clips:

```
let animations: [String: AnimationClip]
```

In `init(name:)`, just before calling `super.init()`, add the following to load the animations:

```
// animations
let assetAnimations = asset.animations.objects.compactMap {
  $0 as? MDLPackedJointAnimation
}
let animations = Dictionary(uniqueKeysWithValues:
assetAnimations.map {
  ($0.name, AnimationComponent.load(animation: $0))
})
self.animations = animations
```

Here you extract all the `MDLPackedJointAnimation` objects from the asset and load them using the provided loading code. This will create a dictionary of animation clips keyed by animation name.

After the previous code, add this:

```
for animation in animations {
  print("Animation: ", animation.key)
}
```

This is to check that you're loading the animation correctly.

Build and run and you should see the skeleton in his bind pose, with `Animation: /skeletonWave/Animations/wave` in the debug console. You can remove the previous `for` loop and `print` statement now.

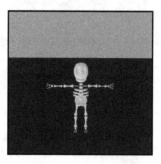

You've just loaded a set of animations listing all rotations and translations on joints. Now to set up the meshes' skeletons.

In `Mesh`, create a new property:

```
let skeleton: Skeleton?
```

At the **top** of `init(mdlMesh:mtkMesh:)`, initialize the skeleton using `mdlMesh`'s `MDLAnimationBindComponent`:

```
let skeleton =
    Skeleton(animationBindComponent:
        (mdlMesh.componentConforming(to: MDLComponent.self)
        as? MDLAnimationBindComponent))
self.skeleton = skeleton
```

You've now loaded up a skeleton with joints. When rendering the skeleton, you'll be able to access the model's current animation and apply it to the mesh's skeleton joints.

Add a print statement to show the joints:

```
skeleton?.jointPaths.map {
    print($0)
}
```

Build and run, and in the debug console you should see a listing of the four skeleton model's joints:

```
/body
/body/upperarm_L
/body/upperarm_L/forearm_L
/body/upperarm_L/forearm_L/hand_L
```

These correspond to the bones that that you previously saw in Blender. You can remove that `print` code now.

Loading the animation

To update the skeleton's pose every frame, you'll create a method that takes the animation clip and iterates through the joints to update each joint's position for the frame. First you'll create a method on `AnimationClip` that gets the pose for a joint at a particular time. This will use the interpolation methods that you've already created in `Animation`.

The main difference is that these poses will be in **joint space**. For example, in this animation, the forearm swings by 45°. All the other joints' rotations and translations will be 0.

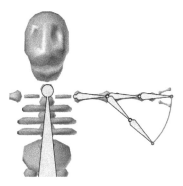

Open **AnimationClip.swift** and create this method:

```
func getPose(at time: Float, jointPath: String) -> float4x4? {
  guard
    let jointAnimation = jointAnimation[jointPath] ?? nil
    else { return nil }
  let rotation =
      jointAnimation.getRotation(at: time) ?? simd_quatf()
  let translation =
      jointAnimation.getTranslation(at: time)
              ?? float3(repeating: 0)
  let pose = float4x4(translation: translation)
              * float4x4(rotation)
  return pose
}
```

Here you retrieve the interpolated rotation and translation for a given joint. You then create a transformation matrix and return it as the pose. This is much the same code as you used earlier for retrieving a transform at a particular time. You return a matrix that combines the translation and rotation for a joint for the current time.

> **Note:** A full transform should include `scale` as well. The starter code for the following chapter will have `scale` keys included.

Joint matrix palette

You're now able to get the pose of a joint. However, each vertex is weighted to up to four joints. You saw this in the earlier elbow example, where some vertices belonging to the lower arm joint would get 50% of the upper arm joint's rotation.

Shortly, you'll change the default vertex descriptor to load vertex buffers with four joints and four weights for each vertex. This set of joints and weights is called the **joint matrix palette**.

The vertex function will sample from each of these joint matrices and, using the weights, will apply the transformation matrix to each vertex.

The following image shows a vertex that is assigned 50% to joint 2 and 50% to joint 3. The other two joint indices are unused.

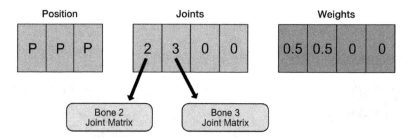

In the vertex function, after multiplying the vertex by the projection, view and model matrices, the vertex function will multiply the vertex by a weighting of each of the joint transforms. Using the example in the image above, the vertex is multiplied with a weighting of 50% of Bone 2's joint matrix and 50% of Bone 3's joint matrix.

In **Skeleton.swift**, in `Skeleton`, create a new method:

```
func updatePose(animationClip: AnimationClip,
                at time: Float) {
}
```

This method, when you've completed it, will iterate through the joints and fill a joint matrix palette buffer with the current pose for each joint.

You'll send this buffer to the GPU's vertex function, so that each vertex will be able to access all of the joint matrices that it is weighted to.

Add the following to the method:

```
guard let paletteBuffer = jointMatrixPaletteBuffer
    else { return }
var palettePointer =
    paletteBuffer.contents().bindMemory(to: float4x4.self,
                           capacity: jointPaths.count)
palettePointer.initialize(repeating: .identity(),
                    count: jointPaths.count)
var poses = [float4x4](repeatElement(.identity(),
                count: jointPaths.count))
```

This initializes the buffer pointer and a matrix array containing the current poses for each joint.

Now, to iterate through the skeleton's joints, add the following:

```
for (jointIndex, jointPath) in jointPaths.enumerated() {
  // 1
  let pose =
      animationClip.getPose(at: time * animationClip.speed,
                       jointPath: jointPath)
                       ?? restTransforms[jointIndex]
  // 2
  let parentPose: float4x4
  if let parentIndex = parentIndices[jointIndex] {
    parentPose = poses[parentIndex]
  } else {
    parentPose = .identity()
  }
  poses[jointIndex] = parentPose * pose
}
```

Going through this code:

1. You retrieve the transformation pose, if there is one, for the joint for this frame. `restTransform` gives a default pose for the joint.

2. The poses array is in flattened hierarchical order, so you can be sure that the parent of any joint has already had its pose updated. You retrieve the current joint's parent pose, concatenate the pose with the current joint's pose and save it in the poses array.

The inverse bind matrix

Examine the properties held on `Skeleton`. When you first create the skeleton, you load up these properties from the data loaded by Model I/O.

One of the properties on `Skeleton` is `bindTransforms`. This is an array of matrices, one element for each joint, that transforms vertices into the local joint space.

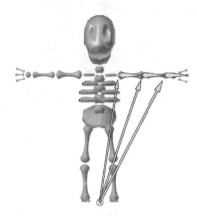

When all the joint transforms are set to identity, that's when you'll get the bind pose. If you apply the inverse bind matrix to each joint, it will move to the origin. The following image shows the skeleton's joints all multiplied by the inverse bind transform matrix:

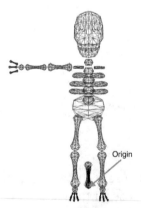

Why is this useful? Each joint should rotate around its base. To rotate an object around a particular point, you first need to translate the point to the origin, then do the rotation, then translate back again. (Review Chapter 4, "Coordinate Spaces" if you're unsure of this rotation sequence.)

In the following image, the vertex is located at (4, 1) and bound 100% to Bone 2. With rotations 10° on Bone 1 and 40° on Bone 2, the vertex should end up at about (3.2, 0) as shown in the right-hand image.

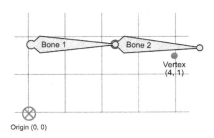

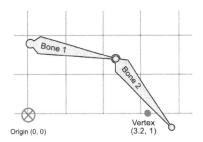

Before applying the pose   After applying the pose

When you currently render your vertices, you multiply each vertex position by the projection, view and model matrices in the vertex function. To get this example vertex in the correct position for the right-hand image, you'll also have to multiply the vertex position by both Bone 1's transform and Bone 2's transform.

Add this to the end of the previous for loop:

```
palettePointer.pointee =
    poses[jointIndex] * bindTransforms[jointIndex].inverse
palettePointer = palettePointer.advanced(by: 1)
```

Here you translate the pose back to the origin with the the inverse bind transform, and combine it with the current pose into the final joint palette matrix.

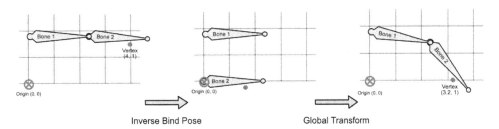

Inverse Bind Pose   Global Transform

With all the frame data set up, you can now set the pose. In **Model.swift**, in update(deltaTime), replace the existing animation code:

```
for mesh in meshes {
  mesh.transform?.setCurrentTransform(at: currentTime)
}
```

...with:

```
for mesh in meshes {
  if let animationClip = animations.first?.value {
    mesh.skeleton?.updatePose(animationClip: animationClip,
                              at: currentTime)
    mesh.transform?.currentTransform = .identity()
  } else {
    mesh.transform?.setCurrentTransform(at: currentTime)
  }
}
```

Here you take the first animation in the list of animations and, if there is an animation, update the pose for the current time. If there is no animation, do the transform animation as you were doing before.

> **Note:** You're using the first animation for simplicity. The starter code for the following chapter will refactor the animation code so that you can send a named animation to the model.

All the meshes are now in position and ready to render.

In `render(renderEncoder:uniforms:fragmentUniforms:)`, at the top of the loop for `mesh in meshes`, add this:

```
if let paletteBuffer = mesh.skeleton?.jointMatrixPaletteBuffer {
  renderEncoder.setVertexBuffer(paletteBuffer, offset: 0,
                                index: 22)
}
```

Here you set up the joint matrix palette buffer so that the GPU can read it. The vertex shader function will take in this palette and apply the matrices to the vertices.

In **Shaders.metal**, add two attributes to `VertexIn`:

```
ushort4 joints [[attribute(Joints)]];
float4 weights [[attribute(Weights)]];
```

The attribute constants `Joints` and `Weights` were set up for you in the starter project in Common.h.

To match `VertexIn`, you'll need to update `Model`'s vertex descriptor. In **VertexDescriptor.swift**, uncomment the three extra vertex attributes. Model I/O will now save color, joint index and joint weight information in the model's vertex buffers.

However, now you have the problem that you saw in the previous chapter - some models will have skeletons and some won't. You can solve this with function constants.

Vertex function constants

In **Shaders.metal**, add a new function constant after importing Common.h.

```
constant bool hasSkeleton [[function_constant(5)]];
```

The function constant is number 5, as 1 through 4 are taken by the fragment textures. You could set these up as named constants in Common.h. Just as you did for textures in the previous chapter, add the joint matrix palette as a conditional parameter to the vertex function:

```
vertex VertexOut
     vertex_main(const VertexIn vertexIn [[stage_in]],
  constant float4x4 *jointMatrices [[buffer(22),
                          function_constant(hasSkeleton)]],
    constant Uniforms &uniforms [[buffer(BufferIndexUniforms)]])
```

At the top of the function, add this:

```
float4 position = vertexIn.position;
float4 normal = float4(vertexIn.normal, 0);
```

This is to save the vertex position and vertex normal.

After this, add the following to combine the joint matrix and weight data with the position and normal:

```
if (hasSkeleton) {
  float4 weights = vertexIn.weights;
  ushort4 joints = vertexIn.joints;
  position =
      weights.x * (jointMatrices[joints.x] * position) +
      weights.y * (jointMatrices[joints.y] * position) +
      weights.z * (jointMatrices[joints.z] * position) +
      weights.w * (jointMatrices[joints.w] * position);
  normal =
      weights.x * (jointMatrices[joints.x] * normal) +
      weights.y * (jointMatrices[joints.y] * normal) +
      weights.z * (jointMatrices[joints.z] * normal) +
      weights.w * (jointMatrices[joints.w] * normal);
}
```

Here you take each joint to which the vertex is bound, calculate the final position and normal, and then take the weighted part of that calculation.

If the function constant `hasSkeleton` is false, you'll just use the original `position` and `normal`.

Change `VertexOut` out assignment so that it looks like this:

```
VertexOut out {
  .position = uniforms.projectionMatrix * uniforms.viewMatrix
              * uniforms.modelMatrix * position,
  .worldPosition = (uniforms.modelMatrix * position).xyz,
  .worldNormal = uniforms.normalMatrix * normal.xyz,
  .worldTangent = 0,
  .worldBitangent = 0,
  .uv = vertexIn.uv
};
```

This uses `position` and `normal` instead of `vertexIn.position` and `vertexIn.normal`. You should also pre-multiply by the tangent and bitangent as well here, but for brevity, you've set `worldTangent` and `worldBitangent` properties to zero.

In Swift, you'll need to tell the pipeline that it has to conditionally prepare two different vertex functions, depending on whether the mesh has a skeleton or not.

In **Submesh.swift**, add a boolean parameter to `init(mdlSubmesh:mtkSubmesh:)`:

```
init(mdlSubmesh: MDLSubmesh, mtkSubmesh: MTKSubmesh,
     hasSkeleton: Bool) {
```

Add a parameter to `makePipelineState(textures:)`:

```
static func makePipelineState(textures: Textures,
                              hasSkeleton: Bool)
  -> MTLRenderPipelineState {
```

In `init(mdlSubmesh:mtkSubmesh:hasSkeleton:)`, update the `pipelineState` assignment:

```
pipelineState =
    Submesh.makePipelineState(textures: textures,
                              hasSkeleton: hasSkeleton)
```

In **Mesh.swift**, in init(mdlMesh:mtkMesh:), add the new parameter when initializing Submesh:

```
Submesh(mdlSubmesh: mesh.0 as! MDLSubmesh,
        mtkSubmesh: mesh.1,
        hasSkeleton: skeleton != nil)
```

In **Submesh.swift**, you'll find an existing function called makeVertexFunctionConstants(hasSkeleton:) to create the vertex function constants for the skeleton option. This is the same procedure as you did for the fragment function constants in Chapter 7, "Maps and Materials".

In makePipelineState, change the vertexFunction definition to:

```
let vertexFunction: MTLFunction?
```

Inside the do where you assign fragmentFunction, add this:

```
let constantValues =
    makeVertexFunctionConstants(hasSkeleton: hasSkeleton)
vertexFunction =
    try library?.makeFunction(name: "vertex_main",
                              constantValues: constantValues)
```

Here you create Metal shaders for the two possibilities - whether the model has a skeleton or not.

Phew! You've now set up all the matrices with animated poses and read in the joint and weight painted data. There's just one more thing to change.

Now that you're taking into account animation data, the skeleton's poses depend upon the transformation matrices derived from each frame's pose. These don't take into account scaling, and there is currently scaling information in the USDZ file's animation data.

In **Renderer.swift**, change the initial rotation of the skeleton:

```
skeleton.rotation = [0, .pi, 0]
```

To:

```
skeleton.rotation = [.pi / 2, .pi, 0]
skeleton.scale = [100, 100, 100]
```

Build and run, and you'll see your friendly skeleton waving.

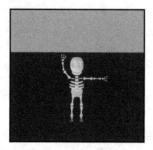

> **Note:** Depending on the power of your device, your animation may glitch. This is because you're taking too long to render a frame, and they sometimes overlap. You can temporarily fix this in `Renderer`'s `draw(in:)`, by adding `commandBuffer.waitUntilCompleted()` after committing the command buffer. Later, you'll find out how to optimize your CPU / GPU synchronization.

Where to go from here?

This chapter took you through the basics of character animation. But don't stop there! There are so many different topics that you can investigate. For instance, you can:

- Learn how to animate your own characters in Blender and import them into your renderer. Start off with a simple robot arm, and work upward from there.

- Download models from http://sketchfab.com, convert them to USD and see what works and what doesn't.

- Watch Disney and Pixar movies... call it research. No, seriously! Animation is a skill all of its own. Watch how people move; good animators can capture personality in a simple walk cycle.

Congratulations, you reached the end of the first section, and you now have a rendering engine in which you can render both simple props and complicated rigged characters. Sweet!

In the next section, you'll move on to creating a game engine where you can build game scenes with their own logic. You'll also discover how to improve your scenes' environments with terrains and skyboxes. Then, you'll examine alternative lighting methods and how to improve performance and use every millisecond available.

Section II: The Scene

With the basics under your belt, you can move on to creating game scenes with scenery, skies and terrains. You'll be able to add multiple models to a scene, and move around the scene and explore it.

- **Chapter 9: The Scene Graph**: Organize your scene models into a scene hierarchy and use different scenes for different levels of your game. You'll drive a car around a large scene and create a simple collision engine to prevent you driving straight through trees.

- **Chapter 10: Fragment Post-Processing**: Some simple techniques will improve your renders with transparency, antialiasing and blending.

- **Chapter 11: Tessellation & Terrains**: The hardware tessellator can add vertices to a low poly model during rendering. Find out how to create detailed mountainous terrains with just a few vertices, a texture and tessellation.

- **Chapter 12: Environment**: Add a 360° sky to your scene. Using the sky to help light your models will integrate them more into their environment. Understand more about physically based rendering and how it can improve the look of your game.

- **Chapter 13: Instancing & Procedural Generation**: Create a vegetation system where you can render hundreds of thousands of blades of grass in your scene. Use morph targets to add variety to rock shapes and create your own procedural system to generate random buildings.

- **Chapter 14: Multipass & Deferred Rendering**: You'll want shadows in your game, which means adding a second render pass to each frame. Using multiple passes, explore a lighting technique where you defer lighting calculations until the final render pass. With this technique, you'll be able to add many more lights to a scene.

- **Chapter 15: GPU-Driven Rendering**: Move your CPU-driven rendering pipeline to the GPU. You'll learn how to use Argument Buffers and Resource Heaps to manage your textures more effectively. With Indirect Command Buffers, you'll generate a list of draw calls, and then create and schedule them on the GPU.

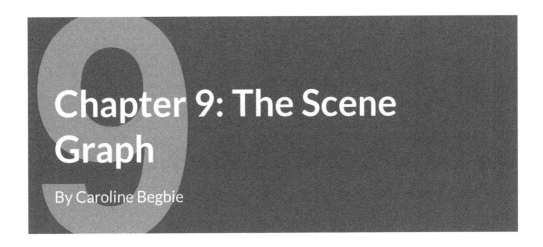

Chapter 9: The Scene Graph

By Caroline Begbie

In this chapter, you'll modify your rendering engine and begin architecting your game engine by abstracting rendering code away from scene management. Game engines can include features such as physics engines and sound. The game engine you'll produce in this chapter doesn't have any high-end features, but it'll help you understand how to integrate other components as well as give you the foundation needed to add complexity later.

For this exercise, you'll create a scene with a drivable car and a controllable player. This should whet your appetite and provide inspiration for making your own games, which is, after all, what this book is all about!

Scenes

A scene can consist of one or more cameras, lights and models. In the scene you'll be building, each model can be a prop or a character.

Of course, you can add these objects in your `Renderer`, but what happens when you want to add some game logic or have them interact with other things? One option is to add this interaction in `update(deltaTime:)`. However, doing so tends to get more impractical as additional interactions are needed. A better way is to create a `Scene` class and abstract the game logic from the rendering code.

To accomplish this, you'll first recreate the starter project's initial render using a `Scene` class. Once you have that, you'll be able to move the skeleton around and drive the car without worrying about what Metal and the GPU are doing behind the curtain.

The starter project

Open the starter project for this chapter. For the most part, this project is similar to the previous chapter's project; however, there are a few changes.

- The main addition is an input controller located in the **Utility** group.

- The storyboard's `MTKView` is subclassed to be a `GameView`, which captures key presses.

- `GameView` passes the user interaction to `InputController` (more on that later!), which then handles the key presses. Because you'll be dealing with the keyboard in this chapter, the iOS target is not included, however, there is a **combined-targets** sample project that uses Core Motion for steering in iOS.

The other significant change is in `Model`. In the previous chapter, you were only able to play one animation. With a few small changes, you can now play, pause and stop named animations, of which **skeleton.usda** has four: **walk**, **wave**, **sit** and **idle**.

Build and run the starter project. If all goes well, you'll see the ground and car, as well as the skeleton running an idle animation. (This "animation" is a still pose.)

The Scene class

To understand how everything will work together, examine the following diagram:

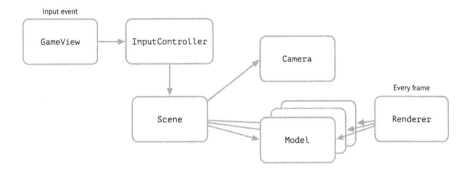

`GameView` will process all of the inputs and pass them along to `InputController`. `Scene` will have an opportunity to intercept and process touch, mouse and keyboard events. `Scene` will also hold references to all `Model`s and `Camera`s. `Renderer` will hold a reference to the current `Scene`. For each frame, `Renderer` will ask `Scene` to update its models' transforms, and then `Renderer` will process each model, which will render itself.

In your starter project, create a new Swift file named **Scene.swift**. This will be a base class that you can subclass for your specific game scenes.

In the base class, you need to include the elements that all subclasses of `Scene`s will require:

- A default `Camera`. You'll create an array of cameras from which the player can choose.

- A reference to `InputController`.

- A list of `Renderable`s in the scene.

- Stub methods that your `Scene` subclasses can override. These methods will be used to alter the setup and the updating on each frame.

- Finally, because the `Scene` controls the cameras, it will also need to hold `Uniforms`.

In **Scene.swift**, add this code:

```swift
class Scene {
  var sceneSize: CGSize

  init(sceneSize: CGSize) {
    self.sceneSize = sceneSize
    setupScene()
  }

  func setupScene() {
    // override this to add objects to the scene
  }
}
```

This initializes the scene with the size of the metal view that you'll pass in from `ViewController`. When you create a new scene subclass, you'll override `setupScene()` to add the objects for each specific game scene.

In `Scene`, add the following:

```swift
var cameras = [Camera()]
var currentCameraIndex = 0
var camera: Camera  {
  return cameras[currentCameraIndex]
}
```

This creates an array of cameras and sets one as the default. For the moment, you only have one camera, but later you'll set up another camera with an alternative viewing position.

The scene graph

In your game, you may want to have trees, houses and animated characters. Some of these objects may depend upon other objects. For example, a car may contain a driver and its passengers. As the car moves, its occupants should move along at the same speed, as if they were inside the car.

While it's possible to move each individual object, you can (and in most cases, should) only move the car, getting the people to automatically follow along. The scene graph is a transform hierarchy that defines the spatial relationships of objects in the scene.

Any children of a parent will move with the parent; however, children can still have their own independent movement within the parent.

The scene you're about to create will have a scene graph that looks like this:

Scene will hold a rootNode, which is the top of the hierarchy. The objects, Model and Camera, are all derived from the Node class, which you already have. Most nodes are Renderable, meaning, you'll render a prop and a character, but not a camera.

Using this tree structure, you'll be able to group Nodes together.

A group is a non-renderable Node that lets you move the group, and all of its children along with it, while still letting you move each node independently within the group.

> **Note**: To better understand groups and their movement, let's say you create a swarm of killer bees and want each to have its own flight pattern within the swarm. With scene graphs and groups, you can do exactly that.

In the following image, on the left-hand side, the skeleton and the car move independently of one another.

On the right, as the car moves, so does the skeleton. However, as in the bee example, the skeleton inside the car still has independent movement (and should be able to duck when those killer bees attack!).

To transform Node into a hierarchical tree, you need to add parent and child properties.

Open **Node.swift** and add these properties to Node:

```
var parent: Node?
var children: [Node] = []
```

Each Node can now have a single parent Node and multiple child Nodes.

Next, add the following methods to handle adding and removing nodes from the tree structure:

```
final func add(childNode: Node) {
  children.append(childNode)
  childNode.parent = self
}

final func remove(childNode: Node) {
  for child in childNode.children {
    child.parent = self
    children.append(child)
  }
  childNode.children = []
  guard let index = (children.firstIndex {
    $0 === childNode
  }) else { return }
  children.remove(at: index)
  childNode.parent = nil
}
```

The first method, add(childNode:), adds the node to the array of children and sets the child node's parent to the current node.

The second method, remove(childNode:), has to adjust the parent/child relationship before removing the node. It does this by adding any children of the removed node to the children of the current node. When that's all done, it sets the parent of these nodes to the current node.

> **Note**: You can read up on tree structures at https://www.raywenderlich.com/138190/swift-algorithm-club-swift-tree-data-structure

You can now create a hierarchy of Nodes in your Scene.

While the transform hierarchy is a parent-child relationship, rendering is not. Later on, you may want to render objects in a particular order — keeping them in a flat array makes this task easier and more flexible.

In **Scene.swift**, add these properties to Scene:

```
let rootNode = Node()
var renderables: [Renderable] = []
var uniforms = Uniforms()
var fragmentUniforms = FragmentUniforms()
```

It's time to replace the current update(deltaTime:) in Renderer with one you'll add to Scene. These new update methods will handle updating the nodes before they are rendered, which requires traversing through the hierarchy.

Still in **Scene.swift**, add the following methods to handle updating the nodes:

```
final func update(deltaTime: Float) {
  uniforms.projectionMatrix = camera.projectionMatrix
  uniforms.viewMatrix = camera.viewMatrix
  fragmentUniforms.cameraPosition = camera.position

  updateScene(deltaTime: deltaTime)
  update(nodes: rootNode.children, deltaTime: deltaTime)
}

private func update(nodes: [Node], deltaTime: Float) {
  nodes.forEach { node in
    node.update(deltaTime: deltaTime)
    update(nodes: node.children, deltaTime: deltaTime)
  }
}
```

```
func updateScene(deltaTime: Float) {
  // override this to update your scene
}
```

Here, you update all of the node transforms, recursively. You also create
updateScene(deltaTime:) as an overridable method for your subclassed game
scenes.

You also need methods to add and remove objects from the scene.

Add the following code to Scene:

```
final func add(node: Node, parent: Node? = nil,
               render: Bool = true) {
  if let parent = parent {
    parent.add(childNode: node)
  } else {
    rootNode.add(childNode: node)
  }
  guard render == true,
    let renderable = node as? Renderable else {
    return
  }
  renderables.append(renderable)
}
```

This method adds a node to the scene. When adding objects to the scene, you can
optionally choose the parent of the object and also whether the object is renderable.
Calling add(node:parent:render:), without the two optional parameters, will add
the object to the scene and render it as you did previously in Renderer.

Now, create the removal method:

```
final func remove(node: Node) {
  if let parent = node.parent {
    parent.remove(childNode: node)
  } else {
    for child in node.children {
      child.parent = nil
    }
    node.children = []
  }
  guard node is Renderable,
    let index = (renderables.firstIndex {
      $0 as? Node === node
    }) else { return }
  renderables.remove(at: index)
}
```

This calls the Node's removal method to remove it from the node hierarchy. It also removes the node from the array of Renderables.

The scene is now able to add and update scene objects. The next step is to modify Renderer to use Scene.

In **Renderer.swift**, add a scene property to Renderer:

```
var scene: Scene?
```

In draw(in:), add the following to the initial guard statement to ensure that an instance of Scene exists:

```
let scene = scene,
```

Next, since the scene will be handling all the models, you need to replace this:

```
for model in models {
  model.update(deltaTime: deltaTime)
}
```

With this:

```
scene.update(deltaTime: deltaTime)
```

And finally, replace:

```
for model in models {
  renderEncoder.pushDebugGroup(model.name)
  model.render(renderEncoder: renderEncoder,
              uniforms: uniforms,
              fragmentUniforms: fragmentUniforms)
  renderEncoder.popDebugGroup()
}
```

With:

```
for renderable in scene.renderables {
  renderEncoder.pushDebugGroup(renderable.name)
  renderable.render(renderEncoder: renderEncoder,
                  uniforms: scene.uniforms,
                  fragmentUniforms: scene.fragmentUniforms)
  renderEncoder.popDebugGroup()
}
```

You're now processing each Renderable in Scene instead of models held on Renderer.

Because you've given Scene control of the cameras, you need to update the projection matrix when the screen is resized.

In **Scene.swift**, at the end of Scene, add this:

```
func sceneSizeWillChange(to size: CGSize) {
  for camera in cameras {
    camera.aspect = Float(size.width / size.height)
  }
  sceneSize = size
}
```

To properly initialize the scene, call this method at the end of init(sceneSize:):

```
sceneSizeWillChange(to: sceneSize)
```

In **Renderer.swift**, replace mtkView(_:drawableSizeWillChange:) with this:

```
func mtkView(_ view: MTKView,
             drawableSizeWillChange size: CGSize) {
  scene?.sceneSizeWillChange(to: size)
}
```

Excellent! You shifted the responsibility of updating models and cameras to the Scene, and you created a basic game engine.

To create a game scene, all you have to do is subclass Scene and add the nodes and the scene logic. For different game levels, you can create different Scene subclasses.

If you wish, you can clean up Renderer by removing the camera, models and uniforms properties and assignments. You can also delete the lines from Renderer that no longer compile after you've removed these objects.

In **ViewControllerExtension.swift**, in handlePan(gesture:), replace:

```
renderer?.camera.rotate(delta: delta)
```

With:

```
renderer?.scene?.camera.rotate(delta: delta)
```

Create a new Swift file named **GameScene.swift**, and then add the following code to it:

```
class GameScene: Scene {
  let ground = Model(name: "ground.obj")
  let car = Model(name: "racing-car.obj")
```

```
    let skeleton = Model(name: "skeleton.usda")
}
```

This instantiates the three models you'll be adding to your game scene. Override setupScene(), and add these models to your scene in their correct positions:

```
override func setupScene() {
   ground.tiling = 32
   add(node: ground)
   car.rotation = [0, .pi / 2, 0]
   car.position = [-0.8, 0, 0]
   add(node: car)
   skeleton.position = [1.6, 0, 0]
   skeleton.rotation = [0, .pi, 0]
   add(node: skeleton)
   skeleton.runAnimation(name: "idle")
   camera.position = [0, 1.2, -4]
}
```

This code adds the models to the scene in the same position they were located at initially in Renderer.

In **ViewController.swift**, create this new scene at the end of viewDidLoad():

```
let scene = GameScene(sceneSize: metalView.bounds.size)
renderer?.scene = scene
```

Build and run, and you'll see much the same render as start of the chapter. The difference, however, is that you have abstracted the scene logic from the rendering logic, making it easier to set up new scenes with different models and different game logic. You can no longer move the camera, as you've also changed the default camera class, so that it is no longer an ArcballCamera.

Grouping nodes

To get an idea of how to update the scene logic, you're going to have the skeleton drive the car off to the right. But there's a hitch! You're only going to move the car model each frame, not the skeleton.

Start by adding this to GameScene:

```
override func updateScene(deltaTime: Float) {
   car.position.x += 0.02
}
```

This overrides the method that Scene calls on every frame, which allows its subclasses to update models further. Build and run the project.

Oh no! This scene must be haunted; the car's driving off on its own, leaving its skeleton driver behind.

To solve this problem (and rid yourself of this haunting), you can make the car a parent of the skeleton so that whenever the car moves, the skeleton automatically follows along.

In GameScene, in setupScene(), change:

```
add(node: skeleton)
skeleton.runAnimation(name: "idle")
```

To:

```
add(node: skeleton, parent: car)
skeleton.runAnimation(name: "sit")
```

This adds the skeleton to the car as a child of the node and changes the animation so the skeleton doesn't look like he's walking when he's supposed to be driving.

Next, you need to update the hierarchy of node transforms, recursively, so that any change to the base node will update all of the transforms of the child nodes.

Add this to Node, in **Node.swift**:

```
var worldTransform: float4x4 {
  if let parent = parent {
    return parent.worldTransform * self.modelMatrix
  }
  return modelMatrix
}
```

This computed property goes up through the node hierarchy, recursively, and returns the final matrix for the model.

In `Model`, in `render(renderEncoder:uniforms:fragmentUniforms:)`, change:

```
uniforms.modelMatrix = modelMatrix * currentLocalTransform
```

To:

```
uniforms.modelMatrix = worldTransform * currentLocalTransform
```

Build and run.

Well that's progress. Your skeleton now travels with the car, but he's not positioned correctly.

When you initially placed the skeleton in the scene, you placed him relative to the scene coordinates, but now his position in the scene needs to be relative to the car instead.

In `GameScene`, in `setupScene()`, change the skeleton's position and rotation to:

```
skeleton.position = [−0.35, −0.2, −0.35]
skeleton.rotation = [0, 0, 0]
```

The axes are not the scene's axes, but rather the car's axes. So when you move the skeleton negatively on the x-axis, you're effectively moving the skeleton further left in the car.

Build and run, and the skeleton is now driving the car, sitting properly in the driver's seat.

First-person camera

In this section, you'll create a first-person camera which places *you* in the driving seat. Once inside the car, you'll be able to drive around the scene using the traditional W-A-S-D keys. Before you begin, take a moment to review some important files.

The main view class in **Main.storyboard** is a GameView, which is a subclass of MTKView. Located in the **SceneGraph-macOS** group, open **GameView.swift**. Notice it has events for key presses and mouse movement, and it forwards these events to an instance of InputController.

The keys you're dealing with are:

- **W**: Move forward
- **A**: Strafe left
- **S**: Move backward
- **D**: Strafe right
- **Right and left arrows (or Q and E)**: Rotate left and right

In the **Utility** group, locate and open **InputController.swift**. Close to the bottom of the file you'll find InputState. This is an enum for the state of the key and is used to track the keypress status. There's also KeyboardControl, which contains a list of valid keys.

With the file review out of the way, it's time to add a **player** into the scene.

Your games will have only one player which the input controller will update using the detected key presses.

In **InputController.swift**, create a property in `InputController`:

```
var player: Node?
```

`player` can be any `Node` type - a `Model` or even a `Camera`.

Next, you need to integrate the input controller into your base `Scene` class.

Add this property to `Scene` in **Scene.swift**:

```
let inputController = InputController()
```

In **InputController.swift**, create a new method to update the player:

```
public func updatePlayer(deltaTime: Float) {
    guard let player = player else { return }
}
```

This method is where you'll calculate how to update the player's transform. Xcode displays a compiler warning until after you've done that.

On every frame, the scene will tell the input controller to update the player transforms according to which keys are pressed.

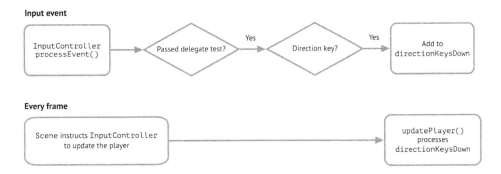

In **Scene.swift**, create a new method to update the player. This is a separate method as this process of updating the player will get more complex:

```
private func updatePlayer(deltaTime: Float) {
    inputController.updatePlayer(deltaTime: deltaTime)
}
```

Add this at the beginning of `update(deltaTime:)`:

```
updatePlayer(deltaTime: deltaTime)
```

You still need to connect the `GameView` input with the `Scene` in `ViewController`. So, in **ViewController.swift**, add this to the end of `viewDidLoad()`:

```
if let gameView = metalView as? GameView {
  gameView.inputController = scene.inputController
}
```

The first player that you'll move around the scene will be the camera. Here's what to expect:

- When you move through the scene, you'll be moving along the x and z axes.

- Your camera will have a direction vector, and when the **W** key is pressed, you'll move along the z-axis in a positive direction.

- If you have the **W** and **D** keys pressed simultaneously, you'll move diagonally.

- When you press the left and right arrow keys (or **Q** and **E**), you'll rotate in that direction.

In **Node.swift**, create a forward vector computed property based on the current rotation of the node:

```
var forwardVector: float3 {
  return normalize([sin(rotation.y), 0, cos(rotation.y)])
}
```

This is an example of forward vectors when `rotation.y` is 0° and 45°:

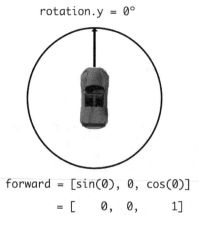

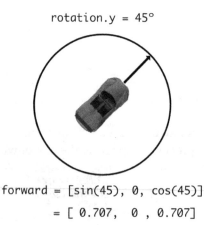

rotation.y = 0°

rotation.y = 45°

forward = [sin(0), 0, cos(0)]
     = [0, 0,   1]

forward = [sin(45), 0, cos(45)]
     = [0.707, 0 , 0.707]

It's useful to have a transformed right direction vector too, so add this:

```
var rightVector: float3 {
  return [forwardVector.z, forwardVector.y, -forwardVector.x]
}
```

This vector points 90° to the right of the node.

Open **InputController.swift** and add the default properties for translation and rotation speed to InputController:

```
var translationSpeed: Float = 2.0
var rotationSpeed: Float = 1.0
```

These values are per second, so you'll use deltaTime to calculate the correct value for the current frame.

At the end of updatePlayer(deltaTime:), add this to create a desired direction vector from the current keys pressed.

```
let translationSpeed = deltaTime * self.translationSpeed
let rotationSpeed = deltaTime * self.rotationSpeed
var direction: float3 = [0, 0, 0]
for key in directionKeysDown {
  switch key {
  case .w:
    direction.z += 1
  case .a:
    direction.x -= 1
  case.s:
    direction.z -= 1
  case .d:
    direction.x += 1
  case .left, .q:
    player.rotation.y -= rotationSpeed
  case .right, .e:
    player.rotation.y += rotationSpeed
  default:
    break
  }
}
```

This code processes each depressed key and creates a final desired direction vector. For instance, if the game player presses W and A, she wants to go diagonally forward and left. The final direction vector ends up as [-1, 0, 1].

Add this after the previous code:

```
if direction != [0, 0, 0] {
  direction = normalize(direction)
  player.position +=
    (direction.z * player.forwardVector
      + direction.x * player.rightVector)
    * translationSpeed
}
```

Here, you're calculating the player's final position from the player's forward and right vectors and the desired direction.

In **GameScene.swift**, add this to the end of setupScene():

```
inputController.player = camera
```

This sets the camera as the player the input controller will update.

Build and run, and you can now roam about your scene using the W-A-S-D keys. You can rotate using the left and right arrow keys (Q and E also do the rotation).

Follow the animated car off the edge of the scene!

Intercepting key presses

That's cool, but what if you want to drive the car in place of the skeleton? By setting up the **C** key as a special key, you'll be able to jump into the car at any time. But first, you need to remove the driving code that you created earlier.

In **GameScene.swift**, remove the following line of code from updateScene(deltaTime:):

```
car.position.x += 0.02
```

InputController is extensible, meaning you can add keys to the enum and capture the input, which is what you're about to do.

Open **InputController.swift**, locate KeyboardControl at the bottom of the file, and add this to the end of the enum:

```
case c = 8
```

8 is the ASCII value of the **C** key.

In **GameScene.swift**, add the following property:

```
var inCar = false
```

This tracks the C key and toggles whether you're driving the car or not. Now you need to set up GameScene to be InputController's keyboard delegate.

Add this to the end of **GameScene.swift**:

```
extension GameScene: KeyboardDelegate {
  func keyPressed(key: KeyboardControl,
                  state: InputState) -> Bool {
    return true
  }
}
```

Returning false from this method stops InputController from updating direction keys, which you don't want, so you'll return true.

Add this to the start of setupScene():

```
inputController.keyboardDelegate = self
```

You can now intercept key presses and optionally prevent default movement from taking place.

In keyPressed(key:state:), add this before the return:

```
switch key {
case .c where state == .ended:
  let camera = cameras[0]
  if !inCar {
    remove(node: skeleton)
    remove(node: car)
    add(node: car, parent: camera)
    car.position = [0.35, -1, 0.1]
    car.rotation = [0, 0, 0]
    inputController.translationSpeed = 10.0
  }
  inCar = !inCar
  return false
```

```
default:
  break
}
```

This code, when you press the C key and let go, temporarily removes the car and the skeleton from the scene. It then adds the car back to the scene but as a child of the camera. Finally, you set the position of the car so that it looks as if you're in the driving seat, and you also set the speed of the camera to move faster.

Build and run, and you can now drive and explore the entire scene. Sure, there's currently not much to see, but you can add several **treefir.obj** models to the scene if you'd like.

> **Note:** In first-person shooter games, the player carries around a weapon. You now know how to substitute the car model for a gun model, with the gun parented to the camera, to implement your own first-person shooter.

To step out of the car, in keyPressed(key:state:), change this:

```
if !inCar {
```

To:

```
if inCar {
  remove(node: car)
  add(node: car)
  car.position = camera.position + (camera.rightVector * 1.3)
  car.position.y = 0
  car.rotation = camera.rotation
  inputController.translationSpeed = 2.0
} else {
```

This code checks to see if you're in the car. If so, it removes the car from the scene and then adds it back, but as a child of the scene, not the camera. It also sets the car's position to be near the camera's position and decreases the player speed to simulate walking.

Build and run, and you can now drive the car around or get out and walk.

Full games tend to have a lot more code, but with this simple prototype, you made some cool stuff happen without even thinking about rendering in Metal.

But there's still more you can do with the camera — like creating a top-down view.

Orthographic projection

Sometimes it's a little tricky to see what's happening in a scene. To help, you can build a top-down camera that shows you the whole scene without any perspective distortion, otherwise known as **orthographic projection**.

Orthographic projection flattens three dimensions to two dimensions without any perspective distortion.

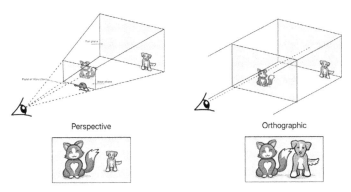

MathLibrary.swift contains a method to return an orthographic matrix of the size of a specified `Rectangle`.

To create a camera with orthographic projection, add this to the end of **Camera.swift**:

```swift
class OrthographicCamera: Camera {
  var rect = Rectangle(left: 10, right: 10,
                       top: 10, bottom: 10)

  override init() {
    super.init()
  }
}
```

```
    init(rect: Rectangle, near: Float, far: Float) {
      super.init()
      self.rect = rect
      self.near = near
      self.far = far
    }

    override var projectionMatrix: float4x4 {
      return float4x4(orthographic: rect, near: near, far: far)
    }
}
```

You can find `Rectangle` and `float4x4(orthographic:near:far:)` defined in
MathLibrary.swift.

This creates a camera similar to the perspective camera that you generally use, but
the projection matrix is an orthographic one. To get the most out of this camera,
you'll set up your scene so that you can switch to this camera by pressing the **1** key
on your keyboard. To switch back to the original first-person camera, you'll use the **0**
key.

In **GameScene.swift**, set up a new property in `GameScene`:

```
let orthoCamera = OrthographicCamera()
```

Add this to the end of `setupScene()`:

```
orthoCamera.position = [0, 2, 0]
orthoCamera.rotation.x = .pi / 2
cameras.append(orthoCamera)
```

Here, you add an orthographic camera that's 2 units up in the air and pointing
straight down.

To set the proper size of the camera, you need to override
`sceneSizeWillChange(to:)`. Add this to the end of `GameScene`:

```
override func sceneSizeWillChange(to size: CGSize) {
  super.sceneSizeWillChange(to: size)
  let cameraSize: Float = 10
  let ratio = Float(sceneSize.width / sceneSize.height)
  let rect = Rectangle(left: -cameraSize * ratio,
                      right: cameraSize * ratio,
                      top: cameraSize,
                      bottom: -cameraSize)
  orthoCamera.rect = rect
}
```

This sets the rectangle for the orthographic projection matrix. It also sets the rotation of the camera to point straight down at the scene and increases its size, so you can show more of the scene.

In keyPressed(key:state:), add this to the switch statement:

```
case .key0:
  currentCameraIndex = 0
case .key1:
  currentCameraIndex = 1
```

This changes the current camera index into the scene's camera array. Key **0** will change to the original camera, and key **1** will take you to top-down view. (That's the numbers above the letters, not the numbers on the numeric keypad. Those keys have different key addresses.)

Build and run, and press **1** to go into top view. Press the **C** key so that the first-person camera becomes the object controlled by the input controller, and the input keys will work to move the car. You can now see what's happening in the overall scene as you drive.

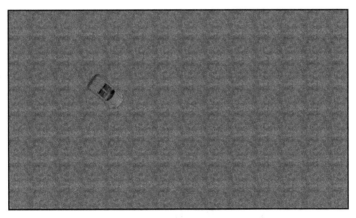

With overhead cameras, you can make things like 2D top-down car racing games.

> **Note:** Notice how you can make the car strafe sideways by using the **A** and **D** keys; this isn't very realistic. If you want to disable these keys, return false from keyPressed(key:state:) when the A and D keys are pressed.

Third-person camera

You wrote the skeleton out of the game, but what if you want to play *as the skeleton*? You still want to be in first-person while driving the car, but when you're out of the car, the skeleton should walk about the scene, and the camera should follow.

In **GameScene.swift**, in `setupScene()`, change the skeleton position, rotation and setup code to:

```
skeleton.position = [1.6, 0, 0]
skeleton.rotation = [0, .pi, 0]
add(node: skeleton)
skeleton.runAnimation(name: "idle")
```

This makes the skeleton a child of the scene rather than the car.

Still in `setupScene()`, change:

```
inputController.player = camera
```

To:

```
inputController.player = skeleton
```

Build and run, and you can move your skeleton around the scene.

The camera is currently fixed, but you can go into top-down view by pressing the **1** key and see the skeleton move.

Speaking of fixed cameras and moving, a third-person camera should really follow the skeleton around. You can fix that now.

Add a new camera class to **Camera.swift**:

```
class ThirdPersonCamera: Camera {
  var focus: Node
```

```
    var focusDistance: Float = 3
    var focusHeight: Float = 1.2

    init(focus: Node) {
      self.focus = focus
      super.init()
    }
}
```

This sets the third-person camera to focus on the player node, positioned by default 3 units back and 1.2 units up.

To calculate the position and rotation of the camera from the position and rotation of the player, all you need to do is override the view matrix property. Add this to `ThirdPersonCamera`:

```
override var viewMatrix: float4x4 {
  position = focus.position - focusDistance
                  * focus.forwardVector
  position.y = focusHeight
  rotation.y = focus.rotation.y
  return super.viewMatrix
}
```

With this code, whenever the renderer asks for the current camera's `viewMatrix`, you update the position of the camera.

In **GameScene.swift**, add this to the end of `setupScene()`:

```
let tpCamera = ThirdPersonCamera(focus: skeleton)
cameras.append(tpCamera)
currentCameraIndex = 2
```

Here, you set the third-person camera as the default rendering camera.

Now build and run the project, and follow your skeleton around the scene.

> **Note**: Pressing the C and 1 keys now do weird things as you've been changing the camera. As a mini-challenge, see if you can make the C key go from the first-person camera (`currentCameraIndex` = 0) to the third-person camera (`currentCameraIndex` = 2), and update the positions of all the nodes correctly.

Animating the player

It's a good idea to animate the skeleton while you're in control of him. **skeleton.usda** includes a walking animation, which is what you'll use. The plan is to animate the skeleton when a key is pressed and freeze him when he's standing still.

> **Note:** In an ideal world, the walk animation would blend into the idle animation, but this is beyond the scope of this chapter.

In **GameScene.swift**, in `setupScene()`, replace:

```
skeleton.runAnimation(name: "idle")
```

With:

```
skeleton.runAnimation(name: "walk")
skeleton.currentAnimation?.speed = 2.0
skeleton.pauseAnimation()
```

The walk animation is a bit slow, so you speed it up to twice its normal speed.

Now to add the start and stop calls based on the key press status.

Add this code to the `switch` statement in `keyPressed()`:

```
case .w, .s, .a, .d:
  if state == .began {
    skeleton.resumeAnimation()
  }
  if state == .ended {
    skeleton.pauseAnimation()
  }
```

Build and run and test out your animation.

Simple collisions

An essential element of games is collision detection. Imagine how boring it would be if platformer games didn't let you collect power-ups like gems and oil cans?

Creating a complete physics engine would take a whole book to describe, so instead, you'll create a simple physics controller so you can understand how to integrate game physics into your engine. This physics controller will test for a simple collision.

The previous chapter touched upon axis-aligned bounding boxes used to check the height of the bouncing ball; these are generally what you use for testing collisions.

Depending on the complexity of your game, you can do several types of collision detection. The most common are:

- **Sphere-to-sphere**: The simplest volume collision test where you add the radius of each sphere and check that the total is greater than the distance between the objects' positions. This is fast and efficient. However, as you'll see when colliding the car, when you have rectangular objects, the collision is not very accurate.

- **AABB**: Axis-aligned bounding box. The AABB is the smallest cubic volume that contains the object. AABB checking is also fast, but if you have many odd rotated shapes, it's not too accurate.

- **OBB**: Oriented bounding box. This is where the bounding volume rotates with the character. It's much more difficult to check the collision.

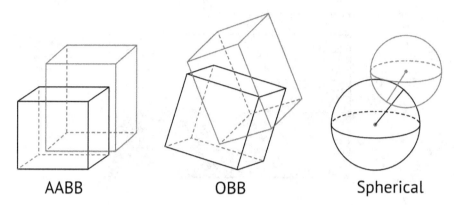

AABB   OBB   Spherical

You'll be doing spherical collision using the bounding box provided by Model I/O. The bounding sphere will have a diameter of the widest side.

If you have many objects in your scene and test collision for every object against every other object, the calculation can seriously overwhelm your processing allowance. If you have this scenario, you would generally separate out your game objects into sections using a space partitioning algorithm such as an **octree**. You'd set this up ahead of time so that you'd only check collisions for objects in the same sections.

In your engine, you'll set only one **dynamic** object which you'll check against every other object. All other objects will be **static** and don't need to be checked against each other.

You'll use a new game scene for this which has a few objects already in the scene. Locate **CarScene.swift** and add it to the macOS target. This is a subclass of Scene that contains some oil cans and trees as well as the car.

In **ViewController.swift**, change:

```
let scene = GameScene(sceneSize: metalView.bounds.size)
```

To:

```
let scene = CarScene(sceneSize: metalView.bounds.size)
```

In the **Utility** folder, open **PhysicsController.swift**. At the top of the file, you'll see this:

```
let debugRenderBoundingBox = false
```

Model has some extra code to render the bounding boxes so that you can visualize them. Change debugRenderBoundingBox to true to switch on this code.

Build and run your new scene and check out the bounding boxes being rendered around the objects:

> **Note**: The bounding boxes are axis-aligned bounding boxes whereas you'll be using a sphere. In top view (key press 1) you can visualize the sphere radius as the largest of the width or height.

In **Scene.swift**, add this property to Scene:

```
let physicsController = PhysicsController()
```

Open **PhysicsController.swift**. PhysicsController currently has a property for the dynamic body and a property to hold all the static bodies. It also has add and remove methods for the static bodies. What it doesn't have is a method for collision detection.

Add a method to check the collision:

```
func checkCollisions() -> Bool {
  return false
}
```

At the moment, you're returning false to indicate that there isn't a collision. At the top of this method add the following code:

```
guard let node = dynamicBody else { return false }
let nodeRadius = max((node.size.x / 2), (node.size.z / 2))
let nodePosition = node.worldTransform.columns.3.xyz
```

Here, you set up the radius for the bounding sphere and the calculated position. Remember that the dynamic node might be a child of another node, so make sure you calculate the true world position.

After the previous code, check the dynamic node against all the static bodies:

```
for body in staticBodies {
  let bodyRadius = max((body.size.x / 2), (body.size.z / 2))
  let bodyPosition = body.worldTransform.columns.3.xyz
  let d = distance(nodePosition, bodyPosition)
  if d < (nodeRadius + bodyRadius) {
    // There's a hit
    return true
  }
}
```

This calculates each static body's radius and world position and checks the distance between the body and the dynamic node. If the distance is less than the combined radii, the spheres overlap and there is a collision, so you return true. You return out of the method on the first collision you find so as not to check all of the other collisions. (In a moment, you'll add an option to check all of the bodies and save the collided ones.)

The base scene class will be responsible for checking for collisions during player transform update. In **Scene.swift**, replace updatePlayer(deltaTime:) with this:

```
private func updatePlayer(deltaTime: Float) {
  guard let node = inputController.player else { return }
  let holdPosition = node.position
  let holdRotation = node.rotation
  inputController.updatePlayer(deltaTime: deltaTime)
  if physicsController.checkCollisions() {
    node.position = holdPosition
    node.rotation = holdRotation
  }
}
```

Here, you hold the position before the update. If the player collides with an object, you want to be able to restore the position, so the player doesn't move forward.

In **CarScene.swift**, at the end of setupScene(), add the following to set up the physics bodies:

```
physicsController.dynamicBody = car
for body in bodies {
  physicsController.addStaticBody(node: body)
}
```

Build and run and check out your collisions. (Hint: It's easier to see them in top view.)

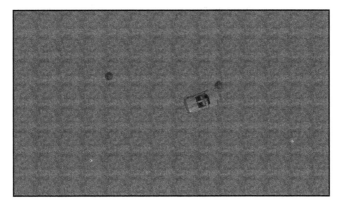

With the oil cans, you can check for collisions and create power-ups in your game. In this case, you'll remove the oil can from the scene to indicate the can's been collected.

In **Scene.swift**, add a new method in Scene that your game scene can override:

```
func updateCollidedPlayer() -> Bool {
  // override this
  return false
}
```

You'll be able to override this in your subclassed game scene and return true if player movement should still take place.

In updatePlayer(deltaTime:), change:

```
if physicsController.checkCollisions() {
```

To:

```
if physicsController.checkCollisions()
    && !updateCollidedPlayer() {
```

If the subclassed game scene returns false from updateCollidedPlayer(), you'll restore the held positions, and the player won't update.

In **PhysicsController.swift**, add these new properties to PhysicsController:

```
var holdAllCollided = false
var collidedBodies: [Node] = []
```

This gives you the option to do a quick collision test rather than store the collided bodies. If you hit one object and want to exit the collision testing immediately, set `holdAllCollided` to `false`; otherwise, set it to `true` and `checkCollisions()` will store all of the collided bodies.

In `checkCollisions()`, in the distance test conditional, replace:

```
return true
```

With:

```
if holdAllCollided {
  collidedBodies.append(body)
} else {
  return true
}
```

At the end of `checkCollisions()`, replace:

```
return false
```

With:

```
return collidedBodies.count != 0
```

At the start of `checkCollisions()`, initialize `collidedBodies`:

```
collidedBodies = []
```

You'll now be able to check each body in `CarScene` to see whether the car has hit an oilcan or a tree.

In **CarScene.swift**, at the end of `setupScene()`, add this

```
physicsController.holdAllCollided = true
```

Override `updateCollidedPlayer()` so that you can check if you've collected an oil can.

```
override func updateCollidedPlayer() -> Bool {
    for body in physicsController.collidedBodies {
        if body.name == "oilcan.obj" {
            print("power-up")
            remove(node: body)
            physicsController.removeBody(node: body)
            return true
        }
}
```

```
    }
    return false
}
```

Build and run. When you run over the oil cans, you collect a power-up; when you hit the trees, you stop.

Where to go from here?

In this chapter, you created a simple game engine with an input controller and a physics controller. There are many different architecture choices you can make. The one presented here is overly simplified and only touched the surface of collision detection and physics engines. However, it should give you an idea of how to separate your game code from your Metal rendering code.

In the **resources** folder for this chapter, you'll find **references.markdown**. In it, you'll find some further reading on how to improve your collision detection using the axis aligned bounding box.

Don't forget to check out the **combined-targets** project. You'll be able to drive your car on your iPhone using an accelerator pedal and steering by tilting your device!

Chapter 10: Fragment Post-Processing

By Marius Horga

Before embarking on complex features like tessellation and instancing, it's best to start with simple techniques to improve your render quality. After the fragments have been processed in the pipeline, a series of operations are run on the GPU. These operations are sometimes referred to as **Per-sample Processing** (https://www.khronos.org/opengl/wiki/Per-Sample_Processing), and include: Alpha testing; Depth testing; Stencil testing; Scissor testing; Blending; and Anti-aliasing.

As you go through this chapter, you'll learn about most of these.

Getting started

In the projects directory for this chapter, open the starter playground. Then, run the playground and you'll see this image:

When you move closer to the tree — using either the scroll wheel or the two-finger gesture on your trackpad — you'll notice the leaves have an unpleasant look. In the playground's **Resources** folder, take a look at **treeColor.png**. The area of the texture surrounding the leaf is transparent.

To make the leaves look more natural, you'll render the white part of the texture as transparent. However, before changing anything, it's important to understand the difference between transparent objects and those that are translucent.

Alpha testing

An object that is transparent allows light to entirely pass through it. A translucent object, on the other hand, will distort light when it passes through. Objects like water, glass, and plastic are all translucent. Objects can also be opaque. In fact, most objects in nature are opaque, meaning they don't allow any light to pass through, like trees and rocks.

All digital colors are formed as a combination of the three primary colors: red, green and blue. Hence the color scheme RGB. There's a fourth component that's added to the color definition. It's called **alpha** and it ranges from 0 (fully transparent) to 1 (fully opaque). A common practice in determining transparency is checking the alpha property and ignoring values below a certain threshold. This is called **alpha testing**.

Start by creating a toggle key so you can see the difference for when an effect is on or off. In the playground page's **Sources** folder, in **Renderer.swift**, add this property to Renderer:

```
var transparencyEnabled = false
```

With this Boolean, you'll be able to control transparency.

Because the trees will have additional modifications, you need to create different shaders, which means you also need several different pipeline states for each shader combination. Add the following at the top of Renderer:

```
var treePipelineState: MTLRenderPipelineState!
```

In buildPipelineState, just before the end of the do block, add these lines:

```
// 1
let treeFragmentFunction =
    library.makeFunction(name: "fragment_tree")
descriptor.fragmentFunction = treeFragmentFunction
// 2
treePipelineState =
  try device.makeRenderPipelineState(descriptor: descriptor)
```

Going through this code:

1. You create a function using the name you plan to provide to the Metal library, and you assign it to the pipeline state descriptor; you'll write the fragment_tree() shader shortly. The playground won't run correctly until you've completed the shader function.

2. You then create the pipeline state for the tree using the provided descriptor.

Next, in `draw(in:)`, right below this line:

```
// render tree
```

Add the following code:

```
renderEncoder.setRenderPipelineState(treePipelineState)
renderEncoder.setFragmentBytes(&transparencyEnabled,
               length: MemoryLayout<Bool>.size, index: 0)
```

This tells the render command encoder to use the pipeline state for the next draw call. You also send the current value of `transparencyEnabled` to the fragment shader.

In **MetalView.swift**, add these two methods to `MetalView`, so the view can capture key presses:

```
// 1
public override var acceptsFirstResponder: Bool {
  return true
}

public override func keyDown(with event: NSEvent) {
  enum KeyCode: UInt16 {
    case t = 0x11
  }

  guard
    let renderer = renderer,
    let keyCode = KeyCode(rawValue: event.keyCode)
  else {return}

  // 2
  switch keyCode {
  case .t:
    renderer.transparencyEnabled = !renderer.transparencyEnabled
  }
}
```

Going through the code:

1. You activate key presses by setting `acceptsFirstResponder` to `true`.

2. You check whether the key pressed is a **T** (0x11 is the hexadecimal code for T) and toggle `transparencyEnabled` on or off depending on its previous value.

Finally, in **Shaders.metal**, in the **Resources** group, add this:

```
// 1
fragment float4 fragment_tree(VertexOut vertex_in [[stage_in]],
            texture2d<float> texture [[texture(0)]],
            constant bool & transparencyEnabled [[buffer(0)]])
{
  // 2
  constexpr sampler s(filter::linear);
  float4 color = texture.sample(s, vertex_in.uv);
  // 3
  if (transparencyEnabled && color.a < 0.1) {
    discard_fragment();
  }
  // 4
  return color;
}
```

With this code:

1. The fragment shader gets the processed vertices from the vertex shader, the tree texture and the value of transparencyEnabled from the CPU.

2. It creates a texture sampler with linear filtering and uses it to read the color information from the input texture.

3. If both transparencyEnabled is active and the alpha value of the current pixel is below a 0.1 threshold, it discards this fragment.

4. Otherwise, it returns the color from the sampled texture.

Run the playground again. Click the rendered image so your key strokes will get captured in that window. Then, press the **T** key a few times to watch the alpha testing (transparency) toggle on and off:

That's better! If you get closer to the tree, you'll notice the white background around the leaves is gone.

However, the leaves all look the same color. That's because this scene lacks a directional light. To fix that, you need to write a new vertex function and configure the tree pipeline state again.

In **Shaders.metal**, add this:

```
vertex VertexOut
         vertex_light(const VertexIn vertex_in [[stage_in]],
                  constant float4x4 &mvp_matrix [[buffer(1)]]) {
  VertexOut vertex_out;
  vertex_out.position = mvp_matrix * vertex_in.position;
  vertex_out.uv = vertex_in.uv;
  return vertex_out;
}
```

This is the same code as vertex_main(), but you're going to add any new code to this one from now on.

In **Renderer.swift**, you need to also reference `vertex_light` in the render pipeline descriptor configuration. Right above this line, in `buildPipelineState()`:

```
treePipelineState =
    try device.makeRenderPipelineState(descriptor: descriptor)
```

Add this code:

```
let lightVertexFunction =
    library.makeFunction(name: "vertex_light")
descriptor.vertexFunction = lightVertexFunction
```

This sets the pipeline to use your new vertex function.

Back in **Shaders.metal**, in `vertex_light`, add this code right before `return vertex_out;`:

```
// 1
vertex_out.normal = (mvp_matrix
                        * float4(vertex_in.normal, 0)).xyz;
// 2
float3 light_direction = {1.0, 1.0, -1.0};
float4 light_color = float4(1.0);
// 3
float intensity = dot(normalize(vertex_out.normal),
                      normalize(light_direction));
// 4
vertex_out.color = saturate(light_color * intensity);
```

Going through this code:

1. You calculate the vertex normal.

2. Set the light direction and light color to custom values.

3. Calculate the light intensity as a dot product of the vertex normal and light direction, just as you did in Chapter 5, "Lighting Fundamentals."

4. Calculate the vertex color and clamp the resulting value between 0 and 1.

To include the light value, you need to multiply it with the existing texture color, so add this code inside the `fragment_tree()` function, right above `return color;`:

```
color *= vertex_in.color * 2;
```

Note: You could multiply the color value with various values, including values below 1, and see which one pleases your eye. Here, 2 seems to bring an acceptable brightness level to the color.

Run the playground again. Don't forget to press the **T** key to toggle the transparency.

As you can see, the leaves are now showing their face or back depending on how each of them is oriented with respect to the light direction.

Depth testing

Depth testing compares the depth value of the current fragment to one stored in the framebuffer. If a fragment is farther away than the current depth value, this fragment fails the depth test and is discarded since it's occluded by another fragment. You'll learn more about depth testing in Chapter 14, "Multipass and Deferred Rendering."

Stencil testing

Stencil testing compares the value stored in a stencil attachment to a masked reference value. If a fragment makes it through the mask it's kept; otherwise it's discarded.

Scissor testing

If you only want to render part of the screen, you can tell the GPU to only render within a particular rectangle. This is much more efficient than rendering the whole screen. The scissor test checks whether a fragment is inside a defined 2D area called the **scissor rectangle**. If the fragment falls outside of this rectangle, it's discarded.

In **Renderer.swift**, add this line in draw(in:), right after the // render tree comment:

```
renderEncoder.setScissorRect(MTLScissorRect(x: 500, y: 500,
                                    width: 600, height: 400))
```

Run the playground again.

Ouch! That's not right. Only the tree was affected.

> **Note**: Keep in mind that any objects rendered before you set the scissor rectangle are not affected by it.

Move that last line to right after the // render terrain comment, before you do the terrain draw.

Run the playground again.

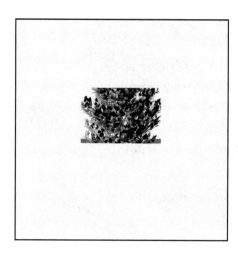

Much better.

You'll need to see the entire scene for the rest of the chapter, so comment out that scissor test line.

Alpha blending

Alpha blending is different from alpha testing in that the latter only works with total transparency. In that case, all you have to do is discard fragments. For translucent or partially transparent objects, discarding fragments is not the solution anymore because you want the fragment color to contribute to a certain extent to the existing framebuffer color. You don't want to just replace it.

The formula for alpha blending is:

$$\vec{C_b} = \alpha_1 * \vec{C_s} + \alpha_2 * \vec{C_d}$$

Going over this formula:

- **Cs**: Source color. The current color you just added to the scene.

- **Cd**: Destination color. The color that already exists in the framebuffer.

- **Cb**: Final blended color.

- **α1** and **α2**: The alpha (opacity) factors for the source and destination color, respectively.

The final blended color is the result of adding the products between the two colors and their opacity factors. The source color is the fragment color you put in front, and the destination color is the color already existing in the framebuffer.

Often the two factors are the inverse of each other transforming this equation into linear color interpolation:

$$\vec{C_b} = \alpha * \vec{C_s} + (1 - \alpha) * \vec{C_d}$$

All right, time to install a glass window in front of the tree.

In **Renderer.swift**, create new texture and pipeline state properties at the top of the class:

```
var windowTexture: MTLTexture?
var windowPipelineState: MTLRenderPipelineState!
```

Next, add this code right before init(metalView:):

```
lazy var window: MTKMesh = {
  do {
    let primitive = self.loadModel(name: "plane")!
    let model = try MTKMesh(mesh: primitive,
                            device: device)
    windowTexture = loadTexture(imageName: "windowColor")
    return model
  } catch {
    fatalError()
  }
}()
var windowTransform = Transform()
```

This code is the same as that for the terrain and tree, however, to quickly recap: you define a new window model using the plane mesh and the **windowColor** texture, and then you create a new transform matrix for this model.

At the end of init(metalView:), add this code:

```
windowTransform.scale = [2, 2, 2]
windowTransform.position = [0, 3, 4]
windowTransform.rotation = [-Float.pi / 2, 0, 0]
```

This code, again, is similar to terrain and tree transforms: First, set the scale to a size factor of 2; then, position the window closer to your eye (the tree is at 6); finally, rotate the window by 90 degrees on the x-axis, so it stands vertically.

> **Note**: The circumference of a circle is 2π, so that means 90° is $\pi / 2$ (a quarter of a circle).

Inside `buildPipelineState()`, at the end of the do block, add these lines:

```
let windowFragmentFunction =
    library.makeFunction(name: "fragment_window")
descriptor.fragmentFunction = windowFragmentFunction
descriptor.vertexFunction = lightVertexFunction
windowPipelineState =
    try device.makeRenderPipelineState(descriptor: descriptor)
```

Here, you configure the pipeline state descriptor with the appropriate functions and then build the pipeline state using this descriptor. You'll write the `fragment_window()` shader in a moment.

Toward the end of `draw(in:)`, add this code right before `renderEncoder.endEncoding()`:

```
// render window
renderEncoder.setRenderPipelineState(windowPipelineState)
modelViewProjectionMatrix = camera.projectionMatrix *
    camera.viewMatrix * windowTransform.matrix
renderEncoder.setVertexBytes(&modelViewProjectionMatrix,
                    length: MemoryLayout<float4x4>.stride,
                    index: 1)
renderEncoder.setVertexBuffer(window.vertexBuffers[0].buffer,
                        offset: 0, index: 0)
renderEncoder.setFragmentTexture(windowTexture, index: 0)
draw(renderEncoder: renderEncoder, model: window)
```

This code draws the window and should be familiar to you by now.

In **Shaders.metal**, add the new fragment function:

```
fragment float4
            fragment_window(VertexOut vertex_in [[stage_in]],
                    texture2d<float> texture [[texture(0)]]) {
    constexpr sampler s(filter::linear);
    float4 color = texture.sample(s, vertex_in.uv);
    return color;
}
```

This function is similar to the earlier one: you create a default sampler, sample the texture to get the pixel color, and finally return the new color.

Run the playground again.

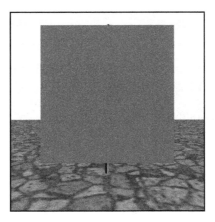

That's a dull, opaque window!

You'll fix that with blending. There are two ways to work with blending: the programmable way and the fixed-function way. In this chapter, you'll learn about fixed-function blending.

In **Renderer.swift**, at the end of `buildPipelineState()`, right before:

```
windowPipelineState =
    try device.makeRenderPipelineState(descriptor: descriptor)
```

Add this code:

```
// 1
guard let attachment = descriptor.colorAttachments[0] else
{ return }
// 2
attachment.isBlendingEnabled = true
// 3
attachment.rgbBlendOperation = .add
// 4
attachment.sourceRGBBlendFactor = .sourceAlpha
// 5
attachment.destinationRGBBlendFactor = .oneMinusSourceAlpha
```

With this code, you:

1. Grab the first color attachment from the render pipeline descriptor. A color attachment is a color render target that specifies the color configuration and color operations associated with a render pipeline. The render target holds the drawable texture where the rendering output goes.

2. Enable blending on the attachment.

3. Specify the blending type of operation used for color. Blend operations determine how a source fragment is combined with a destination value in a color attachment to determine the pixel value to be written.

4. Specify the blend factor used by the source color. A blend factor is how much the color will contribute to the final blended color. If not specified, this value is always 1 (.one) by default.

5. Specify the blend factor used by the destination color. If not specified, this value is always 0 (.zero) by default.

> **Note:** There are quite a few blend factors available to use besides
> sourceAlpha and oneMinusSourceAlpha. For a complete list of options,
> consult Apple's official page for Blend Factors: https://developer.apple.com/
> documentation/metal/mtlblendfactor.

You're almost ready to see blending in action. However, as before, you'll set up a toggle key for blending.

In **Renderer.swift**, add this property to the top of Renderer:

```
var blendingEnabled = false
```

In draw(in:), add this line above the draw call for rendering the window:

```
renderEncoder.setFragmentBytes(&blendingEnabled,
        length: MemoryLayout<Bool>.size, index: 0)
```

In **MetalView.swift**, add a new case to the KeyCode enum in keyDown(with:) for the **B** key:

```
case b = 0xB
```

Then, check for this case in the `switch` statement, and toggle the status of **blendingEnabled**, just like you did for transparency:

```
case .b:
  renderer.blendingEnabled = !renderer.blendingEnabled
```

In **Shaders.metal** change `fragment_window`'s definition to:

```
fragment float4
          fragment_window(VertexOut vertex_in [[stage_in]],
              constant bool &blendingEnabled [[buffer(0)]],
                texture2d<float> texture [[texture(0)]])
```

Now, add this code to `fragment_window`, right before `return color;`:

```
if (blendingEnabled) {
   color.a = 0.5;
}
```

If blending is enabled, you set the `alpha` component of the current pixel to 0.5 (semi-transparent). Run the playground again. Click in the rendered image to make sure key strokes are captured there. Then, press the **B** key a few times to watch the blending toggle on and off:

How about some more fun by adding a second window?

You'll reuse the window's mesh and texture, so in **Renderer.swift**, add this code right before `init(metalView:)`:

```
var window2Transform = Transform()
```

At the end of init(metalView:), set the size, position and rotation for the second window by adding this code:

```
window2Transform.scale = [3, 2, 2]
window2Transform.position = [0, 3, 5]
window2Transform.rotation = [-Float.pi / 2, 0, 0]
```

In draw(in:), while keeping the same pipeline state, add this code right before renderEncoder.endEncoding() to send information about the second window to the GPU:

```
modelViewProjectionMatrix = camera.projectionMatrix *
    camera.viewMatrix * window2Transform.matrix
renderEncoder.setVertexBytes(&modelViewProjectionMatrix,
                    length: MemoryLayout<float4x4>.stride,
                    index: 1)
draw(renderEncoder: renderEncoder, model: window)
```

This block of code is almost identical to the one you used for the first window, except for the transform matrix, which is different for the second window.

Run the playground again and toggle blending on.

Whoa! What happened? It's like looking through one single window instead of two windows. You know for sure the windows are not overlapped because one is positioned at Z = 4 and the other at Z = 5. So what happened?

Note: When blending is enabled, you should always be careful to render objects in a strict order, from back to front. You're currently rendering the first window before rendering the second one, however, the first window is in front of the second one.

In this case, the tree pipeline state doesn't have blending enabled, so it's only important that you render the two windows in order. You have two options:

- Switch the two window rendering blocks inside draw(in:).

- Or move the second window in front of the first.

Option one is a simple cut and paste. Option two isn't too difficult either, so, in **Renderer.swift**, in init(metalView:), change the second window's transform as follows:

```
window2Transform.scale = [2, 2, 2]
window2Transform.position = [0, 2.75, 3]
window2Transform.rotation = [-Float.pi / 2, 0, 0]
```

Run the playground again and toggle blending on.

That's more like it!

You may notice the overlapped portion of the second window is a bit darker than the rest of the window. This has a logical explanation.

Because you're using an alpha value of 0.5 for each window, when blending is enabled, every window linearly interpolates the rendered result halfway closer to the solid green color in the windowColor texture. It's the same idea as looking through multiple panes of green glass; put enough of them in front of each other, and all you'd see is pure green!

As previously mentioned, the other method of blending is programmable, where the developer does everything in the fragment shader. You can use the pipeline attachment's **[[color(0)]]** attribute in the fragment shader to obtain the current color from the framebuffer and then combine it with the current fragment color.

Antialiasing

Often, rendered models show slightly jagged edges that are visible if you zoom in a few times. This is called **aliasing** and is caused by the rasterizer when generating the fragments. If you look at the edge of a triangle, or any straight line — especially one with a slope — you'll notice the line doesn't always go precisely through the center of a pixel; some pixels will be colored above the line and some below it.

The solution to fixing aliasing is called **antialiasing**, as you might have guessed, and it consists of techniques to render smoother edges. By default, the pipeline uses one sample point (subpixel) for each pixel that is close to the line to determine if they meet. It is, however, possible to use 4 or more points for increased accuracy of intersection determination. This is called **Multisample Antialiasing** (MSAA), and it is more expensive to compute.

Next, you're going to configure the fixed-function MSAA on the pipeline and enable antialiasing on both the tree and the windows.

In **Renderer.swift**, add these properties to `Renderer`:

```
var antialiasingEnabled = false
var treePipelineStateAA: MTLRenderPipelineState!
var windowPipelineStateAA: MTLRenderPipelineState!
```

You'll create two different pipeline states for the tree (same for the windows) so that you can toggle between aliased and antialiased.

In `buildPipelineState()`, right below this line:

```
treePipelineState =
  try device.makeRenderPipelineState(descriptor: descriptor)
```

Add this code:

```
descriptor.sampleCount = 4
treePipelineStateAA =
  try device.makeRenderPipelineState(descriptor: descriptor)
descriptor.sampleCount = 1
```

This second pipeline state is the same as `treePipelineState` with the number of samples changed. You also set the sample count back to 1 so the window pipeline state is not affected.

Now, it's time to do the same for the windows.

In `buildPipelineState()`, right below this line:

```
windowPipelineState =
   try device.makeRenderPipelineState(descriptor: descriptor)
```

Add this code:

```
descriptor.sampleCount = 4
windowPipelineStateAA =
   try device.makeRenderPipelineState(descriptor: descriptor)
descriptor.sampleCount = 1
```

In `draw(in:)`, change this code where you set the tree's pipeline state:

```
renderEncoder.setRenderPipelineState(treePipelineState)
```

To:

```
view.sampleCount = antialiasingEnabled ? 4 : 1
var aaPipelineState = antialiasingEnabled ?
                      treePipelineStateAA! : treePipelineState
renderEncoder.setRenderPipelineState(aaPipelineState!)
```

When you press the appropriate toggle key, the pipeline switches between the two different pipelines and also sets the view's sample count to match.

Now do the same for the windows. Change the code where you set the window's pipeline state from:

```
renderEncoder.setRenderPipelineState(windowPipelineState)
```

To:

```
aaPipelineState = antialiasingEnabled ?
                  windowPipelineStateAA : windowPipelineState
renderEncoder.setRenderPipelineState(aaPipelineState!)
```

To add the antialiasing toggle key, in **MetalView.swift**, add another new case to the KeyCode enum in `keyDown(with:)`; this time for the **A** key:

```
case a = 0
```

Add the check for it in the `switch` statement, toggling the status of `antialiasingEnabled` accordingly.

```
case .a:
  renderer.antialiasingEnabled = !renderer.antialiasingEnabled
```

Run the playground again and zoom right into the tree. Now tap the rendered image, so key strokes are captured in there. Press the **A** key a few times to watch the antialiasing being toggled on and off. If you have a retina screen, this effect may be quite hard to see. Look for diagonals on the leaves with transparency off.

Fog

If you still haven't had enough fun in this chapter, why don't you add some fog to the scene to make it even more interesting?

Fog is quite useful in rendering for a couple of reasons. First, it serves as a `far` delimiter for rendered content. The renderer can ignore objects that get lost in the fog since they're not visible anymore. Second, fog helps with avoiding the popping-up effect for objects that just appeared in the scene from a distance, making their appearance into the scene more gradual.

As before, you'll add a toggle key for fog.

In **Renderer.swift**, add this property at the top of the class:

```
var fogEnabled = false
```

You'll need to add the fog to fragment shaders if you want all of the objects to be in the fog.

In `draw(in:)`, before the first draw call, add this:

```
renderEncoder.setFragmentBytes(&fogEnabled,
                               length: MemoryLayout<Bool>.size,
                               index: 1)
```

This sends the `fogEnabled` boolean variable to the GPU using `index: 1`. Because no other resource is using this index, it'll stay in the argument table at that index for all the subsequent draw calls.

In **MetalView.swift**, in `keyDown(with:)`, add one last `KeyCode` case:

```
case f = 0x3
```

In the `switch` statement, check for a press of the **F** key to toggle the status of `fogEnabled`.

```
case .f:
  renderer.fogEnabled = !renderer.fogEnabled
```

Finally, in **Shaders.metal**, add the following argument to all three fragment shader definitions:

```
constant bool &fogEnabled [[buffer(1)]]
```

Then, create a new function in **Shaders.metal**, before any of the fragment functions:

```
float4 fog(float4 position, float4 color) {
  // 1
  float distance = position.z / position.w;
  // 2
  float density = 0.2;
  float fog = 1.0 - clamp(exp(-density * distance), 0.0, 1.0);
  // 3
  float4 fogColor = float4(1.0);
  color = mix(color, fogColor, fog);
  return color;
}
```

With this code, you:

1. Calculate the depth of the fragment position.

2. Define a distribution function that the fog will use next. It's the inverse of the clamped (between 0 and 1) product between the fog density and the depth calculated in the previous step.

3. Mix the current color with the fog color (which you deliberately set to white) using the distribution function defined in the previous step.

Now, add the following code at the end of all three fragment shaders before `return color;`:

```
if (fogEnabled) {
  color = fog(vertex_in.position, color);
}
```

This code calls the fog function. Run the playground again, and toggle the fog with the **F** key:

As you can see, the entire scene is now in the fog. The closer you get to the tree, the less dense the fog. The same happens to the ground.

You see more of it as you go ahead. Go closer to the tree, and you'll see the tree more clearly:

> **Note**: Notice the cream sky is not affected by fog. This is because the cream color is coming from the MTKView instead of being rendered. Later, you'll be creating a textured sky.

Challenge

I hope you had a blast playing with various fragment processing techniques. I know I did!

If you're in for a few challenges:

1. Set the fog density to a lower, then higher value to see how that looks different.

2. Use different texture colors for the two windows to see how different colors blend.

3. Change the alpha value for one or both of the colors to see how this change influences the blended color.

Where to go from here?

In this chapter, you only looked into fixed-function blending and antialiasing. Per-fragment or per-sample **programmable blending** is possible by using the [[color]] attribute, which identifies the color attachment, as an argument to the fragment function.

Similarly, **programmable antialiasing** is possible via programmable sample positions which allow you to set custom sample positions for different render passes, unlike fixed-function antialiasing where the same sample positions apply to all render passes. For further reading, you can review the Programmable Sample Positions page at https://developer.apple.com/documentation/metal/graphics_rendering/render_targets/using_programmable_sample_positions.

Chapter 11: Tessellation & Terrains

By Caroline Begbie

So far you've used normal map trickery in the fragment function to show the fine details of your low poly models. To achieve a similar level of detail *without using normal maps* requires a change of model geometry by adding more vertices. The problem with adding more vertices is that when you send them to the GPU, it chokes up the pipeline. A hardware tessellator in the GPU can create vertices on the fly, adding a greater level of detail and thereby using fewer resources.

In this chapter, you're going to create a detailed terrain using a small number of points. You'll send a flat ground plane with a grayscale texture describing the height, and the tessellator will create as many vertices as needed. The vertex function will then read the texture and **displace** these new vertices vertically; in other words, move them upwards.

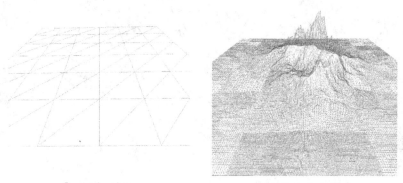

Control points   Tessellated vertices
                                  with displacement

Notice how many vertices the tessellator creates. In this example, the number of vertices depends on how close the control points are to the camera. You'll learn more about that later.

Tessellation

Instead of sending vertices to the GPU, you send patches. These patches are made up of control points — a minimum of three for a triangle patch, or four for a quad patch. The tessellator can convert each quad patch into a certain number of triangles: up to 4,096 triangles on a recent iMac and 256 triangles on an iPhone that's capable of tessellation.

> **Note**: Tessellation is available on all Macs since 2012 and on iOS 10 GPU Family 3 and up; this includes the iPhone 6s and newer devices. Tessellation is not, however, available on the iOS simulator.

With tessellation, you can:

- Send less data to the GPU. Because the GPU doesn't store tessellated vertices in graphics memory, it's more efficient on resources.

- Make low poly objects look less low poly by curving patches.

- Displace vertices for fine detail instead of using normal maps to fake it.

- Decide on the level of detail based on the distance from the camera. The closer an object is to the camera, the more vertices it contains.

The starter project

Before creating a tessellated terrain, you'll tessellate a single four-point patch. Open and run the starter project for this chapter. The code in this project is the minimum needed for a simple render of six vertices to create a quad.

Your task is to convert this quad to a tessellated patch quad made up of many vertices.

Instead of sending six vertices to the GPU, you'll send the positions of the four corners of the patch. You'll give the GPU **edge factors** and **inside factors** which tell the tessellator how many vertices to create. So you can see the vertices added by the tessellator, you'll render in line mode.

To convert the quad, you'll do the following on the CPU side:

On the GPU side, you'll set up a **tessellation kernel** that processes the edge and inside factors. You'll also set up a **post-tessellation vertex** shader that handles the vertices generated by the hardware tessellator.

Tessellation patches

A patch consists of a certain number of control points, generally:

- **bilinear**: Four control points, one at each corner

- **biquadratic**: Nine control points

- **bicubic**: Sixteen control points

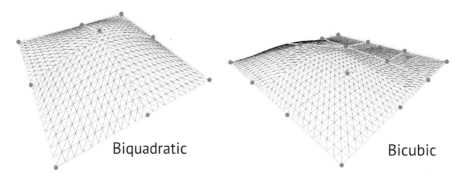

Biquadratic   Bicubic

The control points make up a cage which is made up of spline curves. A spline is a parametric curve made up of control points.

There are various algorithms to interpolate these control points, but here, A, B and C are the control points. As point P travels from A to B, point Q travels from B to C. The half way point between P and Q describes the blue curve.

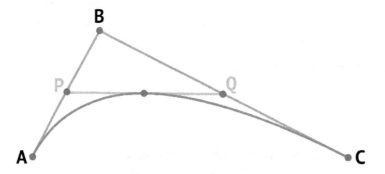

To create the curved patch surface, the vertex function interpolates vertices to follow this parametric curve.

Note: Because the mathematics of curved surfaces is quite involved, you'll only be working with four control points per patch in this chapter.

Tessellation factors

For each patch, you need to specify inside edge factors and outside edge factors. The four-point patch in the following image shows different edge factors for each edge — specified as [2, 4, 8, 16] — and two different inside factors — specified as [8, 16], for horizontal and vertical respectively.

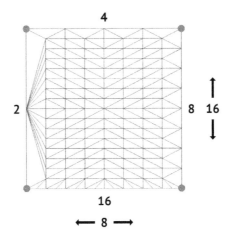

The edge factors specify how many segments an edge will be split into. An edge factor of 2 has two segments along the edge. For the inside factors, look at the horizontal and vertical center lines. In this example, the horizontal center has eight segments, and the vertical center has sixteen.

Although only four control points (shown in red) went to the GPU, the hardware tessellator created a lot more vertices. However, creating more vertices on a flat plane doesn't make the render any more interesting.

Later, you'll find out how to move these vertices around in the vertex function to make a bumpy terrain. But first, you'll discover how to tessellate a single patch.

In **Renderer.swift**, in Renderer, add the following:

```
let patches = (horizontal: 1, vertical: 1)
var patchCount: Int {
  return patches.horizontal * patches.vertical
}
```

This creates a constant for the number of patches you're going to create, in this case, one. `patchCount` is a convenience property that returns the total number of patches.

Now add:

```
var edgeFactors: [Float] = [4]
var insideFactors: [Float] = [4]
```

Here, you're setting up the edge and inside factors as `Float` array properties. These variables indicate four segments along each edge, and four in the middle.

You can specify different factors for different edges by adding them to the array. For each patch, the GPU processes these edge factors and places the amount to tessellate each into a buffer.

Create a lazy property to provide a buffer of the correct length:

```
lazy var tessellationFactorsBuffer: MTLBuffer? = {
  // 1
  let count = patchCount * (4 + 2)
  // 2
  let size = count * MemoryLayout<Float>.size / 2
  return Renderer.device.makeBuffer(length: size,
                              options: .storageModePrivate)
}()
```

1. This is the number of patches multiplied by the four edge factors and two inside factors.

2. This calculates the size of the buffer. In the tessellation kernel, you'll fill the buffer with a special type consisting of half-floats. This type currently has no Swift equivalent.

Now it's time to set up the patch data.

Set up patch data

Instead of an array of six vertices, you'll create a four-point patch with control points at the corners.

Currently, **Data.swift** holds a `vertexBuffer` property that contains the vertices; you'll replace this property with a buffer containing the control points.

In Renderer, add this property:

```
var controlPointsBuffer: MTLBuffer?
```

At the end of init(metalView:), fill the buffer with control points:

```
let controlPoints = createControlPoints(patches: patches,
                                          size: (2, 2))
controlPointsBuffer =
  Renderer.device.makeBuffer(bytes: controlPoints,
    length: MemoryLayout<float3>.stride * controlPoints.count)
```

Data.swift contains a function, createControlPoints(patches:size:). This function takes in the number of patches, and the unit size of the total number of patches. It then returns an array of xyz control points. Here, you're creating a patch with one corner at [-1, 0, 1], and the diagonal at [1, 0, -1]. This is a flat horizontal plane, but Renderer rotates the patch by 90° so you can see the patch vertices.

Set up the render pipeline state

You can configure the tessellator by changing the pipeline state properties. Until now, you've been processing vertices, however, you'll modify the vertex descriptor so it processes patches instead.

In buildRenderPipelineState(), where you set up vertexDescriptor, add this:

```
vertexDescriptor.layouts[0].stepFunction = .perPatchControlPoint
```

With the old setup, you were using a default stepFunction of .perVertex. With that setup, the vertex function fetches new attribute data every time a new *vertex* is processed.

Now that you've moved on to processing patches, you need to fetch new attribute data for every *control point*.

Kernel (compute) functions

You're accustomed to setting up a render pipeline state for rendering, but **compute** allows you to do different tasks on different threads.

> **Note**: The kernel function you'll create in this section is quite simple. However, in Chapter 16, "Particle Systems," you'll investigate compute in depth.

Vertex and fragment shaders run the same task on all vertices or pixels, so there is no granular control over each thread. You'll need to set up a compute pipeline state that points to a **tessellation kernel** shader function.

Add this new method to `Renderer`:

```
static func buildComputePipelineState()
                    -> MTLComputePipelineState {
  guard let kernelFunction =
    Renderer.library?.makeFunction(name: "tessellation_main")
else {
      fatalError("Tessellation shader function not found")
  }
  return try!
      Renderer.device.makeComputePipelineState(
                        function: kernelFunction)
}
```

This creates a compute pipeline state and expects a function that is of a `kernel` type rather than a `vertex` or `fragment` type. With kernel functions, you can, for example, process data in Metal buffers before rendering them.

Next, add a new property to `Renderer`:

```
var tessellationPipelineState: MTLComputePipelineState
```

In `init(metalView:)`, before `super.init()`, add this:

```
tessellationPipelineState = Renderer.buildComputePipelineState()
```

Here you instantiate the pipeline state for the compute pipeline to use.

Compute pass

You've set up a compute pipeline state and an `MTLBuffer` containing the patch data. You also created an empty buffer which the tessellation kernel will fill with the edge and inside factors. Next, you need to create a **compute command encoder**. This encoder is similar to a render command encoder in that you add commands to the encoder and then send it off to the GPU.

In draw(in:), add the following below the comment // tessellation pass:

```
let computeEncoder = commandBuffer.makeComputeCommandEncoder()!
computeEncoder.setComputePipelineState(
                        tessellationPipelineState)
computeEncoder.setBytes(&edgeFactors,
    length: MemoryLayout<Float>.size * edgeFactors.count,
    index: 0)
computeEncoder.setBytes(&insideFactors,
    length: MemoryLayout<Float>.size * insideFactors.count,
    index: 1)
computeEncoder.setBuffer(tessellationFactorsBuffer, offset: 0,
                        index: 2)
```

This creates a compute command encoder and binds the edge and inside factors to the compute function (the tessellation kernel).

If you have multiple patches, the compute function will operate in parallel on each patch, on different threads.

To tell the GPU how many threads you need, continue by adding this code:

```
let width = min(patchCount,
                tessellationPipelineState.threadExecutionWidth)
computeEncoder.dispatchThreadgroups(MTLSizeMake(patchCount,
                                    1, 1),
    threadsPerThreadgroup: MTLSizeMake(width, 1, 1))
computeEncoder.endEncoding()
```

MTLSizeMake defines a three-dimensional grid with width, height and depth. The number of patches you have is small, so you only use one dimension. If you were processing pixels in an image, you'd use both width and height.

With the commands the GPU needs for the compute function in place, you end the encoder by calling endEncoding().

Before changing the render encoder so it'll draw patches instead of vertices, you'll need to create the tessellation kernel.

The tessellation kernel

Open **Shaders.metal**. Currently, this file contains simple vertex and fragment functions. You'll add the tessellation kernel here.

Add this function:

```
kernel void
  tessellation_main(constant float* edge_factors [[buffer(0)]],
                    constant float* inside_factors [[buffer(1)]],
                    device MTLQuadTessellationFactorsHalf*
                              factors [[buffer(2)]],
                    uint pid [[thread_position_in_grid]]) {
}
```

`kernel` specifies the type of shader. The function operates on all threads (i.e., all patches) and receives the three things you sent over: the edge factors, inside factors and the tessellation factor buffer that you're going to fill out in this function.

The fourth parameter is the patch ID with its thread position in the grid. The tessellation factors buffer consists of an array of edge and inside factors for each patch; this gives you the patch index into this array.

Inside the kernel function, add the following:

```
factors[pid].edgeTessellationFactor[0] = edge_factors[0];
factors[pid].edgeTessellationFactor[1] = edge_factors[0];
factors[pid].edgeTessellationFactor[2] = edge_factors[0];
factors[pid].edgeTessellationFactor[3] = edge_factors[0];

factors[pid].insideTessellationFactor[0] = inside_factors[0];
factors[pid].insideTessellationFactor[1] = inside_factors[0];
```

This fills in the tessellation factors buffer with the edge factors that you sent over. The edge and inside factors array you sent over only had one value each, so you put this value into all factors.

Filling out a buffer with values is a trivial thing for a kernel to do. However, as you get more patches and more complexity on how to tessellate these patches, you'll understand why sending the data to the GPU for parallel processing is a useful step.

After the compute pass is done, the render pass takes over.

Render pass

Back in **Renderer.swift**, before doing the render, you need to tell the render encoder about the tessellation factors buffer that you updated during the compute pass.

In `draw(in:)`, locate the `// draw` comment. Just after that, add this:

```
renderEncoder.setTessellationFactorBuffer(
                tessellationFactorsBuffer,
```

```
                     offset: 0, instanceStride: 0)
```

The post-tessellation vertex function reads from this buffer that you set up during the kernel function.

Instead of drawing triangles from the vertex buffer, you need to draw the patch using patch control points from the control points buffer. Replace:

```
renderEncoder.setVertexBuffer(vertexBuffer, offset: 0, index: 0)
```

With:

```
renderEncoder.setVertexBuffer(controlPointsBuffer,
                             offset: 0, index: 0)
```

Replace the `drawPrimitives` command with this:

```
renderEncoder.drawPatches(numberOfPatchControlPoints: 4,
                          patchStart: 0, patchCount: patchCount,
                          patchIndexBuffer: nil,
                          patchIndexBufferOffset: 0,
                          instanceCount: 1, baseInstance: 0)
```

The render command encoder tells the GPU that it's going to draw one patch with four control points.

The post-tessellation vertex function

Open **Shaders.metal** again. The vertex function is called after the tessellator has done its job of creating the vertices and will operate on each one of these new vertices. In the vertex function, you'll tell each vertex what its position in the rendered quad should be.

Rename `VertexIn` to `ControlPoint`. The definition of `position` remains the same.

Because you used a vertex descriptor to describe the incoming control point data, you can use the `[[stage_in]]` attribute.

The vertex function will then check the vertex descriptor from the current pipeline state, find that the data is in buffer 0 and use the vertex descriptor layout to read in the data.

Replace the vertex function `vertex_main` with:

```
// 1
[[patch(quad, 4)]]
// 2
vertex VertexOut
// 3
  vertex_main(patch_control_point<ControlPoint>
    control_points [[stage_in]],
// 4
              constant float4x4 &mvp [[buffer(1)]],
// 5
              float2 patch_coord [[position_in_patch]]) {
}
```

This is the post-tessellation vertex function where you return the correct position of
the vertex for the rasterizer. Going through the code:

1. The function qualifier tells the vertex function that the vertices are coming from
    tessellated patches. It describes the type of patch, `triangle` or quad, and the
    number of control points, in this case, four.

2. The function is still a vertex shader function as before.

3. `patch_control_point` is part of the Metal Standard Library and provides the
    per-patch control point data.

4. The model-view-projection matrix you passed in.

5. The tessellator provides a uv coordinate between 0 and 1 for the tessellated patch
    so that the vertex function can calculate its correct rendered position.

To visualize this, you can temporarily return the uv coordinates as the position and
color.

Add this to the vertex function:

```
float u = patch_coord.x;
float v = patch_coord.y;

VertexOut out;
out.position = float4(u, v, 0, 1);
out.color = float4(u, v, 0, 1);
return out;
```

Here you give the vertex a position as interpolated by the tessellator from the four
patch positions, and a color of the same value for visualization.

Build and run.

See how the patch is tessellated with vertices between 0 and 1? (Normalized Device Coordinates (NDC) are between -1 and 1 which is why all the coordinates are at the top right.)

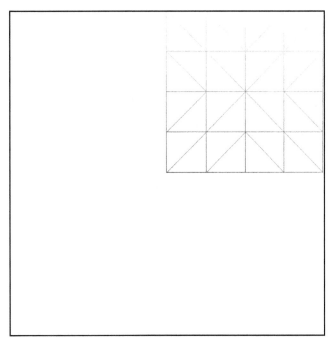

To have your vertex positions depend on the patch's actual position rather than between 0 and 1, you need to interpolate the patch's control points depending on the uv values.

In `vertex_main`, after assigning the u and v values, add this:

```
float2 top = mix(control_points[0].position.xz,
                 control_points[1].position.xz, u);
float2 bottom = mix(control_points[3].position.xz,
                    control_points[2].position.xz, u);
```

This interpolates values horizontally along the top of the patch and the bottom of the patch. Notice the index ordering: the patch indices are 0 to 3 clockwise.

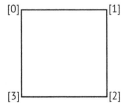

You can change this by setting the pipeline descriptor property `tessellationOutputWindingOrder` to `.counterClockwise`.

Change the the following:

```
out.position = float4(u, v, 0, 1);
```

To:

```
float2 interpolated = mix(top, bottom, v);
float4 position = float4(interpolated.x, 0.0,
                         interpolated.y, 1.0);
out.position = mvp * position;
```

This code interpolates the vertical value between the top and bottom values and multiplies it by the model-view-projection matrix to position the vertex in the scene. Currently, you're leaving y at `0.0` to keep the patch two-dimensional. Build and run to see your tessellated patch:

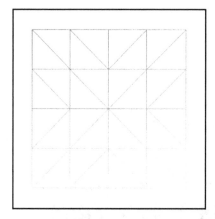

> **Note**: Experiment with changing the edge and inside factors until you're comfortable with how the tessellator subdivides. For example, change the edge factors array to `[2, 4, 8, 16]`, and change the kernel function so that the appropriate array value goes into each edge.

Multiple patches

Now that you know how to tessellate one patch, you can tile the patches and choose edge factors that depend on dynamic factors, like distance.

At the top of Renderer, change patches to:

```
let patches = (horizontal: 2, vertical: 2)
```

Build and run to see the four patches joined together:

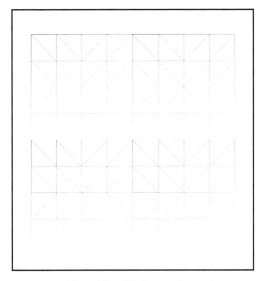

In the vertex function, you can identify which patch you're currently processing using the [[patch_id]] attribute.

In **Shaders.metal**, add this parameter to the vertex function:

```
uint patchID [[patch_id]],
```

Change the assignment of out.color to:

```
out.color = float4(0);
if (patchID == 0) {
  out.color = float4(1, 0, 0, 1);
}
```

Build and run. Notice how it colors the bottom left patch red. This is the first patch in the control points array.

Note: You can click or tap the window to toggle render modes from wireframe and solid fill.

Tessellation by distance

In this section, you're going to create a terrain with patches that are tessellated according to the distance from the camera. When you're close to a mountain, you need to see more detail; when you're farther away, less. Having the ability to dial in the level of detail is where tessellation comes into its own. By setting the level of detail, you save on how many vertices the GPU has to process in any given situation.

In **Common.h**, add the following:

```
typedef struct {
  vector_float2 size;
  float height;
  uint maxTessellation;
} Terrain;
```

This sets up a new struct to describe the size and maximum tessellation of the terrain. You'll use height for scaling vertices on the y-axis later.

In **Renderer.swift**, add a new constant to Renderer:

```
static let maxTessellation = 16
```

This sets maxTessellation to 16. On iOS devices, currently the maximum amount you can tessellate per patch is 16, but on new Macs, the maximum is 64.

Add a new property:

```
var terrain = Terrain(size: [2, 2], height: 1,
        maxTessellation: UInt32(Renderer.maxTessellation))
```

Locate where you set up controlPoints in init(metalView:), and change it to this:

```
let controlPoints = createControlPoints(patches: patches,
                        size: (width: terrain.size.x,
                               height: terrain.size.y))
```

Because your terrains are going to be much larger, you'll use the terrain constant to create the control points.

To calculate edge factors that are dependent on the distance from the camera, you need to send the camera position, model matrix and control points to the kernel.

In draw(in:), `ellation pass with the compute encoder, before dispatching threads, add this:

```
var cameraPosition = viewMatrix.columns.3
computeEncoder.setBytes(&cameraPosition,
                        length: MemoryLayout<float4>.stride,
                        index: 3)
var matrix = modelMatrix
computeEncoder.setBytes(&matrix,
                        length: MemoryLayout<float4x4>.stride,
                        index: 4)
computeEncoder.setBuffer(controlPointsBuffer,
                         offset: 0, index: 5)
computeEncoder.setBytes(&terrain,
                        length: MemoryLayout<Terrain>.stride,
                        index: 6)
```

This code extracts the camera position from the view matrix and sends it, along with the model matrix, the control points buffer and the terrain information to the tessellation kernel.

To accept these buffers, add these parameters to the tessellation_main function header in **Shaders.metal**:

```
constant float4 &camera_position [[buffer(3)]],
constant float4x4 &modelMatrix   [[buffer(4)]],
constant float3* control_points  [[buffer(5)]],
constant Terrain &terrain        [[buffer(6)]],
```

With these constants, you can compute the distance of the edges from the camera.

You'll set the edge and inside tessellation factors differently for each patch edge instead of sending a constant 4 for all of the edges. The further the patch edge is from the camera, the lower the tessellation on that edge. These are the edge and control point orders for each patch:

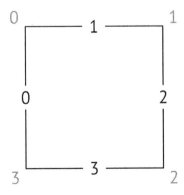

To calculate the tessellation of an edge, you need to know the transformed mid-point of two control points. To calculate edge 2, for example, you get the midpoint of points 1 and 2 and find out the distance of that point from the camera. Where two patches join, it's imperative to keep the tessellation level for the joined edges the same; otherwise you get cracks. By calculating the distance of the mid-point, you end up with the same result for the overlapping edges.

In **Shaders.metal**, create a new function *before* tessellation_main:

```
float calc_distance(float3 pointA, float3 pointB,
                    float3 camera_position,
                    float4x4 modelMatrix) {
  float3 positionA = (modelMatrix * float4(pointA, 1)).xyz;
  float3 positionB = (modelMatrix * float4(pointB, 1)).xyz;
  float3 midpoint = (positionA + positionB) * 0.5;

  float camera_distance = distance(camera_position, midpoint);
  return camera_distance;
}
```

This function takes in two points, the camera position and the model matrix, finds the mid-point between the two points and calculates the distance from the camera.

Remove all of the code from tessellation_main.

Add this to calculate the correct index into the tessellation factors array:

```
uint index = pid * 4;
```

4 is the number of control points per patch, and pid is the patch ID. To index into the control points array for each patch, you skip over four control points at a time.

Add this to keep a running total of tessellation factors:

```
float totalTessellation = 0;
```

Add a for loop for each of the edges:

```
for (int i = 0; i < 4; i++) {
   int pointAIndex = i;
   int pointBIndex = i + 1;
   if (pointAIndex == 3) {
     pointBIndex = 0;
   }
   int edgeIndex = pointBIndex;
}
```

With this code, you're cycling around four corners: 0, 1, 2, 3. On the first iteration, you calculate edge 1 from the mid-point of points 0 and 1. On the fourth iteration, you use points 3 and 0 to calculate edge 0.

At the end of the `for` loop, call the distance calculation function:

```
float cameraDistance =
      calc_distance(control_points[pointAIndex + index],
                    control_points[pointBIndex + index],
                    camera_position.xyz,
                    modelMatrix);
```

Then, set the tessellation factor for the current edge:

```
float tessellation =
    max(4.0, terrain.maxTessellation / cameraDistance);
factors[pid].edgeTessellationFactor[edgeIndex] = tessellation;
totalTessellation += tessellation;
```

You set a minimum edge factor of 4. The maximum depends upon the camera distance and the maximum tessellation amount you specified for the terrain.

After the `for` loop, add this:

```
factors[pid].insideTessellationFactor[0] =
      totalTessellation * 0.25;
factors[pid].insideTessellationFactor[1] =
      totalTessellation * 0.25;
```

This sets the two inside tessellation factors to be an average of the total tessellation for the patch.

Lastly, you need to revise some of the default render pipeline state tessellation parameters.

In **Renderer.swift**, in `buildRenderPipelineState()`, add this before creating the pipeline state:

```
// 1
descriptor.tessellationFactorStepFunction = .perPatch
// 2
descriptor.maxTessellationFactor = Renderer.maxTessellation
// 3
descriptor.tessellationPartitionMode = .fractionalEven
```

1. The step function was previously set to a default `.constant`, which sets the same edge factors on all patches. By setting this to `.perPatch`, the vertex function uses each patch's edge and inside factors information in the tessellation factors array.

2. You set the maximum number of segments per patch for the tessellator.

3. The partition mode describes how these segments are split up. The default is `.pow2`, which rounds up to the nearest power of two. Using `.fractionalEven`, the tessellator rounds up to the nearest even integer, so it allows for much more variation of tessellation.

Build and run, and rotate and zoom your patches. As you reposition the patches, the tessellator recalculates their distance from the camera and tessellates accordingly. Tessellating is a neat superpower!

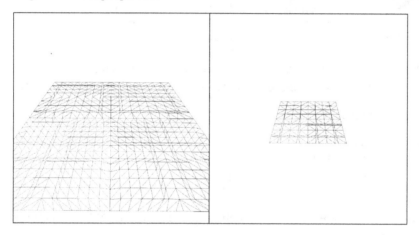

Check where the patches join; the triangles of each side of the patch should connect.

Now that you've mastered tessellation, you'll be able to add detail to your terrain.

Displacement

You've used textures for various purposes in earlier chapters. Now you'll use a height map to change the height of each vertex.

Height maps are grayscale images where you can use the texel value for the Y vertex position, with white being high and black being low.

There are several height maps in **Textures.xcassets** you can experiment with.

In **Renderer.swift**, create a property to hold the height map:

```
let heightMap: MTLTexture
```

In `init(metalView:)`, before calling `super.init()`, initialize `heightMap`:

```
do {
  heightMap = try Renderer.loadTexture(imageName: "mountain")
} catch {
  fatalError(error.localizedDescription)
}
```

Here, you're loading the height map texture from the asset catalog.

In `draw(in:)`, you need to send the texture to the GPU.

Add this before the draw call:

```
renderEncoder.setVertexTexture(heightMap, index: 0)
renderEncoder.setVertexBytes(&terrain,
                 length: MemoryLayout<Terrain>.stride,
                 index: 6)
```

You're already familiar with sending textures to the fragment shader; this makes the texture available to the vertex shader in the same way. You also send the terrain setup details.

In **Shaders.metal**, add the following to the `vertex_main` function parameters to read in the texture and terrain information:

```
texture2d<float> heightMap [[texture(0)]],
constant Terrain &terrain [[buffer(6)]],
```

You're currently only using the x and z position coordinates for the patch and leaving the y coordinate as zero. You'll now map the y coordinate to the height indicated in the texture.

Just as you used u and v fragment values to read the appropriate texel in the fragment function, you use the x and z position coordinates to read the texel from the height map in the vertex function.

After setting `position`, but *before* multiplying by the model-view-projection matrix, add this:

```
// 1
float2 xy = (position.xz + terrain.size / 2.0) / terrain.size;
// 2
```

```
constexpr sampler sample;
float4 color = heightMap.sample(sample, xy);
out.color = float4(color.r);

// 3
float height = (color.r * 2 - 1) * terrain.height;
position.y = height;
```

Going through the code:

1. You convert the patch control point values to be between 0 and 1 to be able to sample the height map. You include the terrain size because, although your patch control points are currently between -1 and 1, soon you'll be making a larger terrain.

2. Create a default sampler and read the texture as you have done previously in the fragment function. The texture is a grayscale texture, so you only use the .r value.

3. color is between 0 and 1, so for the height, shift the value to be between -1 and 1, and multiply it by your terrain height scale setting. This is currently set to 1.

Next, remove the following code from the end of the vertex function, because you're now using the color of the height map.

```
out.color = float4(0);
if (patchID == 0) {
  out.color = float4(1, 0, 0, 1);
}
```

Renderer currently rotates your patches by 90°, so in **Renderer.swift** change the rotation property initialization to:

```
var rotation = float3(Float(-20).degreesToRadians, 0, 0)
```

Build and run to see the height map displacing the vertices. Notice how the white vertices are high and the black ones are low:

This doesn't yet have much detail, but that's about to change.

In **Renderer.swift**, change the maxTessellation constant to:

```
static let maxTessellation: Int = {
  #if os(macOS)
  return 64
  #else
  return 16
  #endif
} ()
```

These are the maximum values for each OS. Because the maximum tessellation on iOS is so low, you may want to increase the number of patches rendered on iOS.

Change patches and terrain to:

```
let patches = (horizontal: 6, vertical: 6)
var terrain = Terrain(size: [8, 8], height: 1,
                 maxTessellation:
UInt32(Renderer.maxTessellation))
```

You're now creating thirty-six patches over sixteen units.

Build and run to see your patch height-mapped into a magnificent mountain. Don't forget to click the wireframe to see your mountain render in its full glory.

Now it's time to render your mountain with different colors and textures depending on height.

Shading by height

In the last section, you sampled the height map in the vertex function, and the colors are interpolated when sent to the fragment function. For maximum color detail, you need to sample from textures per fragment, not per vertex.

For that to work, you need to set up three textures: snow, cliff and grass. You'll send these textures to the fragment function and test the height there.

In **Renderer.swift**, in Renderer, add three new texture properties:

```
let cliffTexture: MTLTexture
let snowTexture: MTLTexture
let grassTexture: MTLTexture
```

In init(metalView:), in the do closure where you create the height map, add this:

```
cliffTexture =
    try Renderer.loadTexture(imageName: "cliff-color")
snowTexture = try Renderer.loadTexture(imageName: "snow-color")
grassTexture =
    try Renderer.loadTexture(imageName: "grass-color")
```

These textures are in the asset catalog.

To send the textures to the fragment function, in draw(in:), add this before the renderEncoder draw call:

```
renderEncoder.setFragmentTexture(cliffTexture, index: 1)
renderEncoder.setFragmentTexture(snowTexture, index: 2)
renderEncoder.setFragmentTexture(grassTexture, index: 3)
```

In **Shaders.metal**, add two new properties to VertexOut:

```
float height;
float2 uv;
```

At the end of vertex_main, before the return, set the value of these two properties:

```
out.uv = xy;
out.height = height;
```

You send the height value from the vertex function to the fragment function so that you can assign fragments the correct texture for that height.

Add the textures to the fragment_main parameters:

```
texture2d<float> cliffTexture [[texture(1)]],
texture2d<float> snowTexture  [[texture(2)]],
texture2d<float> grassTexture [[texture(3)]]
```

Replace the fragment function code with:

```
constexpr sampler sample(filter::linear, address::repeat);
float tiling = 16.0;
float4 color;
if (in.height < -0.5) {
  color = grassTexture.sample(sample, in.uv * tiling);
} else if (in.height < 0.3) {
  color = cliffTexture.sample(sample, in.uv * tiling);
} else {
  color = snowTexture.sample(sample, in.uv * tiling);
}
return color;
```

You create a tileable texture sampler and read in the appropriate texture for the height. Height is between -1 and 1, as set in `vertex_main`. You then tile the texture by 16 — an arbitrary value based on what looks best here.

Build and run. Click the wireframe render to see your textured mountain.

You have grass at low altitudes and snowy peaks at high altitudes.

As you zoom and rotate, notice how the mountain seems to ripple. This is the tessellation level of detail being over-sensitive. One way of dialing this down is to change the render pass's tessellation partition mode.

In **Renderer.swift**, in `buildRenderPipelineState()`, change the `descriptor.tessellationPartionMode` assignment to:

```
descriptor.tessellationPartitionMode = .pow2
```

Build and run. As the tessellator rounds up the edge factors to a power of two, there's a larger difference in tessellation between the patches now, however, the change in tessellation won't occur so frequently, and the ripple disappears.

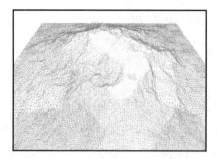

Shading by slope

The snow line in your previous render is unrealistic. By checking the slope of the mountain, you can show the snow texture in flatter areas, and show the cliff texture where the slope is steep.

An easy way to calculate slope is to run a **Sobel filter** on the height map. A Sobel filter is an algorithm that looks at the gradients between neighboring pixels in an image. It's useful for edge detection in computer vision and image processing, but in this case, you can use the gradient to determine the slope between neighboring pixels.

Metal Performance Shaders

The Metal Performance Shaders framework contains many useful, highly optimized shaders for image processing, matrix multiplication, machine learning and raytracing. You'll read more about them in Chapter 21, "Metal Performance Shaders."

The shader you'll use here is `MPSImageSobel` which takes a source image texture and outputs the filtered image into a new grayscale texture. The whiter the pixel, the steeper the slope.

> **Note**: In the challenge for this chapter, you'll use the Sobel-filtered image, and apply the three textures to your mountain depending on slope.

At the top of **Renderer.swift**, import the Metal Performance Shaders framework:

```
import MetalPerformanceShaders
```

Create a new method to process the height map:

```
static func heightToSlope(source: MTLTexture) -> MTLTexture {
}
```

Next, you'll send the height map to this method and return a new texture. To create the new texture, you first need to create a texture descriptor where you can assign the size, pixel format and tell the GPU how you will use the texture.

Add this to `heightToSlope(source:)`:

```
let descriptor =
  MTLTextureDescriptor.texture2DDescriptor(
        pixelFormat: source.pixelFormat,
        width: source.width,
        height: source.height,
        mipmapped: false)
descriptor.usage = [.shaderWrite, .shaderRead]
```

This creates a descriptor for textures that you want to both read and write. You'll write to the texture in the MPS shader and read it in the fragment shader.

Continue adding to the method:

```
guard let destination =
      Renderer.device.makeTexture(descriptor: descriptor),
  let commandBuffer = Renderer.commandQueue.makeCommandBuffer()
      else { fatalError() }
```

This creates the texture and the command buffer for the MPS shader.

Now, add this code:

```
let shader = MPSImageSobel(device: Renderer.device)
shader.encode(commandBuffer: commandBuffer,
            sourceTexture: source,
            destinationTexture: destination)
commandBuffer.commit()
return destination
```

This runs the MPS shader and returns the texture. That's all there is to running a Metal Performance Shader on a texture!

Note: The height maps in the asset catalog have a pixel format of **8 Bit Normalized - R**, or R8Unorm. Using the default pixel format of RGBA8Unorm with `MPSImageSobel` crashes. In any case, for grayscale texture maps that only

> use one channel, using R8Unorm as a pixel format is more efficient.

To hold the terrain slope in a texture, add a new property to Renderer:

```
let terrainSlope: MTLTexture
```

In init(metalView:), before calling super.init(), initialize the texture:

```
terrainSlope = Renderer.heightToSlope(source: heightMap)
```

The texture when created will look like this:

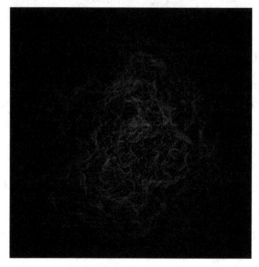

In the challenge, once you send this texture to the vertex shader, you'll be able to see it using the Capture GPU Frame icon. The white parts are the steep slopes.

Challenge

Your challenge for this chapter is to use the slope texture from the Sobel filter to place snow on the mountain on the parts that aren't steep. Because you don't need pixel perfect accuracy, you can read the slope image in the vertex function and send that value to the fragment function.

This is more efficient as there will be fewer texture reads in the vertex function than in the fragment function.

If everything goes well, you'll render an image like this:

Notice how the grass blends into the mountain. This is done using the `mix()` function.

Currently, you have three zones, in other words, the heights where you render the three different textures. The challenge project has four zones:

- **grass**: < -0.6 in height

- **grass blended with mountain**: -0.6 to -0.4

- **mountain**: -0.4 to -0.2

- **mountain with snow on the flat parts**: > -0.2

See if you can get your mountain to look like the challenge project in the projects directory for this chapter.

Where to go from here?

With very steep displacement, there can be lots of texture stretching between vertices. There are various algorithms to overcome this, and you can find one in Apple's excellent sample code: Dynamic Terrain with Argument Buffers at https://developer.apple.com/documentation/metal/fundamental_components/gpu_resources/dynamic_terrain_with_argument_buffers. This is a complex project that showcases argument buffers, but the dynamic terrain portion is interesting.

There's another way to do blending. Instead of using `mix()`, the way you did in the challenge, you can use a texture map to define the different regions.

This is called **texture splatting**. You create a **splat map** with the red, blue and green channels describing up to three textures and where to use them.

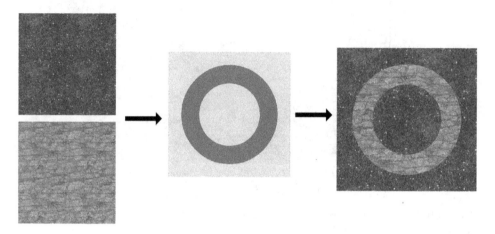

With all of the techniques for reading and using textures that you've learned so far, texture splatting shouldn't be too difficult to implement.

In the next chapter you'll do some realistic rendering in a scene with a complete environment using sky textures for the lighting.

Chapter 12: Environment

By Caroline Begbie

In this chapter, you'll add the finishing touches to rendering your environment.

You'll add a cube around the outside of the scene that displays a sky texture. That sky texture will then light the models within the scene, making them appear as if they belong.

Look at the following comparison of two renders.

This comparison demonstrates how you can use the same shader code, but change the sky image to create different lighting environments.

Getting started

Open the starter project for this chapter. For the most part, this project is similar to the engine you created in Chapter 9, "Scene Graph." There are, however, a few notable changes:

- You can add a fragment function string name to the Model initializer, letting you test different rendering styles for different props.

- The racing car asset and the Textures asset catalog includes metallic and ambient occlusion maps.

Build and run the project, and you'll see the car rendered using physically based shading, as described in Chapter 7, "Maps and Materials". Chapter 8, "Character Animation", and Chapter 9, "Scene Graph" used this same shading, but sneakily used a scaling factor in the fragment shader to lighten the shadows.

Aside from the darkness of the lighting, there are some glaring problems with the render:

- All metals, such as the metallic wheel hubs, aren't looking shiny. Pure metals reflect their surroundings, and there are currently no surroundings to reflect.

- As you move around the car using the keyboard, notice where the light doesn't directly hit the car, the color is black. This happens because the app doesn't provide any ambient light. Later on in the chapter, you'll use the skylight as global ambient light.

> **Note:** If you're using macOS, use the keyboard keys **WASD** to move, and use the **QE** or **right** and **left** arrow keys to rotate.

The skybox

Currently, the sky is a single color, which looks unrealistic. By adding a 360° image surrounding the scene, you can easily place the action in a desert or have snowy mountains as a backdrop.

To do this, you'll create a skybox cube that surrounds the entire scene.

This skybox cube is the same as an ordinary model, but instead of viewing it from the outside, the camera is at the center of the cube looking out. You'll texture the cube with a **cube texture**, which gives you a cheap way of creating a complete environment.

You may think the cube will be distorted at the corners, but as you'll see, each fragment of the cube will render at an effectively infinite distance, and no distortion will occur. Cube maps are much easier to create than spherical ones and are hardware optimized.

Create a new Swift file for the skybox class named **Skybox.swift**. Remember to add the file to both the iOS and macOS targets. This class holds the geometry of the cube, and also the necessary pipeline and sky textures.

Replace the default code with:

```
import MetalKit

class Skybox {

  let mesh: MTKMesh
  var texture: MTLTexture?
  let pipelineState: MTLRenderPipelineState
  let depthStencilState: MTLDepthStencilState?

  init(textureName: String?) {

  }
}
```

You created the Skybox class and some properties:

- mesh: A cube that you'll create using a Model I/O primitive.

- texture: A cube texture of the name given in the initializer.

- pipelineState: The skybox needs a simple vertex and fragment function, therefore it needs its own pipeline.

- depthStencilState: Each pixel of the skybox will be positioned at the very edge of normalized clip space. Renderer's current depth stencil state only adds the fragment if the fragment is less than the current depth value. The skybox depth stencil should test less than or equal to the current depth value. You'll see why shortly.

Your class currently doesn't compile because you need to initialize those properties. Add the following code to init(textureName:):

```
let allocator = MTKMeshBufferAllocator(device: Renderer.device)
let cube = MDLMesh(boxWithExtent: [1,1,1], segments: [1, 1, 1],
                   inwardNormals: true,
                   geometryType: .triangles,
                   allocator: allocator)
do {
  mesh = try MTKMesh(mesh: cube,
                     device: Renderer.device)
} catch {
  fatalError("failed to create skybox mesh")
}
```

Here, you create a cube mesh. Notice that you set the normals to face inwards. That's because the whole scene will appear to be *inside* the cube.

Add a new static method to create the pipeline state:

```
private static func
    buildPipelineState(vertexDescriptor: MDLVertexDescriptor)
                               -> MTLRenderPipelineState {
  let descriptor = MTLRenderPipelineDescriptor()
  descriptor.colorAttachments[0].pixelFormat =
      Renderer.colorPixelFormat
  descriptor.depthAttachmentPixelFormat = .depth32Float
  descriptor.vertexFunction =
      Renderer.library?.makeFunction(name: "vertexSkybox")
  descriptor.fragmentFunction =
      Renderer.library?.makeFunction(name: "fragmentSkybox")
  descriptor.vertexDescriptor =
      MTKMetalVertexDescriptorFromModelIO(vertexDescriptor)
  do {
    return
      try Renderer.device.makeRenderPipelineState(
          descriptor: descriptor)
  } catch {
    fatalError(error.localizedDescription)
  }
}
```

There's nothing new here. You create a pipeline state with the cube's Model I/O vertex descriptor, pointing to two shader functions that you'll write shortly.

Add a new static method to create the depth stencil state:

```
private static func buildDepthStencilState()
            -> MTLDepthStencilState? {
  let descriptor = MTLDepthStencilDescriptor()
  descriptor.depthCompareFunction = .lessEqual
  descriptor.isDepthWriteEnabled = true
  return Renderer.device.makeDepthStencilState(
      descriptor: descriptor)
}
```

This creates the depth stencil state with the less than or equal comparison method mentioned earlier.

Complete the initialization by adding this to the end of init(textureName:):

```
pipelineState =
    Skybox.buildPipelineState(vertexDescriptor:
cube.vertexDescriptor)
depthStencilState = Skybox.buildDepthStencilState()
```

Your project should now compile.

Rendering the skybox

Still in **Skybox.swift**, create a new method to perform the skybox rendering:

```
func render(renderEncoder: MTLRenderCommandEncoder, uniforms:
Uniforms) {

}
```

Add these render encoder commands to the new method:

```
renderEncoder.pushDebugGroup("Skybox")
renderEncoder.setRenderPipelineState(pipelineState)
// renderEncoder.setDepthStencilState(depthStencilState)
renderEncoder.setVertexBuffer(mesh.vertexBuffers[0].buffer,
                    offset: 0, index: 0)
```

Here, you set up the render encoder with all of the properties you initialized. Leave the depth stencil state line commented out for the moment.

After this code, set up `uniforms`:

```
var viewMatrix = uniforms.viewMatrix
viewMatrix.columns.3 = [0, 0, 0, 1]
var viewProjectionMatrix = uniforms.projectionMatrix
                            * viewMatrix
renderEncoder.setVertexBytes(&viewProjectionMatrix,
              length: MemoryLayout<float4x4>.stride,
              index: 1)
```

As a reminder, when you render a scene, you multiply each model's matrix with the view matrix and the projection matrix. When you move through the scene, it appears as if the camera is moving through the scene, but in fact, the whole scene is moving around the camera. You don't want the skybox to move, so you zero out column 3 of `viewMatrix` to remove the camera's translation.

However, you do still want the skybox to rotate with the rest of the scene, and also render with projection, so you multiply the view and projection matrices and send them to the GPU.

Add the following the previous code to do the draw:

```
let submesh = mesh.submeshes[0]
renderEncoder.drawIndexedPrimitives(type: .triangle,
  indexCount: submesh.indexCount,
  indexType: submesh.indexType,
  indexBuffer: submesh.indexBuffer.buffer,
  indexBufferOffset: 0)
```

The skybox shader functions

In the **Metal Shaders** group, add a new Metal file named **Skybox.metal**. Again, add this file to both the macOS and iOS targets.

Add the following code to the new file:

```
#import "Common.h"

struct VertexIn {
  float4 position [[ attribute(0) ]];
};

struct VertexOut {
  float4 position [[ position ]];
};
```

The structs are simple so far — you need a position in and a position out.

Add the shader functions:

```
vertex VertexOut vertexSkybox(const VertexIn in [[stage_in]],
                         constant float4x4 &vp [[buffer(1)]]) {
  VertexOut out;
  out.position = (vp * in.position).xyww;
  return out;
}

fragment half4 fragmentSkybox(VertexOut in [[stage_in]]) {
  return half4(1, 1, 0, 1);
}
```

Two very simple shaders — the vertex function moves the vertices to the projected position, and the fragment function returns yellow. This is a temporary color, which is startling enough that you'll be able to see where the skybox renders.

Notice in the vertex function that you **swizzled** the xyzw position to xyww. To place the sky as far away as possible, it needs to be at the very edge of NDC.

During the change from clip space to NDC, the coordinates are all divided by w during the perspective divide stage.

This will now result in the z coordinate being 1, which will ensure that the skybox renders *behind* everything else within the scene.

The following diagram shows the skybox in camera space rotated by 45°. After projection and the perspective divide, the vertices will be flat against the far NDC plane.

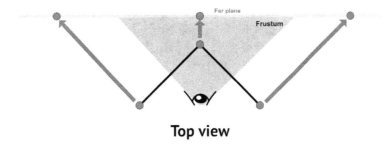

Top view

Integrating the skybox into the scene

Open **Scene.swift**, and add a new property to Scene:

```
var skybox: Skybox?
```

Open **SkyScene.swift**. This is the scene that contains the car and the ground. Add a skybox at the top of `setupScene()`:

```
skybox = Skybox(textureName: nil)
```

You haven't written the code for the skybox texture yet, but soon you'll set it up so that `nil` will give you a physically simulated sky, and a texture name will load a sky texture.

In **Renderer.swift**, in `draw(in:)`, toward the end of the method, add the following after the `// render skybox` comment:

```
scene.skybox?.render(renderEncoder: renderEncoder,
                     uniforms: scene.uniforms)
```

It may seem odd that you're rendering the skybox last, after rendering the models, when it's going to be the object that's behind everything else. Remember early-Z testing from Chapter 3, "The Rendering Pipeline": when objects are rendered, most of the skybox fragments will be behind them and will fail the depth test. Therefore, it's more efficient to render the skybox last.

You've now integrated the skybox into the rendering process.

Build and run to see the new yellow sky.

As you can see from this image, not all of the sky is yellow. As you rotate the scene, the yellow sky flickers and shows the blue of the metal view's clear color. This happens because the current depth stencil state is from `Renderer`, and it's comparing new fragments to *less* than the current depth buffer. The skybox coordinates are right on the edge, so sometimes they're *equal* to the edge of clip space.

In **Skybox.swift**, in render(renderEncoder:uniforms:), uncomment renderEncoder.setDepthStencilState(depthStencilState), and build and run the app again.

This time, the depth comparison is correct, and the sky is the solid yellow returned from the skybox fragment shader.

Procedural skies

Yellow skies might be appropriate on a different planet, but how about a procedural sky? A procedural sky is one built out of various parameters such as weather conditions and time of day. Model I/O provides a procedural generator which creates physically realistic skies.

Before exploring this API further, open and run **skybox.playground** in the **projects** folder for this chapter. This scene contains only a ground plane and a skybox. Use your mouse or trackpad to reorient the scene, and experiment with the sliders under the view to see how you can change the sky depending on:

- **turbidity**: Haze in the sky. 0.0 is a clear sky. 1.0 spreads the sun's color.

- **sun elevation**: How high the sun is in the sky. 0.5 is on the horizon. 1.0 is overhead.

- **upper atmosphere scattering**: Atmospheric scattering influences the color of the sky from reddish through orange tones to the sky at midday.

- **ground albedo**: How clear the sky is. 0 is clear, while 10 can produce intense colors. It's best to keep turbidity and upper atmosphere scattering low if you have high albedo.

As you move the sliders, the result is printed in the debug console so you can record these values for later use. See if you can create a sunrise:

This playground uses Model I/O to create an `MDLSkyCubeTexture`. From this, the playground creates an `MTLTexture` and applies this as a cube texture to the sky cube. You'll do this in your starter project.

Cube textures

Cube textures are similar to the 2D textures that you've already been using. 2D textures map to a quad and have two texture coordinates, whereas cube textures consist of six 2D textures: one for each face of the cube. You sample the textures with a 3D vector.

The easiest way to load a cube texture into Metal is to use Model I/O's `MDLTexture` initializer. When creating cube textures, you can arrange the images in various combinations:

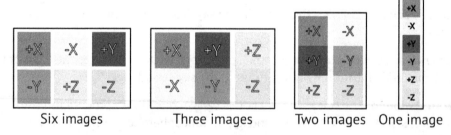

Six images   Three images   Two images   One image

Alternatively, you can create a cube texture in an asset catalog and load the six images there. Back in your starter project, open **Textures.xcassets** in the **Textures** group. This is pre-loaded with a sky texture complete with mipmaps.

The sky should always render on the base mipmap level 0, but you'll see later how to use the other mipmaps.

Aside from there being six images to one texture, moving the images into the asset catalog and creating the mipmaps is the same process as described in Chapter 7, "Maps and Materials".

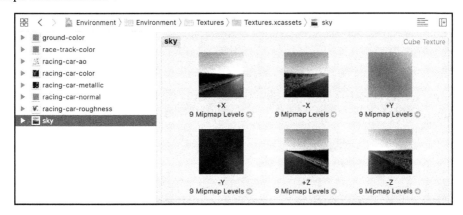

Adding the procedural sky

You'll use these sky textures shortly, but for now, you'll add a procedural sky to the scene in the starter project. In **Skybox.swift**, add these properties to `Skybox`:

```
struct SkySettings {
  var turbidity: Float = 0.28
  var sunElevation: Float = 0.6
  var upperAtmosphereScattering: Float = 0.1
  var groundAlbedo: Float = 4
}

var skySettings = SkySettings()
```

You can use the values from the appropriate sliders in the playground if you prefer.

Now add the following method:

```
func loadGeneratedSkyboxTexture(dimensions: int2) -> MTLTexture?
{
  var texture: MTLTexture?
  let skyTexture = MDLSkyCubeTexture(name: "sky",
      channelEncoding: .uInt8,
      textureDimensions: dimensions,
      turbidity: skySettings.turbidity,
      sunElevation: skySettings.sunElevation,
      upperAtmosphereScattering:
```

```
                skySettings.upperAtmosphereScattering,
        groundAlbedo: skySettings.groundAlbedo)
  do {
    let textureLoader =
          MTKTextureLoader(device: Renderer.device)
    texture = try textureLoader.newTexture(texture: skyTexture,
                                           options: nil)
  } catch {
    print(error.localizedDescription)
  }
  return texture
}
```

This uses the settings to create the sky texture using Model I/O. That's all there is to creating a procedurally generated sky texture! Call this method at the end of init(textureName:):

```
if let textureName = textureName {

} else {
  texture = loadGeneratedSkyboxTexture(dimensions: [256, 256])
}
```

You'll add the if part of this conditional shortly and load the named texture. The nil option provides a default sky.

To render the texture, you'll change the skybox shader function and ensure that the texture gets to the GPU.

Still in **Skybox.swift**, in render(renderEncoder:uniforms:), add this before the draw call:

```
renderEncoder.setFragmentTexture(texture,
                index: Int(BufferIndexSkybox.rawValue))
```

The starter project already has the necessary enum indices set up in **Common.h** for the skybox textures.

In **Skybox.metal**, add this to the VertexOut struct:

```
float3 textureCoordinates;
```

Generally, when you load a model, you also load its texture coordinates. However, when sampling texels from a cube texture, instead of using a uv *coordinate*, you use a 3D *vector*.

For example, a vector from the center of any cube passes through the far top left corner at [-1, 1, 1].

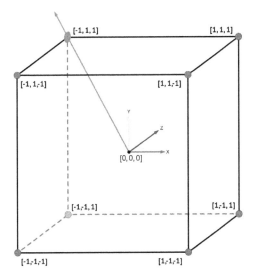

Conveniently, even though the skybox's far top-left vertex position is [-0.5, 0.5, 0.5], it still lies on the same vector, so you can use the skybox vertex position for the texture coordinates. You don't even need to normalize this vector to read the cube texture.

Add this to `vertexSkybox` before the `return`:

```
out.textureCoordinates = in.position.xyz;
```

Change the fragment shader to:

```
fragment half4
      fragmentSkybox(VertexOut in [[stage_in]],
                     texturecube<half> cubeTexture
                       [[texture(BufferIndexSkybox)]]) {
  constexpr sampler default_sampler(filter::linear);
  half4 color = cubeTexture.sample(default_sampler,
                                   in.textureCoordinates);
  return color;
}
```

Accessing a cube texture is similar to accessing a 2D texture. You mark the cube texture as `texturecube` in the shader function parameters and sample it using the `textureCoordinates` vector that you set up in the vertex function.

Build and run, and you now have a realistic sky, simulating physics:

Custom sky textures

As mentioned earlier, you can use your own 360° sky textures. The textures included in the starter project were downloaded from http://hdrihaven.com, a great place to find environment maps. The HDRI has been converted into six tone mapped sky cube textures before adding them to the asset catalog.

> **Note**: If you want to create your own skybox textures or load HDRIs (high dynamic range images), you can find out how to do it in **references.markdown** included with this chapter's files.

Loading a cube texture is almost the same as loading a 2D texture. Open **Texturable.swift**, and examine the method loadCubeTexture(imageName:). Just as with loadTexture(imageName:), you can load either a **cube** texture from the asset catalog or one 2D image consisting of the six faces vertically.

In **Skybox.swift**, add this to the end of the file so you can access the cube texture loading method:

```
extension Skybox: Texturable {}
```

At the end of init(textureName:), in the first half of the incomplete conditional, use the bound textureName to load the cube texture.

```
do {
  texture = try Skybox.loadCubeTexture(imageName: textureName)
} catch {
  fatalError(error.localizedDescription)
}
```

In **SkyScene.swift**, you want to load the sky texture, so change the skybox initialization to:

```
skybox = Skybox(textureName: "sky")
```

Build and run to see your new sky texture.

Notice that as you move about the scene, although the skybox rotates with the rest of the scene, it does not reposition.

You should be careful that the sky textures you use don't have objects that appear to be close, as they will always appear to stay at the same distance from the camera. Sky textures should be for background only. This sky texture is not perfect as it has utility poles behind the car.

Reflection

Now that you have something to reflect, you can easily implement reflection of the sky onto the car. When rendering the car, all you have to do is take the camera view direction, reflect it about the surface normal, and sample the skycube along the reflected vector for the fragment color for the car.

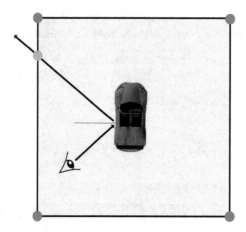

The starter project has the capability of choosing which fragment shader to render a particular object, so in **SkyScene.swift**, change car's initialization to:

```
let car = Model(name: "racing-car.obj",
                fragmentFunctionName: "skyboxTest")
```

In **Shaders.metal**, create a new fragment shader at the end of the file:

```
fragment float4 skyboxTest(VertexOut in [[stage_in]],
  constant FragmentUniforms &fragmentUniforms
    [[buffer(BufferIndexFragmentUniforms)]],
  texturecube<float> skybox [[texture(BufferIndexSkybox)]]) {
  return float4(0, 1, 1, 1);
}
```

You'll temporarily use this shader for rendering the car. The cyan return color is to ensure that you have the shader working.

Build and run to check that the car renders out fully in cyan and that your new shader is working.

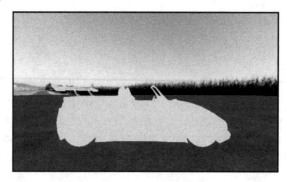

To send the skybox texture to the car's new fragment shader, in **Skybox.swift**, in Skybox, add this new method:

```
func update(renderEncoder: MTLRenderCommandEncoder) {
  renderEncoder.setFragmentTexture(texture,
                  index: Int(BufferIndexSkybox.rawValue))
}
```

You'll add other skybox textures to this method soon.

In **Renderer.swift**, in draw(in:), locate // render models, and add this just before the scene.renderables for loop:

```
scene.skybox?.update(renderEncoder: renderEncoder)
```

The sky texture is now available to the new fragment function.

You now calculate the camera's reflection vector about the surface normal to get a vector for sampling the skybox texture. To get the camera's view vector, you subtract the fragment world position from the camera position.

In **Shaders.metal**, replace the code in skyboxTest with:

```
float3 viewDirection = in.worldPosition.xyz -
                          fragmentUniforms.cameraPosition;
float3 textureCoordinates = reflect(viewDirection,
                          in.worldNormal);
```

Here, you calculate the view vector and reflect it about the surface normal to get the vector for the cube texture coordinates.

Now, add this code:

```
constexpr sampler defaultSampler(filter::linear);
float4 color = skybox.sample(defaultSampler,
                          textureCoordinates);
float4 copper = float4(0.86, 0.7, 0.48, 1);
color = color * copper;
return color;
```

Here, you sample the skybox texture for a color and multiply it by a copper color.

Build and run. The car now appears to be made of beautifully shiny copper. Walk about the scene and around the car to see the sky reflected on the car.

Note: This is not a true reflection; you're only reflecting the sky texture. If you place any objects in the scene, they won't be reflected. You can see this at the rear of the car where the road from the skybox texture instead of the ground node is reflected on the passenger side. However, this reflection is a fast and easy effect, and often sufficient.

Image-based lighting

At the beginning of the chapter, there were two problems with the original car render. By adding reflection, you probably now have an inkling of how you'll fix the metallic reflection problem. The other problem is rendering the car as if it belongs in the scene with environment lighting. **IBL** or **Image Based Lighting** is one way of dealing with this problem.

Using the sky image you can extract lighting information. For example, the parts of the car that face the sun in the sky texture should shine more than the parts that face away. The parts that face away shouldn't be entirely dark but should have ambient light filled in from the sky texture.

Epic Games developed a technique for *Fortnite*, which they adapted from Disney's research, and this has become the standard technique for IBL in games today. If you want to be as physically correct as possible, there's a link to their article on how to achieve this included with the **references.markdown** for this chapter.

You'll be doing an approximation of their technique, making use of Model I/O for the diffuse.

Diffuse reflection

Light comes from all around us. Sunlight bounces around and colors reflect. When rendering an object, you should take into account the color of the light coming from every direction.

This is somewhat of an impossible task, but you can use **convolution** to compute a cube map called an **irradiance map** from which you can extract lighting information. You won't need to know the mathematics behind this: Model I/O comes to the rescue again!

Included in the starter project is a fragment shader already set up in **IBL.metal**. Look at `fragment_IBL` in that file. The shader reads all of the possible textures for a `Model` and sets values for:

- base color
- normal
- roughness
- metallic (this should be 0 or 1)
- ambient occlusion

All of these maps for the car will interact with the sky texture and provide a beautiful render. Currently, the fragment function returns just the base color.

To use the fragment function, in **SkyScene.swift**, change `car`'s initialization to:

```
let car = Model(name: "racing-car.obj",
                fragmentFunctionName: "fragment_IBL")
```

Build and run, and you'll get a basic flat color render:

The diffuse reflection for the car will come from a second texture derived from the sky texture. In **Skybox.swift**, add a new property to hold this diffuse texture:

```
var diffuseTexture: MTLTexture?
```

To create the diffuse irradiance texture, add this temporary method:

```
func loadIrradianceMap() {
  // 1
  let skyCube =
      MDLTexture(cubeWithImagesNamed: ["cube-sky.png"])!
  // 2
  let irradiance =
      MDLTexture.irradianceTextureCube(with: skyCube,
                          name: nil, dimensions: [64, 64],
                          roughness: 0.6)
  // 3
  let loader = MTKTextureLoader(device: Renderer.device)
  diffuseTexture = try! loader.newTexture(texture: irradiance,
                                      options: nil)
}
```

Going through this code:

1. Model I/O currently doesn't load cube textures from the asset catalog, so your project has an image named **cube-sky.png** with the six faces included in it.

2. Use Model I/O to create the irradiance texture. It doesn't have to be a large texture, as the diffuse color is spread out.

3. Load the resultant MDLTexture to the diffuseTexture MTLTexture.

To call this method, add the following to the end of init(textureName:):

```
loadIrradianceMap()
```

Still in **Skybox.swift**, in update(renderEncoder:), add the following:

```
renderEncoder.setFragmentTexture(diffuseTexture,
  index: Int(BufferIndexSkyboxDiffuse.rawValue))
```

This will send the diffuse texture to the GPU.

In **IBL.metal**, add the two skybox textures to the parameter list for fragment_IBL:

```
texturecube<float> skybox [[texture(BufferIndexSkybox)]],
texturecube<float> skyboxDiffuse
                   [[texture(BufferIndexSkyboxDiffuse)]]
```

At the end of fragment_IBL, replace the return with:

```
float4 diffuse = skyboxDiffuse.sample(textureSampler, normal);
return diffuse * float4(baseColor, 1);
```

The diffuse value doesn't depend on the angle of view, so you sample the diffuse texture using the surface normal. You then multiply the result by the base color.

Build and run the app. Because of the irradiance convolution, the app may take a minute or so to start. As you walk about the car, you'll notice it's slightly brighter where it faces the sun.

Click the **Capture GPU frame** icon to enter the GPU Debugger, and look at the generated irradiance map.

You can choose the different faces below the texture.

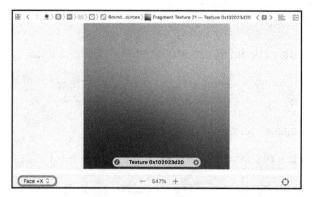

Instead of generating the irradiance texture each time, you can save the irradiance map to a file and load it from there. Included in the **resources** folder for this chapter is a project named **IrradianceGenerator**. You can use this app to generate your irradiance maps.

In the starter project, there's an irradiance map named **irradiance.png** to match the sky textures. It's time to switch to using this irradiance map for the diffuse texture instead of generating it.

In **Skybox.swift**, in `init(textureName:)`, locate where you load `texture` in the `do...catch`, and add this immediately after loading `texture`:

```
diffuseTexture =
    try Skybox.loadCubeTexture(imageName: "irradiance.png")
```

Remove `loadIrradianceMap()` and the code where you called that method at the end of `init(textureName)`.

Build and run to ensure you have the same result as you did *before* swapping to the prebuilt irradiance map.

Specular reflection

The irradiance map provides the diffuse and ambient reflection, but the specular reflection is a bit more difficult.

You may remember from Chapter 5, "Lighting Fundamentals," that, whereas the diffuse reflection comes from all light directions, specular reflection depends upon the angle of view and the roughness of the material.

See the difference in the light's reflection:

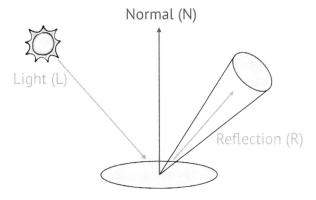

In Chapter 7, "Maps and Materials", you had a foretaste of physically based rendering using the Cook-Torrance microfacet specular shading model. This model is defined as:

$$f(l, v) = \frac{D(h)F(v, h)G(l, v, h)}{4(n \cdot l)(n \cdot v)}$$

Where you provide the light direction **(l)**, view direction **(v)** and the half vector **(h)** between **l** and **v**. As described in Chapter 7, "Maps and Materials", the functions are:

- **D**: Geometric slope distribution

- **F**: Fresnel

- **G**: Geometric attenuation

Just as with the diffuse light, to get the accuracy of the incoming specular light, you need to take many samples, which is impractical in real-time rendering. Epic Games's approach in their paper <u>Real Shading in Unreal Engine 4</u> is to split up the shading model calculation. They prefilter the sky cube texture with the geometry distribution for various roughness values. For each roughness level, the texture gets smaller and blurrier, and you can store these prefiltered environment maps as different mipmap levels in the sky cube texture.

> **Note:** In the resources for this chapter, there's a project named **Specular**, which uses the code from Epic Games's paper. This project takes in six images — one for each cube face — and will generate prefiltered environment maps for as many levels as you specify in the code. The results are placed in a subdirectory of **Documents** named **specular**, which you should create before

> running the project. You can then add the created .png files to the mipmap
> levels of the sky cube texture in your asset catalog.

The **sky** texture in the starter project already contains the prefiltered environment maps.

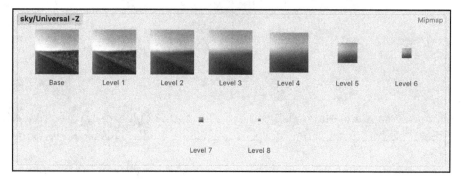

BRDF look-up table

During runtime, you supply a look-up table with the actual roughness of the model and the current viewing angle and receive back the scale and bias for the Fresnel and geometric attenuation contributions to the final color. You can represent this two-dimensional look-up table as a texture that behaves as a two-dimensional array. One axis is the roughness value of the object, and the other is the angle between the normal and the view direction. You input these two values as the UV coordinates and receive back a color. The red value contains the scale, and the green value contains the bias.

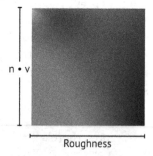

The more photorealistic you want your scene to be, the higher the level of mathematics you'll need to know. In **references.markdown**, there are links with suggested reading that explain the Cook-Torrance microfacet specular shading model.

The starter project contains functions provided by Epic Games to create the BRDF look-up texture. You can find these in the **Utilities** group.

In **Skybox.swift**, add a property for the new texture:

```
var brdfLut: MTLTexture?
```

At the end of `init(textureName:)`, call the method supplied in the starter project to build the texture:

```
brdfLut = Renderer.buildBRDF()
```

This method will use a **compute shader** to create a new texture. You'll find out how to create and use compute shaders in Chapter 16, "Particle Systems".

In `update(renderEncoder:)`, add the following to send the texture to the GPU:

```
renderEncoder.setFragmentTexture(brdfLut,
                index: Int(BufferIndexBRDFLut.rawValue))
```

Build and run the app, and click the **Capture GPU frame** icon to verify the look-up texture created by the BRDF compute shader is available to the GPU.

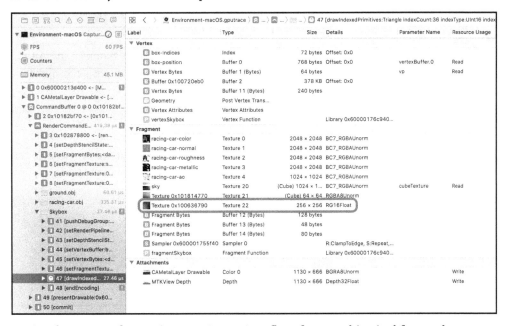

Notice the texture format is `RG16Float`. As a float format, this pixel format has a greater accuracy than `RGBA8Unorm`.

All the necessary information is now on the GPU, so you need to receive the new BRDF look-up texture into the fragment shader and do the shader math.

In **IBL.metal**, add this as a parameter to `fragment_IBL`:

```
texture2d<float> brdfLut [[texture(BufferIndexBRDFLut)]]
```

At the end of `fragment_IBL`, before the `return`, add this:

```
// 1
float3 viewDirection = in.worldPosition.xyz -
                       fragmentUniforms.cameraPosition;
float3 textureCoordinates = reflect(viewDirection, normal);
// 2
constexpr sampler s(filter::linear, mip_filter::linear);
float3 prefilteredColor =
     skybox.sample(s, textureCoordinates,
                   level(roughness * 10)).rgb;
// 3
float nDotV = saturate(dot(normal, normalize(-viewDirection)));
float2 envBRDF = brdfLut.sample(s, float2(roughness, nDotV)).rg;
```

Going through the code:

1. Calculate the view direction and the view direction reflected about the surface normal. This is the same code as you used earlier for reflection.

2. Read the skybox texture along this reflected vector as you did earlier. Using the extra parameter `level(n)`, you can specify the mip level to read. You sample the appropriate mipmap for the roughness of the fragment.

3. Calculate the angle between the view direction and the surface normal, and use this as one of the UV coordinates to read the BRDF look-up texture. The other coordinate is the roughness of the surface. You receive back the red and green values which you'll use to calculate the second part of the Cook Torrence equation.

Fresnel reflectance

When light hits an object straight on, some of the light is reflected. The amount of reflection is called Fresnel zero, or **F0**, and you can calculate this from the material's index of refraction, or **IOR**.

When you view an object, at the viewing angle of 90°, the surface becomes nearly 100% reflective. For example, when you look across the water, it's reflective; but when you look straight down into the water, it's non-reflective.

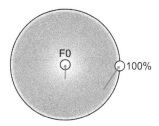

Most dielectric (non-metal) materials have an F0 of about 4%, so most rendering engines use this amount as standard. For metals, F0 is the base color.

Add this after the previous code:

```
float3 f0 = mix(0.04, baseColor.rgb, metallic);
float3 specularIBL = f0 * envBRDF.r + envBRDF.g;
```

Here, you choose F0 as 0.04 for non-metals and the base color for metals. `metallic` **should** be a binary value of 0 or 1, but it's best practice to avoid conditional branching in shaders, so you use `mix()`. You then calculate the second part of the rendering equation using the values from the look-up table.

Replace the `return` line with the following:

```
float3 specular = prefilteredColor * specularIBL;
float4 color = diffuse * float4(baseColor, 1)
                + float4(specular, 1);
return color;
```

You're now including the diffuse and base colors. Build and run.

Your car render is almost complete. Non-metals take the roughness value — the seats are matte, and the car paint is shiny.

Metals reflect but take on the base color — the base color of the wheel hubs and the steel bar behind the seats is gray.

Being able to tweak shaders gives you complete power over how your renders look.

Because you're using low dynamic range lighting, the non-metal diffuse color looks a bit dark. You can tweak the color very easily.

Add this to the end of `fragment_IBL`, right after setting `diffuse` from the diffuse texture:

```
diffuse = mix(pow(diffuse, 0.5), diffuse, metallic);
```

This raises the power of the diffuse value but only for non-metals. Build and run, and the car body is a lot brighter.

The finishing touch will be to add a fake shadow effect. At the rear of the car, the exhausts look as if they are self-lit:

They should be shadowed because they are recessed. This is where ambient occlusion maps come in handy.

Ambient occlusion maps

Ambient occlusion is a technique that approximates how much light should fall on a surface. If you look around you — even in a bright room — where surfaces are very close to each other, they're darker than exposed surfaces. In Chapter 19, "Advanced Shadows", you'll learn how to generate global ambient occlusion using ray marching, but assigning pre-built local ambient occlusion maps to models is a fast and effective alternative.

Apps such as *Substance Painter* can examine the model for proximate surfaces and produce an ambient occlusion map. This is the AO map for the car, which is included in the starter project.

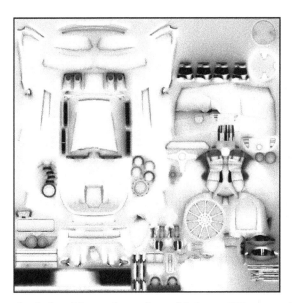

The white areas on the left, with a color value of 1.0, are UV mapped to the car paint. These are fully exposed areas. When you multiply the final render color by 1.0, it'll be unaffected. However, you can identify the wheel at the bottom right of the AO map, where the spokes are recessed. Those areas have a color value of perhaps 0.8, which darkens the final render color.

The ambient occlusion map is all set up in the starter project and ready for you to use. In `fragment_IBL`, just before the final `return`, add this:

```
color *= ambientOcclusion;
```

Build and run. Now compare the exhaust pipes to the previous render.

All of the recessed areas are darker, which gives more natural lighting to the model.

Challenge

On the first page of this chapter is a comparison of the car rendered in two different lighting situations. Your challenge is to create the red lighting scene.

Provided in the **resources** directory are six cube face png images converted from an HDRI downloaded from HDRIHaven.com.

1. Create an irradiance map using the included **IrradianceGenerator** project, and import the generated map into the project.

2. Create specular mipmap levels using the included **Specular** project.

3. Create a new cube texture in the asset catalog.

4. Assign this new cube texture the appropriate generated mipmap images.

There's no code to change; it's all imagery! You'll find the completed project in the challenge directory for this chapter.

Where to go from here?

You've dipped a toe into the water of the great sea of realistic rendering, and you'll read about more advanced concepts of lighting and reflectivity in Chapter 20, "Advanced Lighting." If you want to explore more about realistic rendering, **references.markdown** for this chapter contains links to interesting articles and videos.

This chapter did not touch on spherical harmonics, which is an alternative method to using an irradiance texture map for diffuse reflection. Mathematically, you can approximate that irradiance map with 27 floats. Hopefully, the links in **references.markdown** will get you interested in this amazing technique.

Before you try to achieve the ultimate realistic render, one question you should ask yourself is whether your game will benefit from realism. One way to stand out from the crowd is to create your own rendering style. Games such as *Fortnite* aren't entirely realistic and have a style all of their own. Experiment with shaders to see what you can create.

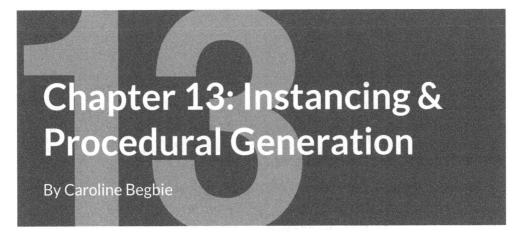

Chapter 13: Instancing & Procedural Generation

By Caroline Begbie

Now that you have an environment with a sky that you can populate with models, you'll want to add some randomness to your scene. Trees and grass make the scene more natural, but they can take up a lot of valuable resources without adding any player action to your game.

In this chapter, you'll first find out how to efficiently render many trees and blades of grass using **instancing**. You'll then render instanced rocks, and you'll use **morphing** for different shapes. Finally, you'll create a procedural house system that will create a row of houses whose size and style will change every time you run the app.

As well as all that, you'll improve your versatility and proficiency in handling GPU resources which will enable you to access any data in MTLBuffers with confidence.

The starter project

Open the starter project for this chapter. This is almost the same project as the previous chapter, with a few skybox tweaks, but it includes a new GameScene that renders 100 trees in random places. Each tree consists of 9,119 vertices, with a color texture of size 8 MB and 2048×2048 pixels.

> **Note**: You generally wouldn't spend 9,119 vertices just on a tree, unless you wanted some fine detail. Low-poly trees are much more efficient. However, this example will show you just how important instancing is.

The project also contains two other scenes with supporting files for later sections in which you'll create a rock system and perform procedural house generation.

Build and run the app. If your device can't handle 100 trees, you might need to reduce instanceCount in GameScene.

In Xcode, check the Debug navigator. This is the result on a 2015 iMac:

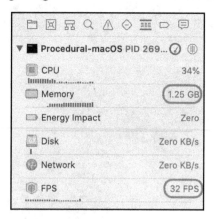

Your aim in the first part of this chapter is to reduce that huge memory footprint, and maybe even address that terrible frame rate.

> **Note**: If you're using faster hardware and are seeing 60 FPS, you might consider increasing the number of trees to 200 or even 300 for the purpose of this exercise – set `instanceCount` in GameScene accordingly.

Instancing

> **Note**: Instance drawing for iOS is available for GPU Family 3 and up - that's a minimum hardware device of the iPhone 6s.

In your scene, there's a lot of duplicated data going to the GPU. For each tree render, you're sending a texture and 9,119 vertices.

This texture and geometry are the same for every tree, and by using instancing, the GPU can use one texture and geometry for multiple models. In this scene, it will mean 24 fewer texture and geometry resources transferred to the GPU.

Each instance of the model will have unique data. The unique data for each tree is its position, rotation and scale, which you set in GameScene. Instead of rendering many Models, you'll render one Model many times using the unique instance data.

The following diagram shows Model with its existing properties of geometry (the vertex buffer), textures and position and rotation. You'll add a new array of Transforms containing the position and rotation for all the instances.

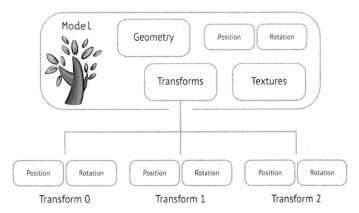

Open **Transform.swift**. This holds a single struct that contains position, rotation and scale information. There are two computed properties that return matrices. You'll hold an array of Transforms in Model - one for each instance.

Open **Model.swift** in the **Nodes** group. Add properties for the array of transforms and the instance count:

```
private var transforms: [Transform]
let instanceCount: Int
```

transforms will hold the transform data for each tree, and instanceCount the total number of trees. Your app won't compile until you've initialized these new properties.

Add an extra optional parameter to init to accept an instance count, so that the function parameters are:

```
init(name: String,
     vertexFunctionName: String = "vertex_main",
     fragmentFunctionName: String = "fragment_IBL",
     instanceCount: Int = 1) {
```

If you don't specify a count when creating a Model, the default number of instances is 1.

Create a new type method to initialize transforms:

```
static func buildTransforms(instanceCount: Int) -> [Transform] {
  return [Transform](repeatElement(Transform(),
                    count: instanceCount))
}
```

This method creates an array for the number of instances required.

In init, before super.init(), initialize the new properties:

```
self.instanceCount = instanceCount
transforms = Model.buildTransforms(instanceCount: instanceCount)
```

Your project will now compile.

Create the instance MTLBuffer

The GPU only requires matrices, not the position and rotation data, so instead of sending all the transform data to the GPU, you'll only send a buffer of matrices.

When you update the position or rotation of an instance, at the same time you'll update the model matrix and the normal matrix in this new buffer.

In **Model.swift**, create a new property to hold the matrices:

```
var instanceBuffer: MTLBuffer
```

In **Common.h**, in the **Metal Shaders** group, define a struct that will format the data for both Swift and your shader functions:

```
struct Instances {
  matrix_float4x4 modelMatrix;
  matrix_float3x3 normalMatrix;
};
```

Back in **Model.swift**, initialize the instances buffer with this new type method:

```
static func buildInstanceBuffer(transforms: [Transform]) ->
MTLBuffer {
// 1
  let instances = transforms.map {
      Instances(modelMatrix: $0.modelMatrix,
          normalMatrix: float3x3(normalFrom4x4: $0.modelMatrix))
  }
// 2
  guard let instanceBuffer =
      Renderer.device.makeBuffer(bytes: instances,
          length: MemoryLayout<Instances>.stride
                      * instances.count) else {
    fatalError("Failed to create instance buffer")
  }
  return instanceBuffer
}
```

With this code, you:

1. Convert the position and rotation data in transforms into an array of Instances.

2. Create the instances buffer and initialize it with this new array.

In init, before super.init(), initialize instanceBuffer:

```
instanceBuffer =
    Model.buildInstanceBuffer(transforms: transforms)
```

Your project will now compile again.

Accessing MTLBuffer data

An MTLBuffer contains bytes, which can be of any data type. Swift is a strongly typed language, meaning that Swift can only access the data in the buffer if you tell Swift what type the data is. You do this by **binding** the data to a type. In this case, the type is Instances.

When you bind the memory to the MTLBuffer contents, you're given a pointer of type UnsafeMutablePointer<Instances>, which points to the first instance in the buffer.

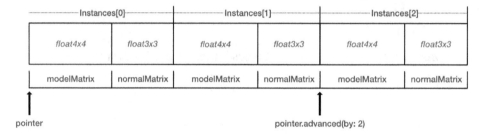

Unsafe means that the buffer is unsafe to read from unless it's correctly typed. You can bind to the data with any type you want, and Swift has no way of knowing whether the formatting is correct. You could bind instanceBuffer.contents() to Int.self, for example, which is incorrect in this case, but Swift will still allow you to access the buffer as if it is made up of Ints. Take care to bind the buffer to the correct type!

In **Model.swift**, create a new method to update a single transform:

```
func updateBuffer(instance: Int, transform: Transform) {
  transforms[instance] = transform
}
```

At the end of this method, add the following:

```
var pointer =
    instanceBuffer.contents().bindMemory(to: Instances.self,
                              capacity: transforms.count)
```

This binds instanceBuffer to a pointer, and formats the data so that Swift knows that the data is of type Instances, and what the specific number of Instances is. Using the pointer's pointee property, you can access the data in the buffer directly.

Continue adding to `updateBuffer(instance:transform:)`:

```
pointer = pointer.advanced(by: instance)
pointer.pointee.modelMatrix = transforms[instance].modelMatrix
pointer.pointee.normalMatrix = transforms[instance].normalMatrix
```

First, you advance the pointer to the correct instance. You then place the matrix information directly into `instanceBuffer`.

You also need to send `instanceBuffer` to the GPU. Add this to `render(renderEncoder:uniforms:fragmentUniforms:)` at the top of the method, just after setting `uniforms`:

```
renderEncoder.setVertexBuffer(instanceBuffer, offset: 0,
                index: Int(BufferIndexInstances.rawValue))
```

The index was already set up for you in the starter project.

Here's the hardware magic where you tell the GPU how many instances to render. In `render(renderEncoder:submesh:)`, change the draw call to the following:

```
renderEncoder.drawIndexedPrimitives(type: .triangle,
        indexCount: mtkSubmesh.indexCount,
        indexType: mtkSubmesh.indexType,
        indexBuffer: mtkSubmesh.indexBuffer.buffer,
        indexBufferOffset: mtkSubmesh.indexBuffer.offset,
        instanceCount: instanceCount)
```

This includes the number of instances. `instanceCount` alerts the GPU that it has to call the vertex shader `indexCount` times for each `instanceCount`.

GPU instances

So you can access the instance array on the GPU side, you'll change the vertex shader.

In **Shaders.metal**, add these two parameters to `vertex_main`:

```
constant Instances *instances [[buffer(BufferIndexInstances)]],
uint instanceID [[instance_id]]
```

The first parameter is the array of matrices, and the second — with the `[[instance_id]]` Metal Shading Language attribute — holds the index into the `instances` array.

> **Note**: If you're rendering a grid of grass plants, for example, you could also use `[[instance_id]]` to calculate the position in the grid instead of sending position data in a buffer.

Change the initialization of `out` to include the matrices for the particular instance:

```
Instances instance = instances[instanceID];
VertexOut out {
  .position = uniforms.projectionMatrix * uniforms.viewMatrix
      * uniforms.modelMatrix * instance.modelMatrix * position,
  .worldPosition = (uniforms.modelMatrix *
          instance.modelMatrix * position).xyz,
  .worldNormal = uniforms.normalMatrix *
          instance.normalMatrix * normal.xyz,
  .worldTangent = uniforms.normalMatrix *
          instance.normalMatrix * tangent.xyz,
  .worldBitangent = uniforms.normalMatrix *
          instance.normalMatrix * bitangent.xyz,
  .uv = vertexIn.uv
};
```

You include the matrices for each instance in the position and normal calculations. With this separation of `Model modelMatrix` and `instance modelMatrix`, you can treat the `Model` as a group.

By changing the transform of the `Model`, it will affect all the instances, so that you can, for example, move an entire patch of grass or a forest at once. Each instance is then offset by its own `modelMatrix`.

You've completely set up an instancing system, and you can now use it in your scene. In **GameScene.swift**, change the `for` loop to:

```
let tree = Model(name: "tree.obj", instanceCount: instanceCount)
add(node: tree)
for i in 0..<instanceCount {
  var transform = Transform()
  transform.position.x = .random(in: -10..<10)
  transform.position.z = .random(in: -10..<10)
  let rotationY: Float = .random(in: -.pi..<Float.pi)
  transform.rotation = [0, rotationY, 0]
  tree.updateBuffer(instance: i, transform: transform)
}
```

Here, you create one `Model` for the group of trees and set transform data for each instance of a tree.

Build and run, and you'll see almost the same result as your starter project. Your tree positions are randomized, so they won't be in the same place.

Check the Debug navigator. Notice the memory footprint has gone way down. That's because you're now only using one texture and one set of vertices for all the trees. You should also be rendering at 60 frames per second again.

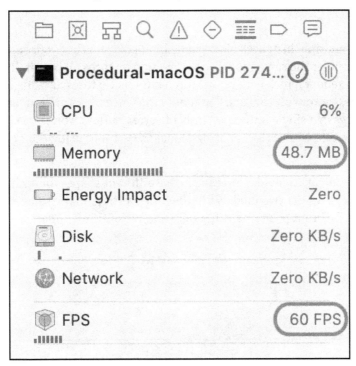

Using the Capture GPU frame tool, you can check that only one **tree** model, instead of twenty-five, is in the list of render encoder commands:

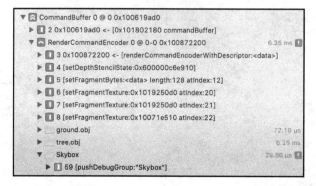

Instancing is a powerful and easy way of improving performance. Whenever you render more than one of a particular model, consider rendering them all as instances.

Morphing

You rendered multiple instances of the same high poly tree, but your scene will look boring if you render the same model with the same textures all over it. In this section, you'll render a rock with one of three random textures and one of three random shapes, or **morph targets**. You'll hold the vertex information for these three different shapes in a single buffer: an array of vertex buffers. You'll also learn how to render vertices that you've read in using Model I/O without using the stage_in attribute.

Using **homeomorphic** models, you can choose different shapes for each model. Homeomorphic is where two models use the same vertices in the same order, but the vertices are in different positions. A famous example of this is *"Spot the cow"* by *Keenan Crane*:

Spot uses the same number and order of vertices as a sphere. The uv coordinates don't change either.

Morph targets are commonly used for human figures. The 3D content supplier **Daz 3D** has a figure named **Genesis**, a generic human model, but you can purchase morph targets to change how the model looks.

You can turn the base model from a toon to a muscled super-hero just by switching the morph target mesh. You can also use morph targets for animating expressions from a frown to a smile, for example.

The only prerequisite for a morph target is that it has been built from a base mesh by rearranging the vertices, not by adding or removing any.

For this next section, you'll use three differently shaped rocks that were modeled from a sphere. You'll find a Blender file with the three rocks and a UV-mapped sphere in the resources for this chapter. You could experiment with making your own rock shapes from the sphere.

> **Note**: The base shape, although it looks like a sphere, is actually a subdivided cube. It's much easier to UV map a cube than a sphere, so before the artist subdivided the cube, she made the UV maps. Rocks are simple shapes, so small imperfections don't show too much.

Because you'll build up a fairly complex class, the starter project contains a `Nature` class, which is a cut-down version of the instanced `Model` that you just built. Open and examine **Nature.swift**. You'll initialize the class with an array of texture names and an array of OBJ file names for the morph targets, but nothing here should be new to you.

Common.h contains a struct named `NatureInstance` that will describe each rock instance. Each rock instance has a morph target ID and a texture ID that will tell the GPU which morph target and texture to use. The class `Nature` has an instance buffer for each rock, and currently only renders a single base color texture and single shape for all the rocks.

An important thing to note is that to make things simpler, Nature assumes that all of the OBJ files have just one material submesh and that the vertex descriptor has only position, normal and uv data. This class does not hold tangent information for normal map usage.

Open **ViewController.swift**, and change the initialization of scene from GameScene to RocksScene:

```
let scene = RocksScene(sceneSize: metalView.bounds.size)
```

Open **RocksScene.swift**. It's almost an exact copy of GameScene.swift, but it's using Nature instead of Model. The scene lists three morph target OBJ files and three textures, but it currently only uses one.

Build and run the app to see instanced rocks:

All of the rocks are the same color and shape, but you'll soon fix that!

Vertex descriptors and stage_in

So far, to render OBJ models, you've been using the [[stage_in]] attribute to describe vertex buffers in the vertex shader function.

The following image shows what Model I/O reads into the vertex MTLBuffer:

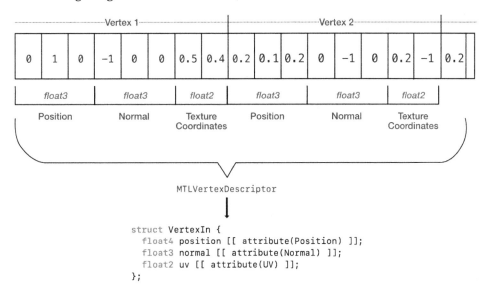

There are two float3s and a float2 for each vertex. The MTLVertexDescriptor describes this layout and assigns the position, normal and texture coordinate fields. The vertex descriptor stride describes the number of bytes between the start of one vertex and the start of the next.

When you use a parameter with a stage_in attribute, the vertex shader uses the layout from the vertex descriptor to read the buffer. These don't have to be the same lengths as the data in the buffer, as the shader will automatically convert. Notice that, whereas the position is a float3 in the buffer, the vertex shader can map it to the Position attribute and read it in as a float4.

You're going to be using one of three different vertex buffers for the three differently shaped rocks, and the stage_in conversion can only be used on one buffer. Because of this, you'll read the raw buffer bytes in the vertex shader. You'll have to match the actual format of the buffer data in the shader, not the struct format in VertexIn that the shader currently uses.

In **Nature.metal**, change VertexIn to:

```
struct VertexIn {
    float3 position;
    float3 normal;
    float2 uv;
};
```

If you're familiar with reading MTLBuffers in shaders, you may be aware that this particular struct will cause you problems. Unfortunately, the format of this struct is a common mistake, so you'll deliberately make this mistake to see what happens; you'll correct it later.

Change the first parameter of vertex_nature to:

```
constant VertexIn *in [[buffer(0)]],
uint vertexID [[vertex_id]],
```

You've changed the [[stage_in]] parameter to a pointer to an array of VertexIns. The [[vertex_id]] attribute gives you the current vertex so that you can retrieve the position from the array.

Add this at the top of the vertex function:

```
VertexIn vertexIn = in[vertexID];
```

This gives you the current vertex.

You'll get a compile error because position is now a float3. Change the assignment of position to:

```
float4 position = float4(vertexIn.position, 1);
```

Build and run, and you'll get one of those interesting and generally frustrating renders where the vertices aren't in their proper places:

This usually means that the struct format in the vertex shader doesn't match the contents of the MTLBuffer, which you'll fix now.

Packed floats

In Apple's Metal Shading Language Specification, available at https://developer.apple.com/metal/Metal-Shading-Language-Specification.pdf, you can see the size and alignment of vector data types.

Type	Size (in bytes)	Alignment (in bytes)
float3	16	16
float4	16	16
packed_float3	12	4
packed_float4	16	4

A float3 has an alignment of 16 bytes; each field of the struct must start at the alignment offset, and the compiler inserts padding where needed. This will change the size of the stride of VertexIn, so the vertex shader doesn't read the data correctly. Your VertexIn struct currently contains float types, and you'll need to change these to packed_float types.

The packed_float3 type has an alignment of only 4 bytes with a size of 12 bytes, so the stride will be consistent with the actual data in the buffer.

This is one problem; however, there is another problem: The vertex descriptor currently has a stride of 40 bytes, as you may have noticed printing out in the debug console. The actual stride in the buffer is 32 bytes: 12 + 12 + 8.

In **Nature.swift**, where you define the mdlVertexDescriptor property, after:

```
var offset = 0
```

Add this:

```
let packedFloat3Size = MemoryLayout<Float>.stride * 3
```

After both Position and Normal, change:

```
offset += MemoryLayout<float3>.stride
```

To:

```
offset += packedFloat3Size
```

Instead of using the size of a float3, which is 16 bytes, you're now using the size of three Floats which is 12 bytes. You don't need to change the offset for float2, as the size is 8 bytes, whether it's packed or not.

In **Nature.metal**, change VertexIn to:

```
struct VertexIn {
  packed_float3 position;
  packed_float3 normal;
  float2 uv;
};
```

Build and run, and you'll see in the debug console that the vertex descriptor stride is now 32 bytes, and your rocks will render correctly.

MTLBuffer array

You're now able to render a single rock shape. In Swift, if you were going to have several rock shapes, you'd probably consider putting each shape into an array. However C++ does not allow variable length arrays, and you want to have the ability to add a variable number of morph targets to your Nature system.

You'll append each morph target into a single MTLBuffer. Because the different rock models all have the same number of vertices, you can easily calculate the offset to the correct rock shape for the current instance. Each instance will have a random morph target ID from 0 to 2.

> **Note:** You can track the contents of the buffer that you send to the GPU by using the Capture GPU Frame icon. On the Debug navigator, choose the Rocks

command folder and view the contents of Vertex Buffer 0. You'll see there are
currently 1649 rows - one for the position, normal and uv of each vertex.

In **Nature.swift**, in `Nature`, create a new property to hold the number of vertices in
each morph target:

```
var vertexCount: Int
```

This needs to be a `var`, not a constant, as you'll be sending this to the GPU in a buffer
later.

In `init`, locate where you load up the first morph target into a buffer. This is where
you'll concatenate all of the morph target buffers into the single `MTLBuffer`
`vertexBuffer`. Change:

```
vertexBuffer = mesh.vertexBuffers[0].buffer
```

To:

```
let bufferLength = mesh.vertexBuffers[0].buffer.length
vertexBuffer = Renderer.device.makeBuffer(length: bufferLength
  * morphTargetNames.count)!
```

You've already loaded the first OBJ and saved the submesh index data from it. All the
morph targets will have the same index data, so you only need to save this once.

You can use the loaded buffer to find out the length of the morph target data for each
element. Similar to the submesh index data, all of the morph targets will have the
same number of vertices, so each vertex buffer will be the same length for each
morph target.

Following on from the previous code, calculate the number of vertices:

```
let layout = mesh.vertexDescriptor.layouts[0]
                as! MDLVertexBufferLayout
vertexCount = bufferLength / layout.stride
```

To extract the vertex count from the mesh, you divide the length of the vertex buffer
by the layout stride taken from the vertex descriptor.

The Blit Command Encoder

You'll copy each morph target vertex buffer into the single `MTLBuffer` using a **blit** operation. You were introduced to a render command encoder in Chapter 1, "Introduction to Metal," and then briefly to a compute encoder in Chapter 11, "Tessellation". You are now learning about yet another type of encoder. A blit command encoder does a fast copy between resources such as textures and buffers. Just like with an `MTLRenderCommandEncoder`, you create an `MTLBlitCommandEncoder` and issue commands to the command buffer.

After the previous code, add this to create the command buffer and blit encoder:

```
let commandBuffer = Renderer.commandQueue.makeCommandBuffer()
let blitEncoder = commandBuffer?.makeBlitCommandEncoder()
```

Process all of the OBJ files and blit each vertex buffer into the single `MTLBuffer`. Continue by adding this code:

```
for i in 0..<morphTargetNames.count {
  guard let mesh = Nature.loadMesh(name: morphTargetNames[i])
else {
    fatalError("morph target not loaded")
  }
  let buffer = mesh.vertexBuffers[0].buffer
  blitEncoder?.copy(from: buffer, sourceOffset: 0,
                  to: vertexBuffer,
                  destinationOffset: buffer.length * i,
                  size: buffer.length)
}
```

The offset of each morph target vertex buffer is the length of the original morph target buffer multiplied by the current morph target array index.

Finish off the blit operation just as you would a render pass:

```
blitEncoder?.endEncoding()
commandBuffer?.commit()
```

Note: If you build and run now, click the Capture GPU Frame icon and inspect the vertex buffer in the Rocks folder, you'll see that the buffer now contains 4947 entries, which is 3 times 1649 vertices.

Random rock shape

In **Nature.swift**, change updateBuffer(instance:transform:) to receive a random number for both the morph target and the texture:

```
func updateBuffer(instance: Int, transform: Transform,
                  textureID: Int, morphTargetID: Int)
```

Add a check at the top of the method to make sure that the morph target or texture id is not out of range:

```
guard textureID < textureCount
      && morphTargetID < morphTargetCount else {
  fatalError("ID is too high")
}
```

Add this at the end of the method to update the instance data with the index ids. You'll randomly generate these in the scene:

```
pointer.pointee.textureID = UInt32(textureID)
pointer.pointee.morphTargetID = UInt32(morphTargetID)
```

Now, correct the compile errors. You call updateBuffer in two places. At the end of init(name:instanceCount:textureNames:morphTargetNames:), add the two extra parameters:

```
updateBuffer(instance: 0, transform: Transform(),
             textureID: 0, morphTargetID: 0)
```

In **RocksScene.swift**, in setupScene(), also add the two extra parameters:

```
let textureID = Int.random(in: 0..<textureNames.count)
let morphTargetID = Int.random(in: 0..<morphTargetNames.count)
rocks.updateBuffer(instance: i, transform: transform,
                   textureID: textureID,
                   morphTargetID: morphTargetID)
```

As well as adding the two parameters, you create a random index to access the data in the texture and morph target arrays.

On the GPU side, in **Nature.metal**, you're currently using vertexID to access the currently rendered vertex. To access the next morph target in the buffer, you'll have to add the number of vertices for each morph target to vertexID.

In the below example, where each morph target has 1649 vertices, the first vertex for the second morph target should be vertex ID 1649.

VERTICES

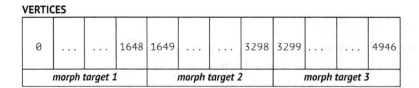

0	...	...	1648	1649	...	...	3298	3299	...	...	4946
morph target 1				*morph target 2*				*morph target 3*			

In **Nature.swift**, in render(renderEncoder:uniforms:fragmentUniforms:), add the following code below // set vertex buffer:

```
renderEncoder.setVertexBytes(&vertexCount,
                            length: MemoryLayout<Int>.stride,
                            index: 1)
```

Here, you send the GPU the vertex count so that the vertex shader will be able to calculate the morph target offset.

Now, open **Nature.metal** to receive this buffer length variable. Add this extra parameter to vertex_nature:

```
constant int &vertexCount [[buffer(1)]],
```

Still in vertex_nature, change:

```
VertexIn vertexIn = in[vertexID];
NatureInstance instance = instances[instanceID];
```

To:

```
NatureInstance instance = instances[instanceID];
uint offset = instance.morphTargetID * vertexCount;
VertexIn vertexIn = in[vertexID + offset];
```

This calculates the offset of each morph using the morph target ID and the vertex count.

Build and run, and you now get randomly positioned and shaped rocks:

Texture arrays

Accessing a random texture is slightly easier than a random morph target since you can load the textures into an MTLTexture with a textureType of type2DArray. All of the textures are held in one MTLTexture, with each element of the array being called a **slice**.

You need to create a method to load up the textures into a temporary array of MTLTextures. This is a useful method, so you'll add it to the Texturable protocol so that you can use it with any class that conforms to Texturable. In **Texturable.swift**, add this:

```
static func loadTextureArray(textureNames: [String]) ->
MTLTexture? {
}
```

Add this to the new method:

```
var textures: [MTLTexture] = []
for textureName in textureNames {
  do {
    if let texture =
        try Nature.loadTexture(imageName: textureName) {
      textures.append(texture)
    }
  }
  catch {
    fatalError(error.localizedDescription)
  }
}
guard textures.count > 0 else { return nil }
```

Here, you load up an array of textures.

Following on from that code, create a new texture array:

```
let descriptor = MTLTextureDescriptor()
descriptor.textureType = .type2DArray
descriptor.pixelFormat = textures[0].pixelFormat
descriptor.width = textures[0].width
descriptor.height = textures[0].height
descriptor.arrayLength = textures.count
let arrayTexture =
    Renderer.device.makeTexture(descriptor: descriptor)!
```

You use the first texture in the array for the pixel format, width and height. `textureType` indicates that this texture will have **slices**. These are equivalent to array elements: each texture will go into a slice.

Continue with this code to blit the `textures` into `arrayTexture`:

```
let commandBuffer = Renderer.commandQueue.makeCommandBuffer()!
let blitEncoder = commandBuffer.makeBlitCommandEncoder()!
let origin = MTLOrigin(x: 0, y: 0, z: 0)
let size = MTLSize(width: arrayTexture.width,
                   height: arrayTexture.height, depth: 1)
for (index, texture) in textures.enumerated() {
  blitEncoder.copy(from: texture,
                   sourceSlice: 0, sourceLevel: 0,
                   sourceOrigin: origin, sourceSize: size,
                   to: arrayTexture, destinationSlice: index,
                   destinationLevel: 0,
                   destinationOrigin: origin)
}
blitEncoder.endEncoding()
commandBuffer.commit()
return arrayTexture
```

You create the command buffer and blit command encoder as before. For each texture, you copy it to the correct slice of `arrayTexture`. The copy command has a large number of parameters, which gives you total control over the copy. You can copy a corner of one texture to another corner of a second texture, for example. In this case, you want to copy the whole texture, so you use a zero origin with the full texture size.

`sourceLevel` is the mipmap level. Previously, you have filled mipmaps using the asset catalog, but this is how you can set the mipmap texture for each level in code.

This method now takes in a list of strings, loads up single textures, and then combines them all into one 2D texture array and returns this texture.

Back in **Nature.swift**, in
`init(name:instanceCount:textureNames:morphTargetNames:)`, locate `// load the texture` and replace:

```
do {
  baseColorTexture =
      try Nature.loadTexture(imageName: textureNames[0])
} catch {
  fatalError(error.localizedDescription)
}
```

With:

```
baseColorTexture =
    Nature.loadTextureArray(textureNames: textureNames)
```

You're now loading all of the three rock textures into `baseColorTexture`.

In **Nature.metal**, in `fragment_nature`, replace the `baseColorTexture` parameter with:

```
texture2d_array<float> baseColorTexture [[texture(0)]]
```

The fragment function is now set up to receive the texture array. The compile error in the fragment function means that you're not indicating which slice of the texture array to use.

Previously, you were using a single 2D texture which doesn't have slices, but now when you sample the texture array, you have to specify the slice. You'll pass the texture ID from the vertex shader to the fragment shader.

Add this variable to `VertexOut`:

```
uint textureID [[flat]];
```

The `[[flat]]` Metal Shading Language attribute prevents the rasterizer from interpolating the value between vertices so that the fragment shader will receive the value exactly as the vertex shader set it.

At the end of `vertex_nature`, before the return, load up the variable with the instance's random texture:

```
out.textureID = instance.textureID;
```

In `fragment_nature` replace the `baseColor` assignment with:

```
float4 baseColor = baseColorTexture.sample(s, in.uv,
                                            in.textureID);
```

You give `textureID` as the index into the texture array to get the base color. Your project should now compile.

Build and run to see your new rock system. Each of your rocks has one of three shapes and one of three textures.

Procedural systems

With the techniques you've learned so far, you have the power to load random objects into your scene and make each scene unique. However, you're currently limited to having a single mesh size. In games such as *No Man's Sky*, each planet and all of the animals that you meet on the planets are **procedurally generated** using many different meshes.

Procedural generation essentially means that you send a system some random parameters, such as integers or even noise, and the system generates a new and unique model or game level.

In this section, you'll use a similar technique to procedural animal generation in *No Man's Sky* and create a house system consisting of a row of houses.

Each house will have a random number of floors, and each floor will use a random model. However, even though the system might use a floor model or a roof model several times in different houses, for better efficiency, there will only be one instance of the model geometry.

Rules

The secret to procedural systems is having a set of rules. For example, if you're procedurally generating animals out of multiple parts, you don't want to be attaching heads to leg joints; this isn't *The Island of Doctor Moreau* after all.

So, in this case, you'd have a rule that *heads* only attach to *head joints*.

Your houses will consist of a first (ground) floor, middle floors and an optional roof. The rules for the house system are:

- First floors are a ground model.

- Roofs are only on the top floor.

- Maximum number of floors.

- Minimum and maximum gap between the houses.

- Maximum number of houses.

These are the models for each floor type, created by Kenney at https://kenney.nl:

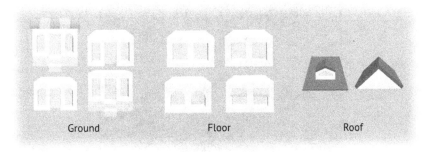

The Houses scene

Add **HousesScene.swift**, **Houses.swift** and **Houses.metal** to the targets by Cmd-Selecting all three files, and on the **File inspector**, check **Target Membership** for both macOS and iOS targets.

> **Note:** These files were not part of the original targets because Houses has a reference to house.instanceBuffer, which you only added at the beginning of this chapter.

Open **ViewController.swift**, and change the initialization of scene from RocksScene to HousesScene:

```
let scene = HousesScene(sceneSize: metalView.bounds.size)
```

Look at **Houses.swift**. Houses is a subclass of Node and contains an array of Models. render(renderEncoder:uniforms:fragmentUniforms:) renders this array with currently only one Model.

In **Houses.metal**, the vertex and fragment shaders are very simple. vertex_house extracts the current instance from the Model's instance array just as you set it up in the earlier part of this chapter. fragment_house uses the material colors from the Model's submesh with just a single sunlight for lighting.

HousesScene.swift simply loads the Houses system. Build and run the app to see the lone house:

You'll now create rules to add houses to your Houses system.

Determine the rules

In **Houses.swift**, add an enum to Houses to lay down the rules with constants:

```
enum Rule {
  // gap between houses
  static let minGap: Float = 0.3
  static let maxGap: Float = 1.0

  // number of OBJ files for each type
  static let numberOfGroundFloors = 4
  static let numberOfUpperFloors = 4
  static let numberOfRoofs = 2

  // maximum houses
  static let maxHouses: Int = 5

  // maximum number of floors in a single house
  static let maxFloors: Int = 6
}
```

The number of OBJ files reflects the models held in the group **Models ▸ Houses**. These are carefully named for easy loading.

Add the following instance variable to Houses:

```
var floorsRoof: Set<Int> = []
```

This is a set of integers holding the indices of the roof OBJs in houses. If the system selects a floor with an element index in this set, then it is a roof, and no further building of that house can take place.

Load the OBJ files

Create a new method to read all the house OBJ files and place them into a Swift array.

```
func loadOBJs() -> [Model] {
  var houses: [Model] = []
  func loadHouse(name: String) {
    houses.append(Model(name: name + ".obj",
                      vertexFunctionName: "vertex_house",
                      fragmentFunctionName: "fragment_house"))
  }
  for i in 1...Rule.numberOfGroundFloors {
    loadHouse(name: String(format: "houseGround%d", i))
  }
  for i in 1...Rule.numberOfUpperFloors {
```

```
    loadHouse(name: String(format: "houseFloor%d", i))
  }
  for i in 1...Rule.numberOfRoofs {
    loadHouse(name: String(format: "houseRoof%d", i))
    floorsRoof.insert(houses.count-1)
  }
  return houses
}
```

Here, you use the constant values to load each of the OBJ types into the array of Models. If you were to print out the index and names of the Models in the array, this is what you'd see:

```
0 :  houseGround1
1 :  houseGround2
2 :  houseGround3
3 :  houseGround4
4 :  houseFloor1
5 :  houseFloor2
6 :  houseFloor3
7 :  houseFloor4
8 :  houseRoof1
9 :  houseRoof2
```

For the two roofs, you insert the indices into floorsRoof so that you can determine later whether a particular OBJ is a roof.

In init(), replace:

```
houses.append(Model(name: "houseGround1.obj",
                    vertexFunctionName: "vertex_house",
                    fragmentFunctionName: "fragment_house"))
```

With:

```
houses = loadOBJs()
```

All of the house OBJ files are now loaded and ready for use. You'll generate arrays of integers to index to the correct house.

Create the first (ground) floors

Create two new properties in Houses:

```
var remainingHouses: Set<Int> = []
var housefloors: [[Int]] = []
```

When you create the first (ground) floors, you'll add each house to the remainingHouses set. When the house is complete, you'll remove it from the set.

When the set is empty, then your procedural job is done, and all of the houses will be complete.

`housefloors` is a two-dimensional array. The first dimension is for each house and the second for the floors within each house.

Add this code at the end of `init()`:

```
let numberOfHouses = 5
for _ in 0..<numberOfHouses {
  let random = Int.random(in: 0..<Rule.numberOfGroundFloors)
  housefloors.append([random])
  let lastIndex = housefloors.count - 1
  remainingHouses.insert(lastIndex)
}
```

You set `numberOfHouses` to 5, but you could, of course, randomize this number. For each house choose a random number between 0 and 3 (or the number of ground floor OBJ files you have). This number will index into `houses`. Remember that you loaded the ground floor OBJ files first, so they are elements 0 to 3. You insert the floor into `remainingHouses` to keep track of whether the house is complete.

Iterate through the houses and add floors while `remainingHouses` still contains elements. Add this after the previous code:

```
while remainingHouses.count > 0 {
  for i in 0..<housefloors.count {
    // 1
    if remainingHouses.contains(i) {
      let offset = Rule.numberOfGroundFloors
      let upperBound =
          offset + Rule.numberOfUpperFloors + Rule.numberOfRoofs
      let random = Int.random(in: offset..<upperBound)
      housefloors[i].append(random)

      // 2
      if floorsRoof.contains(random) ||
        housefloors[i].count >= Rule.maxFloors ||
        Int.random(in: 0...3) == 0 {
        // 3
        remainingHouses.remove(i)
      }
    }
  }
}
// 4
print(housefloors)
```

Going through this code:

1. If the house index is still in `remainingHouses`, then it doesn't yet have a roof, so is not yet complete. Add a random index number that will index into `houses` for a new floor. This index number has to be greater than the first few elements that contain only the first (ground) floors.

2. Finish up the house if the floor is a roof, or if the house has reached the maximum number of floors, or, for more randomness, a 1 in 4 chance.

3. Remove the house from `remainingHouses` if it is complete.

4. Temporarily print out `housefloors` to examine its contents.

Build and run the app to examine your progress.

This is a render of five first floors all in one place.

You'll see something like this in the debug console (yours will be different as it's all random):

[[2, 5], [0, 8], [0, 4, 7, 5], [1, 9], [0, 4, 9]]

This is the contents of the multidimensional array `housefloors`. Using these indices, you'll be able to access the correct model in `houses` for each entry. In this example (which will change every time, as it's random), there are 5 houses in the array which contain several floors each. House 0 has a first floor index of 2, meaning use the `Model` **houseGround3**. House 0's upper floor is 5, which uses **houseFloor2**. House 2 has four floors, and house 4 has 3 floors with **houseRoof2** on top.

You'll now create a final one-dimensional array: `floors`, which will contain a list of all the floors. In `Houses`, create a new property for the array:

```
struct Floor {
  var houseIndex: Int = 0
  var transform = Transform()
}
var floors: [Floor] = []
```

Each floor indexes to the correct Model in houses. You'll also calculate the correct position for each floor.

Replace the print statement at the end of init() with:

```
var width: Float = 0
var height: Float = 0
var depth: Float = 0
for house in housefloors {
  var houseHeight: Float = 0

  // add inner for loop here to process all the floors

  let house = houses[house[0]]
  width += house.size.x
  height = max(houseHeight, height)
  depth = max(house.size.z, depth)
  boundingBox.maxBounds = [width, height, depth]
  width += Float.random(in: Rule.minGap...Rule.maxGap)
}
```

You set up variables for the bounding box of the entire house system and process each house. houseHeight will keep the height of the current house so that you know where to locate the next floor. After processing all of the floors, you'll update the width and depth from each first (ground) floor, and the height from all the floors. You also add to the total width of the system a random gap between each house.

Add the inner for loop — where you commented in the previous code — to process each floor of the current house:

```
for floor in house {
  var transform = Transform()
  transform.position.x = width
  transform.position.y = houseHeight
  floors.append(Floor(houseIndex: floor, transform: transform))
  houseHeight += houses[floor].size.y
}
```

You assign a transform and the house index to each floor and update houseHeight for the next floor.

Now, you'll update the render loop. In render(renderEncoder:uniforms:fragmentUniforms:), replace:

```
for house in houses {
```

With:

```
for floor in floors {
  let house = houses[floor.houseIndex]
```

You'll render each floor instance using the floor's transform. Replace
`uniforms.modelMatrix` and `uniforms.normalMatrix` assignments with:

```
uniforms.modelMatrix = modelMatrix * floor.transform.modelMatrix
uniforms.normalMatrix =
  float3x3(normalFrom4x4: modelMatrix *
floor.transform.modelMatrix)
```

Build and run. You now have a procedural house system:

The arrangement of houses and floors will be different every time you run the app.
Notice that a roof is always the top story, the first floor OBJ models are always on the
ground, and the height of the houses doesn't exceed the maximum number of floors.

This is a simplified procedural system, but you can explore **procgen** (procedural
generation) much further with the links in **references.markdown** for this chapter.

Challenge

Using the **Nature** system that you set up for the rocks, you can easily create a field
full of blades of grass.

Your challenge is to use the grass OBJ files in the **Models ▸ Grass** group and the
grass textures in **Textures.xcassets**. The grass OBJ files all have the same number
and order of vertices, so you can use them as morph targets.

This will be a similar exercise to creating the rocks system earlier. You'll create a new
scene and a Nature system with the textures and morph targets.

The project in the challenge folder shows lush grass as far as the eye can see, but still running at 60fps on a 2015 iMac.

For the record, it doesn't perform as well on an iPhone 6s, or even a 2018 iPad Pro.

The app achieves this with a bit of trickery. GrassScene creates several grass systems with reduced amounts of grass the further you go back into the scene. By tracking where the camera goes, you can place grass with higher level of detail closer to the camera, and sparse low detail grass further away.

Where to go from here?

Procedural systems are fun to create. Later in this book, you'll encounter **Perlin noise**, and if you use this noise for your randomness, you can generate infinite terrains, or even dynamic wind or animation.

You're currently generating your systems on the CPU, but in a few chapters, you'll learn how to use compute kernels, and you'll be able to create more massive systems in parallel. A particle system is an excellent example of a procedural system, and in just a few short chapters you'll also master particles.

One of the sections in **references.markdown** is about **Lindenmayer systems**. Using L-systems for creating plants is interesting and approachable. Now that you know how to manipulate vertices more comfortably, you might want to try your hand at generating 3D plants.

The next chapter will take you further into lighting techniques. You'll find out how to render to a texture without immediately putting it onto the screen.

Chapter 14: Multipass & Deferred Rendering

By Marius Horga

Up to this point, you've been running projects and playgrounds that only had one render pass. In other words, you used a single command encoder to submit all of your draw calls to the GPU.

For more complex apps, you may need multiple render passes before presenting the texture to the screen, letting you use the result of one pass in the next one. You may even need to render content offscreen for later use.

With multiple render passes, you can render a scene with multiple lights and shadows, like this:

Take note, because in this chapter, you'll be creating that scene. Along the way, you'll learn a few key concepts, such as:

- Shadow maps.

- Multipass rendering.

- Deferred rendering with a G-buffer.

- The blit command encoder.

You'll start with shadows first.

Shadow maps

A shadow represents the absence of light on a surface. A shadow is present on an object when another surface or object obscures it from the light. Having shadows in a project makes your scene look more realistic and provides a feeling of depth.

Shadow maps are nothing more than textures containing shadow information about the scene. When a light shines on an object, anything that is behind that object gets a shadow cast on it.

Typically you render the scene from the location of your camera, but to build a shadow map, you need to render your scene from the location of the light source - in this case the sun.

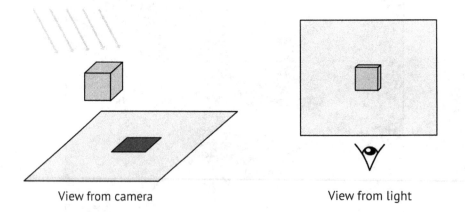

View from camera   View from light

The image on the left shows a render from the position of the camera with the directional light pointing down. The image on the right shows a render from the position of the directional light.

The eye shows where the camera was positioned in the first image.

You'll do two render passes:

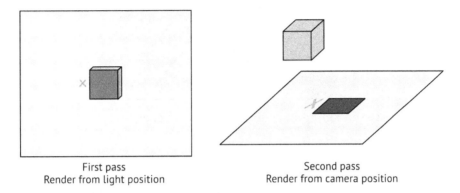

First pass
Render from light position

Second pass
Render from camera position

- **First pass**: Using a separate view matrix holding the sun's position, you'll render from the point of view of the light. Because you're not interested in color at this stage, only the depth of objects that the sun can see, you'll only render a depth texture in this pass. This is a grayscale texture, with the gray value indicating depth. Black is close to the light and white is far away.

- **Second pass**: You'll render using the camera as usual, but you'll compare the camera fragment with each depth map fragment. If the fragment's depth is lighter in color than the depth map at that position, it means the fragment is in the shadow. The light can "see" the blue x in the above image, so it is not in shadow.

Shadows and deferred rendering are complex subjects, so there's a starter project available for this chapter. Open it in Xcode and take a look around.

The code is similar to what's available at the end of Chapter 5, "Lighting Fundamentals".

For simplicity, you'll be working on the diffuse color only; specularity and ambient lighting are not included with this project.

Build and run the project, and you'll see a train and a tree model, both on top of a plane:

Add these properties in **Renderer.swift**, at the top of Renderer:

```
var shadowTexture: MTLTexture!
let shadowRenderPassDescriptor = MTLRenderPassDescriptor()
```

Later, when you create the render command encoder for drawing the shadow, you'll use this render pass descriptor. Each render pass descriptor can have up to eight color textures attached to it, plus a depth texture and a stencil texture. The shadowRenderPassDescriptor points to shadowTexture as a depth attachment.

You'll need several textures through the course of the chapter, so create a helper method for building them.

Add this new method to Renderer:

```
func buildTexture(pixelFormat: MTLPixelFormat,
                  size: CGSize,
                  label: String) -> MTLTexture {
  let descriptor = MTLTextureDescriptor.texture2DDescriptor(
                           pixelFormat: pixelFormat,
                           width: Int(size.width),
                           height: Int(size.height),
                           mipmapped: false)
  descriptor.usage = [.shaderRead, .renderTarget]
  descriptor.storageMode = .private
  guard let texture =
    Renderer.device.makeTexture(descriptor: descriptor) else {
    fatalError()
  }
  texture.label = "\(label) texture"
  return texture
}
```

In this method, you configure a texture descriptor and create a texture using that descriptor. Textures used by render pass descriptors have to be configured as **render targets**. Render targets are memory buffers or textures that allow offscreen rendering for cases where the rendered pixels don't need to end up in the framebuffer. The storage mode is private, meaning the texture is stored in memory in a place that only the GPU can access.

Next, add the following to the bottom of the file:

```
private extension MTLRenderPassDescriptor {
  func setUpDepthAttachment(texture: MTLTexture) {
    depthAttachment.texture = texture
    depthAttachment.loadAction = .clear
    depthAttachment.storeAction = .store
    depthAttachment.clearDepth = 1
  }
}
```

This creates a new extension on `MTLRenderPassDescriptor` with a new method that sets up the depth attachment of a render pass descriptor and configures it to store the provided texture. This is where you'll attach `shadowTexture` to `shadowRenderPassDescriptor`.

You're creating a separate method because you'll have other render pass descriptors later in the chapter. The load and store actions describe what action the attachment should take at the start and end of the render pass. In this case, you clear the texture at the beginning of the pass and store the texture at the end of the pass.

Now, add the following to the `Renderer` class:

```
func buildShadowTexture(size: CGSize) {
  shadowTexture = buildTexture(pixelFormat: .depth32Float,
                               size: size, label: "Shadow")
  shadowRenderPassDescriptor.setUpDepthAttachment(
                               texture: shadowTexture)
}
```

This builds the depth texture by calling the two helper methods you just created. Next, call this method at the end of `init(metalView:)`:

```
buildShadowTexture(size: metalView.drawableSize)
```

Also, call it at the end of `mtkView(_:drawableSizeWillChange:)` so that when the user resizes the window, you can rebuild the textures with the correct size:

```
buildShadowTexture(size: size)
```

Build and run the project to make sure everything works. You won't see any visual changes yet; you're just verifying things are error-free before moving onto the next task.

Multipass rendering

A render pass consists of sending commands to a command encoder. The pass ends when you end encoding on that command encoder. Multipass rendering uses multiple command encoders and facilitates rendering content in one render pass and using the output of this pass as the input of the next render pass.

Why would you need two passes here? Because in this case, you'll render the shadow from the light's position, not from the camera's position. You'll then save the output to a shadow texture and give it to the next render pass which combines the shadow with the rest of the scene to make up a final image.

Since you already have code that renders the scene, you can easily refactor this code into a new function that you can reuse for shadows as well.

The shadow pass

During the shadow pass, you'll be rendering from the point of view of the sun, so you'll need a new view matrix.

In **Common.h**, add this to the `Uniforms` struct:

```
matrix_float4x4 shadowMatrix;
```

You'll also need a new pipeline state to hold the different vertex function you'll be calling.

Add this property to `Renderer`:

```
var shadowPipelineState: MTLRenderPipelineState!
```

Now add the following to the end of `Renderer`:

```
func renderShadowPass(renderEncoder: MTLRenderCommandEncoder) {
  renderEncoder.pushDebugGroup("Shadow pass")
  renderEncoder.label = "Shadow encoder"
  renderEncoder.setCullMode(.none)
  renderEncoder.setDepthStencilState(depthStencilState)
  // 1
  renderEncoder.setDepthBias(0.01, slopeScale: 1.0, clamp: 0.01)
  // 2
  uniforms.projectionMatrix = float4x4(orthoLeft: -8, right: 8,
                                       bottom: -8, top: 8,
                                       near: 0.1, far: 16)
  let position: float3 = [sunlight.position.x,
                          sunlight.position.y,
                          sunlight.position.z]
  let center: float3 = [0, 0, 0]
  let lookAt = float4x4(eye: position, center: center,
                        up: [0,1,0])
  uniforms.viewMatrix = lookAt
  uniforms.shadowMatrix =
      uniforms.projectionMatrix * uniforms.viewMatrix

  renderEncoder.setRenderPipelineState(shadowPipelineState)
  for model in models {
    draw(renderEncoder: renderEncoder, model: model)
  }
  renderEncoder.endEncoding()
  renderEncoder.popDebugGroup()
}
```

Going through this code:

1. This adjusts the depth values in the pipeline by a scaling factor and a scaling bias, clamping the bias to a maximum amount.

2. Here, you create an orthographic projection matrix. You previously used an orthographic matrix in Chapter 9, "The Scene Graph", to render the scene from above. Because sunlight is a directional light, this is the correct projection type for shadows caused by sunlight. If instead you used a spotlight, for example, you would use the perspective projection matrix. You also use a `lookAt` matrix to set the direction vector of the sun vector.

Now you need to call this method for every frame.

Add the following code in `draw(in:)`, right below `// shadow pass`:

```
guard let shadowEncoder =
commandBuffer.makeRenderCommandEncoder(
              descriptor: shadowRenderPassDescriptor) else {
```

```
    return
  }
  renderShadowPass(renderEncoder: shadowEncoder)
```

Next, create a new method after init(metalView:):

```
func buildShadowPipelineState() {
  let pipelineDescriptor = MTLRenderPipelineDescriptor()
  pipelineDescriptor.vertexFunction =
      Renderer.library.makeFunction(name: "vertex_depth")
  pipelineDescriptor.fragmentFunction = nil
  pipelineDescriptor.colorAttachments[0].pixelFormat = .invalid
  pipelineDescriptor.vertexDescriptor =
      MTKMetalVertexDescriptorFromModelIO(
              Model.defaultVertexDescriptor)
  pipelineDescriptor.depthAttachmentPixelFormat = .depth32Float
  do {
    shadowPipelineState =
      try Renderer.device.makeRenderPipelineState(
                      descriptor: pipelineDescriptor)
  } catch let error {
    fatalError(error.localizedDescription)
  }
}
```

This creates a pipeline state without a color attachment or fragment function. Remember, at this point, you're only interested in depth information, not color information.

Call this method at the end of init(metalView:):

```
buildShadowPipelineState()
```

As you may have noticed, you're referencing a shader function named vertex_depth which does not exist yet.

In the **Shaders** group, using the **Metal File** template, create a new file named **Shadow.metal**. Make sure to check both macOS and iOS targets. Then, add this code to the newly created file:

```
#import "../Utility/Common.h"

struct VertexIn {
  float4 position [[ attribute(0) ]];
};

vertex float4
        vertex_depth(const VertexIn vertexIn [[ stage_in ]],
                     constant Uniforms &uniforms [[buffer(1)]]) {
```

```
    matrix_float4x4 mvp =
          uniforms.projectionMatrix * uniforms.viewMatrix
          * uniforms.modelMatrix;
    float4 position = mvp * vertexIn.position;
    return position;
}
```

Note that you have to put the correct relative path to **Common.h**.

This simple code receives a vertex position, and returns the transformed position.

Build and run the project.

Whoa! What happened to the scene?

Don't worry. This happened because you used the orthographic projection matrix for the shadow pass; to correct things, the main pass needs to use the perspective projection matrix again, so add this line in draw(in:) before the for loop where you process models:

```
    uniforms.projectionMatrix = camera.projectionMatrix
```

Build and run the project, and you should see the starter scene rendered again.

Ok, that's nice! But where's the shadow?

Click the **Capture GPU Frame** button on the debug bar (circled in red below):

In the **Debug navigator**, click on the **Shadow pass** group:

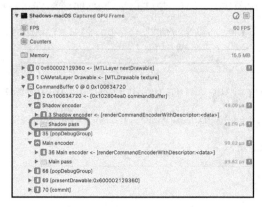

Excellent, the app window shows the shadow map. Yay! :D

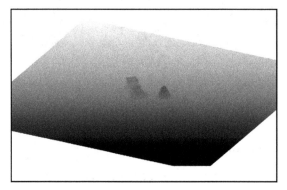

This is the scene rendered from the light's position. You used the shadow pipeline state, which you configured not to have a fragment shader, so the color information is not processed here at all — it's purely depth. Lighter colors are further away, and darker colors are closer.

The main pass

Now that you have the shadow map saved to a texture, all you need to do is send it to the next pass — the main pass — so you can use the texture in lighting calculations in the fragment function.

In draw(in:), before the for loop of the main pass, add this line:

```
renderEncoder.setFragmentTexture(shadowTexture, index: 0)
```

You're passing the shadow texture to the main pass's fragment function.

In **Main.metal**, add a new member to the `VertexOut` struct:

```
float4 shadowPosition;
```

You'll hold two transformed positions for each vertex. One transformed within the scene from the camera's point of view, and the other from the sun's point of view. You'll be able to compare them in the fragment function.

Add this line in `vertex_main`, before `return;`:

```
out.shadowPosition =
    uniforms.shadowMatrix * uniforms.modelMatrix
    * vertexIn.position;
```

The rest of the work happens in `fragment_main`. First, add one more function parameter after `&material`:

```
depth2d<float> shadowTexture [[texture(0)]]
```

Unlike the textures you've used in the past which have a type of `texture2d`, the texture type of a depth texture is `depth2d`.

Then, add this code before the `return` statement:

```
// 1
float2 xy = in.shadowPosition.xy;
xy = xy * 0.5 + 0.5;
xy.y = 1 - xy.y;
// 2
constexpr sampler s(coord::normalized, filter::linear,
                    address::clamp_to_edge,
                    compare_func:: less);
float shadow_sample = shadowTexture.sample(s, xy);
float current_sample =
    in.shadowPosition.z / in.shadowPosition.w;
// 3
if (current_sample > shadow_sample ) {
  diffuseColor *= 0.5;
}
```

Going through this code, you:

1. Determine a coordinate pair from the shadow position that will serve as a screen space pixel locator on the shadow texture. Then, you normalize the coordinates from [-1, 1] to [0, 1]. Finally, you reverse the Y coordinate since it's upside down.

2. Create a sampler to use with the shadow texture, and sample the texture at the coordinates you just created. Get the depth value for the currently processed pixel.

3. Compare the current depth value to the shadow depth value, and you set a darker grey for pixels that have the depth greater than the shadow value stored in the texture.

Build and run the project, and you'll finally see models with shadows! :]

> **Note**: If you're not entirely pleased about the quality of your shadows, there are some common techniques you can use to improve shadow maps at: https://msdn.microsoft.com/en-us/library/windows/desktop/ee416324(v=vs.85).aspx.

Deferred rendering

Before this chapter you've only been using **forward rendering** but assume you have a hundred models (or instances) and a hundred lights in the scene. Suppose it's a metropolitan downtown where the number of buildings and street lights could easily amount to the number of the objects in this scene.

With forward rendering, you render all of the models and process all of the lights in the fragment shader, for every single fragment, even though the final render may exclude a particular fragment. This can easily become a quadratic runtime problem that seriously decreases the performance of your app.

Deferred rendering, on the other hand, does two things:

- It collects information such as material, normals and positions from the models and stores them in a special buffer — traditionally named the **G-buffer** where *G* is for Geometry — for later processing in the fragment shader; by that time, the GPU only keeps visible fragments, so unnecessary calculation does not occur.

- It processes all of the lights in a fragment shader, but only on the final visible fragments.

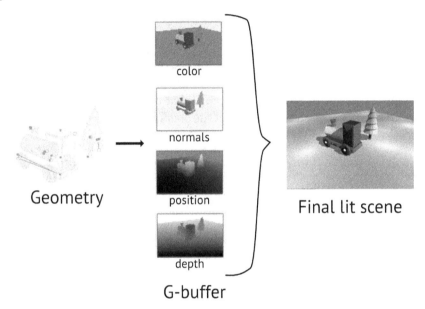

This approach takes the quadratic runtime down to linear runtime since the lights' processing loop is only performed once, and not for each model.

Here's a breakdown of the steps:

- A first pass renders the shadow map. You've already done this.

- A second pass reads the framebuffer attachments and constructs G-buffer textures containing these values: material color (or albedo), world space normals and positions and shadow information.

- A third and final pass using a full-screen quad combines all of this information into one final composited texture.

The G-buffer pass

All right, time to build that `G-buffer` up! First, create four new textures. Add this code at the top of `Renderer`:

```
var albedoTexture: MTLTexture!
var normalTexture: MTLTexture!
var positionTexture: MTLTexture!
var depthTexture: MTLTexture!
```

Define the `G-buffer` pass descriptor and pipeline state:

```
var gBufferPipelineState: MTLRenderPipelineState!
var gBufferRenderPassDescriptor: MTLRenderPassDescriptor!
```

Create a new method after `init(metalView:)` that builds the four textures using the convenience method you created earlier in the shadow pass:

```
func buildGbufferTextures(size: CGSize) {
  albedoTexture = buildTexture(pixelFormat: .bgra8Unorm,
                       size: size, label: "Albedo texture")
  normalTexture = buildTexture(pixelFormat: .rgba16Float,
                       size: size, label: "Normal texture")
  positionTexture = buildTexture(pixelFormat: .rgba16Float,
                       size: size, label: "Position texture")
  depthTexture = buildTexture(pixelFormat: .depth32Float,
                       size: size, label: "Depth texture")
}
```

Create another method within `private extension MTLRenderPassDescriptor` that will allow you to attach a texture to a render pass descriptor color attachment:

```
func setUpColorAttachment(position: Int, texture: MTLTexture) {
  let attachment: MTLRenderPassColorAttachmentDescriptor =
    colorAttachments[position]
  attachment.texture = texture
  attachment.loadAction = .clear
  attachment.storeAction = .store
  attachment.clearColor = MTLClearColorMake(0.73, 0.92, 1, 1)
}
```

This is similar to the depth attachment you created earlier. This time, you're dealing with a color attachment, so you can set the clear color. The scene depicts a sunny day with sharp shadows, so you're setting the color to sky blue.

Create another function in `Renderer`, that configures the G-buffer render pass descriptor using all of the convenience functions you've created:

```swift
func buildGBufferRenderPassDescriptor(size: CGSize) {
  gBufferRenderPassDescriptor = MTLRenderPassDescriptor()
  buildGbufferTextures(size: size)
  let textures: [MTLTexture] = [albedoTexture,
                                normalTexture,
                                positionTexture]
  for (position, texture) in textures.enumerated() {
    gBufferRenderPassDescriptor.setUpColorAttachment(
        position: position, texture: texture)
  }
  gBufferRenderPassDescriptor.setUpDepthAttachment(
        texture: depthTexture)
}
```

Here, you attach three color textures and a depth texture to the render pass descriptor.

Call this method at the end of `mtkView(_:drawableSizeWillChange:)`:

```swift
buildGBufferRenderPassDescriptor(size: size)
```

When the user resizes the window, all of the render pass descriptor attachment textures will now get resized too. Next, in `Renderer`, create a method to build the G-buffer pipeline state:

```swift
func buildGbufferPipelineState() {
  let descriptor = MTLRenderPipelineDescriptor()
  descriptor.colorAttachments[0].pixelFormat = .bgra8Unorm
  descriptor.colorAttachments[1].pixelFormat = .rgba16Float
  descriptor.colorAttachments[2].pixelFormat = .rgba16Float
  descriptor.depthAttachmentPixelFormat = .depth32Float
  descriptor.label = "GBuffer state"

  descriptor.vertexFunction =
    Renderer.library.makeFunction(name: "vertex_main")
  descriptor.fragmentFunction =
    Renderer.library.makeFunction(name: "gBufferFragment")
  descriptor.vertexDescriptor =
    MTKMetalVertexDescriptorFromModelIO(
              Model.defaultVertexDescriptor)
  do {
    gBufferPipelineState = try
      Renderer.device.makeRenderPipelineState(
              descriptor: descriptor)
  } catch let error {
    fatalError(error.localizedDescription)
  }
}
```

Previously, you only configured `colorAttachment[0].pixelFormat` and `depthAttachmentPixelFormat`. Now that you're storing an extra two attachments on the render pass descriptor, you'll specify their pixel formats in the pipeline state. `bgra8Unorm` has the format of four 8-bit unsigned components, which is all that's necessary to hold color values between 0 and 255. However, you'll need to store the position and normal values in higher precision than the color values by using `rgba16Float`.

You can reuse `vertex_main` from the main render pass, as all this does is transform the positions and normals. However, you'll need a new fragment function that stores the position and normal data into textures and doesn't process the lighting.

At the end of `init(metalView:)`, call this function:

```
buildGbufferPipelineState()
```

At the end of `Renderer`, add this function to perform the G-buffer pass:

```
func renderGbufferPass(renderEncoder: MTLRenderCommandEncoder) {
  renderEncoder.pushDebugGroup("Gbuffer pass")
  renderEncoder.label = "Gbuffer encoder"

  renderEncoder.setRenderPipelineState(gBufferPipelineState)
  renderEncoder.setDepthStencilState(depthStencilState)

  uniforms.viewMatrix = camera.viewMatrix
  uniforms.projectionMatrix = camera.projectionMatrix
  fragmentUniforms.cameraPosition = camera.position
  renderEncoder.setFragmentTexture(shadowTexture, index: 0)
  renderEncoder.setFragmentBytes(&fragmentUniforms,
              length: MemoryLayout<FragmentUniforms>.stride,
              index: 3)
  for model in models {
    draw(renderEncoder: renderEncoder, model: model)
  }
  renderEncoder.endEncoding()
  renderEncoder.popDebugGroup()
}
```

This pass is similar to the old main render pass, which you'll be removing shortly. You set the G-buffer's pipeline state, passing all of the fragment shader information the main pass used, except for the lights. Lighting will take place in the composition pass.

To perform the G-buffer pass, add this code in `draw(in:)`, under `// g-buffer pass`:

```
guard let gBufferEncoder =
commandBuffer.makeRenderCommandEncoder(
                descriptor: gBufferRenderPassDescriptor)
```

```
else {
  return
}
renderGbufferPass(renderEncoder: gBufferEncoder)
```

Now, to create the G-buffer fragment shader!

In the **Shaders** group, create a new file named **Gbuffer.metal** using the **Metal File** template. As usual, make sure to check both macOS and iOS targets. Then, add this code to the newly created file:

```
#import "../Utility/Common.h"

struct VertexOut {
  float4 position [[position]];
  float3 worldPosition;
  float3 worldNormal;
  float4 shadowPosition;
};

struct GbufferOut {
  float4 albedo [[color(0)]];
  float4 normal [[color(1)]];
  float4 position [[color(2)]];
};
```

VertexOut is the same as in **Main.metal**.

GbufferOut is a return from the fragment function. Instead of returning a float4 containing the color of the fragment, you'll return a color for each of the render pass descriptor attachments. That's what the [[color(i)]] attribute indicates.

Add the fragment function:

```
fragment GbufferOut gBufferFragment(VertexOut in [[stage_in]],
             depth2d<float> shadow_texture [[texture(0)]],
             constant Material &material [[buffer(1)]]) {
  GbufferOut out;
  // 1
  out.albedo = float4(material.baseColor, 1.0);
  out.albedo.a = 0;
  out.normal = float4(normalize(in.worldNormal), 1.0);
  out.position = float4(in.worldPosition, 1.0);

  // 2
  // copy from fragment_main
  float2 xy = in.shadowPosition.xy;
  xy = xy * 0.5 + 0.5;
  xy.y = 1 - xy.y;
  constexpr sampler s(coord::normalized, filter::linear,
```

```
                        address::clamp_to_edge,
                        compare_func:: less);
   float shadow_sample = shadow_texture.sample(s, xy);
   float current_sample =
         in.shadowPosition.z / in.shadowPosition.w;

   // 3
   if (current_sample > shadow_sample ) {
     out.albedo.a = 1;
   }
   return out;
}
```

Going through this code:

1. You populate the G-buffer struct for each fragment with the provided information. You're currently only using RGB values for the albedo, so you can use the alpha channel to save shadow information.

2. This is the same shadow code from `fragment_main` in **Main.metal**.

3. This sets the alpha channel for the albedo struct member to 1 for pixels that have the depth value greater than the shadow value stored in the texture. Only the pixels not supposed to be in the shadow will retain the value 0.

Build and run the project. You should see the same scene you rendered after the main pass. That's because you rendered to multiple render targets with gBufferEncoder and not to the framebuffer directly.

That said, look in the GPU Debugger and click the Gbuffer encoder group, then the Gbuffer pass group; this lets you see the four textures to which you just rendered.

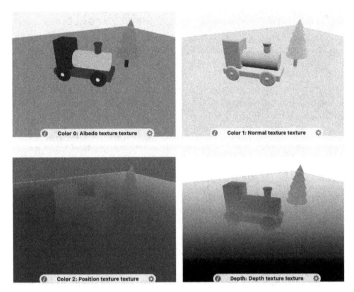

If you don't see the textures, click the **Navigate to Related items** icon at the top left of the center pane and choose **Automatic ▸ Attachments**.

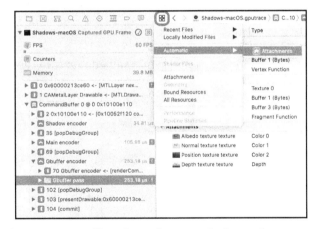

You can render these textures directly to the app window using a type of encoder called the **blit command encoder**.

The Blit Command Encoder

To blit means to copy from one part of memory to another. You use a blit command encoder on resources such as textures and buffers. It's generally used for image processing, but you can (and will) also use it to copy image data that is rendered offscreen.

In **Renderer.swift**, add this code in draw(in:) under // blit:

```
guard let blitEncoder = commandBuffer.makeBlitCommandEncoder()
else {
  return
}
blitEncoder.pushDebugGroup("Blit")
blitEncoder.label = "Blit encoder"
let origin = MTLOriginMake(0, 0, 0)
let size = MTLSizeMake(Int(view.drawableSize.width),
Int(view.drawableSize.height), 1)
blitEncoder.copy(from: albedoTexture, sourceSlice: 0,
                 sourceLevel: 0,
                 sourceOrigin: origin, sourceSize: size,
                 to: drawable.texture, destinationSlice: 0,
                 destinationLevel: 0, destinationOrigin: origin)
blitEncoder.endEncoding()
blitEncoder.popDebugGroup()
```

Here, you create a blit command encoder and copy from the albedo texture to the view's current drawable.

In init(metalView:), add this line to allow the view to render blitted textures:

```
metalView.framebufferOnly = false
```

Build and run the project, and you should see the albedo texture rendered to the window this time:

You can see how fast the blit is — it's happening every frame without a glitch. However, the holy grail of Deferred Rendering is having multiple lights in the scene, so time to work on lights next!

The Lighting pass

Up to this point, you've rendered the scene color attachments to multiple render targets, saving them for later use in the fragment shader. This assured that only the visible fragments get processed, thus reducing the amount of calculation that you would have otherwise done for all the geometry in the models in the scene.

Computing hundreds or thousands of lights would not be possible in a forward renderer while also preserving performance.

By rendering a full-screen quad, you'll render to every fragment on the screen. This allows you to process each fragment from your three textures and calculate lighting for each fragment. The results of this composition pass will end up in the view's drawable.

At the top of Renderer, declare a new render pipeline state, two quad buffers and create two arrays to hold the coordinates for the quad vertices and its texture:

```
var compositionPipelineState: MTLRenderPipelineState!

var quadVerticesBuffer: MTLBuffer!
var quadTexCoordsBuffer: MTLBuffer!

let quadVertices: [Float] = [
  -1.0,  1.0,
   1.0, -1.0,
  -1.0, -1.0,
  -1.0,  1.0,
   1.0,  1.0,
   1.0, -1.0
]

let quadTexCoords: [Float] = [
  0.0, 0.0,
  1.0, 1.0,
  0.0, 1.0,
  0.0, 0.0,
  1.0, 0.0,
  1.0, 1.0
]
```

At the end of init(metalView:), create the two quad buffers you declared above:

```
quadVerticesBuffer =
    Renderer.device.makeBuffer(bytes: quadVertices,
        length: MemoryLayout<Float>.size * quadVertices.count,
        options: [])
quadVerticesBuffer.label = "Quad vertices"
```

```
quadTexCoordsBuffer =
    Renderer.device.makeBuffer(bytes: quadTexCoords,
        length: MemoryLayout<Float>.size * quadTexCoords.count,
        options: [])
quadTexCoordsBuffer.label = "Quad texCoords"
```

At the end of Renderer, create a new function for the composition pass that will combine lights with the G-buffer information:

```
func renderCompositionPass(
                renderEncoder: MTLRenderCommandEncoder) {
    renderEncoder.pushDebugGroup("Composition pass")
    renderEncoder.label = "Composition encoder"
    renderEncoder.setRenderPipelineState(compositionPipelineState)
    renderEncoder.setDepthStencilState(depthStencilState)
    // 1
    renderEncoder.setVertexBuffer(quadVerticesBuffer,
                                  offset: 0, index: 0)
    renderEncoder.setVertexBuffer(quadTexCoordsBuffer,
                                  offset: 0, index: 1)
    // 2
    renderEncoder.setFragmentTexture(albedoTexture, index: 0)
    renderEncoder.setFragmentTexture(normalTexture, index: 1)
    renderEncoder.setFragmentTexture(positionTexture, index: 2)
    renderEncoder.setFragmentBytes(&lights,
        length: MemoryLayout<Light>.stride * lights.count,
        index: 2)
    renderEncoder.setFragmentBytes(&fragmentUniforms,
        length: MemoryLayout<FragmentUniforms>.stride,
        index: 3)
    // 3
    renderEncoder.drawPrimitives(type: .triangle,
                                 vertexStart: 0,
                                 vertexCount: quadVertices.count)
    renderEncoder.endEncoding()
    renderEncoder.popDebugGroup()
}
```

Going through this code:

1. Send the quad information to the vertex shader.

2. Send the G-buffer textures and lights array to the fragment shader.

3. Draw the quad. Notice that you're not looping through scene models anymore! :]

In draw(in:), comment out the entire block of code for both the main pass and the blit encoder (but not the g-buffer pass).

Then, add this code under `// composition pass`:

```
guard let compositionEncoder =
    commandBuffer.makeRenderCommandEncoder(
                        descriptor: descriptor) else {
  return
}
renderCompositionPass(renderEncoder: compositionEncoder)
```

Add the following method to the end of `Renderer`:

```
func buildCompositionPipelineState() {
  let descriptor = MTLRenderPipelineDescriptor()
  descriptor.colorAttachments[0].pixelFormat =
      Renderer.colorPixelFormat
  descriptor.depthAttachmentPixelFormat = .depth32Float
  descriptor.label = "Composition state"
  descriptor.vertexFunction = Renderer.library.makeFunction(
    name: "compositionVert")
  descriptor.fragmentFunction = Renderer.library.makeFunction(
    name: "compositionFrag")
  do {
    compositionPipelineState =
      try Renderer.device.makeRenderPipelineState(
          descriptor: descriptor)
  } catch let error {
    fatalError(error.localizedDescription)
  }
}
```

This create the composition pipeline state and is similar to the ones you created for the other two pipeline states. The main thing to note is the two shaders that you're going to create next.

But first, call this method at the end of `init(metalView:)`:

```
buildCompositionPipelineState()
```

Finally, you now need to create the composition shaders.

In the **Shaders** group, create a new file from the **Metal File** template named **Composition.metal** and ensure you check both iOS and macOS targets.

In your new file, create a struct to hold the processed vertices:

```
#import "../Utility/Common.h"

struct VertexOut {
  float4 position [[position]];
```

```
    float2 texCoords;
};
```

Next, create the vertex shader which assigns the proper position and texture
coordinate to each vertex:

```
vertex VertexOut compositionVert(
  constant float2 *quadVertices [[buffer(0)]],
  constant float2 *quadTexCoords [[buffer(1)]],
  uint id [[vertex_id]]) {
  VertexOut out;
  out.position = float4(quadVertices[id], 0.0, 1.0);
  out.texCoords = quadTexCoords[id];
  return out;
}
```

Finally, create the fragment shader.

First copy the entire lighting function `diffuseLighting` from **Main.metal** to
Composition.metal, and rename it `compositeLighting`.

> **Note:** In a real-world project, this would be a common function, but duplicate
> it here for convenience.

In **Composition.metal**, create a new fragment function:

```
fragment float4 compositionFrag(VertexOut in [[stage_in]],
    constant FragmentUniforms &fragmentUniforms [[buffer(3)]],
    constant Light *lightsBuffer [[buffer(2)]],
    texture2d<float> albedoTexture [[texture(0)]],
    texture2d<float> normalTexture [[texture(1)]],
    texture2d<float> positionTexture [[texture(2)]],
    depth2d<float> shadowTexture [[texture(4)]]) {
  // 1
  constexpr sampler s(min_filter::linear, mag_filter::linear);
  float4 albedo = albedoTexture.sample(s, in.texCoords);
  float3 normal = normalTexture.sample(s, in.texCoords).xyz;
  float3 position = positionTexture.sample(s, in.texCoords).xyz;
  float3 baseColor = albedo.rgb;
  // 2
  float3 diffuseColor = compositeLighting(normal, position,
                          fragmentUniforms,
                          lightsBuffer, baseColor);
  // 3
  float shadow = albedo.a;
  if (shadow > 0) {
    diffuseColor *= 0.5;
```

```
    }
    return float4(diffuseColor, 1);
  }
```

Going through this code, you:

1. Create a sampler and read in the values from the passed-in textures.

2. Call the same lighting function as you did in the main pass. This time you're
   sending values from the textures as parameters.

3. Look at the value of the albedo's alpha channel where the shadow information is,
   and if this value is non-negative, make the diffuse color darker.

Build and run the project, and you should see the same scene as you started with.

Well, that's not very exciting! But don't worry, this is where the fun begins. Because
you're now doing deferred rendering, you can load up your scene with models and
lights, and they'll all be processed more efficiently than with forward rendering.
Don't believe it? Read on…

There's a pre-defined method in **RenderExtension.swift** to create a random number
of point lights, so you'll start by adding thirty point lights to the scene.

In **Renderer.swift**, in init(metalView:), after this line:

```
  lights.append(sunlight)
```

Add the following line to create thirty lights in the scene, moderately packed near
the center of the scene:

```
  createPointLights(count: 30, min: [-3, 0.3, -3], max: [1, 2, 2])
```

This creates lots of extra light in the scene, so you can reduce the intensity of the sun. Find where you set up the property `sunlight`, and change `light.intensity` to **0.8**.

In `draw(in:)`, right before the shadow pass, add this line to rotate the train and show off those new lights and shadows:

```
models[0].rotation.y += 0.01
```

Build and run, and you'll see thirty point lights in your scene rendering — without a glitch!

So far so good, but what if you wanted to render hundreds of light instead of just a few dozen?

To render more lights, you first need to replace `setFragmentBytes(_:length:index:)` with `setFragmentBuffer(_:offset:index:)` in `renderCompositionPass(renderEncoder:)` because you're only allowed to send up to 4KB in an extemporary buffer.

Add a new buffer for lights at the top of `Renderer`:

```
var lightsBuffer: MTLBuffer!
```

At the end of `init(metalView:)`, initialize the buffer:

```
lightsBuffer = Renderer.device.makeBuffer(bytes: lights,
    length: MemoryLayout<Light>.stride * lights.count,
    options: [])
```

In `renderCompositionPass(renderEncoder:)`, replace this line:

```
renderEncoder.setFragmentBytes(&lights,
  length: MemoryLayout<Light>.stride * lights.count,
  index: 2)
```

With:

```
renderEncoder.setFragmentBuffer(lightsBuffer,
                        offset: 0, index: 2)
```

In `init(metalView:)`, update the call to `createPointLights(count:min:max:)` with the following:

```
createPointLights(count: 300, min: [-10, 0.3, -10],
                  max: [10, 2, 20])
```

This will render **300** lights instead of just 30. Build and run the project, and you'll see a lot more lights now:

What a fantastic journey through multipass rendering!

You've seen, tried and learned so much. Let's recap:

- You started with a simple shadow pass where you learned that rendering is not always from a camera's position but also possible from the light's position.

- Then, you learned about multipass rendering and how you can use a shadow map that was saved in a first pass during a second pass.

- Next, you learned what a G-buffer is and how deferred rendering works.

- You also learned how to improve your app's performance by processing lights based on the visibility of the fragments affected.

- Finally, you learned there's another type of command encoder other than the rendering one — the blit command encoder.

Where to go from here?

If you're trying to improve your app performance, you can try a few approaches. One is to render the lights as light volumes and use stencil tests to select only lights that are affecting the fragments and only render those lights instead of all.

In the next chapter, you're in for some more advanced GPU topics!

Chapter 15: GPU-Driven Rendering

By Caroline Begbie

So far, you've created an engine where you can load complex models with textures and materials, animate or update them per frame and render them. Your scenes will start to get more and more complicated as you develop your game, and you'll want to find more performant ways of doing things.

In this chapter, you'll take a simple scene and instead of organizing the render command codes on the CPU on each frame, you'll set up a list of all the commands before you even start the rendering loop. Along the way, you'll learn about argument buffers, resource heaps and indirect command buffers. Finally you'll move the command list creation to the GPU, and have a fully GPU-driven pipeline.

As you progress through the chapter, you may not see the immediate gains. However, once you've centralized your rendering at the end of the chapter, your app will have more complex initial loading, but much simpler rendering.

If you feel that you haven't spent enough time so far digging around inside buffers and examining memory, then this is the chapter for you.

> **Note:** Indirect command buffers are supported by: iOS - Apple A9 devices and up; iMacs - models from 2015; and MacBook and MacBook Pro - models from 2016. As you're going to be delving deep into using the hardware directly, much of this chapter won't work on the iOS simulator.

Argument buffers

In previous chapters, you sent up to five textures to the fragment shader - the base color, normals, roughness, metalness and ambient occlusion textures. During the frame render loop, each of these incurs a `renderEncoder.setFragmentTexture(texture:at:)` command. Using **argument buffers**, you can group five pointers to these five textures into one buffer, and set this buffer on the render command encoder with just one command. This argument buffer doesn't only have to contain textures, it can contain any other data necessary to render the frame.

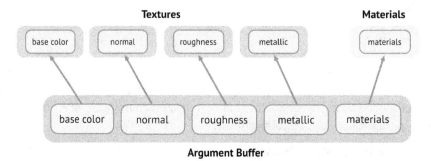

Argument Buffer

When you come to draw time, instead of setting the five fragment textures on the render command encoder, you set the single argument buffer. You then perform `renderEncoder.useResource(_:usage:)` for each texture, which places all five textures onto the GPU as **indirect resources**.

Once you've set up an argument buffer, you can refer to it in a shader, using a `struct` as a parameter to the shader function.

The starter project

With the concepts under your belt, open up the starter project for this chapter and examine the project. The project is minimal and it's not the most exciting scene, but the two models have very few vertices, and you can examine the loaded model buffers more easily. The barn has a color texture, and the grass has color and normal textures.

Model loading takes place, as usual, in Model. For simplicity, all rendering takes place in Renderer's draw(in:).

1. Model only loads one mesh and one submesh, with two textures - the color and normal. You hold the minimum objects needed to render each model:

- a pipeline state object

- a vertex buffer mesh

- an index buffer

- a color texture and optionally a normal texture

- model parameters - a model matrix and tiling for the fragment textures

2. Uniforms are split up between per-frame constants, being the projection and view matrix, and per-model constants, being the model matrix and tiling. You'll see the reason for this later in the chapter.

3. The focus of this chapter will be shader function parameters and data passed to the GPU. As a result, the bodies of the two shader functions in Shaders.metal are extremely simple. The normal texture is not used in the fragment shader - it's included simply as illustration of the concept of passing multiple textures.

In **Shaders.metal**, the fragment function has two parameters for textures. You're going to combine both of these into one struct, and use the struct as the parameter.

Create the struct

Combine both textures into a new struct. Add this before fragment_main:

```
struct Textures {
  texture2d<float> baseColorTexture;
```

```
    texture2d<float> normalTexture;
};
```

This struct currently holds only two textures, but could be a list of all the textures you need for rendering the model, including roughness, metallic, etc. It could also include other data buffers such as materials.

You can now replace the two textures in the fragment function header with a parameter that points to this struct. Replace:

```
texture2d<float> baseColorTexture [[texture(BaseColorTexture)]],
texture2d<float> normalTexture [[texture(NormalTexture)]],
```

With:

```
constant Textures &textures [[buffer(BufferIndexTextures)]],
```

Instead of receiving the textures directly, you'll just receive one struct containing all the textures needed for the model.

Change the assignment to baseColor to:

```
float3 baseColor =
  textures.baseColorTexture.sample(textureSampler,
                        in.uv * modelParams.tiling).rgb;
```

Create the argument buffer

To pass these textures, you create an **argument buffer** that matches the struct.

Open **Model.swift** and add a new argument buffer property:

```
var texturesBuffer: MTLBuffer!
```

This is a simple MTLBuffer which will contain pointers to the textures. In this chapter, for brevity's sake, you'll use implicitly unwrapped optionals on all of your buffers. In a real world app, you should include error checking.

Create a new method to create the argument buffer. You're creating it in a method so that it's easier to change the code later in the chapter.

```
func initializeTextures() {
  // 1
  let textureEncoder = fragmentFunction.makeArgumentEncoder(
    bufferIndex: Int(BufferIndexTextures.rawValue))
```

```
  // 2
  texturesBuffer =
    Renderer.device.makeBuffer(
            length: textureEncoder.encodedLength,
            options: [])!
  texturesBuffer.label = "Textures"
  //3
  textureEncoder.setArgumentBuffer(texturesBuffer, offset: 0)
  textureEncoder.setTexture(colorTexture, index: 0)
  if let normalTexture = normalTexture {
    textureEncoder.setTexture(normalTexture, index: 1)
  }
}
```

Going through the code:

1. `init(name:)` initializes `fragmentFunction` with the Metal library function `fragment_main`. You create a texture encoder using this fragment function and use the same buffer index that you used for your `textures` struct in `fragment_main`. The encoder refers to this argument and can work out how many elements there are in the struct, and therefore how long the length of the new argument buffer should be.

2. Create an `MTLBuffer` of the texture encoder's length. With the added complexity that you'll have with many buffers, it's sensible to label each buffer as you create it.

3. Set the argument buffer and the textures on the texture encoder. During the render loop, setting the textures on the render command encoder incurs some internal verifying of the textures. This verifying will now take place here, when the textures are initially set into the texture encoder. Anything you can move outside of the render loop is a gain.

In `init(name:)`, call this method after `super.init()` to initialize the argument buffer:

```
initializeTextures()
```

You've now set up two textures into an argument buffer. Instead of sending the textures to the fragment shader during the render loop, you'll send this single argument buffer.

The draw call

In **Renderer.swift**, in draw(in:), change:

```
renderEncoder.setFragmentTexture(model.colorTexture,
                    index: Int(BaseColorTexture.rawValue))
renderEncoder.setFragmentTexture(model.normalTexture,
                    index: Int(NormalTexture.rawValue))
```

To:

```
renderEncoder.setFragmentBuffer(model.texturesBuffer,
                    offset: 0,
                    index: Int(BufferIndexTextures.rawValue))
```

Here you send the textures argument buffer to the GPU. BufferIndexTextures is the index that links the argument buffer between the render encoder and the fragment function.

Build and run. The render may look exactly the same as before, although on the iPhone, you will probably receive many errors. Click the Capture GPU frame icon, and take a look behind the scenes. The result of the capture will resemble this:

It may not be an exact replica, because when you have GPU memory errors, weird things can happen on the display. Debugging GPU errors can be frustrating when your display locks up because you have accessed memory that you're not supposed to.

With the second draw call under plane.obj selected, choose **Automatic ▸ Attachments** from the top left navigator icon. You'll see that the textures aren't rendered correctly. Choose **Bound Resources** to show the list of resources currently on the GPU.

The following image shows Bound Resources on the left and Attachments on the right.

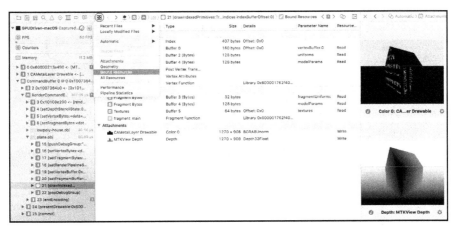

Under **Fragment**, double click the **Textures** buffer. `Textures` is the name of the label that you set on your model's argument buffer. You'll see that neither of these textures is a valid texture.

You've set up a level of indirection with the argument buffer pointing to the textures, but you still have to tell the GPU to *load* these textures. When dealing with indirection and buffer data, it's often easy to omit this vital step, so if you have errors at any time, check in the GPU debugger that the resource is available in the indirect resource list, but also check that you are using the resource in the render command encoder command list.

Back in **Renderer.swift**, under the previous code where you set the textures argument buffer, add this:

```
if let colorTexture = model.colorTexture {
  renderEncoder.useResource(colorTexture, usage: .read)
}
if let normalTexture = model.normalTexture {
  renderEncoder.useResource(normalTexture, usage: .read)
}
```

This tells the GPU that you're going to read from these textures. Build and run again, and in the GPU debugger, check that the Textures buffer now points to the textures:

You'll also see that your textures are listed under **Indirect Resources**, and are available for any shader function to use:

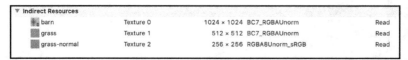

You've now set up your app to use argument buffers for the textures instead of sending them individually. This may not feel like a win yet, and you've increased overhead by adding a new buffer. But you've reduced overhead on the render command encoder. Instead of having to validate the textures each frame, the textures are validated when they are first placed into the argument buffer, while you're still initializing your app data. In addition to this, you're grouping your textures together into the one struct, and the one parameter to the fragment function. If you have many parameters that you can group together, this will save time too.

Resource heaps

You've grouped textures into an argument buffer, but you can also combine all your app's textures into a resource **heap**.

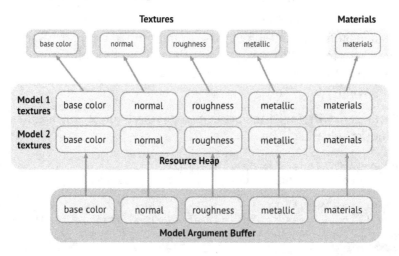

A resource heap is simply an area of memory where you bundle resources. These can be textures or data buffers. To make your textures available on the GPU, instead of having to perform `renderEncoder.useResource(_:usage:)` for every single texture, you can perform `renderEncoder.useHeap(_:)` once per frame instead. That's one step further in the quest for reducing render commands.

You're going to create a `TextureController` which takes care of all your app's textures and the texture heap.

> **Note:** For simplicity, you'll create `TextureController` as a singleton, but you could easily hold it as an instance per scene in a larger app. As an added feature of centralizing textures into the texture controller, there's a performance improvement. You may have previously loaded some of Apple's usdz sample models from https://developer.apple.com/augmented-reality/quick-look/. These are split up into many submeshes, and so far, the engine code loads one texture per submesh. As a result, each of the sample models takes up a huge amount of memory. You could create a method that checks whether `Texture Controller` already holds a texture, and so load a texture only once, no matter how many submeshes refer to it.

Create a new Swift file called **TextureController.swift**. Don't forget to add it to both the iOS and macOS targets. Replace the code with:

```
import MetalKit

class TextureController {
  static var textures: [MTLTexture] = []
}
```

`TextureController` will round up all the textures used by your models and hold them in an array. `Model`, instead of holding a reference to a texture, will hold an index into this texture array.

Add a new method to `TextureController`:

```
static func addTexture(texture: MTLTexture?) -> Int? {
  guard let texture = texture else { return nil }
  TextureController.textures.append(texture)
  return TextureController.textures.count - 1
}
```

Here, you receive a texture, add it to the central texture array and return an index to the texture.

In **Model.swift**, change:

```
let colorTexture: MTLTexture?
let normalTexture: MTLTexture?
```

To:

```
let colorTexture: Int?
let normalTexture: Int?
```

Instead of holding the texture on Model, you'll hold the index to the texture held in TextureController's textures array. Your code won't compile until you've changed all the places where you refer to these textures.

In init(name:), replace:

```
colorTexture = textures.baseColor
normalTexture = textures.normal
```

With:

```
colorTexture =
    TextureController.addTexture(texture: textures.baseColor)
normalTexture =
    TextureController.addTexture(texture: textures.normal)
```

Also, in initializeTextures(), update the argument buffer code that doesn't compile, to reference the correct textures:

```
if let index = colorTexture {
  textureEncoder.setTexture(TextureController.textures[index],
                            index: 0)
}
if let index = normalTexture {
  textureEncoder.setTexture(TextureController.textures[index],
                            index: 1)
}
```

In **Renderer.swift**, in draw(in:), change:

```
if let colorTexture = model.colorTexture {
  renderEncoder.useResource(colorTexture, usage: .read)
}
if let normalTexture = model.normalTexture {
  renderEncoder.useResource(normalTexture, usage: .read)
}
```

To:

```
if let index = model.colorTexture {
  renderEncoder.useResource(TextureController.textures[index],
                            usage: .read)
}
```

```
if let index = model.normalTexture {
   renderEncoder.useResource(TextureController.textures[index],
                             usage: .read)
}
```

Your code should compile again, so build and run to make sure everything still works. Your textures should render, only now they are all held centrally in `TextureController`. In this app, there's no performance gain here, but if you use this technique on models that have many submeshes accessing the same texture, it will be a huge memory usage reduction.

This modification means that instead of sending a texture to the GPU per model, you're ready to gather up all the textures into a heap and move the whole heap at one time to the GPU.

In `TextureController`, create a new property:

```
static var heap: MTLHeap?
```

Create a new type method to build the heap:

```
static func buildHeap() -> MTLHeap? {
   let heapDescriptor = MTLHeapDescriptor()

   // add code here

   guard let heap =
       Renderer.device.makeHeap(descriptor: heapDescriptor)
     else { fatalError() }
   return heap
}
```

You build a heap from a heap descriptor. This descriptor will need to know the size of all the textures. Unfortunately `MTLTexture` doesn't hold that information, but you can retrieve the size of a texture from a texture descriptor.

In **Extensions.swift**, there's an extension on `MTLTextureDescriptor` that will provide a descriptor based on an `MTLTexture`.

In **TextureController.swift**, in `buildHeap()`, add this under `// add code here`

```
let descriptors = textures.map { texture in
   MTLTextureDescriptor.descriptor(from: texture)
}
```

Here, you create an array of texture descriptors to match the array of textures. Now you can add up the size of all these descriptors. Following on from the previous code, add this:

```
let sizeAndAligns = descriptors.map {
  Renderer.device.heapTextureSizeAndAlign(descriptor: $0)
}
heapDescriptor.size = sizeAndAligns.reduce(0) {
  $0 + $1.size - ($1.size & ($1.align - 1)) + $1.align
}
if heapDescriptor.size == 0 {
  return nil
}
```

Here you calculate the size of the heap using size and correct alignment within the heap. As long as `align` is a power of two, `(size & (align - 1))` will give you the remainder when size is divided by alignment. For example, if you have a size of 129 bytes, and you want to align it to memory blocks of 128 bytes, this is the result of `$1.size - ($1.size & ($1.align - 1)) + $1.align`:

```
129 - (129 & (128 - 1)) + 128 = 256
```

This result shows that if you want to align blocks to 128, you'll need a 256 byte block to fit 129 bytes.

You have an empty heap, but you need to populate it with the textures. You'll iterate through the texture array and create a new array of textures that you'll store in the heap. For each texture you'll create a new texture resource and then copy the original texture contents to the new resource using a blit command encoder.

At the end of the method, but before the return, add this:

```
let heapTextures = descriptors.map { descriptor -> MTLTexture in
  descriptor.storageMode = heapDescriptor.storageMode
  return heap.makeTexture(descriptor: descriptor)!
}
```

Here you create an array of new texture resources using the texture descriptors. These are empty texture resources, so you need to copy the model texture information to the heap texture resources.

Add this to create a blit command encoder:

```
guard
  let commandBuffer = Renderer.commandQueue.makeCommandBuffer(),
  let blitEncoder = commandBuffer.makeBlitCommandEncoder()
```

```
  else {
    fatalError()
  }
```

You've used the blit command encoder to do fast copies of memory several times previously. You'll copy each texture to the heap texture. Add this code to do the copy:

```
zip(textures, heapTextures).forEach { (texture, heapTexture) in
  var region = MTLRegionMake2D(0, 0, texture.width,
                                     texture.height)
  for level in 0..<texture.mipmapLevelCount {
    for slice in 0..<texture.arrayLength {
      blitEncoder.copy(from: texture,
                  sourceSlice: slice,
                  sourceLevel: level,
                  sourceOrigin: region.origin,
                  sourceSize: region.size,
                  to: heapTexture,
                  destinationSlice: slice,
                  destinationLevel: level,
                  destinationOrigin: region.origin)
    }
    region.size.width /= 2
    region.size.height /= 2
  }
}
```

Here you copy each texture to a heap texture. Within each texture, you copy each level and slice. Levels contain the texture mipmaps, which is why you halve the region each loop, and slices will contain texture arrays, if there are any.

Before returning the heap from the method, add the following:

```
blitEncoder.endEncoding()
commandBuffer.commit()
TextureController.textures = heapTextures
```

This ends the encoding, commits the command buffer and replaces the original textures with the heap textures. Models will now point to a heap texture with their texture index, instead of to the original texture. The models' texture argument buffers, however, point to textures that no longer exist. You'll fix that up in a moment.

You've created a class method to create the heap. To use this method, open **Renderer.swift**. Create a new method to initialize the heap. You'll add other initializations to this method shortly.

```
func initialize() {
```

```
    TextureController.heap = TextureController.buildHeap()
}
```

Call this new method at the end of `init(metalView:)`

```
initialize()
```

Now you've created a texture controller, and centralized the texture allocations.
Before rendering any models, you can send the textures to the GPU at the start of the
frame to be all ready and waiting for processing.

In `draw(in:)`, remove:

```
if let index = model.colorTexture {
  renderEncoder.useResource(TextureController.textures[index],
                            usage: .read)
}
if let index = model.normalTexture {
  renderEncoder.useResource(TextureController.textures[index],
                            usage: .read)
}
```

At the top of `draw(in:)`, after setting the depth stencil state on the render command
encoder, add this:

```
if let heap = TextureController.heap {
  renderEncoder.useHeap(heap)
}
```

Instead of having a `useResource` command for every texture, you perform one
`useHeap` every frame. This could be a huge saving on the number of commands in a
render command encoder, and so a reduction of the number of commands that a GPU
has to process each frame.

The models' argument buffers are still pointing to the old texture, and not the new
heap texture, so you need to re-initialize the argument buffers.

Still in **Renderer.swift**, at the end of `initialize()`, add this:

```
models.forEach { model in
  model.initializeTextures()
}
```

This will call the method you wrote earlier to create the argument buffer and set the
textures. In **Model.swift**, remove `initializeTextures()` from the end of
`init(name:)`.

Build and run, and your render should be exactly the same as it was.

Take a look at the GPU debugger via the Capture GPU frame button.

Under `CommandBuffer` \ `RenderCommandEncoder`, select the `useHeap` command that you set at the start of the frame. Select **Bound Resources** using the navigator icon at the top left of the pane. The three textures in the heap are at this point available in Indirect Resources for any draw call to use. There's one color texture for the barn, and a color and normal texture for the grass.

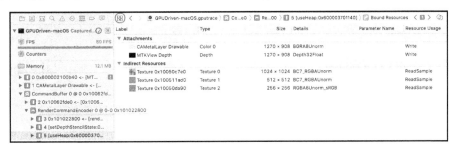

Locate the `drawIndexedPrimitives` command under `plane.obj`, and, in the Bound Resources, under **Fragment**, locate `Textures`. Double click `Textures`, and you'll see a pointer to the `grass` texture. Click on the arrow, and it will show you the texture. As before, you can check the mipmaps at the bottom left of that pane.

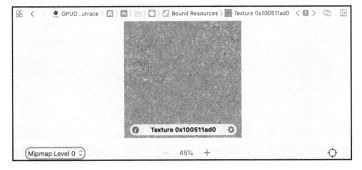

You've now separated out your textures from your rendering code, with a level of indirection via the argument buffer. But have you seen any performance improvement? In this example, probably not. But the more textures you load, the better the improvement, as there will be fewer render commands.

In addition, your app is more flexible and you can schedule more complicated events, which will have an overall impact on performance.

Indirect Command Buffers

You've created several levels of indirection with your textures by using an argument buffer and a heap, but you can also create indirection with commands on command encoders.

At the start of this chapter, your rendering process was this:

You loaded all the model data, materials and pipeline states at the start of the app. Each frame, you created a render command encoder and issued commands to that encoder, ending with a draw call.

But instead of creating these commands per frame, you can create them all at the start of the app using an **indirect command buffer** with a list of commands. You'll set up each command with pointers to the relevant uniform, texture and vertex buffers, and specify how to do the draw.

With that one initialization process, at the start of the app, to set up the per-frame command list, during the render loop, you can just issue one execute command to the render command encoder, and the encoder will send the list of commands, all at once, off to the GPU.

Your process will then look like this:

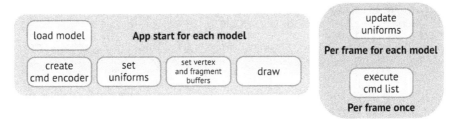

Remember that your aim is to do as much as you can when your app first loads, and as little as you have to per frame. To achieve this, you'll:

1. Place all your uniform data in buffers. As the indirect commands need to point to buffers at the start of the app, you can't send ad hoc bytes to the GPU. You can still update the buffers each frame. For the model constants containing the model matrix for the model, you'll hold an array of model constants and update the model matrices for all models at the start of each frame.

2. Set up an Indirect Command Buffer. This buffer will hold all the draw commands.

3. Loop through the models and set up the indirect commands.

4. Clean up the render loop and use the resources you referred to in the indirect commands to send them to the GPU.

5. Change the shader functions to use the array of model constants.

6. Execute the command list.

1. Uniform buffers

In **Renderer.swift**, create three new properties to hold the uniforms and model constants in buffers:

```
var uniformsBuffer: MTLBuffer!
var fragmentUniformsBuffer: MTLBuffer!
var modelParamsBuffer: MTLBuffer!
```

Add this at the end of `initialize()`:

```
var bufferLength = MemoryLayout<Uniforms>.stride
uniformsBuffer =
  Renderer.device.makeBuffer(length: bufferLength, options: [])
uniformsBuffer.label = "Uniforms"
bufferLength = MemoryLayout<FragmentUniforms>.stride
```

```
fragmentUniformsBuffer =
  Renderer.device.makeBuffer(length: bufferLength, options: [])
fragmentUniformsBuffer.label = "Fragment Uniforms"
bufferLength = models.count * MemoryLayout<ModelParams>.stride
modelParamsBuffer =
  Renderer.device.makeBuffer(length: bufferLength, options: [])
modelParamsBuffer.label = "Model Parameters"
```

Here, you set up three empty buffers ready to take the uniform data. draw(in:) calls updateUniforms() at the start of each frame, and that's where you'll update the contents of these buffers.

Add this code to the end of updateUniforms().

```
// 1
var bufferLength = MemoryLayout<Uniforms>.stride
uniformsBuffer.contents().copyMemory(from: &uniforms,
                                     byteCount: bufferLength)
bufferLength = MemoryLayout<FragmentUniforms>.stride
fragmentUniformsBuffer.contents().copyMemory(
            from: &fragmentUniforms,
            byteCount: bufferLength)

// 2
var pointer =
  modelParamsBuffer.contents().bindMemory(to: ModelParams.self,
                                          capacity: models.count)
// 3
for model in models {
  pointer.pointee.modelMatrix = model.modelMatrix
  pointer.pointee.tiling = model.tiling
  pointer = pointer.advanced(by: 1)
}
```

Going through this code:

1. You copy the uniforms and fragment uniforms data from the struct to the MTLBuffers.

2. For the model data, you'll need to iterate through the models to get each model matrix, so you bind a pointer to the buffer.

3. Iterate through the models and fill the buffer.

2. Indirect command buffer

You're now ready to create some indirect commands. Take a look at `draw(in:)` to refresh your memory on all the render commands that you set in the rendering `for` loop. You're going to move all these commands to an indirect command list. You'll set up this command list at the start of the app, and simply call `executeCommandsInBuffer` on the render command encoder each frame. This will execute the entire command list with just that one command.

At the top of `Renderer`, create a property for the Indirect Command Buffer (**ICB**).

```
var icb: MTLIndirectCommandBuffer!
```

Create a new method where you'll build up the command list in an indirect command buffer:

```
func initializeCommands() {
  let icbDescriptor = MTLIndirectCommandBufferDescriptor()
  icbDescriptor.commandTypes = [.drawIndexed]
  icbDescriptor.inheritBuffers = false
  icbDescriptor.maxVertexBufferBindCount = 25
  icbDescriptor.maxFragmentBufferBindCount = 25
  icbDescriptor.inheritPipelineState = false
}
```

Here you create an Indirect Command Buffer descriptor. You specify that (eventually) the GPU should expect an indexed draw call. That's a draw call that uses an index buffer for indexing into the vertices. You set the maximum number of buffers that the ICB can bind to in the vertex and fragment shader parameters to 25. This is far too many, but it's somewhere to start.

You set `inheritPipelineState` to false. In simple apps, like this one, that only use one vertex shader and one fragment shader, you could set one pipeline state at the start of the frame. In that case you'd set `inheritPipelineState` to true. In this app, though, you'll find out how to set a different pipeline state for each draw call, so you won't be inheriting a pipeline state.

Following on from that code, create the indirect command buffer:

```
guard let icb =
  Renderer.device.makeIndirectCommandBuffer(
    descriptor: icbDescriptor,
    maxCommandCount: models.count,
    options: [])
  else { fatalError() }
self.icb = icb
```

The ICB will need one command per draw call. In this app, you're only performing one draw call per model, but in a more complex app where you're doing a draw call for every submesh, you'd have to iterate through the models prior to setting up the ICB to find out how many draw calls you'll do.

3. Indirect commands

Now that you've set up an indirect command buffer, you'll add the list of commands to it. Add this to `initializeCommands()`

```
for (modelIndex, model) in models.enumerated() {
  let icbCommand = icb.indirectRenderCommandAt(modelIndex)
  icbCommand.setRenderPipelineState(model.pipelineState)
  icbCommand.setVertexBuffer(uniformsBuffer, offset: 0,
    at: Int(BufferIndexUniforms.rawValue))
  icbCommand.setFragmentBuffer(fragmentUniformsBuffer,
    offset: 0,
    at: Int(BufferIndexFragmentUniforms.rawValue))
  icbCommand.setVertexBuffer(modelParamsBuffer, offset: 0,
    at: Int(BufferIndexModelParams.rawValue))
  icbCommand.setFragmentBuffer(modelParamsBuffer, offset: 0,
    at: Int(BufferIndexModelParams.rawValue))

  icbCommand.setVertexBuffer(model.vertexBuffer, offset: 0,
    at: Int(BufferIndexVertices.rawValue))
  icbCommand.setFragmentBuffer(model.texturesBuffer, offset: 0,
    at: Int(BufferIndexTextures.rawValue))
}
```

This may look familiar to you from the render loop in `draw(in:)`. You use the model index to keep track of the command list, and you set all the necessary data for each draw call.

The one thing missing is the actual draw call. Add this to the end of the `for` loop:

```
icbCommand.drawIndexedPrimitives(.triangle,
  indexCount: model.submesh.indexCount,
  indexType: model.submesh.indexType,
  indexBuffer: model.submesh.indexBuffer.buffer,
  indexBufferOffset: model.submesh.indexBuffer.offset,
  instanceCount: 1,
  baseVertex: 0,
  baseInstance: modelIndex)
```

This draw command is very similar to the one that you've already been using. There are a couple of extra arguments:

• `baseVertex` - the vertex in the vertex buffer to start rendering from.

- `baseInstance` - the instance to start rendering from. You have set up an array of `modelParams`, one for each model. Using `baseInstance`, in the shader, you can index into the array to get the correct element.

The command list is now complete. Call this method at the end of `init(metalView:)`:

```
initializeCommands()
```

4. Update the render loop

You can now remove most of the render encoder commands from `draw(in:)`. Remove all the code after setting the heap down to, but not including, `renderEncoder.endEncoding()`.

`draw(in:)` should look like this:

```
func draw(in view: MTKView) {
  guard
    let descriptor = view.currentRenderPassDescriptor,
    let commandBuffer =
      Renderer.commandQueue.makeCommandBuffer() else {
      return
  }

  updateUniforms()
  guard let renderEncoder =
  commandBuffer.makeRenderCommandEncoder(descriptor: descriptor)
      else { return }
  renderEncoder.setDepthStencilState(depthStencilState)
  if let heap = TextureController.heap {
    renderEncoder.useHeap(heap)
  }

  renderEncoder.endEncoding()
  guard let drawable = view.currentDrawable else {
    return
  }
  commandBuffer.present(drawable)
  commandBuffer.commit()
}
```

Build and run to make sure that your app still works after all this time. As you only create the command list but don't execute it, you should expect to see just a clear blue sky. However, there's an error:

```
failed assertion `Setting a pipeline that does not have
supportIndirectCommandBuffers = YES is invalid'
```

When you use a pipeline state in an indirect command list, you have to tell it that it should support indirect command buffers. Open **Model.swift**, and, in `buildPipelineState(vertexFunction:fragmentFunction:)`, add this before do:

```
pipelineDescriptor.supportIndirectCommandBuffers = true
```

Build and run again, and you should get a plain clear background.

So much potential

Currently none of your resources are making their way to the GPU. To fix this, open **Renderer.swift**. In `draw(in:)`, before `renderEncoder.endEncoding()`, add this:

```
renderEncoder.useResource(uniformsBuffer, usage: .read)
renderEncoder.useResource(fragmentUniformsBuffer, usage: .read)
renderEncoder.useResource(modelParamsBuffer, usage: .read)
for model in models {
  renderEncoder.useResource(model.vertexBuffer, usage: .read)
  renderEncoder.useResource(model.submesh.indexBuffer.buffer,
                            usage: .read)
  renderEncoder.useResource(model.texturesBuffer, usage: .read)
}
```

These will move each model's buffers to the GPU as indirect resources ready for the GPU to access.

5. Update the shader functions

Both `vertex_main` and `fragment_main` use `modelParams`, which holds each model's matrix and the tiling of textures for the model. You've changed the single instance of `modelParams` to be an array, so now you'll change the shader functions to match the incoming buffers and access the correct element in the model parameters array.

Open **Shaders.metal**. In `vertex_main`, change:

```
constant ModelParams &modelParams
[[buffer(BufferIndexModelParams)]]
```

To:

```
constant ModelParams *modelParamsArray
                [[buffer(BufferIndexModelParams)]],
uint baseInstance [[base_instance]]
```

Here you change the parameter to receive an array in the buffer, and also receive the model index using the `base_instance` attribute. This matches the `baseInstance` parameter in the draw call.

At the start of `vertex_main`, add this to get the parameters for the current model:

```
ModelParams modelParams = modelParamsArray[baseInstance];
```

To pass the model index to the fragment function, add this to `VertexOut`:

```
uint modelIndex [[flat]];
```

The `[[flat]]` attribute ensures that the value won't be interpolated between the vertex and fragment function.

In `vertex_main`, add the model index to the `VertexOut` `out` assignment:

```
.modelIndex = baseInstance
```

That's dealt with the vertex function, now for the fragment function. As you did before, replace:

```
constant ModelParams &modelParams
[[buffer(BufferIndexModelParams)]]
```

With:

```
constant ModelParams *modelParamsArray
[[buffer(BufferIndexModelParams)]]
```

Add this to the start of the fragment_main:

```
ModelParams modelParams = modelParamsArray[in.modelIndex];
```

That's fixed up the shader functions so that they'll read an array of parameters instead of a single instance.

6. Execute the command list

All the code you have written in this chapter so far has been building up to one command. Drum roll....

In **Renderer.swift**, in draw(in:), add this before renderEncoder.endEncoding:

```
renderEncoder.executeCommandsInBuffer(icb,
                                      range: 0..<models.count)
```

This will execute all the commands in the indirect command buffer's list within the range specified here. If you specify a range of 0..<1, then only the first draw call would be performed.

Build and run, and you should get the same render as at the start of the chapter. Very little is happening in your render loop, and all the heavy lifting is done at the very start of the app. Success :].

As before, examine everything in the GPU Debugger, and make sure you understand what's happening. At the bottom of the Bound Resources, you'll see the Indirect Command Buffer. Double click this to see the two commands listed, one for each model.

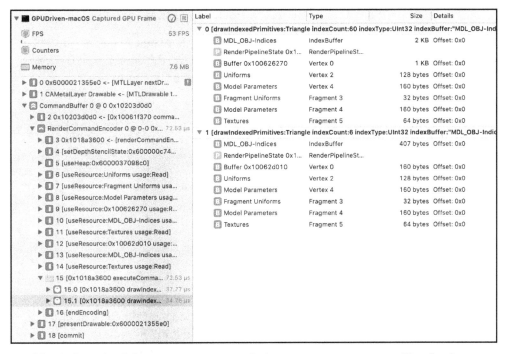

Double click each of the resources to see their contents. `Textures` will only show floats. It's not until it's received into `fragment_main` that the debugger formats it into the `Textures` struct.

> **Note:** to see the debugger, you may have to run the app on macOS. It doesn't always work on devices.

GPU driven rendering

You've achieved indirect CPU rendering, by setting up a command list and rendering it. However, you can go one better, and get the GPU to create this command list. Open **Renderer.swift** and take a look at the for loop in initializeCommands().

This for loop executes serially on the CPU, but is one that you can easily parallelize. Each command executes one after another, but by moving this loop to the GPU, you can create each command at the same time over multiple GPU cores.

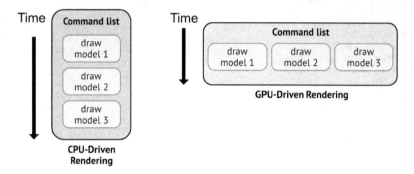

When you come to write real-world apps, setting up the render loop at the very start of the app is impractical. In each frame you'll be determining which models to render. Are the models in front of the camera? Is the model occluded by another model? Should you render a model with lower level of detail? By creating the command list every frame, you have complete flexibility in which models you should render, and which you should ignore. As you'll see, the GPU is amazingly fast at creating these render command lists, so you can include this process each frame.

In Chapter 16, "Particle Systems", you're going to learn all about compute programming, or GPGPU (general purpose GPU programming). But you're going to have a gentle preview in this chapter. Compute is very good at performing multi-threaded tasks in parallel. You may not understand yet how it all works, but all you need to know in this chapter is that you'll perform a compute shader function using one thread for each model.

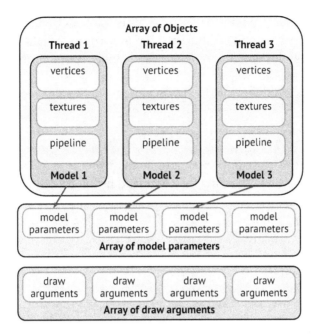

This compute shader function is very similar to the vertex and fragment function in that you set up a pipeline state pointing to the compute function. You set buffers on a compute command encoder, just as you do on a render command encoder, to pass data to the compute function. The compute function will need all the data that you used during the `initializeCommands()` for loop:

* uniform and model parameter buffers

* the indirect command buffer

For the models' vertex buffers and textures, you'll create a `Model` struct for the compute function in Metal, and an argument buffer in Swift, containing, for each model:

* the vertex buffer

* the index buffer

* the texture argument buffer

* the pipeline state

You'll set up an array of `Model`s in one single buffer and pass this to the compute function.

There's one more array you'll need to send. This is the draw arguments for each model. Each model's draw call is different from every other. You have to specify, for example, what the index buffer is and what is the index count. Fortunately Apple have created a format that you can use for this, called `MTLDrawIndexedPrimitivesIndirectArguments`. That's some mouthful!

Compute shader function

You'll start by creating the compute shader, so that you can see what data you have to pass. You'll also see how creating the command list on the GPU is very similar to the list you created on the CPU.

Create a new Metal file called **ICB.metal**. Remember to add it to both the iOS and macOS targets.

Add the following code:

```
#import "Common.h"

struct ICBContainer {
  command_buffer icb [[id(0)]];
};

struct Model {
  constant float *vertexBuffer;
  constant uint *indexBuffer;
  constant float *texturesBuffer;
  render_pipeline_state pipelineState;
};
```

Here you set up a struct to hold the indirect command buffer. On the Swift side, you'll create an argument buffer to hold the ICB. You also create a struct for the model. This holds all the necessary data for the model's draw call. Note that you can use `[[id(n)]]` to assign a custom index number. In `Model`, the index numbers will run from 0 to 3.

Create the compute shader function:

```
kernel void encodeCommands(
  uint modelIndex [[thread_position_in_grid]],
  constant Uniforms &uniforms [[buffer(BufferIndexUniforms)]],
  constant FragmentUniforms &fragmentUniforms
    [[buffer(BufferIndexFragmentUniforms)]],
  constant MTLDrawIndexedPrimitivesIndirectArguments
    *drawArgumentsBuffer [[buffer(BufferIndexDrawArguments)]],
  constant ModelParams *modelParamsArray
    [[buffer(BufferIndexModelParams)]],
```

```
    constant Model *modelsArray [[buffer(BufferIndexModels)]],
    device ICBContainer *icbContainer [[buffer(BufferIndexICB)]])
{
}
```

Notice the keyword `kernel`. This sets it apart from `vertex` and `fragment` shader functions. Each GPU thread will process one model, and you get the model's index from the thread position. You receive the uniform buffers just as you did in a vertex function. You also set an array for the draw arguments, the model constants and the models. Lastly, you receive the ICB in `device` space, which allows you to write to it within the shader function.

In `encodeCommands`, first extract the elements from the arrays using the model index:

```
Model model = modelsArray[modelIndex];
MTLDrawIndexedPrimitivesIndirectArguments drawArguments
  = drawArgumentsBuffer[modelIndex];
render_command cmd(icbContainer->icb, modelIndex);
```

Here you extract the model and the model's draw arguments for its draw call. You also get an indirect render command object from the ICB, using the model's index.

Set all the buffers for the command:

```
cmd.set_render_pipeline_state(model.pipelineState);
cmd.set_vertex_buffer(&uniforms, BufferIndexUniforms);
cmd.set_fragment_buffer(&fragmentUniforms,
                        BufferIndexFragmentUniforms);
cmd.set_vertex_buffer(modelParamsArray, BufferIndexModelParams);
cmd.set_fragment_buffer(modelParamsArray,
                        BufferIndexModelParams);
cmd.set_vertex_buffer(model.vertexBuffer, 0);
cmd.set_fragment_buffer(model.texturesBuffer,
                        BufferIndexTextures);
```

This looks very similar to your original render loop. You set the model's pipeline state, the uniforms, the vertex buffer and the textures buffer on the render command object.

Next you encode the draw call using the draw arguments:

```
cmd.draw_indexed_primitives(
  primitive_type::triangle,
  drawArguments.indexCount,
  model.indexBuffer + drawArguments.indexStart,
  drawArguments.instanceCount,
```

```
    drawArguments.baseVertex,
    drawArguments.baseInstance);
```

This draw command is almost exactly the same as the one on the Swift side, minus the argument labels.

You've now encoded a complete draw call, and that's all that's required for the compute function. Your next task is to set up the compute function on the CPU side, with a compute pipeline state and pass all the data to the compute function.

> **Note:** You're not performing any extra logic here to see whether the model should be rendered this frame. But if you determine that the model shouldn't be rendered, instead of doing a draw call, you'd create an empty command with cmd.reset().

The compute pipeline state

In **Renderer.swift**, create these new properties:

```
let icbPipelineState: MTLComputePipelineState
let icbComputeFunction: MTLFunction
```

You'll need a new compute pipeline state which uses the compute function you just created.

Create a new type method to build the pipeline state:

```
static func buildComputePipelineState(function: MTLFunction) ->
  MTLComputePipelineState {
  let computePipelineState: MTLComputePipelineState
  do {
    computePipelineState = try
      Renderer.device.makeComputePipelineState(
                function: function)
  } catch {
    fatalError(error.localizedDescription)
  }
  return computePipelineState
}
```

In init(metalView:), before calling super.init(), add this:

```
icbComputeFunction =
  Renderer.library.makeFunction(name: "encodeCommands")!
```

```
icbPipelineState =
  Renderer.buildComputePipelineState(function:
icbComputeFunction)
```

This creates the compute function in the Metal library, and also the compute pipeline state.

The argument buffers

In the compute shader, you created two structs — one for the ICB, and one for the model. In Renderer, create two buffer properties for the argument buffers to match these structs:

```
var icbBuffer: MTLBuffer!
var modelsBuffer: MTLBuffer!
```

In initializeCommands(), remove the for loop. You're going to be creating the commands on the GPU each frame now.

Add this code at the end of initializeCommands():

```
let icbEncoder = icbComputeFunction.makeArgumentEncoder(
                bufferIndex: Int(BufferIndexICB.rawValue))
icbBuffer = Renderer.device.makeBuffer(
            length: icbEncoder.encodedLength,
            options: [])
icbEncoder.setArgumentBuffer(icbBuffer, offset: 0)
icbEncoder.setIndirectCommandBuffer(icb, index: 0)
```

Just as you did in the first part of this chapter, you create an argument encoder for the compute function, and assign an argument buffer, that will contain the command list, to the encoder. You also set the indirect command buffer.

You'll now create an argument buffer for each model and hold it in an array. Add this, following on from the previous code:

```
var mBuffers: [MTLBuffer] = []
var mBuffersLength = 0
for model in models {
  let encoder = icbComputeFunction.makeArgumentEncoder(
                bufferIndex: Int(BufferIndexModels.rawValue))
  let mBuffer = Renderer.device.makeBuffer(
                length: encoder.encodedLength, options: [])!
  encoder.setArgumentBuffer(mBuffer, offset: 0)
  encoder.setBuffer(model.vertexBuffer, offset: 0, index: 0)
  encoder.setBuffer(model.submesh.indexBuffer.buffer,
                offset: 0, index: 1)
```

```
    encoder.setBuffer(model.texturesBuffer!, offset: 0, index: 2)
    encoder.setRenderPipelineState(model.pipelineState, index: 3)
    mBuffers.append(mBuffer)
    mBuffersLength += mBuffer.length
}
```

Here you create an array of argument buffers to match the Model struct you created in ICB.metal. You also keep track of the total buffer length.

Now that you've created an array of argument buffers, you'll create one large buffer to hold all these buffers. Add this code:

```
modelsBuffer = Renderer.device.makeBuffer(length:
mBuffersLength,
                                          options: [])
modelsBuffer.label = "Models Array Buffer"
```

This is an empty buffer. You can't directly assign the array to the Metal buffer, but you can copy the bytes. You'll iterate through mBuffers and copy each MTLBuffer element into modelsBuffer.

Add this after the previous code:

```
var offset = 0
for mBuffer in mBuffers {
  var pointer = modelsBuffer.contents()
  pointer = pointer.advanced(by: offset)
  pointer.copyMemory(from: mBuffer.contents(), byteCount:
mBuffer.length)
  offset += mBuffer.length
}
```

This copies each MTLBuffer into modelsBuffer. You keep track of the offset in the buffer to copy to.

You've created the compute pipeline state and the argument buffers. The last item to create is the draw arguments for the model.

Draw arguments

At the top of Renderer, create a new buffer property for the draw arguments:

```
var drawArgumentsBuffer: MTLBuffer!
```

At the end of initializeCommands(), create this buffer:

```
let drawLength = models.count *
  MemoryLayout<MTLDrawIndexedPrimitivesIndirectArguments>.stride
drawArgumentsBuffer =
    Renderer.device.makeBuffer(length: drawLength,
                                    options: [])!
drawArgumentsBuffer.label = "Draw Arguments"
```

To fill the draw arguments buffer, add this:

```
// 1
var drawPointer =
  drawArgumentsBuffer.contents().bindMemory(
    to: MTLDrawIndexedPrimitivesIndirectArguments.self,
    capacity: models.count)
// 2
for (modelIndex, model) in models.enumerated() {
  var drawArgument = MTLDrawIndexedPrimitivesIndirectArguments()
  drawArgument.indexCount = UInt32(model.submesh.indexCount)
  drawArgument.instanceCount = 1
  drawArgument.indexStart =
      UInt32(model.submesh.indexBuffer.offset)
  drawArgument.baseVertex = 0
  drawArgument.baseInstance = UInt32(modelIndex)
  // 3
  drawPointer.pointee = drawArgument
  drawPointer = drawPointer.advanced(by: 1)
}
```

Going through this code:

1. You bind a pointer to the buffer, of the type
    `MTLDrawIndexedPrimitivesIndirectArguments`.

2. You iterate through the models and provide the draw arguments. These are
    exactly the same as you set for the draw call in the command list that you
    commented out.

3. Set the draw argument into the buffer and advance the pointer.

The compute command encoder

You've done all the preamble and setup code. All that's left to do now is create a
compute command encoder to run the compute shader function. This will create a
render command to render every model.

In draw(in:), after updateUniforms(), add this:

```
guard
  let computeEncoder = commandBuffer.makeComputeCommandEncoder()
  else { return }
computeEncoder.setComputePipelineState(icbPipelineState)
computeEncoder.setBuffer(uniformsBuffer, offset: 0,
  index: Int(BufferIndexUniforms.rawValue))
computeEncoder.setBuffer(fragmentUniformsBuffer, offset: 0,
  index: Int(BufferIndexFragmentUniforms.rawValue))
computeEncoder.setBuffer(drawArgumentsBuffer, offset: 0,
  index: Int(BufferIndexDrawArguments.rawValue))
computeEncoder.setBuffer(modelParamsBuffer, offset: 0,
  index: Int(BufferIndexModelParams.rawValue))
computeEncoder.setBuffer(modelsBuffer, offset: 0,
  index: Int(BufferIndexModels.rawValue))
computeEncoder.setBuffer(icbBuffer, offset: 0,
  index: Int(BufferIndexICB.rawValue))
```

Here you create a compute command encoder, and, just as you have previously with render command encoders, you set a pipeline state and then pass all the buffers.

Add this code:

```
computeEncoder.useResource(icb, usage: .write)
computeEncoder.useResource(modelsBuffer, usage: .read)

if let heap = TextureController.heap {
  computeEncoder.useHeap(heap)
}

for model in models {
  computeEncoder.useResource(model.vertexBuffer, usage: .read)
  computeEncoder.useResource(model.submesh.indexBuffer.buffer,
                            usage: .read)
  computeEncoder.useResource(model.texturesBuffer!,
                            usage: .read)
}
```

Just as before, when you use argument buffers, you have to use the resources.

Complete the command encoder. Add this:

```
let threadExecutionWidth = icbPipelineState.threadExecutionWidth
let threads = MTLSize(width: models.count, height: 1, depth: 1)
let threadsPerThreadgroup = MTLSize(width: threadExecutionWidth,
                                    height: 1, depth: 1)
computeEncoder.dispatchThreads(threads,
  threadsPerThreadgroup: threadsPerThreadgroup)
computeEncoder.endEncoding()
```

The next chapter will go into compute threads in depth. Just notice for now, that there's `models.count` number of threads in the threads per threadgroup width. That means that the compute shader function will execute `models.count` number of times.

Finally, optimize your ICB commands with a blit command encoder:

```
let blitEncoder = commandBuffer.makeBlitCommandEncoder()!
blitEncoder.optimizeIndirectCommandBuffer(icb,
                              range: 0..<models.count)
blitEncoder.endEncoding()
```

This will remove any empty commands, if you have them.

You're using all the resources and sending them to the GPU for the compute function, so remove all the `use` commands off `renderEncoder`. The only commands on the render encoder should be:

```
renderEncoder.setDepthStencilState(depthStencilState)
renderEncoder.executeCommandsInBuffer(icb,
                              range: 0..<models.count)
renderEncoder.endEncoding()
```

Before you build and run, save all the documents you have open. When you're programming GPUs and moving around blocks of memory, sometimes you can accidentally set memory blocks in areas where you're not supposed to. When this happens, your display may go crazy with flickering and drawing weirdness, and you'll have to restart your computer. Hopefully, you have followed this chapter correctly, and this won't happen to you. Not until you start experimenting, anyway :].

Build and run, capture the frame using the Capture GPU frame button, and examine both the compute command list and the render command list and take note where exactly the resources load. Notice how few commands there are on the render command coder.

Congratulations! You've learned a number of new techniques in this chapter.

- You started out collecting resources into argument buffers, which means passing fewer parameters to shaders.

- You gathered your textures into a resource heap. The heap you created is static, but you can reuse space on the heap where you use different textures at different times.

- You explored indirect commands on the CPU. For simple static rendering work, this works fine.

- Finally you took creating your indirect commands from the CPU to a compute function on the GPU. You created indirect render commands in this chapter, but WWDC 2019 introduced indirect compute commands also.

Where to go from here?

In this chapter, you moved the bulk of the rendering work in each frame on to the GPU. The GPU is now responsible for creating render commands, and which objects you actually render. Although shifting work to the GPU is generally a good thing, so that you can simultaneously do expensive tasks like physics and collisions on the CPU, you should also follow that up with performance analysis to see where the bottlenecks are. You can read more about this at the end of the next section.

GPU-driven rendering is a recent concept, and the best resources are Apple's WWDC sessions:

- WWDC 2018 Metal for Game Developers https://developer.apple.com/videos/play/wwdc2018/607/

- WWDC 2019 Modern Rendering with Metal https://developer.apple.com/videos/play/wwdc2019/601/

Metal for Game Developers has a wide range of sample code using argument buffers, heaps and GPU encoding.

Section III: The Effects

In this section, you'll use compute shaders to create many different effects. You'll trace rays to render objects with more realism than the rasterization techniques you've used up to now.

- **Chapter 16: Particle Systems:** Create fireworks, snow storms and flames with particle systems. Use a compute shader to track particle life and movement and learn how to manage GPU threads and threadgroups.

- **Chapter 17: Particle Behavior:** Make your particles swarm by assigning behavior to them.

- **Chapter 18: Rendering with Rays**: Ray marching is an alternative rendering technique to rasterization. March infinite spheres, learn about Perlin noise and then use it to create clouds.

- **Chapter 19: Advanced Shadows**: Apply the distance techniques you learned in the previous chapter for advanced shadow techniques. You'll find out how much more realistic shadows and screen space ambient occlusion can be.

- **Chapter 20: Advanced Lighting**: Learn about global illumination and how to render water with advanced lighting effects such as reflection and refraction.

- **Chapter 21: Metal Performance Shaders**: This framework is a large collection of shaders for image processing, matrix operations and ray tracing. Post-process a rendered scene with bloom, and explore MPS-accelerated ray tracing — the rendering technique of the future.

- **Chapter 22: Integrating with SpriteKit & SceneKit**: Sometimes you'll want to use Metal with other APIs. You'll create a Metal toon shader to use with a simple SceneKit project, and a game HUD using SpriteKit. To wrap up the chapter, you'll post-process an entire rendered scene with Core Image using a Metal Shader.

- **Chapter 23: Debugging & Profiling**: Whether it's objects in the scene you seem to have accidentally lost, or maybe more lights and shadows you want to render, you'll get to use some of Xcode's excellent tools to find out what's happening on the GPU, as well as find ways to optimize your game to run at blazing speeds.

- **Chapter 24: Performance Optimization**: In this final chapter, you'll learn more ways to optimize the performance of your game. You'll understand how to categorize GPUs, how to manage memory, how to synchronize resources between the CPU and GPU, how to move your game on multiple threads and what are the best practices for a smooth rendering.

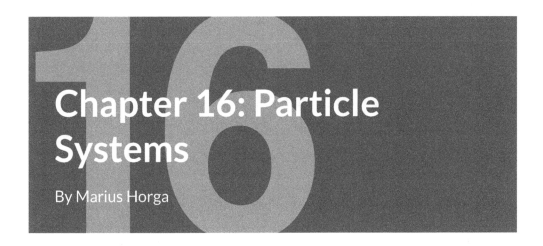

Chapter 16: Particle Systems

By Marius Horga

One of the many ways to create art and present science in code is by making use of particles. A **particle** is a tiny graphical object that carries basic information about itself such as color, position, life, speed and direction of movement.

Nothing explains a visual effect better than an image showing what you'll be able to achieve at the end of this chapter.

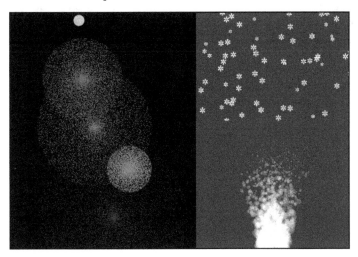

Particle systems are widely used in:

- Video games and animation: hair, cloth, fur.

- Modeling of natural phenomena: fire, smoke, water, snow.

- Scientific simulations: galaxy collisions, cellular mitosis, fluid turbulence.

> **Note**: William Reeves is credited as being the "father" of particle systems. While at Lucasfilm, Reeves created the *Genesis Effect* in 1982 while working on the movie *Star Trek II: The Wrath of Khan*. Later, he joined *Pixar Animation Studios* where he's still creating amazing animations using particles.

In a moment, you'll get your feet wet trying out one such practical application: fireworks. But first, what exactly is a particle?

Particle

Newtonian dynamics describe the relationship between any small body — a particle — and the forces acting upon it, as well as its motion in response to those forces. Newton's three laws of motion define the relationship between them.

The first two laws define motion as a result of either inertia or force interference upon the particle's current state of motion (stationary or moving). You'll be working with them in this chapter.

The third law, however, defines motion as a reaction of two or more particles interacting with each other. You'll work with this law in Chapter 17, "Particle Behavior."

A fourth law, if you wish, is the law of life. It's not one of the Newtonian motion laws, but it does indeed apply to particles. Particles are born; they move and interact with the environment; and then, they die.

Particle Life
Color changes from dark (birth) to white (death)

V: Velocity
G: Gravity

Emitter

You need a particle system to create fireworks. First, however, you need to define a particle that has — at a minimum — a position, direction, speed, color and life.

What makes a particle system cohesive, however, are emitters.

Emitter

An **emitter** is nothing more than a particle generator — in other words, a source of particles. You can make your particle system more exciting by having several emitters shooting out particles from different positions.

Fireworks are sequential explosions that occur a few seconds apart from each other. Emitters fit here perfectly so you'll create one first.

Open **Fireworks.playground** located in the starter folder for this chapter. This playground has an MTKView with a Renderer as the delegate. Currently, the only thing Renderer does is set the background color to (0.5, 0.5, 0.5, 1.0) which is the RGB translation for gray.

In the **Sources** folder, create a new file named **Emitter.swift**, and add this code to it:

```
import MetalKit

struct Particle {
  var position: float2
  var direction: Float
  var speed: Float
  var color: float3
  var life: Float
}
```

This is a struct to hold the particle's properties.

Now, create an emitter with a buffer to hold the particles.

```
public struct Emitter {
  public let particleBuffer: MTLBuffer
}
```

Inside Emitter, add an initializer that will take in the particle count and the particle's lifetime:

```
public init(particleCount: Int, size: CGSize,
            life: Float, device: MTLDevice) {
  let bufferSize = MemoryLayout<Particle>.stride * particleCount
```

```
    particleBuffer = device.makeBuffer(length: bufferSize)!
}
```

Here, you create the buffer with a size that represents the area in which the particles will be drawn.

You'll randomize the initial position and color once for all particles, and then randomize each particle's speed and direction based on the size of the display area.

Add the following code to `init(particleCount:size:life:device)`:

```
var pointer =
    particleBuffer.contents().bindMemory(to: Particle.self,
                                    capacity: particleCount)
let width = Float(size.width)
let height = Float(size.height)
let position = float2(Float.random(in: 0...width),
                    Float.random(in: 0...height))
let color = float3(Float.random(in: 0...life) / life,
                Float.random(in: 0...life) / life,
                Float.random(in: 0...life) / life)

for _ in 0..<particleCount {
  let direction =
    2 * Float.pi * Float.random(in: 0...width) / width
  let speed = 3 * Float.random(in: 0...width) / width
  pointer.pointee.position = position
  pointer.pointee.direction = direction
  pointer.pointee.speed = speed
  pointer.pointee.color = color
  pointer.pointee.life = life
  pointer = pointer.advanced(by: 1)
}
```

Here, you loop through the buffer using a pointer to access each particle object and set their properties.

You've now created lots of particles, each with distinct direction and speed. However, all of them have the same original position, color and life.

Back in `Renderer`, create the following properties:

```
let particleCount = 10000
let maxEmitters = 8
var emitters: [Emitter] = []
let life: Float = 256
var timer: Float = 0
```

Next, you'll set up an array of emitters, each with 10,000 particles. Add this method to Renderer:

```
func update(size: CGSize) {
  timer += 1
  if timer >= 50 {
    timer = 0
    if emitters.count > maxEmitters {
      emitters.removeFirst()
    }
    let emitter = Emitter(particleCount: particleCount,
                          size: size, life: life,
                          device: device)
    emitters.append(emitter)
  }
}
```

You reset a timer variable every time it reaches a threshold (50 in this case). At that point, you add a new emitter and then remove the oldest one.

Call this method at the top of draw(in:), after the guard statement, so that it's called every frame:

```
update(size: view.drawableSize)
```

Run the playground to verify everything compiles. Note, however, you'll see the same solid gray color as you did in the beginning.

The shader function is where the particles' life and position are updated. For this to work, you need more granular control of the GPU threads than you had with render encoding.

Enter **compute** encoding!

Compute

What is compute? Simply put, compute programming is the only other way to use a GPU besides rendering. Compute is also widely known as **General Purpose GPU (GPGPU)** programming.

GPUs transitioned about a decade ago from a fixed-pipeline architecture to programmable pipelines, enabling the many-core GPU architectures to speed up parallel computation needs such as image/video processing, scientific simulations and more recently, machine learning.

Compute uses a **compute command encoder**. This is another encoder type Metal provides, along with the render command encoder and the blit command encoder that you have already used.

All right, time to write some compute code!

In `Renderer`, add this property to the top of the class:

```
let pipelineState: MTLComputePipelineState!
```

Then, update `initializeMetal` to return a value for it:

```
private static func initializeMetal() -> (
  device: MTLDevice, commandQueue: MTLCommandQueue,
  pipelineState: MTLComputePipelineState)? {
  guard let device = MTLCreateSystemDefaultDevice(),
    let commandQueue = device.makeCommandQueue(),
    let path = Bundle.main.path(forResource: "Shaders",
                                ofType: "metal")
      else { return nil }

  let pipelineState: MTLComputePipelineState

  do {
    let input = try String(contentsOfFile: path,
                           encoding: String.Encoding.utf8)
    let library = try device.makeLibrary(source: input,
                                         options: nil)
    guard let function = library.makeFunction(name: "compute")
      else { return nil }
    pipelineState =
        try device.makeComputePipelineState(function: function)
  }
  catch {
    print(error.localizedDescription)
    return nil
  }
  return (device, commandQueue, pipelineState)
}
```

Finally, assign the value in `init()` before calling `super.init()`:

```
pipelineState = initialized?.pipelineState
```

This part should be familiar from previous chapters. You create the Metal library, a kernel function and a pipeline state. However, what's new here is the way in which you create the pipeline state.

Notice that you didn't need a pipeline state descriptor anymore but instead created the pipeline state directly from the *kernel function* — the third (and last) type of shader function Metal provides, along with the vertex and fragment functions.

You'll learn more about the kernel function shortly.

Threads and threadgroups

Next, you'll create a compute pass. For that, you need to specify how many times you want the kernel function to run. To determine this, you need to know the size of the array, texture or volume you want to process. This size is known as the **grid** and consists of **threads** organized into **threadgroups**.

The grid is defined in three dimensions: width, height and depth — but often, especially when you're processing images, you'll only work with a 1D or 2D grid. Every point in the grid runs one instance of the kernel function, each on a separate thread.

In this example, you have an image of 512 by 384 pixels. This **grid** is split up into 384 **threadgroups** — that's 16 by 24 threadgroups. Each threadgroup has 512 **threads** — that's 32 by 16 threads.

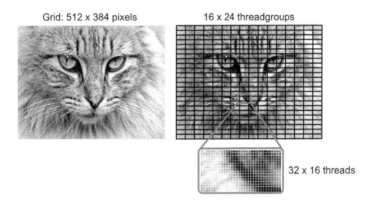

Grid: 512 x 384 pixels   16 x 24 threadgroups

32 x 16 threads

See how a threadgroup can only affect a tiny part of the grid and process it independently from other threadgroups?

Threadgroups have the advantage of executing a group of threads together and also share a small chunk of memory. Even though sometimes threads run independently of each other, it's also common to organize threads into threadgroups so they can work on smaller parts of the problem, independently from other threadgroups.

You can choose how you split up the group. In the following image, a 16 by 12 grid is split first into 2×3 threadgroups and secondly into 4×4 thread groups.

Grid: 16 x 12

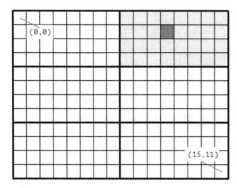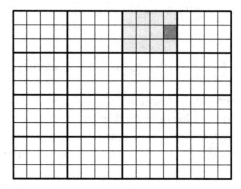

Threadgroups: 2 x 3   Threadgroups: 4 x 4

Within each grid, you can locate each pixel. The red pixel in both grids is located at (11, 1). You can also uniquely identify each thread within the threadgroup. The blue threadgroup on the left is located at (1, 0), and on the right at (2, 0). The red pixels in both grids are threads located within their threadgroup at (3, 1).

You have control over the number of threadgroups. However, you need to add an extra threadgroup to the size of the grid to make sure at least one threadgroup will execute.

The following code demonstrates how you could set up the threads and threadgroups to process the cat image above. It is only for exemplification, and **you don't** need to put it into your project:

```
let width = 32
let height = 16
let threadsPerThreadgroup = MTLSizeMake(width, height, 1)
let gridWidth = Int(view.drawableSize.width)
let gridHeight = Int(view.drawableSize.height)
let threadGroupCount =
    MTLSizeMake((gridWidth + width - 1) / width,
                (gridHeight + height - 1) / height,
                1)
computeEncoder.dispatchThreadgroups(threadGroupCount,
            threadsPerThreadgroup: threadsPerThreadgroup)
```

You specify the threads per threadgroup. In this case, the threadgroup will consist of 32 threads wide, 16 threads high and 1 thread deep. This is a typical threadgroup for processing a 2D image. You calculate the threadgroup count from the grid (image) width and height. In this case, the image size is 512 by 384 pixels, so threadGroupCount will be calculated as (16, 24, 1). You then tell the compute command encoder to dispatch this batching information to the GPU.

In this example, the threads and threadgroups work out evenly across the grid, but if the size of your data does not match the size of the grid, you may have to perform boundary checks in the kernel function.

In the following example, with a threadgroup size of 32 by 16 threads, the number of threadgroups necessary to process the image would be 10 by 13. You'd have to check that the threadgroup is not using threads that are off the edge of the image.

Threads: 32 x 16   Grid: 300 x 200 pixels   Threadgroups:10 x 13 threads
                                                                  (9.375 x 12.5)

The threads that are off the edge, are **underutilized threads**; that is, threads that you dispatched but there was no work for them to do.

In the most recent version of iOS and macOS, it's now possible to only specify the size of your grid and the size of a threadgroup. From there, Metal will figure out the number of threadgroups for you to use.

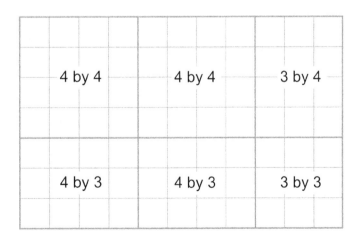

This is an excellent feature because Metal will provide **nonuniform threadgroups** if the grid size is not a multiple of the threadgroup size:

Threadgroups: nonuniform

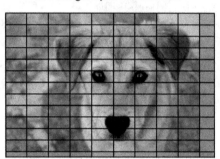

You calculate the number of threads per threadgroup based on two compute pipeline state properties:

- `maxTotalThreadsPerThreadgroup`: its name is self-explanatory

- `threadExecutionWidth`: represents the number of threads scheduled to execute in parallel on the GPU.

> **Note**: `maxTotalThreadsPerThreadgroup` depends on the device, kernel register usage and thread group memory usage.
> `maxTotalThreadsPerThreadgroup` will not change once you created the compute pipeline state but two compute pipeline states on the same device may have different `maxTotalThreadsPerThreadgroup` values. Also, for the most efficient execution of the kernel function, you should set the number of threads in the threadgroup as a multiple of `threadExecutionWidth`.

Back to code! In **Renderer.swift**, in `draw(in:)`, replace these lines:

```
let renderEncoder = makeRenderCommandEncoder(commandBuffer,
                                             drawable.texture)
renderEncoder.endEncoding()
```

With this code:

```
// 1
guard let computeEncoder =
commandBuffer.makeComputeCommandEncoder()
        else { return }
```

```
computeEncoder.setComputePipelineState(pipelineState)
computeEncoder.setTexture(drawable.texture, index: 0)
// 2
var width = pipelineState.threadExecutionWidth
var height = pipelineState.maxTotalThreadsPerThreadgroup / width
let threadsPerThreadgroup = MTLSizeMake(width, height, 1)
width = Int(view.drawableSize.width)
height = Int(view.drawableSize.height)
var threadsPerGrid = MTLSizeMake(width, height, 1)
// 3
computeEncoder.dispatchThreads(threadsPerGrid,
                threadsPerThreadgroup: threadsPerThreadgroup)
computeEncoder.endEncoding()
```

Going through the code:

1. You create the compute command encoder and set its pipeline state. You also send the drawable texture to the GPU at index 0 for writing.

2. You declare the number of threads per group and the number of threads per grid.

3. You dispatch these threads to do the work in parallel on the GPU.

You'll get a compiler warning for the var, but you'll be reusing threadsPerGrid shortly.

> **Note**: A kernel function executes once per thread just like a vertex function executes once per vertex. The main difference between the kernel function and the other two shader functions is that a kernel function's return type is always void so it will never return anything.

In the **Resources** folder, create a new file named **Shaders.metal**, and add the kernel function:

```
#include <metal_stdlib>
using namespace metal;

kernel void compute(texture2d<half, access::read_write>
                                output [[texture(0)]],
                uint2 id [[thread_position_in_grid]]) {
  output.write(half4(0.0, 0.0, 0.0, 1.0), id);
}
```

You create a kernel function that takes, as arguments, the drawable texture you sent from the CPU and the thread index. Then, you write the same color (black) to the drawable texture for each thread/pixel.

The kernel function's index parameter uses the `[[thread_position_in_grid]]` attribute qualifier which uniquely locates a thread within the compute grid and enables it to work distinctly from the others.

The thread index could be 1-, 2- or 3-dimensions depending on how you configured the number of threads per grid before dispatching them. Since you declared the grid would be of *width * height* size back in `Renderer: threadsPerGrid = MTLSizeMake(width, height, 1)`, you match it with a `uint2` (2-dimensional) index in the kernel function for the threads to be correctly dispatched.

Run the playground again and now that you're writing a color to the view's drawable texture, you'll finally see the view color turns from gray to black.

All right, you managed to transition from a rendering pipeline to a compute pipeline fully. So far so good! But what about the particles?

You learned in Chapter 14, "Multipass and Deferred Rendering" how you can use the output of one pass as the input of a second pass. You could apply that concept here and use two pipeline states: one to clear the screen, as you just did, and another one for cool fireworks particles! :]

Fireworks

At the top of `Renderer`, add a new pipeline state:

```
let particlePipelineState: MTLComputePipelineState!
```

Add a `particlePipelineState` to the end of the signature for `initializeMetal`:

```
private static func initializeMetal() -> (
  device: MTLDevice, commandQueue: MTLCommandQueue,
  pipelineState: MTLComputePipelineState,
  particlePipelineState: MTLComputePipelineState)?
```

In `initializeMetal`, before the do block, add this declaration:

```
let particlePipelineState: MTLComputePipelineState
```

Change the end of the do block from the guard onwards to this:

```
guard let function = library.makeFunction(name: "compute"),
  let particleFunction =
      library.makeFunction(name: "particleKernel")
  else { return nil }
```

```
pipelineState =
    try device.makeComputePipelineState(function: function)
particlePipelineState = try
    device.makeComputePipelineState(function: particleFunction)
```

Add `particlePipelineState` to the returned tuple, disambiguating it from `pipelineState` by using labels for each:

```
return (
    device, commandQueue,
    pipelineState: pipelineState,
    particlePipelineState: particlePipelineState)
```

Lastly, assign the value in `init()` before calling `super.init()`:

```
particlePipelineState = initialized?.particlePipelineState
```

In `draw(in:)`, add these lines below `// second command encoder`:

```
// 1
guard let particleEncoder =
commandBuffer.makeComputeCommandEncoder()
              else { return }
particleEncoder.setComputePipelineState(particlePipelineState)
particleEncoder.setTexture(drawable.texture, index: 0)
// 2
threadsPerGrid = MTLSizeMake(particleCount, 1, 1)
for emitter in emitters {
  // 3
  let particleBuffer = emitter.particleBuffer
  particleEncoder.setBuffer(particleBuffer, offset: 0, index: 0)
  particleEncoder.dispatchThreads(threadsPerGrid,
                  threadsPerThreadgroup: threadsPerThreadgroup)
}
particleEncoder.endEncoding()
```

Going through this code:

1. You create a second command encoder and set the particle pipeline state and drawable texture to it.

2. You change the dimensionality from 2D to 1D and set the number of threads per grid to equal the number of particles.

3. You dispatch threads for each emitter in the array.

Since your `threadsPerGrid` is now 1D, you need to match `[[thread_position_in_grid]]` in the shader kernel function with a `uint` parameter. Threads will not be dispatched for each pixel anymore but rather for each particle, so `[[thread_position_in_grid]]` in this case will only affect a particular pixel if there is a particle emitted at the current pixel.

All right, time for some physics chatter!

Particle dynamics

Particle dynamics makes heavy use of Newton's laws of motion. Particles are considered to be small objects approximated as point masses.

Since volume is not something that characterizes particles, scaling or rotational motion will not be considered. Particles will, however, make use of translation motion so they'll always need to have a position.

Besides a position, particles might also have a direction and speed of movement (velocity), forces that influence them (e.g., gravity), a mass, a color and an age.

Since the particle footprint is so small in memory, modern GPUs can generate 4+ million particles, and they can follow the laws of motion at 60 fps!

For now, you're going to ignore gravity, so its value will be 0. Time in this example won't change so it will have a value of 1. As a consequence, velocity will always be the same. You can also assume the particle mass is always 1, for convenience.

To calculate the position, you use this formula:

$$x_2 = x_1 + v_1 t + \frac{1}{2}at^2$$

Where **x2** is the new position, **x1** is the old position, **v1** is the old velocity, **t** is time, and **a** is acceleration.

This is the formula to calculate the new velocity from the old one:

$$v_2 = v_1 + at$$

However, since the acceleration is 0 in this case, the velocity will always have the same value.

As you might remember from Physics class, the formula for velocity is:

```
velocity = speed * direction
```

Plugging all this information into the first formula above gives you the final equation to use in the kernel.

Again, as for the second formula, since acceleration is 0, the last term cancels out:

```
newPosition = oldPosition * velocity
```

Finally, you're creating exploding fireworks, so your firework particles will move in a circle that keeps growing away from the initial emitter origin, so you need to know the equation of a circle:

$$x = a + r\ cos\ t$$
$$y = b + r\ sin\ t$$

Using the angle that the particle direction makes with the axes, you can re-write the velocity equation from the parametric form of the circle equation using the trigonometric functions *sine* and *cosine* as follows:

```
xVelocity = speed * cos(direction)
yVelocity = speed * sin(direction)
```

Great! Why don't you write all this down in code now?

In **Shaders.metal**, add the following:

```
struct Particle {
  float2 position;
  float  direction;
  float  speed;
  float3 color;
  float  life;
};
```

This defines a particle struct to match the one from **Emitter.swift** which you created earlier. Now, add a second kernel function:

```
kernel void particleKernel(texture2d<half, access::read_write>
                           output [[texture(0)]],
  // 1
                   device Particle *particles [[buffer(0)]],
                   uint id [[thread_position_in_grid]]) {
  // 2
  float xVelocity = particles[id].speed
                    * cos(particles[id].direction);
  float yVelocity = particles[id].speed
                    * sin(particles[id].direction) + 3.0;
  particles[id].position.x += xVelocity;
  particles[id].position.y += yVelocity;
  // 3
  particles[id].life -= 1.0;
  half4 color;
```

```
   color.rgb =
      half3(particles[id].color * particles[id].life / 255.0);
   // 4
   color.a = 1.0;
   uint2 position = uint2(particles[id].position);
   output.write(color, position);
   output.write(color, position + uint2(0, 1));
   output.write(color, position - uint2(0, 1));
   output.write(color, position + uint2(1, 0));
   output.write(color, position - uint2(1, 0));
}
```

Going through this code:

1. Get the particle buffer from the CPU and use a 1D index to match the number of threads per grid you dispatched earlier.

2. Compute the velocity and update the position for the current particle according to the laws of motion and using the circle equation as explained above.

3. Update the life variable and compute a new color after each update. The color will fade as the value held by the life variable gets smaller and smaller.

4. Write the updated color at the current particle position, as well as its neighboring particles to the left, right, top and bottom to create the look and feel of a *thicker particle*.

Run the playground once more and finally enjoy the cool fireworks!

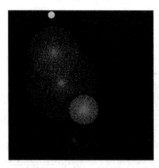

You can improve the realism of particle effects in at least a couple of ways. One of them is to attach a sprite or a texture to each particle. Instead of a dull point, you'll then be able to see a textured point which looks way more lively.

You can practice this technique in the next particle endeavor: a snowing simulation.

Particle systems

Open up the **Particles** starter project. You'll get a warning compile message, but that will disappear when you start adding code.

This project contains the pipeline states you'll need, in addition to an `Emitter` class similar to the struct in your fireworks playground.

Particle systems can be very complex with many different options for particle movement, colors and sizes, but this `Emitter` class is a fairly simple example of a generic particle system where you can create many different types of particles.

For example, you're going to create snow falling, but also a fire blazing upwards. These particle systems will have different speeds, textures and directions.

In **Emitter.swift**, you have a `ParticleDescriptor`. To create a particle system, you create a descriptor which describes all the characteristics of your particle system. Many of the properties in `ParticleDescriptor` are `ClosedRanges`.

For example, as well as `position`, there is a `positionXRange` and `positionYRange`. This allows you to specify a starting position but also allows randomness within limits. If you specify a `position` of [10, 0], and a `positionXRange` of `0...180`, then each particle will be within the range of 10 to 190.

`Emitter` also has a `birthRate` property. This allows you to slowly release particles (like a gentle snow flurry) or send them out more quickly (like a blazing fire).

Each particle has a `startScale` and an `endScale`. By setting the `startScale` to 1 and the `endScale` to 0, you can make the particle get smaller over its lifespan.

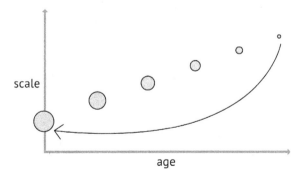

When you create the particle system, you create a buffer the size of all the particles. `emit()` processes each new particle and creates it with the particle settings you set up in `ParticleDescriptor`.

More complex particle systems would maintain a **live** buffer and a **dead** buffer. As particles die, they move from **live** to **dead**, and as the system requires new particles, it recovers them from **dead**. However, in this more simple system, a particle never dies. As soon as a particle's age reaches its life-span, it's reborn with the values it started with.

Snow

You'll attach a texture to each snow particle to improve the realism of your rendering. To render textured particles, as well as having a compute kernel to update the particles, you'll also have a render pipeline with vertex and fragment functions to render them.

To start, open **Renderer.swift** and examine the contents of Renderer. You'll find a method that builds both the pipeline to update the particles with a compute pipeline, and the pipeline for rendering the particles. draw(in:) is just a skeleton that is waiting for you to fill out the passes.

In draw(in:), under // first command encoder, add this:

```
guard let computeEncoder =
    commandBuffer.makeComputeCommandEncoder()
  else { return }
computeEncoder.setComputePipelineState(particlesPipelineState)
let width = particlesPipelineState.threadExecutionWidth
let threadsPerGroup = MTLSizeMake(width, 1, 1)
for emitter in emitters {
  let threadsPerGrid = MTLSizeMake(emitter.particleCount, 1, 1)
  computeEncoder.setBuffer(emitter.particleBuffer,
                      offset: 0, index: 0)
  computeEncoder.dispatchThreads(threadsPerGrid,
                  threadsPerThreadgroup: threadsPerGroup)
}
computeEncoder.endEncoding()
```

Here you create the compute encoder that will update each emitter's particles, and create a 1D grid that dispatches a new set of threads for each emitter.

> **Note**: The previous code, which may create non-uniform threadgroup sizes, will only work on macOS, and iOS devices included in Apple 4 and later GPUs. See Chapter 24, "Performance Optimization" for GPU family breakdown. In addition, the iOS simulator does not support non-uniform threadgroup sizes.

Moving on, below // second command encoder, add the following code for the render command encoder:

```
// 1
let renderEncoder =
  commandBuffer.makeRenderCommandEncoder(descriptor: descriptor)!
renderEncoder.setRenderPipelineState(renderPipelineState)
// 2
var size = float2(Float(view.drawableSize.width),
                  Float(view.drawableSize.height))
renderEncoder.setVertexBytes(&size,
                  length: MemoryLayout<float2>.stride,
                  index: 0)
// 3
for emitter in emitters {
  renderEncoder.setVertexBuffer(emitter.particleBuffer,
                      offset: 0, index: 1)
  renderEncoder.setVertexBytes(&emitter.position,
                  length: MemoryLayout<float2>.stride,
                  index: 2)
  renderEncoder.setFragmentTexture(emitter.particleTexture,
                          index: 0)
  renderEncoder.drawPrimitives(type: .point, vertexStart: 0,
                  vertexCount: 1,
                  instanceCount: emitter.currentParticles)
}
renderEncoder.endEncoding()
```

Going through this code, you:

1. Create a new render command encoder and set the render pipeline state to use the two shader functions.

2. Determine the size of the rendering window and send that size to the vertex shader.

3. For each emitter, you send the emitter buffer and the emitter's position to the vertex shader, set the particle's texture and draw a point primitive for each particle.

Now that you've set up the Swift side, you can build and run to ensure the project works. You should get a blank screen with the gray color of the view set in `init(metalView:)`.

All right, time to configure the shader functions.

Replace the kernel function in **Shaders.metal** with this one:

```
// 1
kernel void compute(device Particle *particles [[buffer(0)]],
                    uint id [[thread_position_in_grid]]) {
```

```
  // 2
  float xVelocity = particles[id].speed
                      * cos(particles[id].direction);
  float yVelocity = particles[id].speed
                      * sin(particles[id].direction);
  particles[id].position.x += xVelocity;
  particles[id].position.y += yVelocity;
  // 3
  particles[id].age += 1.0;
  float age = particles[id].age / particles[id].life;
  particles[id].scale =  mix(particles[id].startScale,
                             particles[id].endScale, age);
  // 4
  if (particles[id].age > particles[id].life) {
    particles[id].position = particles[id].startPosition;
    particles[id].age = 0;
    particles[id].scale = particles[id].startScale;
  }
}
```

This code:

1. Takes in the particle buffer as a shader function argument and sets a 1D index to iterate over this buffer.

2. Calculates the velocity for each particle and then updates its position by adding the velocity to it.

3. Updates the particle's age and scales the particle depending on its age.

4. If the particle's age has reached its total lifespan, reset the particle to its original properties.

Add a new struct for the vertex and fragment shaders:

```
struct VertexOut {
  float4 position    [[position]];
  float  point_size [[point_size]];
  float4 color;
};
```

The only notable change here is the use of the [[point_size]] attribute. By setting this in the vertex function, you can change the point size.

> **Note:** As opposed to [[position]], which is mandatory in a struct that is used as a return type (i.e. VertexOut in your case), you can omit [[point_size]] when not needed. However, you won't be able to access the

point size in the fragment function.

Replace the vertex shader with this one:

```
// 1
vertex VertexOut vertex_particle(
            constant float2 &size [[buffer(0)]],
            const device Particle *particles [[buffer(1)]],
            constant float2 &emitterPosition [[ buffer(2) ]],
            uint instance [[instance_id]]) {
  VertexOut out;
  // 2
  float2 position = particles[instance].position
                          + emitterPosition;
  out.position.xy = position.xy / size * 2.0 - 1.0;
  out.position.z = 0;
  out.position.w = 1;
  // 3
  out.point_size = particles[instance].size
                        * particles[instance].scale;
  out.color = particles[instance].color;
  return out;
}
```

Going through this code:

1. Get the drawable size from the CPU as well as the updated particle buffer and the emitter's position, and use a 1D index to iterate over all particles.

2. Offset the particle position by the emitter's position, and map the particle positions from a [0, 1] range to a [-1, 1] range so that the middle of the screen is now the origin (0, 0).

3. Set the particle's point size and color.

Finally, replace the fragment shader with this code:

```
// 1
fragment float4 fragment_particle(
            VertexOut in [[stage_in]],
            texture2d<float> particleTexture [[texture(0)]],
            float2 point [[point_coord]]) {
  constexpr sampler default_sampler;
  float4 color = particleTexture.sample(default_sampler, point);
  if (color.a < 0.5) {
    discard_fragment();
  }
  color = float4(color.xyz, 0.5);
```

```
    color *= in.color;
    return color;
}
```

Going through this code:

1. Get the processed particle fragments via [[stage_in]] and the snowflake texture from the CPU. The [[point_coord]] attribute is generated by the rasterizer and is a 2D coordinate that indicates where the current fragment is located within a point primitive (in a [0, 1] range).

2. Create a sampler and use it to sample from the given texture at the current fragment position.

3. Apply alpha testing so you can get rid of very low alpha values.

4. Return the texture color combined with the particle color.

You've set up the particle computing and rendering structure — now to set up an emitter for snow particles.

Open **Particles.swift**. fire(size:) is already set up for you, giving you a preview of what your snow emitter is going to look like.

Add this new method:

```
func snow(size: CGSize) -> Emitter {
    let emitter = Emitter()

    // 1
    emitter.particleCount = 100
    emitter.birthRate = 1
    emitter.birthDelay = 20

    // 2
    emitter.particleTexture =
        Emitter.loadTexture(imageName: "snowflake")!

    // 3
    var descriptor = ParticleDescriptor()
    descriptor.position.x = 0
    descriptor.positionXRange = 0...Float(size.width)
    descriptor.direction = -.pi / 2
    descriptor.speedRange =   2...6
    descriptor.pointSizeRange = 80 * 0.5...80
    descriptor.startScale = 0
    descriptor.startScaleRange = 0.2...1.0

    // 4
```

```
    descriptor.life = 500
    descriptor.color = [1, 1, 1, 1]
    emitter.particleDescriptor = descriptor
    return emitter
}
```

Here's what's happening:

1. You tell the emitter how many particles in total should be in the system. `birthRate` and `birthDelay` control how fast the particles emit. With these parameters, you'll emit one snowflake every twenty frames until there are 100 snowflakes in total. If you want a blizzard rather than a few flakes, then you can set the birthrate higher and the delay between each emission less.

2. Load a snowflake texture to render onto the particle.

3. The descriptor describes how each particle should be initialized. You set up ranges for position, speed and scale.

4. A particle has an `age` and a `life`-span. A snowflake particle will remain alive for 500 frames and then recycle. You want the snowflake to travel from the top of the screen all the way down to the bottom of the screen. `life` has to be long enough for this to happen. If you give your snowflake a short life, it will disappear while still on screen.

Particle parameters are really fun to experiment with. Once you have your snowflakes falling, change any of these parameters to see what the effect is.

In **Renderer.swift**, at the end of `init(metalView:)`, set up your snow emitter:

```
let snowEmitter = snow(size: metalView.drawableSize)
snowEmitter.position = [0, Float(metalView.drawableSize.height)]
emitters.append(snowEmitter)
```

This sets the emitter at the top of the screen. Any particles with position (0, 0) will emit from that position.

Add similar code to `mtkView(_:drawableSizeWillChange:)` so that the emitter and particles will update when the screen size changes:

```
func mtkView(_ view: MTKView,
             drawableSizeWillChange size: CGSize) {
  emitters.removeAll()
  let snowEmitter = snow(size: size)
  snowEmitter.position = [0, Float(size.height)]
  emitters.append(snowEmitter)
}
```

At the top of `draw(in:)`, add this to set the emitters emitting:

```
for emitter in emitters {
  emitter.emit()
}
```

The emitters will create all the particles gradually over time, depending on the emitters' `birthRate` and `particleCount`.

Build and run the project, and enjoy the relaxing snow with variable snowflake speeds and sizes:

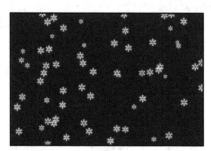

Go back and experiment with some of the particle settings. With `particleCount` of 800, `birthDelay` of 2 and `speedRange` of 4...8, you start off with a gentle snowfall that gradually turns into a veritable blizzard.

Fire

Brrr. That snow is so cold, you need a fire. In **Renderer.swift**, at the end of `init(metalView)` change the snow emitter to:

```
let fireEmitter = fire(size: metalView.drawableSize)
fireEmitter.position = [0, -10]
emitters.append(fireEmitter)
```

This positions the emitter just off the bottom of the screen. Change the code in `mtkView(_:drawableSizeWillChange:)` so that the fire is always in the center of the screen:

```
let fireEmitter = fire(size: size)
fireEmitter.position = [0, -10]
emitters.append(fireEmitter)
```

Look at the `fire` settings in **Particles.swift** and see if you can work out what the particle system will look like.

You're loading more particles than for snow, and a different texture. The birth rate is higher, and there's no delay. The direction is upwards, with a slight variation in range. The particle scales down over its life. The color is fiery orange.

Build and run to see this new particle system in action.

The particles are certainly performing as they should, but it doesn't really look anything like a nice blazing fire with yellow and white heat in the middle of it.

You can achieve this by enabling alpha blending so that particle colors can blend together. Currently, when two particles are in the same position, the top color wins out. However, if you blend the two particles, they'll combine to yellow, and if there are enough blended particles in one position, to white.

Also, you don't care about the order the particles were rendered, so you need to adopt an **order-independent transparency** methodology which uses an additive blending formula that doesn't depend on the order in which particles are rendered. This is needed to create a fluid, homogeneous color.

In **Renderer.swift**, in `buildPipelineStates()` after this line:

```
descriptor.colorAttachments[0].pixelFormat = .bgra8Unorm
```

Add this:

```
// 1
descriptor.colorAttachments[0].isBlendingEnabled = true
descriptor.colorAttachments[0].rgbBlendOperation = .add
// 2
descriptor.colorAttachments[0].sourceRGBBlendFactor
    = .sourceAlpha
descriptor.colorAttachments[0].destinationRGBBlendFactor = .one
```

Going through this code:

1. Enable additive blending.

2. Set the source blending factor to its alpha channel and the destination blending factor to the value of 1 which will be added to the source color.

Build and run the project so you can finally enjoy the burning fire.

Where to go from here?

You've only just begun playing with particles! There are many more particle characteristics you could include in your particle system:

- Color over life.

- Gravity.

- Acceleration.

- Instead of scaling linearly over time, how about scaling slowly then faster?

If you want more ideas, review the links in this chapter's **references.markdown**.

There are some things you haven't yet looked at, like collisions or reaction to acting forces. You have also not read anything about intelligent agents and their behaviors. You'll learn more about all this next, in Chapter 17, "Particle Behavior."

Chapter 17: Particle Behavior

By Marius Horga

As you learned in the previous chapter, particles have been at the foundation of computer animation for years. In computer graphics literature, three major animation paradigms are well defined and have rapidly evolved in the last two decades:

- **Keyframe animation:** Starting parameters are defined as initial frames, and then an interpolation procedure is used to fill the remaining values for in-between frames. This topic was covered in Chapter 8, "Character Animation."

- **Physically based animation:** Starting values are defined as animation parameters, such as a particle's initial position and velocity, but intermediate values are not specified externally. This topic was covered in Chapter 16, "Particle Systems."

- **Behavioral animation:** Starting values are defined as animation parameters. In addition, a cognitive process model describes and influences the way intermediate values are later determined.

In this chapter, you'll focus on the last paradigm as you work through:

- Behavioral animation.

- Swarming behavior.

- Velocity and bounds checking.

- Behavioral rules.

By the end of the chapter, you'll build and control a swarm exhibiting basic behaviors you might see in nature.

Behavioral animation

You can broadly split behavioral animation into two major categories:

- **Cognitive behavior:** This is the foundation of *artificial life* which differs from artificial intelligence in that AI objects do not exhibit behaviors or have their own preferences. It can range from a simple cause-and-effect based system to more complex systems, known as *agents*, that have a psychological profile influenced by the surrounding environment.

- **Aggregate behavior:** Think of this as the overall outcome of a group of agents. This behavior is based on the individual rules of each agent and can influence the behavior of neighbors.

In this chapter, you'll keep your focus on aggregate behavior.

There's a strict correlation between the various types of aggregate behavior entities and their characteristics. In the following table, notice how the presence of a physics system or intelligence varies between entity types.

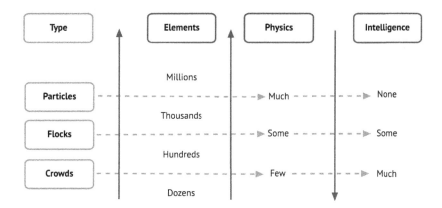

- **Particles** are the largest aggregate entities and are mostly governed by the laws of physics, but they lack intelligence.

- **Flocks** are an entity that's well-balanced between size, physics and intelligence.

- **Crowds** are smaller entities that are rarely driven by physics rules and are highly intelligent.

Working with crowd animation is both a challenging and rewarding experience. However, the purpose of this chapter is to describe and implement a flocking-like system, or to be more precise, a swarm of insects.

Swarming behavior

Swarms are gatherings of insects or other small-sized beings. The swarming behavior of insects can be modeled in a similar fashion as the flocking behavior of birds, the herding behavior of animals or the shoaling behavior of fish.

You know from the previous chapter that particle systems are fuzzy objects whose dynamics are mostly governed by the laws of physics. There are no interactions between particles, and usually, they are unaware of their neighboring particles. In contrast, swarming behavior uses the concept of neighboring quite heavily.

The swarming behavior follows a set of basic movement rules developed in 1986 by *Craig Reynolds* in an artificial flocking simulation program known as *Boids*. Since this chapter is heavily based on his work, the term Boid will be used throughout the chapter instead of "particle".

Initially, this basic set only included three rules: cohesion, separation and alignment. Later, more rules were added to extend the set to include a new type of agent; one that has *autonomous behavior* and is characterized by the fact that it has more intelligence than the rest of the swarm. This led to defining new models such as *follow-the-leader* and *predator-prey*.

Time to transform all of this knowledge into a swarm of quality code!

The project

The starting project is the same as the final one from the previous chapter except this time around, the boids:

- No longer have an age/life.

- Are always the same size (no scaling).

- Have the same color.

There's also no more blending, because it's not relevant to the topics presented in this chapter.

The project is set up in such a way that a `firstPass` kernel function first writes the output texture with the background color — black in this case. A `secondPass` kernel function writes the boids on top of the background color.

Build and run the project, and you'll see this:

There's a problem: a visibility issue. In its current state, the boids are barely distinguishable despite being white on a black background.

There's a neat trick you can apply in cases like this when you don't want to use a texture for boids (like you used in the previous chapter). In fact, scientific simulations and computational fluid dynamics projects very rarely use textures, if ever.

You can't use the `[[point_size]]` attribute here because you're not rendering in the traditional sense. Instead, you're writing pixels in a kernel function directly to the drawable's texture.

The trick is to "paint" the *surrounding neighbors* of each boid, which makes the *current* boid seem larger than it really is.

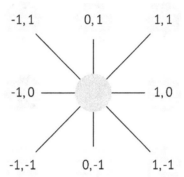

In **Shaders.metal**, add this code at the end of the `secondPass` kernel function:

```
output.write(color, location + uint2( 1, 0));
output.write(color, location + uint2( 0, 1));
output.write(color, location - uint2( 1, 0));
output.write(color, location - uint2( 0, 1));
output.write(color, location + uint2(-1, 1));
output.write(color, location - uint2(-1, 1));
output.write(color, location + uint2( 1,-1));
output.write(color, location - uint2( 1,-1));
```

This code modifies the other eight neighbors of the boid and creates a visual effect which causes the boid to appear larger.

Build and run, and you'll see that the boids are more distinguishable now.

That's a good start, but how do you get them to move around? For that, you need to look into velocity.

Velocity

Velocity is a vector made up of two other vectors: direction and speed. The speed is the magnitude or length of the vector, and the direction is given by the linear equation of the line on which the vector lies.

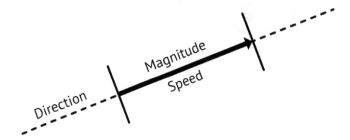

In **Emitter.swift**, add a new member at the end of the `Particle` struct:

```
var velocity: float2
```

Inside the particle loop, add this before the last line where you advance the pointer:

```
let velocity = float2(random(10), random(10))
pointer.pointee.velocity = velocity
```

This gives the particle (boid) a random direction and speed that ranges between `0` and `10`.

In **Shaders.metal**, add velocity as a new member of the `Boid` struct:

```
float2 velocity;
```

In `secondPass`, add this code after the line where you define `position`:

```
float2 velocity = boid.velocity;
position += velocity;
boid.position = position;
boid.velocity = velocity;
boids[id] = boid;
```

This gets the current velocity, updates the current position with the velocity, and then updates the boid data before storing the new values.

Build and run the project, and you'll see that the boids are now moving everywhere on the screen and... uh, wait! It looks like they're disappearing from the screen too. What happened?

Although you set the velocity to random values that will move the boids toward the positive direction on both axes (Y - down and X - to the right), you still need a way to force the boids to stay on the screen. Essentially, you need a way to make the boids bounce back when they hit any of the edges.

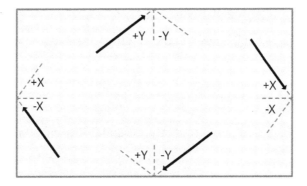

For this function to work, you need to add checks for X and Y to make sure the boids stay in the rectangle defined by the origin and the size of the window, in other words, the width and height of your scene.

In secondPass, add this code right below the line where you initially define velocity:

```
if (position.x < 0 || position.x > output.get_width()) {
    velocity.x *= -1;
}

if (position.y < 0 || position.y > output.get_height()) {
    velocity.y *= -1;
}
```

Here, you check whether a boid coordinate gets outside the screen; if it does, you change the velocity sign, which changes the direction of the moving boid.

Build and run the project, and you'll see that the boids are now bouncing back when hitting an edge.

Currently, the boids only obey the laws of physics. They'll travel to random locations with random velocities, and they'll stay on the window screen because of a few strict physical rules you're imposing on them.

The next stage is to make the boids behave as if they are able to think for themselves.

Behavioral rules

There's a basic set of steering rules that swarms and flocks can adhere to, and it includes:

- Cohesion
- Separation
- Alignment
- Escaping
- Dampening

You'll learn about each of these rules as you implement them in your project.

Cohesion

Cohesion is a steering behavior that causes the boids to stay together as a group. To determine how cohesion works, you need to find the average position of the group, known as the *center of gravity*. Each neighboring boid will then apply a steering force in the direction of this center and converge near the center.

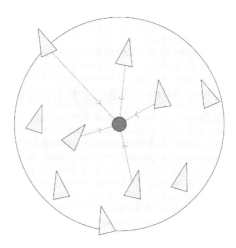

In **Shaders.metal**, at the top of the file, add three global constants:

```
constant float average = 100;
constant float attenuation = 0.1;
constant float cohesionWeight = 2.0;
```

With these constants, you defined:

• **average**: A value that represents a smaller group of the swarm that stays cohesive.

• **attenuation**: A toning down factor that lets you relax the cohesion rule.

• **cohesionWeight**: The contribution made to the final cumulative behavior.

Create a new function for cohesion:

```
float2 cohesion(uint index, device Boid* boids,
                uint particleCount) {
  // 1
  Boid thisBoid = boids[index];
  float2 position = float2(0);
  // 2
  for (uint i = 0; i < particleCount; i++) {
    Boid boid = boids[i];
    if (i != index) {
      position += boid.position;
    }
  }
  // 3
  position /= (particleCount - 1);
  position = (position - thisBoid.position) / average;
  return position;
}
```

Going through the code:

1. Isolate the current boid at the given index from the rest of the group. Define and initialize `position`.

2. Loop through all of the boids in the swarm, and accumulate each boid's position to the `position` variable.

3. Get an average position value for the entire swarm, and calculate another averaged position based on the current boid position and the fixed value `average` that preserves average locality.

In `secondPass`, add this code immediately after defining `velocity`:

```
float2 cohesionVector =
    cohesion(id, boids, particleCount) * attenuation;

// velocity accumulation
velocity += cohesionVector * cohesionWeight;
```

Here, you determine the cohesion vector for the current boid and then attenuate its force. You'll build upon the velocity accumulation line as you go ahead with new behavioral rules. For now, you give cohesion a weight of 2 and add it to the total velocity.

Build and run the project. Notice how the boids are initially trying to get away — following their random directions. Moments later, they're pulled back toward the center of the flock.

Separation

Separation is another steering behavior that allows a boid to stay a certain distance from nearby neighbors. This is accomplished by applying a repulsion force to the current boid when the set threshold for proximity is reached.

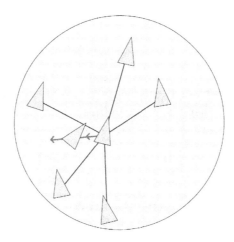

Add two more global constants:

```
constant float limit = 20;
constant float separationWeight = 1.0;
```

Here's what they're for:

- **limit**: A value that represents the proximity threshold that triggers the repulsion force.

- **separationWeight**: The contribution made by the separation rule to the final cumulative behavior.

Then, add the new separation function:

```
float2 separation(uint index, device Boid* boids,
                  uint particleCount) {
  // 1
  Boid thisBoid = boids[index];
  float2 position = float2(0);
  // 2
  for (uint i = 0; i < particleCount; i++) {
    Boid boid = boids[i];
    if (i != index) {
      if (abs(distance(boid.position, thisBoid.position))
          < limit) {
        position =
            position - (boid.position - thisBoid.position);
      }
    }
  }
  return position;
}
```

Going through the code:

1. Isolate the current boid at the given index from the rest of the group. Define and initialize position.

2. Loop through all of the boids in the swarm; if this is a boid other than the isolated one, check the distance between the current and isolated boids. If the distance is smaller than the proximity threshold, update the position to keep the isolated boid within a safe distance.

In secondPass, before the // velocity accumulation comment, add this code:

```
float2 separationVector = separation(id, boids, particleCount)
  * attenuation;
```

Then, update the velocity accumulation to include the separation contribution:

```
velocity += cohesionVector * cohesionWeight
  + separationVector * separationWeight;
```

Build and run the project. Notice that now there's a counter-effect of pushing back from cohesion as a result of the separation contribution.

Alignment

Alignment is the last of the three steering behaviors Reynolds used for his flocking simulation. The main idea is to calculate an average of the velocities for a limited number of neighbors. The resulting average is often referred to as the *desired velocity*.

With alignment, a steering force gets applied to the current boid's velocity to make it align with the group.

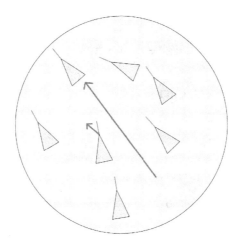

To get this working, add two global constants:

```
constant float neighbors = 8;
constant float alignmentWeight = 3.0;
```

With these, you define:

- **neighbors**: A value that represents the size of the local group that determines the "desired velocity".

- **alignmentWeight**: The contribution made by the alignment rule to the final cumulative behavior.

Then, add the new alignment function:

```
float2 alignment(uint index, device Boid* boids,
                 uint particleCount) {
  // 1
  Boid thisBoid = boids[index];
  float2 velocity = float2(0);
  // 2
  for (uint i = 0; i < particleCount; i++) {
    Boid boid = boids[i];
    if (i != index) {
      velocity += boid.velocity;
    }
  }
  // 3
  velocity /= (particleCount - 1);
  velocity = (velocity - thisBoid.velocity) / neighbors;
  return velocity;
}
```

Going through the code:

1. Isolate the current boid at the given index from the rest of the group. Define and initialize `velocity`.

2. Loop through all of the boids in the swarm, and accumulate each boid's velocity to the `velocity` variable.

3. Get an average velocity value for the entire swarm, and then calculate another averaged velocity based on the current boid velocity and the size of the local group, `neighbors`, which preserves locality.

In `secondPass`, before the `// velocity accumulation` comment, add this code:

```
float2 alignmentVector = alignment(id, boids, particleCount)
  * attenuation;
```

Then, update the velocity accumulation to include the alignment contribution:

```
velocity += cohesionVector * cohesionWeight
  + separationVector * separationWeight
  + alignmentVector * alignmentWeight;
```

Build and run the project. The flock is homogeneous now because the alignment contribution brings balance to the previous two opposed contributions.

Escaping

Escaping is a new type of steering behavior that introduces an agent with autonomous behavior and slightly more intelligence — the *predator*.

In the predator-prey behavior, the predator tries to approach the closest prey on one side, while on the other side, the neighboring boids try to escape.

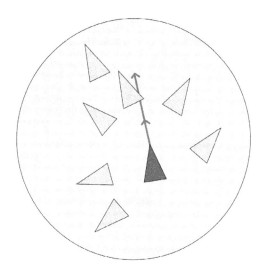

Like before, add a new global constant to indicate the weight of the escaping force:

```
constant float escapingWeight = 0.01;
```

Then, add the new escaping function:

```
float2 escaping(Boid predator, Boid boid) {
  return -attenuation * (predator.position - boid.position)
          / average;
}
```

In this function, you return the averaged position of neighboring boids relative to the predator position. The final result is then attenuated and negated because the escaping direction is the opposite of where the predator is located.

At the top of secondPass, replace this line:

```
Boid boid = boids[id];
```

With this code:

```
Boid predator = boids[0];
Boid boid;
if (id != 0) {
  boid = boids[id];
}
```

Here, you isolate the first boid in the buffer and label it as the predator. For the rest of the boids, you create a new boid object.

Make the predator stand out by coloring it red, and save its current position. Toward the end of `secondPass`, after defining `color`, add this:

```
if (id == 0) {
   color = half4(1.0, 0.0, 0.0, 1.0);
   location = uint2(boids[0].position);
}
```

Before the line where you define `location`, add this code:

```
// 1
if (predator.position.x < 0
      || predator.position.x > output.get_width()) {
   predator.velocity.x *= -1;
}
if (predator.position.y < 0
      || predator.position.y > output.get_height()) {
   predator.velocity.y *= -1;
}
// 2
predator.position += predator.velocity / 2.0;
boids[0] = predator;
```

With this code, you:

1. Check for collisions with the edges of the screen, and change the velocity when that happens.

2. Update the predator position with the current velocity, attenuated to half value to slow it down. Finally, save the predator position and velocity to preserve them for later use.

Before the `// velocity accumulation` comment, add this:

```
float2 escapingVector = escaping(predator, boid) * attenuation;
```

Then, update the velocity accumulation to include the escaping contribution:

```
velocity += cohesionVector * cohesionWeight
   + separationVector * separationWeight
   + alignmentVector * alignmentWeight
   + escapingVector * escapingWeight;
```

Build and run the project. Notice that some of the boids are slightly steering away from the group.

Dampening

Dampening is the last steering behavior you'll looking at in this chapter. Its purpose is to dampen the effect of the escaping behavior, because at some point, the predator will stop its pursuit.

Add one more global constant to represent the weight for the dampening:

```
constant float dampeningWeight = 1.0;
```

Then, add the new dampening function:

```
float2 dampening(Boid boid) {
  // 1
  float2 velocity = float2(0);
  // 2
  if (abs(boid.velocity.x) > limit) {
    velocity.x += boid.velocity.x / abs(boid.velocity.x)
                      * attenuation;
  }
  if (abs(boid.velocity.y) > limit) {
    velocity.y = boid.velocity.y / abs(boid.velocity.y)
                      * attenuation;
  }
  return velocity;
}
```

With this code, you:

1. Define and initialize the velocity variable.

2. Check if the velocity gets larger than the separation threshold; if it does, attenuate the velocity in the same direction.

In secondPass, before the `// velocity accumulation` comment, add this:

```
float2 dampeningVector = dampening(boid) * attenuation;
```

Then, update the velocity accumulation to include the dampening contribution:

```
velocity += cohesionVector * cohesionWeight
    + separationVector * separationWeight
    + alignmentVector * alignmentWeight
    + escapingVector * escapingWeight
    + dampeningVector * dampeningWeight;
```

Build and run the project. Notice the boids are staying together with the group again after the predator breaks pursuit.

Where to go from here?

In this chapter, you learned how to construct basic behaviors and apply them to a small flock. Continue developing your project by adding a colorful background and textures for the boids. Or make it a 3D flocking app by adding projection to the scene. When you're done, add the flock animation to your engine. Whatever you do, the sky is the limit!

This chapter barely scratched the surface of what is widely known as **behavioral animation**. Be sure to review the **references.markdown** file for links to more resources about this wonderful topic.

This chapter concludes the particle series. In the next chapter, you'll continue to build on your compute skills in a new series about ray-based rendering techniques as opposed to the traditional rasterizing technique you've been using so far.

Chapter 18: Rendering with Rays

By Marius Horga

In previous chapters, you worked with a traditional pipeline model, a **raster-model**, which uses a *rasterizer* to color the pixels on the screen. In this chapter, you'll learn about another, somewhat different rendering technique, a **ray-model**, which you'll use to render clouds.

Getting started

In the world of computer graphics, there are two main approaches to rendering graphics: The first one is **geometry -> pixels**. This approach transforms geometry into pixels using the raster-model. The raster-model assumes you know all of the models and their geometry (triangles) beforehand.

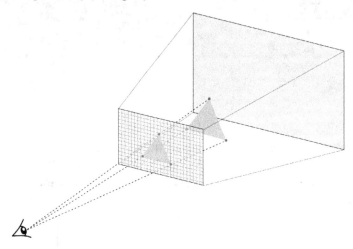

A pseudo-algorithm for the raster-model might look something like this:

```
for each triangle in the scene:
  if visible:
    mark triangle location
    apply triangle color
  if not visible:
    discard triangle
```

The second one is **pixels -> geometry**. This approach involves shooting rays from the camera, *out of the screen and into the scene,* using the ray-model which is what you'll be using for the remainder of this chapter.

A pseudo-algorithm for the ray-model may look something like this:

```
for each pixel on the screen:
  if there's an intersection (hit):
    identify the object hit
    change pixel color
    optionally bounce the ray
  if there's no intersection (miss):
    discard ray
    leave pixel color unchanged
```

In ideal conditions, light travels through the air as a ray following a straight line until it hits a surface. Once the ray hits something, any combination of the following events may happen to the light ray:

- Light gets absorbed into the surface.

- Light gets reflected by the surface.

- Light gets refracted through the surface.

- Light gets scattered from another point under the surface.

When comparing the two models, the raster-model is a faster rendering technique, highly optimized for GPUs. This model scales well for larger scenes and implements antialiasing with ease. If you're creating highly interactive rendered content, such as 1st- and 3rd-person games, the raster-model might be the better choice since pixel accuracy is not paramount.

In contrast, the ray-model is more parallelizable and handles shadows, reflection and refractions more easily. When you're rendering static, far away scenes, using a ray-model might be the better choice.

The ray-model has a few variants; among the most popular are ray casting, ray tracing, path tracing and raymarching. Before you get started, it's important to understand each.

Ray casting

In 1968 *Arthur Appel* introduced ray casting, making it one of the oldest ray-model variants. However, it wasn't until 1992 that it became popular in the world of gaming — that's when *Id Software*'s programmer, *John Carmack*, used it for their *Wolfenstein 3D* game.

With ray casting, the main idea is to cast rays from the camera into the scene looking for surfaces the ray can hit. In *Wolfenstein 3D*, they used a floor map to describe all of the surfaces in the scene.

Because the object height was usually the same across all objects, scanning was fast and simple — only one ray needs to be cast for each vertical line of pixels (column).

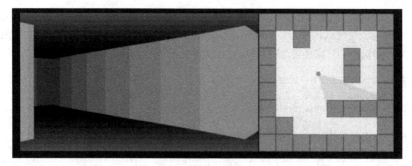

But there's more to the simplicity and fast performance of this algorithm than objects having the same height!

The walls, ceiling and floor each had one specific color and texture, and the light source was known ahead of time. With that information, the algorithm could quickly calculate the shading of an object, especially since it assumes that when a surface faces the light, it will be lit (and not hiding in the shadows).

In its rawest form, a ray casting algorithm states this:

For each cell in the floor map, shoot a ray from the camera, and find the closest object blocking the ray path.

The number of rays cast tends to equal the screen width:

```
For each pixel from 0 to width:
  Cast ray from the camera
  If there's an intersection (hit):
    Color the pixel in object's color
    Stop ray and go to the next pixel
  If there's no intersection (miss):
    Color the pixel in the background color
```

Ray casting has a few advantages:

- It's a high-speed rendering algorithm because it works with scene constraints such as the number of rays being equal to the width of the screen — about a thousand rays.

- It's suitable for real-time, highly interactive scenes where pixel accuracy is not essential.

- The size occupied on disk is small because scenes don't need to be saved since they're rendered so fast.

There are also disadvantages to this algorithm:

- The quality of the rendered image looks blocky because the algorithm uses only primary rays that stop when they hit an object.

- The scene is limited to basic geometric shapes that can be easily intersected by rays.

- The calculations used for intersections are not always precise.

To overcome some of these disadvantages, you'll learn about another variant of the ray-model: ray tracing.

Ray tracing

Ray tracing was introduced in 1979 by Turner Whitted. In contrast to ray casting — which shoots about a thousand rays into the scene — ray tracing shoots a ray for each pixel (width * height), which can easily amount to a million rays!

Advantages of using ray tracing:

- The quality of images rendered is much better than those rendered with ray casting.

- The calculations used for intersections are precise.

- The scene can contain any type of geometric shape, and there are no constraints at all.

Of course, there are also disadvantages of using ray tracing:

- The algorithm is way slower than ray casting.

- The rendered images need to be stored on disk because they take a long time to render again.

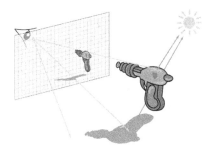

Whitted's approach changes what happens when a ray hits a surface.

Here's his algorithm:

```
For each pixel on the screen:
  For each object in the scene:
    If there's an intersection (hit):
      Select the closest hit object
      Recursively trace reflection/refraction rays
      Color the pixel in the selected object's color
```

The recursive step of the ray tracing algorithm is what adds more realism and quality to ray-traced images. However, the holy grail of realistic rendering is path tracing!

Path tracing

Path Tracing was introduced as a Monte Carlo algorithm to find a numerical solution to an integral part of the rendering equation. James Kajiya presented the rendering equation in 1986. You'll learn more about the rendering equation in Chapter 20, "Advanced Lighting" and you'll implement a path tracer in Chapter 21, "Metal Performance Shaders".

The main idea of the Monte Carlo integration — also known as the Russian Roulette method — is to shoot multiple primary rays for each pixel, and when there's a hit in the scene, shoot just *K* more secondary rays (usually just one more) in a random direction for each of the primary rays shot:

The path tracing algorithm looks like this:

```
For each pixel on the screen:
  Reset the pixel color C.
    For each sample (random direction):
      Shoot a ray and trace its path.
        C += incoming radiance from ray.
      C /= number of samples
```

Path tracing has a few advantages over other ray-model techniques:

- It's a predictive simulation, so it can be used for engineering or other areas that need precision.

- It's photo-realistic if a large enough number of rays are used.

There are some disadvantages too:

- It's slow compared to other techniques, so it is mostly used in *off-line rendering* such as for animated movies.

- It needs precisely defined lights, materials and geometry.

Ah, wouldn't it be great to have a sweet spot where rendering is still close to real-time, and the image quality is more than acceptable? Enter raymarching!

Raymarching

Raymarching is one of the newer approaches to the ray-model. It attempts to make rendering faster than ray tracing by jumping (or marching) in fixed steps along the ray, making the time until an intersection occurs shorter.

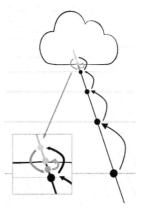

The last jump might end up missing the target. When that happens, you can make another jump back but of a smaller size. If you miss the target again, make yet another jump even smaller than the previous one, and so on until you are getting close enough to the target.

The algorithm is straightforward:

```
For each step up to a maximum number of steps:
  Travel along the ray and check for intersections.
  If there's an intersection (hit):
    Color the pixel in object's color
  If there's no intersection (miss):
    Color the pixel in the background color
  Add the step size to the distance traveled so far.
```

In case the last step is missing the target often, you can retry with a smaller-sized step in the algorithm above. A smaller step improves the accuracy for hitting the target, but it slows down the total marching time.

In 1996, John Hart introduced **sphere tracing** which is a faster raymarching technique used for rendering **implicit surfaces**; it uses geometric distance. Sphere tracing marches along the ray toward the first intersection in steps guaranteed not to go past an implicit surface.

To make a distinction between explicit and implicit surfaces, you need to remember that the raster-model works with geometry stored explicitly as a list of vertices and indices before rendering.

As you can see in the following image, the rasterized circle is made of line segments between vertices:

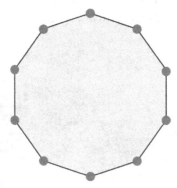

Implicit surfaces, on the other hand, are shapes described by functions rather than by geometry stored before rendering.

So, in this case, the traced circle is perfectly round as each point on the circle is precisely defined by the circle equation:

```
F(X,Y) = X^2 + Y^2 - R^2
```

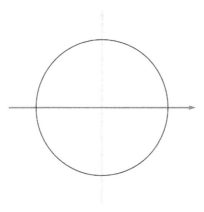

The function that describes a sphere of radius R is straightforward as well:

```
F(X,Y,Z) = X^2 + Y^2 + Z^2 - R^2
```

This type of function can help you estimate the biggest possible sphere that can fit the current marching step. With this technique, you can have variable marching steps which help speed up the marching time.

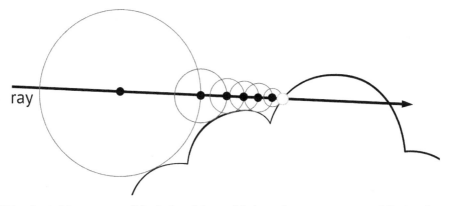

You'll look at this new, modified algorithm a bit later because you need first to learn how to measure the distance from the current step (ray position) to the nearest surface in the scene.

Signed distance functions

Signed Distance Functions (SDF) describe the distance between any given point and the surface of an object in the scene. An SDF returns a negative number if the point is inside that object or positive otherwise.

SDFs are useful because they allow for reducing the number of samples used by ray tracing. The difference between the two techniques is that in ray tracing, the intersection is determined by a strict set of equations, while in raymarching the intersection is approximated.

Using SDFs, you can march along the ray until you get close enough to an object. This is inexpensive to compute compared to precisely determining intersections.

All right, time to finally write some code!

Run the starter playground included with this chapter, and you'll see a light-blue background.

Click on the **SDF** page, and inside the **Resources** folder, open **Shaders.metal**. Within the kernel function, add this code below `// SDF`:

```
// 1
float radius = 0.25;
float2 center = float2(0.0);
// 2
float distance = length(uv - center) - radius;
// 3
if (distance < 0.0) {
  color = float4(1.0, 0.85, 0.0, 1.0);
}
```

Going through the code:

1. Define the radius and center of the circle.

2. Create an SDF that can find the distance to this circle from any point on the screen.

3. Check the sign of the distance variable. If it's negative, it means the point is inside the circle, so change the color to yellow.

> **Note**: You learned earlier that the function that describes a circle is $F(X,Y) = X^2 + Y^2 - R^2$ which is what you used for the SDF. Since the center is at (0,

0) you can more easily recognize the function in this reduced form instead:
`dist = length(uv) - radius.`

Run the playground, and you'll see a yellow circle in the middle of the screen:

Now that you know how to calculate the distance to a circle from any point on the screen, you can apply the same principle and calculate the distance to a sphere too.

The raymarching algorithm

Go to the **Raymarching** playground page. Inside the **Resources** folder, open **Shaders.metal**.

Start by adding the following code above the kernel function to create a struct for the sphere object:

```
struct Sphere {
  float3 center;
  float radius;
  Sphere(float3 c, float r) {
    center = c;
    radius = r;
  }
};
```

The sphere has a center, a radius and a constructor, so you can build a sphere with the provided arguments.

Next, create a struct for the ray you'll march along in the scene. It has the ray origin, direction and a constructor:

```
struct Ray {
  float3 origin;
  float3 direction;
  Ray(float3 o, float3 d) {
    origin = o;
    direction = d;
  }
};
```

Now you need to write an SDF for calculating the distance from a given point to the sphere. The difference from the old function is that your point is now marching along the ray, so you'll use the ray position instead. Add this below the previous code:

```
float distanceToSphere(Ray r, Sphere s) {
  return length(r.origin - s.center) - s.radius;
}
```

Remember the raymarching algorithm you saw earlier?

```
For each step up to a maximum number of steps:
  Travel along the ray and check for intersections.
  If there's an intersection (hit):
    Color the pixel in object's color
  If there's no intersection (miss):
    Color the pixel in the background color
  Add the step size to the distance traveled so far.
```

You can now turn that into code. The first thing you need is a ray to march along with the sphere.

Inside the kernel function, add this code below `// raymarching`:

```
// 1
Sphere s = Sphere(float3(0.0), 1.0);
Ray ray = Ray(float3(0.0, 0.0, -3.0),
              normalize(float3(uv, 1.0)));
// 2
for (int i = 0.0; i < 100.0; i++) {
  float distance = distanceToSphere(ray, s);
  if (distance < 0.001) {
    color = float3(1.0);
    break;
  }
  ray.origin += ray.direction * distance;
}
```

Going through the code:

1. Create a sphere object and a ray. You need to normalize the direction of the ray to make sure its length will always be 1 thus making sure the ray will never miss the object by overshooting the ray beyond the intersection point.

2. Loop enough times to get acceptable precision. On each iteration, calculate the distance from the current position along the ray to the sphere while also checking the distance against `0.001`, a number small enough that's still not zero to make sure you're not yet touching the sphere. If you did, color it white; otherwise, update the ray position by moving it closer to the sphere.

> **Note:** You use `100` in this case, but you can try with an increased number of steps to see how the quality of the rendered image improves — being at the expense of more CPU time used, of course.

That's it! That loop is the essence of raymarching.

Run the playground now, and you'll see a similar image:

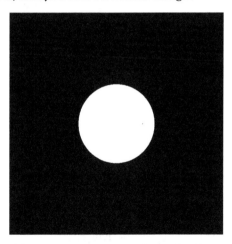

What if you want other objects or even more spheres in the scene? You can do that with a neat instancing trick. ;]

First, set up the sphere and ray. Replace these lines inside the kernel function:

```
Sphere s = Sphere(float3(0.0), 1.0);
Ray ray = Ray(float3(0.0, 0.0, -3.0),
              normalize(float3(uv, 1.0)));
```

With this:

```
Sphere s = Sphere(float3(1.0), 0.5);
Ray ray = Ray(float3(1000.0), normalize(float3(uv, 1.0)));
```

Here, you position the sphere at (1, 1, 1) and set its radius to 0.5. This means the sphere is now contained in the [0.5 - 1.5] range. The ray origin is now much farther away to give you plenty of range for the number of steps you'll use for marching.

Create a function that takes in a ray as the only argument. All you care about now is to find the shortest distance to a complex scene that contains multiple objects.

Place this function below distanceToSphere:

```
float distanceToScene(Ray r, Sphere s, float range) {
  // 1
  Ray repeatRay = r;
  repeatRay.origin = fmod(r.origin, range);
  // 2
  return distanceToSphere(repeatRay, s);
}
```

1. You make a local copy of the ray (a.k.a. that neat trick to do instancing). By using the fmod or modulo function on the ray's origin, you effectively repeat the space throughout the entire screen. This creates an infinite number of spheres, each with its own (repeated) ray. You'll see an example next that should help you understand this better.

2. This uses the repeated ray with the distanceToSphere function and returns the value.

Now call the function from inside the loop. Replace this line:

```
float distance = distanceToSphere(ray, s);
```

With this:

```
float distance = distanceToScene(ray, s, 2.0);
```

You're sending a range of 2.0, so the sphere fits safely inside this range.

Run the playground now, and you'll see this:

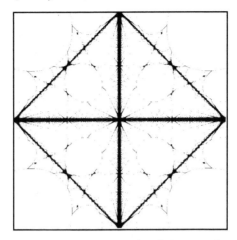

Um, it's interesting, but where is the promised infinite number of spheres?

Replace this line in the kernel:

```
output.write(float4(color, 1.0), gid);
```

With this:

```
output.write(float4(color * abs((ray.origin - 1000.) / 10.0),
                    1.0), gid);
```

That line is complex. What you're doing is multiplying the color with the ray's current position, which is conveniently offset by `1000` to match its initial origin.

Next, you divide by `10.0` to scale down the result, which would be bigger than `1.0` and give you a solid white.

Then, you guard against negative values by using the `abs` function because the left side of the screen x is lower than `0` which would give you a solid black.

So at this moment, your X and Y values are between [0, 1], which is what you need to draw colors, and then these colors are also mirrored top/bottom and left/right.

Run the playground now, and you'll the following:

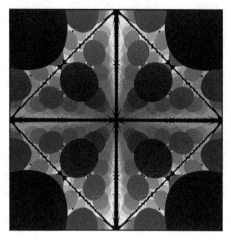

There's one more exciting thing you can do to this scene — animate it!

The kernel function already provides you with a convenient timer variable which Renderer updates on the CPU:

```
constant float &time [[buffer(0)]]
```

To create the sensation of movement, you can plug it into a ray's coordinates. You can even use math functions such as sin and cos to make the movement look like a spiral.

But first, you need to create a camera and make that move along the ray instead.

Inside the kernel function, replace this line:

```
Ray ray = Ray(float3(1000.0), normalize(float3(uv, 1.0)));
```

With these lines:

```
float3 cameraPosition = float3(1000.0 + sin(time) + 1.0,
                               1000.0 + cos(time) + 1.0,
                               time);
Ray ray = Ray(cameraPosition, normalize(float3(uv, 1.0)));
```

You replace the static ray origin with one that changes over time. The X and Y coordinates are making the sphere move in a circular pattern while the Z coordinate moves it more into the screen.

The 1.0 that you added to both X and Y coordinates is there to prevent the camera from crashing into the nearest sphere.

Now, replace this line:

```
output.write(float4(color * abs((ray.origin - 1000.0)/10.0),
                    1.0), gid);
```

With this:

```
float3 positionToCamera = ray.origin - cameraPosition;
output.write(float4(color * abs(positionToCamera / 10.0),
                    1.0), gid);
```

Run the playground, and let yourself mesmerized by the trippy animation. But not for too long. There is still work you need to do!

All right, you need to master one more skill before you can create beautifully animated clouds: random noise.

Creating random noise

Noise, in the context of computer graphics, represents perturbations in the expected pattern of a signal. In other words, noise is everything the output contains but was not expected to be there. For example, pixels with different colors that make them seem misplaced among neighboring pixels.

Noise is useful in creating random procedural content such as fog, fire or clouds. You'll work on creating clouds later, but you first need to learn how to handle noise.

Noise has many variants such as **Value** noise and **Perlin** noise; however, for the sake of simplicity, you'll only work with value noise in this chapter.

Value noise uses a method that creates a lattice of points which are assigned random values. The noise function returns a number based on the interpolation of values of the surrounding lattice points.

Octaves are used in calculating noise to express the multiple irregularities around us. For each octave, you run the noise functions with a different frequency (the period at which data is sampled) and amplitude (the range at which the result can be in).

Multiple octaves of this noise can be generated and then summed together to create a form of fractal noise.

The most apparent characteristic of noise is randomness. Since the *Metal Shading Language* does not provide a random function, you'll need to create one yourself.

You need a random number between [0, 1], which you can get by using the `fract()` function. This returns the fractional component of a number.

You use a *pseudorandom number generator* technique that creates sequences of numbers whose properties approximate the properties of sequences of random numbers. This sequence is not truly random because it's determined by an initial seed value which is the same every time the program runs.

Go to the **Random Noise** playground page. Inside the **Resources** folder, open **Shaders.metal**, and add this above the kernel function:

```
float randomNoise(float2 p) {
   return fract(6791.0 * sin(47.0 * p.x + 9973.0 * p.y));
}
```

The values used in this function are all prime numbers because they are guaranteed not to return the same fractional part for a different number that would otherwise divide it — one of its factors.

Inside the kernel function, replace the last line with this code:

```
float noise = randomNoise(uv);
output.write(float4(float3(noise), 1.0), gid);
```

Run the playground, and you'll see a pretty decent noise pattern like this one:

You can simulate a zooming-in effect by implementing **tiling**. Tiling splits the view into many tiles of equal size, each with its own solid color.

Right above this line:

```
float noise = randomNoise(uv);
```

Add this:

```
float tiles = 8.0;
uv = floor(uv * tiles);
```

Run the playground again, and you'll see the tiles:

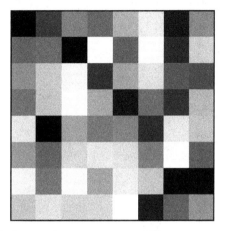

This pattern, however, is far too heterogeneous. What you need is a smoother noise pattern where colors are not so distinctive from the adjacent ones.

To smooth out the noise pattern, you'll make use of **pixel neighborhoods**, also known as convolution kernels in the world of image processing. One such famous convolution grid is the **Von Neumann neighborhood**:

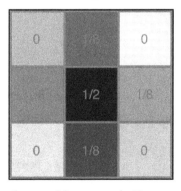

Neighborhood averaging produces a blurry result. You can easily express this grid with code.

In **Shaders.metal**, create a new function:

```
float smoothNoise(float2 p) {
  // 1
  float2 north = float2(p.x, p.y + 1.0);
  float2 east = float2(p.x + 1.0, p.y);
  float2 south = float2(p.x, p.y - 1.0);
  float2 west = float2(p.x - 1.0, p.y);
  float2 center = float2(p.x, p.y);
  // 2
  float sum = 0.0;
  sum += randomNoise(north) / 8.0;
  sum += randomNoise(east) / 8.0;
  sum += randomNoise(south) / 8.0;
  sum += randomNoise(west) / 8.0;
  sum += randomNoise(center) / 2.0;
  return sum;
}
```

Going through the code:

1. Store the coordinates for the central pixel and the neighbors located at the four cardinal points relative to the central pixel.

2. Calculate the value noise for each of the stored coordinates and divide it by its convolution weight. Add each of these values to the total noise value sum.

Now replace this line:

```
float noise = randomNoise(uv);
```

With this:

```
float noise = smoothNoise(uv);
```

Run the playground, and you'll see a smoother noise pattern:

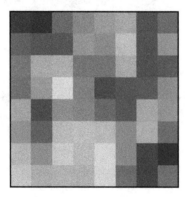

The tiles are still distinctive from one another, but notice how the colors are now more homogeneous.

The next step is to smooth the edges between tiles, making them look borderless. This is done with bilinear interpolation. In other words, you mix the colors at the endpoints of a line to get the color at the middle of the line.

In the following image you have the Q values located in the tile corners; Q11 has a black color; Q21 has a gray color from the tile to its right. The R1 value can be computed by interpolating these two values.

Similarly, for Q12 and Q22, the value for R2 can be obtained. Finally, the value of P will be obtained by interpolating the value of R1 and R2:

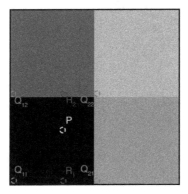

Add this function:

```
float interpolatedNoise(float2 p) {
  // 1
  float q11 = smoothNoise(float2(floor(p.x), floor(p.y)));
  float q12 = smoothNoise(float2(floor(p.x), ceil(p.y)));
  float q21 = smoothNoise(float2(ceil(p.x), floor(p.y)));
  float q22 = smoothNoise(float2(ceil(p.x), ceil(p.y)));
  // 2
  float2 ss = smoothstep(0.0, 1.0, fract(p));
  float r1 = mix(q11, q21, ss.x);
  float r2 = mix(q12, q22, ss.x);
  return mix (r1, r2, ss.y);
}
```

Going through the code:

1. Sample the value noise in each of the four corners of the tile.

2. Use smoothstep for cubic interpolation. Mix the corner colors to get the R and P colors.

In the kernel function, replace these lines:

```
float tiles = 8.0;
uv = floor(uv * tiles);
float noise = smoothNoise(uv);
```

With this:

```
float tiles = 4.0;
uv *= tiles;
float noise = interpolatedNoise(uv);
```

Run the playground, and you'll see an even smoother noise pattern:

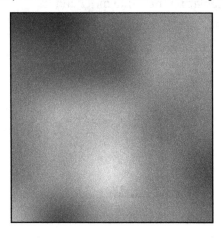

> **Note**: You can read more about noise randomness, smoothing and interpolation in Ray Wenderlich's tutorial *OpenGL ES Pixel Shaders Tutorial* at https://www.raywenderlich.com/70208/opengl-es-pixel-shaders-tutorial

The noise pattern looks good, but you can still improve it with the help of another technique called **fractional Brownian motion (fBm)**.

fBm is also known as the *Random Walk Process* because it consists of steps in a random direction and with an octave (step) that has a characteristic value. What's unique about fBm is that when you zoom in on any part of the function, you'll see a similar random walk in the zoomed-in part.

It's time to create the fBm function. Add this to **Shaders.metal**:

```
float fbm(float2 uv, float steps) {
  // 1
```

```
float sum = 0;
float amplitude = 0.8;
for(int i = 0; i < steps; ++i) {
  // 2
  sum += interpolatedNoise(uv) * amplitude;
  // 3
  uv += uv * 1.2;
  amplitude *= 0.4;
}
return sum;
}
```

Going through the code:

1. Initialize the accumulation variable `sum` to `0` and the `amplitude` factor to a value that satisfies your need for the noise quality (try out different values).

2. At each step, compute the value noise attenuated by amplitude and add it to the sum.

3. Update both the location and amplitude values (again, try out different values).

In the kernel, replace this line:

```
float noise = interpolatedNoise(uv);
```

With this:

```
float noise = fbm(uv, tiles);
```

Here, you used the value of `tiles` in place of `steps` just because they coincidentally have the same value, but you could have just created a new variable named `steps` if you wanted it to be a different value than four. By adding four octaves of noise at different amplitudes, you generated a simple gaseous-like pattern. Run the playground once more, and the output image will look like this:

Fantastic! You're almost done! But there's one more stop: marching clouds.

Marching clouds

All right, it's time to apply what you've learned about signed distance fields, random noise and raymarching by making some marching clouds!

Go to the **Clouds** playground page, and inside the **Resources** folder, open **Shaders.metal**. You already have all of the noise code and a Ray struct, so just add this code:

```
struct Plane {
  float yCoord;
  Plane(float y) {
    yCoord = y;
  }
};

float distanceToPlane(Ray ray, Plane plane) {
  return ray.origin.y - plane.yCoord;
}

float distanceToScene(Ray r, Plane p) {
  return distanceToPlane(r, p);
}
```

This code is similar to what you used in the raymarching section. Instead of a Sphere, however, you create a Plane for the ground, an SDF for the plane and another one for the scene. You're only returning the distance to the plane in the scene at the moment.

Everything else from now on happens inside the kernel. Replace these lines:

```
uv *= tiles;
float3 clouds = float3(fbm(uv));
```

With this:

```
float2 noise = uv;
noise.x += time * 0.1;
noise *= tiles;
float3 clouds = float3(fbm(noise));
```

Run the playground now, and you'll see the noise pattern gently moving to the left side. This happens because you're adding the time variable to the X coordinate, attenuated by 0.1 to slow the movement down a bit.

> **Note:** You make a copy of uv because you only want to affect the noise movement, but you need everything else in the scene to remain static.

Add this code below the lines you just wrote:

```
// 1
float3 land = float3(0.3, 0.2, 0.2);
float3 sky = float3(0.4, 0.6, 0.8);
clouds *= sky * 3.0;
// 2
uv.y = -uv.y;
Ray ray = Ray(float3(0.0, 4.0, -12.0),
              normalize(float3(uv, 1.0)));
Plane plane = Plane(0.0);
// 3
for (int i = 0.0; i < 100.0; i++) {
  float distance = distanceToScene(ray, plane);
  if (distance < 0.001) {
    clouds = land;
    break;
  }
  ray.origin += ray.direction * distance;
}
```

Going through the code:

1. Set the colors for the clouds and the sky; then, add the sky color to the noise for a bluish effect.

2. Since the image is upside down, you reverse the Y coordinate. Create a ray and a plane object.

3. Apply the raymarching algorithm you learned in the previous section.

Run the playground one last time, and you'll see marching clouds above the land:

So. Much. Beautiful.

Where to go from here?

In this chapter, you learned about various rendering techniques such as ray casting, ray tracing, path tracing, and raymarching. You learned about signed distance fields and how to find objects in the scene with them. You learned about noise and how useful it is to define random volumetric content that cannot be easily defined using traditional geometry (meshes). Finally, you learned how to use raymarching and random noise to create dynamic clouds.

With this knowledge, you can render anything you want — from classic shapes, such as spheres and cubes, to complex natural phenomena and scenes. The sky is the limit. No, literally! Once your ray hits the sky, you need to stop following it and cast another one.

In **references.markdown**, there's a list of articles about rendering with rays and creating amazing content.

Chapter 19: Advanced Shadows

By Marius Horga

Shadows and lighting are important topics in Computer Graphics. In Chapter 14, "Multipass & Deferred Rendering," you learned how to render basic shadows in two passes: one to render from the light source location to get a shadow map of the scene; and one to render from the camera location to incorporate the shadow map into the rendered scene.

By the end of this chapter, you'll be able to create various shadow types.

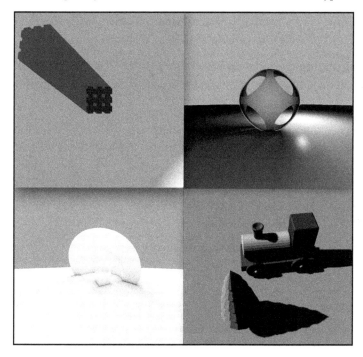

Along the way, you'll work through:

• Hard shadows.

• Soft shadows.

• Ambient Occlusion.

• Percentage Closer Filtering.

Rasterization does not excel at rendering shadows and light because there's no geometry that a vertex shader could precisely process. So now you'll learn how to do it differently.

Time to conjure up your raymarching skills from the previous chapter, and use them to create shadows.

Hard shadows

In this section, you'll create shadows using raymarching instead of using a shadow map like you did in Chapter 14, "Multipass & Deferred Rendering". A shadow map is a non real-time tool that requires you to bake the shadows in a previous pass.

With raymarching, you're making use of **signed distance fields (SDF)**. An SDF is a real-time tool that provides you with the precise distance to a boundary.

This makes calculating shadows easy as they come for "free", meaning that all of the information you need to compute shadows already exists and is available because of the SDF.

The principle is common to both rendering methods: If there's an occluder between the light source and the object, the object is in the shadow; otherwise, it's lit.

Great! Time to put that wisdom down in code.

Open the starter playground, and select the **Hard Shadows** playground page. In the **Resources** folder, open **Shaders.metal**.

Add a new `struct`, so you can create rectangle objects:

```
struct Rectangle {
  float2 center;
  float2 size;
};
```

Next, add a function that gets the distance from any point on the screen to a given rectangle boundary. If its return value is positive, a given point is outside the rectangle; all other values are inside the rectangle.

```
float distanceToRectangle(float2 point, Rectangle rectangle) {
  // 1
  float2 distances =
      abs(point - rectangle.center) - rectangle.size / 2;
  return
    // 2
    all(sign(distances) > 0)
    ? length(distances)
    // 3
    : max(distances.x, distances.y);
}
```

Going through the code:

1. Offset the current point coordinates by the given rectangle center. Then, get the symmetrical coordinates of the given point by using the abs() function, and calculate the signed distance to each of the two edges.

2. If those two distances are positive, then you'll need to calculate the distance to the corner.

3. Otherwise, return the distance to the closer edge.

> **Note:** In this case, rectangle.size / 2 is the distance from the rectangle center to an edge, similar to what a radius is for a circle.

Next is a handy function that lets you subtract one shape from another. Think about Set Theory from back in your school days.

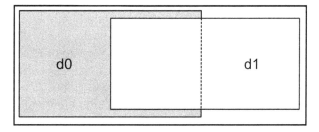

> **Note:** You can find out more about Set Theory here: https://en.wikipedia.org/wiki/Complement_(set_theory)#Relative_complement

Add this function to **Shaders.metal**:

```
float differenceOperator(float d0, float d1) {
  return max(d0, -d1);
}
```

This yields a value that can be used to calculate the difference result from the previous image, where the second shape is subtracted from the first. The result of this function is a signed distance to a compound shape boundary. It'll only be negative when inside the first shape, but outside the second.

Next, design a basic scene:

```
float distanceToScene(float2 point) {
  // 1
  Rectangle r1 = Rectangle{float2(0.0), float2(0.3)};
  float d2r1 = distanceToRectangle(point, r1);
  // 2
  Rectangle r2 = Rectangle{float2(0.05), float2(0.04)};
  float2 mod = point - 0.1 * floor(point / 0.1);
  float d2r2 = distanceToRectangle(mod, r2);
  // 3
  float diff = differenceOperator(d2r1, d2r2);
  return diff;
}
```

Going through the code:

1. Create a rectangle, and get the distance to it.

2. Create a second, smaller rectangle, and get the distance to it. The difference here is that the area is repeated every 0.1 points — which is a 10th of the size of the scene — using a modulo operation. See the note below.

3. Subtract the second repeated rectangle from the first rectangle, and return the resulting distance.

> **Note:** The fmod() function in MSL uses trunc() instead of floor(), so you create a custom mod operator because you also want to use the negative values. You use the GLSL specification for mod() which is x - y * floor(x/y). You need the modulus operator to draw many small rectangles mirrored with a distance of 0.1 from each other.

Finally, use these functions to generate a shape that looks a bit like a fence or a trellis.

At the end of the kernel, replace the `color` assignment with:

```
float d2scene = distanceToScene(uv);
bool inside = d2scene < 0.0;
float4 color = inside ? float4(0.8,0.5,0.5,1.0) :
   float4(0.9,0.9,0.8,1.0);
```

Run the playground, and you'll see something like this:

For shadows to work, you need to:

1. Get the distance to the light.

2. Know the light direction.

3. Step in that direction until you either reach the light or hit an object.

Above the last line in the kernel, add this:

```
float2 lightPos = 2.8 * float2(sin(time), cos(time));
float dist2light = length(lightPos - uv);
color *= max(0.3, 2.0 - dist2light);
```

First, you create a light at position `lightPos`, which you'll animate just for fun using the timer uniform that you passed from the host (API) code.

Then, you get the distance from any given point to `lightPos`, and you color the pixel based on the distance from the light — but only if it's not inside an object. You make the color lighter when closer to the light, and darker when further away with the `max()` function to avoid negative values for the brightness of the light.

Run the playground, and you'll see a similar image. Notice the moving light.

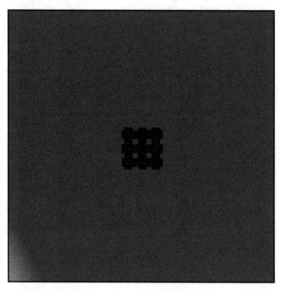

You just took care of the first two steps: light position and direction. Now it's time to handle the third one: the shadow function.

Add this code above the kernel function:

```
float getShadow(float2 point, float2 lightPos) {
  // 1
  float2 lightDir = lightPos - point;
  // 2
  for (float lerp = 0; lerp < 1; lerp += 1 / 300.0) {
    // 3
    float2 currentPoint = point + lightDir * lerp;
    // 4
    float d2scene = distanceToScene(currentPoint);
    if (d2scene <= 0.0) { return 0.0; }
  }
  return 1.0;
}
```

Going through the code:

1. Get a vector from the point to the light.

2. Use a loop to divide the vector into many smaller steps. If you don't use enough steps, you might jump past the object, leaving holes in the shadow.

3. Calculate how far along the ray you are currently, and move along the ray by this lerp distance to find the point in space you are sampling.

4. See how far you are from the surface at that point, and then test if you're inside an object. If yes, return 0, because you're in the shadow; otherwise, return 1, because the ray didn't hit an object.

It's finally time to see some shadows.

Above the last line in the kernel, add this:

```
float shadow = getShadow(uv, lightPos);
color *= 2;
color *= shadow * .5 + .5;
```

A value of 2 is used here to enhance the light brightness and the effect of the shadow. Feel free to play with various values and notice how changes affect it.

Run the playground, and you'll see something like this:

The shadow loop goes in 1-pixel steps, which is not good performance-wise. You can improve that a little by moving along in big steps, provided you don't step past the object. You can safely step in any direction by the distance to the scene instead of a fixed step size, and this way you skip over empty areas fast.

When finding the distance to the nearest surface, you don't know what direction the surface is in, but you have the radius of a circle that intersects with the nearest part of the scene. You can trace along the ray, always stepping to the edge of the circle until the circle radius becomes 0, which means it intersected a surface.

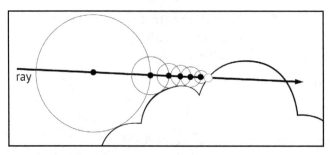

Replace the contents of the getShadow() function with this:

```
float2 lightDir = normalize(lightPos - point);
float shadowDistance = 0.75;
float distAlongRay = 0.0;
for (float i = 0; i < 80; i++) {
  float2 currentPoint = point + lightDir * distAlongRay;
  float d2scene = distanceToScene(currentPoint);
  if (d2scene <= 0.001) { return 0.0; }
  distAlongRay += d2scene;
  if (distAlongRay > shadowDistance) { break; }
}
return 1.0;
```

Run the playground again, and the shadow is now faster and looks more accurate.

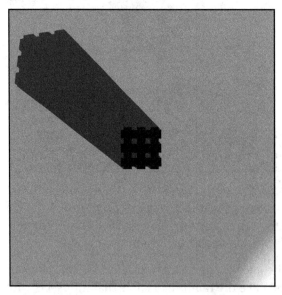

In raymarching, the size of the step depends on the distance from the surface. In empty areas, it jumps big distances, and it can travel a long way. However, if it's parallel to the object and close to it, the distance is always small, so the jump size is also small. That means the ray travels very slowly. With a fixed number of steps, it doesn't travel far. With 80 or more steps you should be safe from getting holes in the shadow.

Congratulations, you made your first hard shadow. Next, you'll be looking into soft shadows. Soft shadows tend to be more realistic and thus, better looking.

Soft shadows

Shadows are not only black or white, and objects aren't just in shadow or not. Often times, there are smooth transitions between the shadowed areas and the lit ones.

In the starter playground, select the **Soft Shadows** playground page. In the **Resources** folder, open **Shaders.metal**.

First, add structs to hold a ray, a sphere, a plane and a light object:

```
struct Ray {
  float3 origin;
  float3 direction;
};

struct Sphere {
  float3 center;
  float radius;
};

struct Plane {
  float yCoord;
};

struct Light {
  float3 position;
};
```

Nothing new or worth noting here, except that for a plane, all you need to know is its Y-coordinate because it's a horizontal plane.

Next, create a few distance operation functions to help you determine distances between elements of the scene:

```
float distToSphere(Ray ray, Sphere s) {
  return length(ray.origin - s.center) - s.radius;
}

float distToPlane(Ray ray, Plane plane) {
  return ray.origin.y - plane.yCoord;
```

```
}

float differenceOp(float d0, float d1) {
  return max(d0, -d1);
}

float unionOp(float d0, float d1) {
  return min(d0, d1);
}
```

Only the union function is new here, which lets you join two areas together.

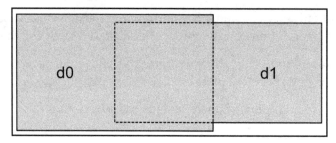

Then, create the distanceToScene() function, which gives you the closest distance to any object in the scene. You can use this function to generate a shape that looks like a hollow sphere with holes in it.

```
float distToScene(Ray r) {
  // 1
  Plane p = Plane{0.0};
  float d2p = distToPlane(r, p);
  // 2
  Sphere s1 = Sphere{float3(2.0), 2.0};
  Sphere s2 = Sphere{float3(0.0, 4.0, 0.0), 4.0};
  Sphere s3 = Sphere{float3(0.0, 4.0, 0.0), 3.9};
  // 3
  Ray repeatRay = r;
  repeatRay.origin = fract(r.origin / 4.0) * 4.0;
  // 4
  float d2s1 = distToSphere(repeatRay, s1);
  float d2s2 = distToSphere(r, s2);
  float d2s3 = distToSphere(r, s3);
  // 5
  float dist = differenceOp(d2s2, d2s3);
  dist = differenceOp(dist, d2s1);
  dist = unionOp(d2p, dist);
  return dist;
}
```

Going through the code:

1. Create a plane and calculate the distance to it from the current ray.

2. Create three spheres: one small one, and two larger ones that are concentric.

3. Create a repeated ray, like you did in the previous chapter, that mirrors the small sphere located between `float3(0)` and 4.0 on each of the three axes. The `fract()` function returns the fractional part of a value.

4. Calculate the distance to the three spheres. The small sphere is created repeatedly every 4.0 units in all directions.

5. Calculate the difference between the two large spheres first, which results in a large hollow sphere. Then, subtract the small one from them, resulting in the large sphere having holes in it. Finally, join the result with the plane to complete the scene.

In Chapter 5, "Lighting Fundamentals," you learned about normals and why they're needed. Next, you'll create a function that finds the normal on any surface. As an example, on your plane, the normal is always pointing up, so its vector is (0, 1, 0); the normal in 3D space is a `float3`, and you need to know its precise position on the ray. A plane, however, is a trivial case.

Assume the ray touches the left side of a sphere situated at the origin. The normal vector is (-1, 0, 0) at that contact point that's pointing to the left, and away from the sphere. If the ray moves slightly to the right of that point, it's inside the sphere (e.g., 0.001). If the ray moves slightly to the left, it's outside the sphere (e.g., 0.001).

If you subtract left from right, you get (-0.001 - 0.001) = -0.002, which still points to the left, so this is your X-coordinate of the normal. Repeat this for Y and Z.

Add this before the kernel:

```
float3 getNormal(Ray ray) {
  float2 eps = float2(0.001, 0.0);
  float3 n = float3(
    distToScene(Ray{ray.origin + eps.xyy, ray.direction}) -
    distToScene(Ray{ray.origin - eps.xyy, ray.direction}),
    distToScene(Ray{ray.origin + eps.yxy, ray.direction}) -
    distToScene(Ray{ray.origin - eps.yxy, ray.direction}),
    distToScene(Ray{ray.origin + eps.yyx, ray.direction}) -
    distToScene(Ray{ray.origin - eps.yyx, ray.direction}));
  return normalize(n);
}
```

eps is a 2D vector, so you can easily do vector swizzling using the chosen value 0.001 for one coordinate, and 0 for the other two coordinates, as needed in each case.

You covered all of the cases and checked that the ray is either inside or outside on all three axes. Finally, you're ready to see some visuals. You'll be writing a raymarching loop again.

Replace the last line of the kernel, `output.write(...)`, with this code:

```
// 1
Ray ray = Ray{float3(0., 4., -12), normalize(float3(uv, 1.))};
// 2
for (int i = 0; i < 100; i++) {
  // 3
  float dist = distToScene(ray);
  // 4
  if (dist < 0.001) {
    col = float3(1.0);
    break;
  }
  // 5
  ray.origin += ray.direction * dist;
}
// 6
float3 n = getNormal(ray);
output.write(float4(col * n, 1.0), gid);
```

Going through the code:

1. Create a ray to travel with inside the scene.

2. Use the loop to divide the ray into many smaller steps. If you don't use enough steps, you might jump past the object.

3. Calculate the new distance to the scene.

4. See how far you are from the surface at that point, and then test if you're inside an object. If yes, break out of the loop.

5. Move along the ray by the distance to the scene to find the point in space you are sampling at.

6. Get the normal so that you can calculate the color of every pixel.

Run the playground, and you'll see the colors representing the normal values.

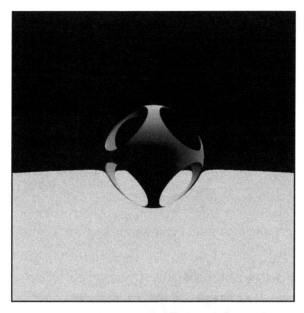

Now that you have normals, you can calculate lighting for each pixel in the scene.

Create a new function named `lighting()`:

```
float lighting(Ray ray, float3 normal, Light light) {
  // 1
  float3 lightRay = normalize(light.position - ray.origin);
  // 2
  float diffuse = max(0.0, dot(normal, lightRay));
  // 3
  float3 reflectedRay = reflect(ray.direction, normal);
  float specular = max(0.0, dot(reflectedRay, lightRay));
  // 4
  specular = pow(specular, 200.0);
  return diffuse + specular;
}
```

Going through the code:

1. Find the direction to the light ray by normalizing the distance between the light position and the current ray origin.

2. For diffuse lighting, you need the angle between the normal and `lightRay`, that is, the dot product of the two. Also, make sure you're never using negative values by making 0 always the minimum value possible.

3. For specular lighting, you need reflections on surfaces, and they depend on the angle you're looking at. You first cast a ray into the scene, reflect it from the surface, and then measure the angle between the reflected ray and `lightRay`.

4. Finally, take a high power of that value to make it much sharper and return the combined light.

Replace the last line, `output.write(...)`, in the kernel with this:

```
Light light = Light{float3(sin(time) * 10.0, 5.0,
                           cos(time) * 10.0)};
float l = lighting(ray, n, light);
output.write(float4(col * l, 1.0), gid);
```

You create a light that circles around in time and use it to calculate the lighting in the scene.

Run the playground, and see the light circling your central sphere:

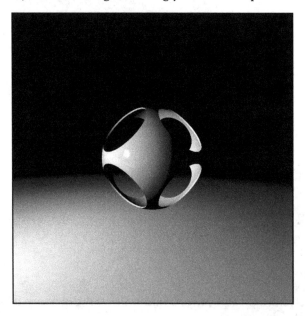

Next, shadows!

Add this function before the kernel:

```
float shadow(Ray ray, Light light) {
  float3 lightDir = light.position - ray.origin;
  float lightDist = length(lightDir);
  lightDir = normalize(lightDir);
  float distAlongRay = 0.01;
```

```
for (int i = 0; i < 100; i++) {
    Ray lightRay = Ray{ray.origin + lightDir * distAlongRay,
                       lightDir};
    float dist = distToScene(lightRay);
    if (dist < 0.001) { return 0.0; }
    distAlongRay += dist;
    if (distAlongRay > lightDist) { break; }
}
return 1.0;
}
```

The shadow function is quite similar to that of hard shadows with a few modifications. You normalize the direction of the light, and then you keep updating the distance along the ray as you march along with it. You also reduce the number of steps to only 100.

Replace the last line in the kernel with this:

```
float s = shadow(ray, light);
output.write(float4(col * l * s, 1.0), gid);
```

Run the playground, and you'll see the light casting shadows.

Time to finally get some soft shadows in the scene.

In real life, a shadow spreads out the farther it gets from an object. For example, where an object touches the floor, you get a sharp shadow; but farther away from the object, the shadow is more blurred.

In other words, you start at some point on the floor, march toward the light, and have either a hit or a miss. Hard shadows are straightforward: you hit something, it's in the shadow. Soft shadows have in-between stages.

Replace shadow() with this:

```
// 1
float shadow(Ray ray, float k, Light l) {
  float3 lightDir = l.position - ray.origin;
  float lightDist = length(lightDir);
  lightDir = normalize(lightDir);
  // 2
  float light = 1.0;
  float eps = 0.1;
  // 3
  float distAlongRay = eps * 2.0;
  for (int i=0; i<100; i++) {
    Ray lightRay = Ray{ray.origin + lightDir * distAlongRay,
                       lightDir};
    float dist = distToScene(lightRay);
    // 4
    light = min(light, 1.0 - (eps - dist) / eps);
    // 5
    distAlongRay += dist * 0.5;
    eps += dist * k;
    // 6
    if (distAlongRay > lightDist) { break; }
  }
  return max(light, 0.0);
}
```

Going through the code, here are the differences from the previous shadow function:

1. Add an attenuator (k) as a function argument, which you'll use to get intermediate values of light.

2. Start with a white light and a small value for **eps**. This is a variable that tells you how much wider the beam is as you go out into the scene. A thin beam means a sharp shadow while a wide beam means a soft shadow.

3. Start with a small distAlongRay, because otherwise, the surface at this point would shadow itself.

4. Compute the light by subtracting the distance from the beam width **eps** and then dividing by it. This gives you the percentage of beam covered. If you invert it (1 - beam width) you get the percentage of beam that's in the light. Then, take the minimum of this new value and light to preserve the darkest shadow as you march along the ray.

5. Move along the ray, and increase the beam width in proportion to the distance traveled and scaled by the attenuator **k**.

6. If you're past the light, break out of the loop. Avoid negative values by returning the maximum between 0.0 and the value of light.

Next, adapt the kernel code to work with the new shadow function. Replace all of the lines after the one where you created the Ray object, with these:

```
// 1
bool hit = false;
for (int i = 0; i < 200; i++) {
  float dist = distToScene(ray);
  if (dist < 0.001) {
    hit = true;
    break;
  }
  ray.origin += ray.direction * dist;
}
// 2
col = float3(1.0);
// 3
if (!hit) {
  col = float3(0.8, 0.5, 0.5);
} else {
  float3 n = getNormal(ray);
  Light light = Light{float3(sin(time) * 10.0, 5.0,
                            cos(time) * 10.0)};
  float l = lighting(ray, n, light);
  float s = shadow(ray, 0.3, light);
  col = col * l * s;
}
// 4
Light light2 = Light{float3(0.0, 5.0, -15.0)};
float3 lightRay = normalize(light2.position - ray.origin);
float fl = max(0.0, dot(getNormal(ray), lightRay) / 2.0);
col = col + fl;
output.write(float4(col, 1.0), gid);
```

Going through the code:

1. Add a boolean that tells you if you whether or not you hit the object. If the distance to the scene is within 0.001, you have a hit.

2. Start with a default white color. This is important, because when you later multiply this color with the value of shadow and that of the light; white will never influence the result because of multiplying by 1.

3. If there's no hit, color everything in a nice sky color, otherwise determine the shadow value.

4. Add another fixed light source in front of the scene to see the shadows in greater detail.

Run the playground, and you'll see a beautiful combination of shadow tones.

Ambient occlusion

Ambient occlusion (AO) is a global shading technique, unlike the Phong local shading technique you learned about in Chapter 5, "Lighting Fundamentals". AO is used to calculate how exposed each point in a scene is to ambient lighting which is determined by the neighboring geometry in the scene.

AO is, however, a weak variant of global illumination. It looks like a scene on a rainy day and feels like a non-directional, diffuse shading effect. For hollow objects, AO makes the interior look darker because the light is even more occluded inside. As you move towards the edges of the object, it looks lighter and lighter.

Only large objects are taken into consideration when computing the amount of ambient light, such as the sky, walls or any other objects that would normally be big enough to cast a shadow if they were lit. AO is usually a fragment post-processing technique. However, you are looking into it in this chapter because AO is a type of shadow.

In the following image, you can see how the base of the curved wall is darker, as well as the base of the box.

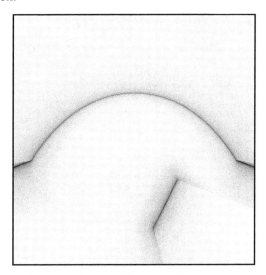

In the starter playground, select the **Ambient Occlusion** playground page. In the **Resources** folder, open **Shaders.metal**.

Add a new box object type:

```
struct Box {
  float3 center;
  float size;
};
```

Next, add a new distance function for Box:

```
float distToBox(Ray r, Box b) {
  float3 d = abs(r.origin - b.center) - float3(b.size);
  return min(max(d.x, max(d.y, d.z)), 0.0)
         + length(max(d, 0.0));
}
```

First, offset the current ray origin by the center of the box. Then, get the symmetrical coordinates of the ray position by using the abs() function. Offset the resulting distance **d** by the length of the box edge.

Second, get the distance to the farthest edge by using max(), and then get the smaller value between 0 and the distance you just calculated. If the ray is inside the box, this value will be negative, so you need to add the larger length between 0 and **d**.

Replace the return line in `distToScene` with this:

```
// 1
Sphere s1 = Sphere{float3(0.0, 0.5, 0.0), 8.0};
Sphere s2 = Sphere{float3(0.0, 0.5, 0.0), 6.0};
Sphere s3 = Sphere{float3(10., -5., -10.), 15.0};
float d2s1 = distToSphere(r, s1);
float d2s2 = distToSphere(r, s2);
float d2s3 = distToSphere(r, s3);
// 2
float dist = differenceOp(d2s1, d2s2);
dist = differenceOp(dist, d2s3);
// 3
Box b = Box{float3(1., 1., -4.), 1.};
float dtb = distToBox(r, b);
dist = unionOp(dist, dtb);
dist = unionOp(d2p, dist);
return dist;
```

Going through the code:

1. Draw two spheres with the same center: one with a radius of 8, and one with a radius of 6. Draw a third, larger sphere at a different location.

2. Subtract the second sphere from the first, resulting in a hollow, thicker sphere. Subtract the third sphere from the hollow sphere to make a cross-section through it.

3. Add a box and a plane to complete the scene.

Run the playground, and you'll see the hollow sphere, box and plane.

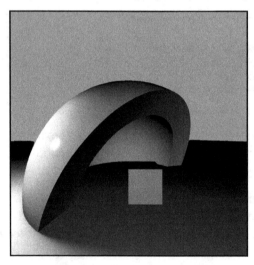

Time to work on the ambient occlusion code.

Create a skeleton function:

```
float ao(float3 pos, float3 n) {
    return n.y * 0.5 + 0.5;
}
```

This function uses the normal's Y component for light and adds 0.5 to it. This makes it look like there's light directly above.

Inside the kernel, since there are no shadows anymore, replace this line:

```
col = col * l * s;
```

With this code:

```
float o = ao(ray.origin, n);
col = col * o;
```

Also, delete or comment out this line:

```
col = col + fl;
```

Run the playground, and you'll see the same scene as before. This time without the shadows, and the surfaces pointing upward are brighter.

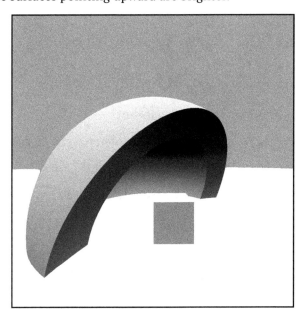

This is a good start. However, it's not yet how ambient occlusion should look.

Ambient means that the light does not come from a well-defined light source, but is rather lighting coming from other objects in the scene, all contributing to the general scene light. **Occlusion** means how much of the ambient light is blocked.

The main idea about ambient occlusion is to use the point where the ray hits the surface and look at what's around it. If there's an object anywhere around it, that will block most of the light nearby, so this will be a dark area. If there's nothing around it, then the area is well lit. For in-between situations, however, you need more precision about how much light was occluded.

Cone tracing is a technique that uses a cone instead of a ray. If the cone intersects an object, you don't just have a simple true/false result. You can find out how much of the cone the object covers at that point. Tracing a cone might be a challenge though. You could make a cone using spheres aligned along a line, small at one end and big at the other end. This would be a good a cone approximation to use. Since you're doubling the sphere size at each step, that means you travel out from the surface very fast, so you need fewer iterations. That also gives you a nice wide cone.

Inside the ao() function, replace the return line with this code:

```
// 1
float eps = 0.01;
// 2
pos += n * eps * 2.0;
// 3
float occlusion = 0.0;
for (float i = 1.0; i < 10.0; i++) {
  // 4
  float d = distToScene(Ray{pos, float3(0)});
  float coneWidth = 2.0 * eps;
  // 5
  float occlusionAmount = max(coneWidth - d, 0.);
  // 6
  float occlusionFactor = occlusionAmount / coneWidth;
  // 7
  occlusionFactor *= 1.0 - (i / 10.0);
  // 8
  occlusion = max(occlusion, occlusionFactor);
  // 9
  eps *= 2.0;
  pos += n * eps;
}
// 10
return max(0.0, 1.0 - occlusion);
```

Going through the code:

1. **eps** is both the cone radius and the distance from the surface.

2. Move away a bit to prevent hitting surfaces you're moving away from.

3. `occlusion` is initially zero (the scene is white).

4. Get the scene distance, and double the cone radius so you know how much of the cone is occluded.

5. Eliminate negative values for the light by using `max()`.

6. Get the amount, or ratio, of occlusion scaled by the cone width.

7. Set a lower impact for more distant occluders; the iteration count provides this.

8. Preserve the highest occlusion value so far.

9. Double **eps**, and then move along the normal by that distance.

10. Return a value that represents how much light reaches this point.

Run the playground, and you'll see ambient occlusion in all of its splendor.

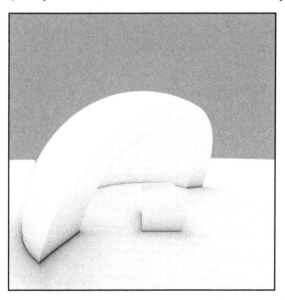

It would be useful to have a camera that moves around the scene. All it needs is a position, a ray that can be used as the camera's direction and a divergence factor which shows how much the ray spreads.

Add a new struct:

```
struct Camera {
  float3 position;
  Ray ray{float3(0), float3(0)};
  float rayDivergence;
};
```

Here, you're setting up a camera using the **look-at** technique. This requires the camera to have a forward direction, an up direction and a left vector. If you're using a right-handed coordinate system, it's a right vector instead.

Add this function before the kernel:

```
Camera setupCam(float3 pos, float3 target,
                float fov, float2 uv, int x) {
  // 1
  uv *= fov;
  // 2
  float3 cw = normalize(target - pos);
  // 3
  float3 cp = float3(0.0, 1.0, 0.0);
  // 4
  float3 cu = normalize(cross(cw, cp));
  // 5
  float3 cv = normalize(cross(cu, cw));
  // 6
  Ray ray = Ray{pos,
              normalize(uv.x * cu + uv.y * cv + 0.5 * cw)};
  // 7
  Camera cam = Camera{pos, ray, fov / float(x)};
  return cam;
}
```

Going through the code:

1. Multiply the **uv** coordinates by the field of view.

2. Calculate a unit direction vector **cw** for the camera's forward direction.

3. The left vector will point orthogonally from an up and forward vector. **cp** is a temporary up vector.

4. The cross product gives you an orthogonal direction, so calculate the left vector **cu** using the forward and up vectors.

5. Calculate the correct up vector **cv** using the left and forward vectors.

6. Create a ray at the given origin with the direction determined by the left vector **cu** for the **X**-axis, by the up vector **cv** for the **Y**-axis and by the forward vector **cw** for the **Z**-axis.

7. Create a camera using the ray you created above. The third parameter is the ray divergence and represents the width of the cone. **x** is the number of pixels inside the field of view (e.g., if the view is 60 degrees wide and contains 60 pixels, each pixel is 1 degree). This is useful for speeding up the SDF when far away, and also for antialiasing.

To initialize the camera, replace this line in the kernel:

```
Ray ray = Ray{float3(0., 4., -12), normalize(float3(uv, 1.))};
```

With this:

```
float3 camPos = float3(sin(time) * 10., 3., cos(time) * 10.);
Camera cam = setupCam(camPos, float3(0), 1.25, uv, width);
Ray ray = cam.ray;
```

Run the playground, and as the camera circles the scene, you can view the ambient occlusion from all directions.

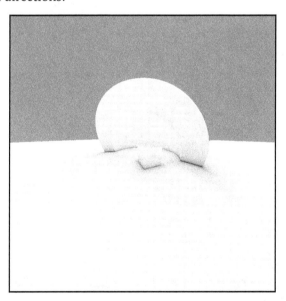

This concludes the raymarching section of the chapter. For the remainder of the chapter, you'll look into a shadow technique that applies to rasterized content.

Percentage closer filtering

If you remember from Chapter 14, "Multipass & Deferred Rendering", you implemented a shadow map.

Even though this technique is quite fast, as you can notice there is a fair amount of aliasing, especially noticeable if you zoom in on the tree shadow. You can easily see all those jaggies on the shadow contour.

Fortunately, there's a technique known as **percentage closer filtering (PCF)** that lets you improve its quality by taking into account the shadow contribution of the neighboring pixels.

In Chapter 14, "Multipass & Deferred Rendering", you learned that the shadow map contains depth values for each pixel which determine whether that pixel is in the shadow or not based on a threshold you set. As an example, you could decide that each pixel with a depth value of z > 10 is in the shadow, and all others are lit.

You'd construct a grid with the depth value of neighboring pixels. This method will still create an aliased line between pixels that are in the shadow and those that are lit, but now you can compare the pixel depth value to those of all the neighboring pixels.

Then, you'd take the average of these values and obtain a filter value. By taking multiple samples around the pixel, you'll know how much the pixel is in the shadow.

Look at the following shadow map.

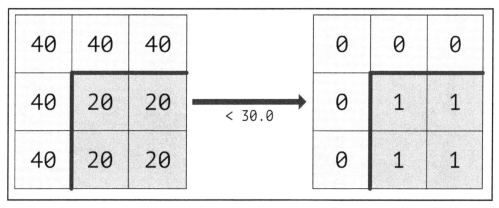

In this example, you set the shadow threshold to 30. Every depth value from the shadow map that's higher than the threshold is considered in shadow, so in the new grid, you give it a value of 0. Everything else is considered lit, so they get a value of 1.

The PCF method assumes you'll do the average of these values, which is 4 / 9 = 0.44, since you have four ones and a total of nine grid cells. The value, 0.44, is what the current pixel will store now.

This method helps you draw a smoother line between light and shadow that's not aliased anymore, because neighboring pixels will now have close values that consist of more than just 0s or 1s.

Are you up for one last fun coding trip?

Open the starter **PCF** project. Build and run, and you'll see a familiar shadowed train and tree.

In the **Shaders** group, in **Main.metal**, replace this code inside `fragment_main`:

```
float shadow_sample = shadowTexture.sample(s, xy);
float current_sample = in.shadowPosition.z /
in.shadowPosition.w;
if (current_sample > shadow_sample ) {
  diffuseColor *= 0.5;
}
return float4(diffuseColor, 1);
```

With this:

```
// 1
const int neighborWidth = 3;
const float neighbors = (neighborWidth * 2.0 + 1.0) *
                        (neighborWidth * 2.0 + 1.0);
// 2
float mapSize = 4096;
float texelSize = 1.0 / mapSize;
float total = 0.0;
for (int x = -neighborWidth; x <= neighborWidth; x++) {
  for (int y = -neighborWidth; y <= neighborWidth; y++) {
    // 3
    float shadow_sample = shadowTexture.sample(
                     s, xy + float2(x, y) * texelSize);
    float current_sample =
        in.shadowPosition.z / in.shadowPosition.w;
    if (current_sample > shadow_sample ) {
      total += 1.0;
    }
  }
}
// 4
total /= neighbors;
float lightFactor = 1.0 - (total * in.shadowPosition.w);
return float4(diffuseColor * lightFactor, 1);
```

Going through the code:

1. Set the grid size, in this case, 7×7.

2. Set the texel size based on the size of the shadow map, and reset the sum of depth values to 0 before entering the loop.

3. For each pixel, get the depth value from the shadow map, and calculate the current depth value. Compare these values, and if the current value is larger than the one from the shadow map, add a 1 to the total sum.

4. Take the average, calculate the light contribution, and apply it to the color of the current pixel.

Build and run the project.

You'll notice that the jaggies are all gone and the shadow now has a smooth edge.

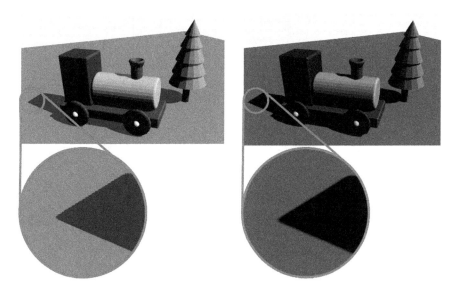

Where to go from here?

This chapter took you through a few advanced shadow techniques, specifically:

- Hard shadows.
- Soft shadows.
- Ambient occlusion.
- Percentage closer filtering.

In addition to these, there are other shadow techniques such as Screen Space Ambient Occlusion and Shadow Volumes. If you're interested in learning about these, review the **references.markdown** for this chapter.

In the next chapter, you'll move on to advanced lighting and learn about important aspects of the physics of light such as reflection, refraction and the rendering equation.

Chapter 20: Advanced Lighting

By Marius Horga

As you've progressed through this book, you've encountered various lighting and reflection models:

- In Chapter 5, "Lighting Fundamentals," you started with the Phong reflection model which defines light as a sum of three distinct components: ambient light, diffuse light and specular light.

- In Chapter 7, "Maps and Materials," you briefly looked at physically based rendering and the Fresnel effect.

- In Chapter 12, "Environment," you implemented skybox-based reflection and image-based lighting, and you used a Bidirectional Reflectance Distribution Function (BRDF) look-up table.

In this chapter, you'll learn about **global illumination** and the famous **rendering equation** that defines it.

While reflection is possible using the local illumination techniques you've seen so far, advanced effects — like refraction, subsurface scattering, total internal reflection, caustics and color bleeding — are only possible with global illumination. By the end of this chapter, you'll be able to render beautiful content like this:

You'll start by examining the rendering equation. From there, you'll move on to reflection and refraction, and you'll render water in two ways: ray marching and rasterization.

The rendering equation

Two academic papers — one by *James Kajiya* and the other by *David Immel et al.* — introduced the rendering equation in 1986. In its raw form, this equation might look intimidating:

$$L_o(\mathbf{x}, \omega_o, \lambda, t) = L_e(\mathbf{x}, \omega_o, \lambda, t) + \int_\Omega f_r(\mathbf{x}, \omega_i, \omega_o, \lambda, t)\, L_i(\mathbf{x}, \omega_i, \lambda, t)\,(\omega_i \cdot \mathbf{n})\, \mathrm{d}\omega_i$$

> **Note**: A friendlier form of it was written recently by *Pixar's Julian Fong* in a tweet. Check **references.markdown** for more information.

The rendering equation is based on the law of conservation of energy, and in simple terms, it translates to an **equilibrium equation** where the sum of all source lights must equal the sum of all destination lights:

```
incoming light + emitted light = transmitted light + outgoing
light
```

If you rearrange the terms of the equilibrium equation, you get the most basic form of the rendering equation:

```
outgoing light = emitted light + incoming light - transmitted
light
```

The incoming light - transmitted light part of the equation is subject to recursion because of multiple light bounces at that point. That recursion process translates to an integral over a unit hemisphere that's centered on the normal vector at the point and which contains all the possible values for the negative direction of the incoming light.

Although the rendering equation might be a bit intimidating, think of it like this: *all the light leaving an object is what remains from all the lights coming into the object after some of them were transmitted through the object.*

The transmitted light can be either absorbed by the surface of the object (material), changing its color; or scattered through the object, which leads to a range of interesting optical effects such as refraction, subsurface scattering, total internal reflection, caustics and so on.

Reflection

Reflection is one of the most common interactions between light and objects. Imagine looking into a mirror. Not only would you see your image being reflected, but you'd also see the reflection of any nearby objects.

Reflection, like any other optical phenomenon, has an equation that depends on three things: the incoming light vector, the incident angle and the normal vector for the surface.

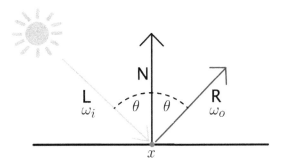

The law of reflection states that the angle at which an incident light hits the surface of an object will be the same as the angle of the light that's being reflected off the normal.

But enough with the theory for now. Time to have some fun coding!

Getting started

Open the starter playground named **AdvancedLighting**, and select the **1. reflection** playground page. Run the playground, and you'll see this:

The code in this playground might look familiar to you, as you've seen it in the two previous chapters. Next, you'll add a checkerboard pattern to the plane and get it to reflect onto the sphere.

Drawing a checkerboard pattern

To draw a pattern on the plane, you first you need to have a way of identifying objects within the scene by comparing their proximity to the camera based on distance.

Inside the **Resources** folder for this playground page, open **Shaders.metal**, and create two constants to identify the two objects in the scene:

```
constant float PlaneObj = 0.0;
constant float SphereObj = 1.0;
```

Then, in distToScene, after this line:

```
float dts = distToSphere(r, s);
```

Add this:

```
float object = (dtp > dts) ? SphereObj : PlaneObj;
```

Here, you check whether the distance to the plane is greater than the distance to the sphere, and you hold the result in `object`.

Include this information in the function return. Replace `return dist;` with:

```
return float2(dist, object);
```

Run the playground to verify the image hasn't changed.

The kernel function `compute` is where you're raymarching the scene. In a `for` loop, you iterate over a considerable number of samples and update the ray color until you attain enough precision. It's in this code block that you'll draw the pattern on the plane.

Inside the `for` loop, locate:

```
float2 dist = distToScene(cam.ray);
```

`distToScene` returns the closest object in `dist.y`.

Immediately after that line, add this:

```
float closestObject = dist.y;
```

After `hit = true;`, add this code:

```
// 1
if (closestObject == PlaneObj) {
  // 2
  float2 pos = cam.ray.origin.xz;
  pos *= 0.1;
  // 3
  pos = floor(fmod(pos, 2.0));
  float check = mod(pos.x + pos.y, 2.0);
  // 4
  col *= check * 0.5 + 0.5;
}
```

Going through the code:

1. Build the checkerboard if the selected object is the plane.

2. Get the position of the camera ray in the horizontal XZ plane since you're interested in intersecting the floor plane only.

3. Create squares. You first alternate between 0s and 1s on both X and Z axes by applying the modulo operator.

At this point, you have a series of pairs containing either 0s or 1s or both. Next, add the two values together from each pair, and apply the modulo operator again.

If the sum is 2, roll it back to 0; otherwise, it will be 1.

4. Apply color. Initially, it's a solid white color. Multiply by 0.5 to tone it down, and add 0.5 back, so you can have both white and grey squares.

If you were to run the playground now, you'd notice a red flag for the missing mod function. However, before adding the missing function, take a moment to understand why you need to implement a separate modulo operation.

The fmod function, as implemented by the Metal Shading Language, performs a **truncated division** where the remainder will have the same sign as the numerator:

```
fmod = numerator - denominator * trunc(numerator / denominator)
```

A second approach, missing from MSL, is called **floored division** where the remainder has the same sign as the denominator:

```
mod = numerator - denominator * floor(numerator / denominator)
```

These two approaches could have entirely different results. When calculating pos, the values need to alternate between 0s and 1s, so taking the floor of the truncated division is enough. However, when you add the two coordinates to determine the check value on the next line, you need to take the floor of their sum.

Add the new floored division function above the kernel function:

```
float mod(float x, float y) {
  return x - y * floor(x / y);
}
```

Run the playground, and you'll see your checkerboard pattern.

All you need to do now is reflect the checkerboard onto the sphere.

Add a new reflection function above `compute`:

```
Camera reflectRay(Camera cam, float3 n, float eps) {
  cam.ray.origin += n * eps;
  cam.ray.dir = reflect(cam.ray.dir, n);
  return cam;
}
```

The MSL standard library provides a `reflect()` function that takes the incoming ray direction and intersecting surface normal as arguments and returns the outgoing (reflected) ray direction. This convenience function returns the `Camera` object, not just its ray direction.

In `compute`, *after* the `if (closestObject == PlaneObj)` block, but *inside* the `if (dist.x < eps)` block, add this code:

```
float3 normal = getNormal(cam.ray);
cam = reflectRay(cam, normal, eps);
```

This gets the normal where the camera ray intersects an object, and reflects it at that point. You move the ray away from the surface, along the normal and not along the ray direction as you might have expected because that could be almost parallel to the surface. You only move away a small distance eps that's precise enough to tell you when there's not a hit anymore.

The bigger eps is, the fewer steps you need to hit the surface, so the faster your tracing is; but it'll also be less accurate. You can play with various values for eps until you find a balance between precision and speed that satisfies your needs.

Run the playground, and you'll see this:

You're successfully reflecting the checkerboard onto the sphere, but the sky is not reflecting. This is because in the starter code you used the boolean hit, which stops and breaks out of the loop when the ray first hits any object.

That's not true anymore, because now you need the ray to keep hitting objects for reflection.

Replace this code:

```
if (!hit) {
  col = mix(float3(.8, .8, .4), float3(.4, .4, 1.),
          cam.ray.dir.y);
} else {
  float3 n = getNormal(cam.ray);
  float o = ao(cam.ray.origin, n);
  col = col * o;
}
```

With this:

```
col *= mix(float3(0.8, 0.8, 0.4), float3(0.4, 0.4, 1.0),
          cam.ray.dir.y);
```

You're now adding the sky color to the scene color globally, not just when a ray failed to hit an object in the scene. You can optionally remove the ao() function and the two lines in compute where hit appears since you're not using them anymore.

Run the playground, and you'll see the sky is now also reflected on the sphere and the floor.

You can spin the camera a little bit to make the reflection look more interesting. Add this parameter to the kernel function:

```
constant float &time [[buffer(0)]]
```

And replace this line:

```
float3 camPos = float3(15.0, 7.0, 0.0);
```

With this:

```
float3 camPos = float3(sin(time) * 15.0,
                       sin(time) * 5.0 + 7.0,
                       cos(time) * 15.0);
```

Run the playground, and you'll see the same image but now nicely animated.

Refraction

Refraction is another common interaction between light and objects that you often see in nature. While it's true that most objects in nature are opaque — thus absorbing most of the light they get — the few objects that are translucent, or transparent, allow for the light to propagate through them.

The law of refraction is a little more complicated than mere equality between the incoming and outgoing light vector angles.

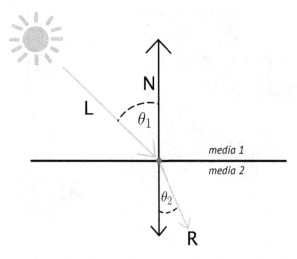

Refraction is dictated by **Snell's law** which states that the ratio of angles equals the reversed ratio of indices of refraction:

$$\frac{sin\ \theta_2}{sin\ \theta_1} = \frac{IOR\ of\ media\ 1}{IOR\ of\ media\ 2}$$

The **index of refraction** (IOR) is a constant that defines how fast light propagates through various media. IOR is defined as the speed of light in a vacuum divided by the phase velocity of light in that particular medium.

> **Note**: There are published lists with IOR values for various media but the ones that interest us here are that of air (IOR = 1) and that of water (IOR = 1.33). https://en.wikipedia.org/wiki/List_of_refractive_indices

If you're trying to find the angle for the refracted light vector through water, for example, all you need to know is the incoming light vector angle which you can use from the reflected light vector, and then you can divide that by the IOR for water (since IOR for air is 1 and does not affect the calculation):

```
sin(theta2) = sin(theta1) / 1.33
```

Time for more coding!

Open the **2. refraction** playground page and run it. The code is the same as the previous section, so you'll see the same animation. Inside the **Resources** folder for this playground page open **Shaders.metal**.

You first need to have a way of knowing when the ray is inside the sphere, as you only do refraction in that case. Add this code to the kernel `compute` function, before the `for` loop:

```
bool inside = false;
```

In the first part of this chapter, you identified objects, so you now know when the ray hits the sphere. This means that you can change the sign of the distance depending on whether the ray enters the sphere, or leaves it. As you know from previous chapters, a negative distance means you're inside the object you are sending your ray towards.

Locate:

```
float2 dist = distToScene(cam.ray);
```

Add this line below it:

```
dist.x *= inside ? -1.0 : 1.0;
```

This adjusts the x value to reflect whether you are inside the sphere or not. Next, you need to adjust the normals. Delete this line:

```
float3 normal = getNormal(cam.ray);
```

Now locate this line:

```
if (dist.x < eps) {
```

And after that line, add the normal definition back:

```
float3 normal = getNormal(cam.ray) * (inside ? -1.0 : 1.0);
```

You now have a normal that points outward when outside the sphere and inward when you're inside the sphere.

Move the following line so that it is inside the inner `if` block because you only want the plane to be reflective from now on:

```
cam = reflectRay(cam, normal, eps);
```

After the inner `if` block, add an `else` block where you make the sphere refractive:

```
// 1
else if (closestObject == SphereObj) {
    inside = !inside;
    // 2
    float ior = inside ? 1.0 / 1.33 : 1.33;
    cam = refractRay(cam, normal, eps, ior);
}
```

Going through the code:

1. Check whether you're inside the sphere. On the first intersection, the ray is now inside the sphere, so turn `inside` to `true` and do the refraction. On the second intersection, the ray now leaves the sphere, so turn `inside` to `false`, and refraction no longer occurs.

2. Set the index of refraction (IOR) based on the ray direction. IOR for water is `1.33`. The ray is first going air-to-water, then it's going water-to-air in which case the IOR becomes `1 / 1.33`.

Add this function above the kernel `compute` function:

```
Camera refractRay(Camera cam, float3 n, float eps, float ior) {
    cam.ray.origin -= n * eps * 2.0;
    cam.ray.dir = refract(cam.ray.dir, n, ior);
    return cam;
}
```

The MSL standard library also provides a `refract()` function, so you're just building a convenience function around it. You subtract the distance this time because the ray is inside the sphere.

You also double the eps value, which is enough to move far enough inside to avoid another collision.

If it were still the old value, the ray might stop and consider it another collision with the object since eps was defined precisely for this purpose: precision. Doubling it will make the ray pass just over the point that was already a collision point before.

Run the playground, and you'll see the sphere now being refractive.

Raytraced water

It's relatively straightforward to create a cheap, fake water-like effect on the sphere.

Open the **3. water** playground page and run it. You'll see the same animation from the previous section. Inside the **Resources** folder for this playground page, open **Shaders.metal**. In the distToScene function, locate:

```
float object = (dtp > dts) ? SphereObj : PlaneObj;
```

And add this code afterward:

```
if (object == SphereObj) {
  // 1
  float3 pos = r.origin;
  pos += float3(sin(pos.y * 5.0),
                sin(pos.z * 5.0),
                sin(pos.x * 5.0)) * 0.05;
  // 2
  Ray ray = Ray{pos, r.dir};
  dts = distToSphere(ray, s);
}
```

Going through the code:

1. Get the ray's current position, and apply ripples to the surface of the sphere by altering all three coordinates. Use `0.05` to attenuate the altering. A value of `0.001` is not large enough to make an impact, while `0.01` is too much of an impact.

2. Construct a new ray using the altered position as the new ray origin while preserving the old direction. Calculate the distance to the sphere using this new ray.

In the kernel `compute` function, replace this line:

```
cam.ray.origin += cam.ray.dir * dist.x;
```

With this:

```
cam.ray.origin += cam.ray.dir * dist.x * 0.5;
```

You added an attenuation factor of `0.5` to make the animation slower but more precise.

Run the playground, and you'll see a water-like ball.

For more realistic water you need a flat, larger surface, with reflection, refraction and a Fresnel effect. You are going to do that next.

Rasterized water

From this point on, and until the end of the chapter, you'll work on adapting an exemplary algorithm for creating realistic water developed by *Michael Horsch* in 2005 (for more information, see **references.markdown**). This realistic water algorithm is purely based on lighting and its optical properties, as opposed to having a water simulation based on physics.

Here's the plan on how you'll proceed:

1. Create a large horizontal quad that will be the surface of the water.

2. Render the scene to a reflection texture.

3. Use a clipping plane to limit what geometry you render.

4. Distort the reflection using a normal map to create ripples on the surface.

5. Render the scene to a refraction texture.

6. Apply the Fresnel effect so that the dominance of each texture will change depending on the viewing angle.

7. Add smoothness to the water depth visibility using a depth texture.

Ready? It's going to be a wild ride but stick around until the end, because you won't want to miss this.

Open the starter project named **Water**. Build and run, and you'll see this:

Because the water construction is reasonably complex, the project has been stripped to the bare minimum.

- **RendererDraws.swift**: Contains methods for separate draw calls for the house, terrain and skybox. Each of these has separate shaders and requires its own pipeline state.

- **RendererExtension.swift**: Contains texture and model loading methods, as well as the camera control. Using your mouse or trackpad, you can drag the camera around a stationary point. You can raise and lower the camera along its Y-axis with the mouse scroll wheel or with a two-finger swipe gesture on the trackpad. On iOS, use a drag or pinch gestures instead.

- **RenderPass.swift**: Contains the necessary details for a render-to-texture pass. It includes the render pass descriptor, color attachment texture and depth attachment texture.

1. Create the water surface

First, you'll create a plane for the water surface. In **Renderer.swift**, add these properties to `Renderer`:

```
lazy var water: MTKMesh = {
  do {
    let mesh = Primitive.plane(device: Renderer.device)
    let water = try MTKMesh(mesh: mesh, device: Renderer.device)
    return water
  } catch let error {
    fatalError(error.localizedDescription)
  }
}()

var waterTransform = Transform()
var waterPipelineState: MTLRenderPipelineState!
```

You create the water mesh from a plane primitive; a transform object, so you can position, rotate and scale the mesh; and a render pipeline state for the water plane.

In `buildPipelineState()`, at the end of the do block, add this code:

```
// water pipeline state
descriptor.vertexFunction =
  library.makeFunction(name: "vertex_water")
descriptor.fragmentFunction =
  library.makeFunction(name: "fragment_water")
descriptor.colorAttachments[0].pixelFormat = .bgra8Unorm
descriptor.vertexDescriptor =
  MTKMetalVertexDescriptorFromModelIO(water.vertexDescriptor)
try waterPipelineState =
  device.makeRenderPipelineState(descriptor: descriptor)
```

With this code, you build the water pipeline state using a reconfigured render pass descriptor that uses its own shader functions and vertex descriptor.

In **RendererDraws.swift**, add this new method to render the water:

```
func renderWater(renderEncoder: MTLRenderCommandEncoder) {
  renderEncoder.pushDebugGroup("water")
  renderEncoder.setRenderPipelineState(waterPipelineState)
  renderEncoder.setVertexBuffer(water.vertexBuffers[0].buffer,
                                offset: 0, index: 0)
  uniforms.modelMatrix = waterTransform.matrix
  renderEncoder.setVertexBytes(&uniforms,
                  length: MemoryLayout<Uniforms>.stride,
                  index: Int(BufferIndexUniforms.rawValue))
  for submesh in water.submeshes {
    renderEncoder.drawIndexedPrimitives(type: .triangle,
              indexCount: submesh.indexCount,
              indexType: submesh.indexType,
              indexBuffer: submesh.indexBuffer.buffer,
              indexBufferOffset: submesh.indexBuffer.offset)
  }
  renderEncoder.popDebugGroup()
}
```

This configures the render encoder by setting its render pipeline state, vertex buffer and uniforms. For each submesh, you issue a draw call as you've done in other chapters.

Back in **Renderer.swift**, in draw(in:), add this code before ending the render encoding:

```
renderWater(renderEncoder: renderEncoder)
```

Next, create the water shaders. In the **Shaders** group, create a new Metal file named **Water.metal**. Remember to add it to both the macOS and iOS targets.

Add this code to the newly created file:

```
#import "Common.h"

struct VertexIn {
  float4 position [[attribute(0)]];
  float2 uv [[attribute(2)]];
};

struct VertexOut {
  float4 position [[position]];
  float2 uv;
};
```

```
vertex VertexOut
    vertex_water(const VertexIn vertex_in [[stage_in]],
                 constant Uniforms &uniforms
                           [[buffer(BufferIndexUniforms)]]) {
  VertexOut vertex_out;
  float4x4 mvp = uniforms.projectionMatrix * uniforms.viewMatrix
                    * uniforms.modelMatrix;
  vertex_out.position = mvp * vertex_in.position;
  vertex_out.uv = vertex_in.uv;
  return vertex_out;
}

fragment float4
    fragment_water(VertexOut vertex_in [[stage_in]]) {
  return float4(0.0, 0.3, 0.5, 1.0);
}
```

This is a minimal configuration for rendering the water surface quad and giving it a bluish color.

Build and run, and you'll see this image with your new water plane.

2. The reflection render pass

The water plane should reflect its surroundings. In Chapter 12, "Environment," you reflected the skybox onto objects, but this time you're also going to reflect the house and terrain on the water.

You're going to render the scene to a texture from a point underneath the water pointing upwards. You'll then take this texture and render it flipped on the water surface.

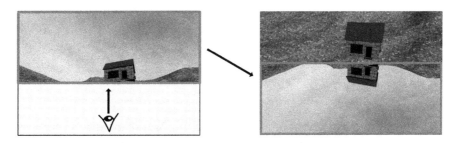

To do this, you'll first create a new render pass.

In **Renderer.swift**, add this new property to Renderer:

```
let reflectionRenderPass: RenderPass
```

In init(metalView:), before calling super.init(), add this:

```
reflectionRenderPass = RenderPass(name: "reflection",
                                  size: metalView.drawableSize)
```

RenderPass will create a render pass descriptor with a texture and a depth texture.

You need reflectionRenderPass to update the size of these textures on resize of the view, so in mtkView(_:drawableSizeWillChange:), add:

```
reflectionRenderPass.updateTextures(size: size)
```

Now that you have set up the render pass, create an encoder, and render the whole scene to the reflection render pass texture.

In draw(in:), add this code below // Water render:

```
// 1
let reflectEncoder =
  commandBuffer.makeRenderCommandEncoder(
        descriptor: reflectionRenderPass.descriptor)!
reflectEncoder.setDepthStencilState(depthStencilState)
// 2
reflectionCamera.transform = camera.transform
reflectionCamera.transform.position.y =
-camera.transform.position.y
reflectionCamera.transform.rotation.x =
-camera.transform.rotation.x
```

```
uniforms.viewMatrix = reflectionCamera.viewMatrix
// 3
renderHouse(renderEncoder: reflectEncoder)
renderTerrain(renderEncoder: reflectEncoder)
renderSkybox(renderEncoder: reflectEncoder)
reflectEncoder.endEncoding()
```

Going through the code:

1. Create a new render command encoder for reflection, and set its depth stencil state.

2. This is the unique part about rendering reflection. You're using a separate camera specially for reflection, and you set its position to the main camera's negated values because you want the camera to be below the surface of the water and capture what's above the surface of the water.

3. Render all of the elements of the scene before ending the rendering encoding.

> **Note**: You can build and run at this point, capture the GPU frame, and check that you have two RenderCommandEncoders. The first RenderCommandEncoder is the texture captured from the reflectionCamera position. It's half-size because you don't need the reflection texture to be completely accurate. Save on memory where you can.

If you build and run the project again, it'll look as it did before — which is nice, but where's that reflection?

In **RendererDraws.swift**, add this line to renderWater(renderEncoder:) before the for loop:

```
renderEncoder.setFragmentTexture(reflectionRenderPass.texture,
                                 index: 0)
```

This sends the texture from the reflection render pass to the water shader.

Now, in **Water.metal**, add a new parameter to the fragment function:

```
texture2d<float> reflectionTexture [[texture(0)]]
```

Replace the return line with this code:

```
// 1
constexpr sampler s(filter::linear, address::repeat);
```

```
// 2
float width = float(reflectionTexture.get_width() * 2.0);
float height = float(reflectionTexture.get_height() * 2.0);
float x = vertex_in.position.x / width;
float y = vertex_in.position.y / height;
float2 reflectionCoords = float2(x, 1 - y);
// 3
float4 color = reflectionTexture.sample(s, reflectionCoords);
color = mix(color, float4(0.0, 0.3, 0.5, 1.0), 0.3);
return color;
```

Going through the code:

1. Create a new sampler with linear filtering and repeat addressing mode.

2. Determine the reflection coordinates which will use an inverted Y value because the reflected image is a mirror of the scene above the water surface. Notice you multiplied by 2.0. You did this because the texture is only half-size.

3. Sample the color from the reflection texture, and mix it a little with the previous bluish color the water plane had before.

Build and run, and you'll see the house, terrain and sky reflected on the water surface.

Nice. But move the camera slightly up the Y-axis by scrolling the mouse wheel or by swiping with two fingers on the trackpad. Oh no! What happened to the reflection?

On the left is the result you see after moving the camera up its Y-axis; on the right is the reflection texture from the reflection render pass. If you want, you can see this texture in the GPU debugger.

As the main camera moves *up* the Y-axis, the reflection camera moves *down* the Y-axis to below the terrain surface which blocks the view to the sky. You could temporarily solve this by culling the terrain's back faces when you render, but this will only introduce other rendering artifacts. A better way of dealing with this issue is to clip the geometry you don't want to render.

3. Clipping planes

A clipping plane, as its name suggests, clips the scene using a plane. It's hardware accelerated, meaning that if geometry is not within the clip range, the GPU immediately discards it and doesn't put it through the rasterizer.

This technique is also a significant performance boost as half of the geometry will not need to get processed by the shaders anymore.

For the reflection texture, you only need to render half the scene, flip it, and add it to the final render.

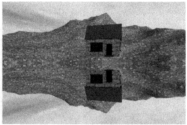

Placing the clipping plane in the center of the view ensures that only half the scene geometry is rendered.

In **Common.h**, add a new member to Uniforms:

```
vector_float4 clipPlane;
```

In **Skybox.metal**, add a new member to the VertexOut struct:

```
float clip_distance [[clip_distance]] [1];
```

Notice the new MSL attribute, [[clip_distance]], which is one of the built-in attributes exclusively used by vertex shaders. The clip_distance built-in attribute is an array of distances, and the [1] argument represents its size — a 1 in this case because you declared this variable as one float only.

> **Note**: You can read more about this in the Metal Shading Language specification, in Section 5.7.1 "Vertex-Fragment Signature Matching."

You may have noticed that here, and in **Shaders.metal**, that FragmentIn is a duplicate of VertexOut. [[clip_distance]] is a vertex-only attribute, so you duplicate the struct so the fragment shader can use it.

Keep FragmentIn the same as VertexOut, by adding the following new member to the FragmentIn struct:

```
float clip_distance;
```

In vertex_skybox, add this line before the return statement:

```
vertex_out.clip_distance[0] =
    dot(uniforms.modelMatrix * vertex_in.position,
        uniforms.clipPlane);
```

Any negative result in vertex_out.clip_distance[0] will result in the vertex being clipped.

Repeat the last three steps in **Shaders.metal** as well: modify the VertexOut struct, the FragmentIn struct and vertex_main accordingly.

Back in **Renderer.swift**, add this line in draw(in:) below // Water render:

```
var clipPlane = float4(0, 1, 0, 0.1)
uniforms.clipPlane = clipPlane
```

This sets a clipping plane before rendering the reflected scene. The clipping plane XYZ is a direction vector that denotes the clipping direction. The last component, 0.1 in this case, represents the distance from the clipping plane that you want to capture — something close to 0 will do.

Below // Main render, add this code:

```
clipPlane = float4(0, -1, 0, 6)
uniforms.clipPlane = clipPlane
```

Build and run the project, and you'll see this:

Whoops! What happened? It seems the fourth component of the clipping plane, the value 6, still affects part of the scene that you want rendered. Increase the clipping distance from 6 to 100:

```
clipPlane = float4(0, -1, 0, 100)
```

Build and run, and your water reflection appears smooth and calm. As you move the camera up and down, the reflection is now consistent.

Still water, no matter how calming, isn't realistic. Time to give that water some ripples.

4. Rippling normal maps

The project contains a tiling normal map for the water ripples.

You'll tile this map across the water and move it, perturbing the water normals, which will make the water appear to ripple.

In **Renderer.swift**, and this new property to Renderer:

```
var waterTexture: MTLTexture?
```

Inside the declaration for the water variable, add this line before the return to load up the normal texture:

```
waterTexture =
    try Renderer.loadTexture(imageName: "normal-water.png")
```

In **RendererDraws.swift**, add this code to renderWater(renderEncoder:) before the for loop:

```
renderEncoder.setFragmentTexture(waterTexture, index: 2)
renderEncoder.setFragmentBytes(&timer,
                               length: MemoryLayout<Float>.size,
                               index: 3)
```

Here, you send the normal map and a timer variable to the fragment shader. Renderer's draw(in:) maintains this timer.

In **Water.metal**, add two new parameters for the texture, and timer to fragment_water:

```
texture2d<float> normalTexture [[texture(2)]],
constant float& timer [[buffer(3)]]
```

Add this code before the line where color is defined:

```
// 1
float2 uv = vertex_in.uv * 2.0;
// 2
float waveStrength = 0.1;
float2 rippleX = float2(uv.x + timer, uv.y);
float2 rippleY = float2(-uv.x, uv.y) + timer;
float2 ripple =
    ((normalTexture.sample(s, rippleX).rg * 2.0 - 1.0) +
     (normalTexture.sample(s, rippleY).rg * 2.0 - 1.0))
        * waveStrength;
reflectionCoords += ripple;
// 3
reflectionCoords = clamp(reflectionCoords, 0.001, 0.999);
```

Going through the code:

1. Get the texture coordinates and multiply them by a tiling value. For 2 you get huge, ample ripples while for something like 16 you get quite small ripples. Pick a value that suits your needs.

2. Calculate ripples by distorting the texture coordinates with the timer value. Only grab the R and G values from the sampled texture because they are the U and V coordinates that determine the horizontal plane where the ripples will be, so the B value is not important here. `waveStrength` is an attenuator value, that gives you weaker or stronger waves.

3. Clamp the reflection coordinates to eliminate anomalies around the margins of the screen.

Build and run, and you'll see gorgeous ripples on the water surface.

5. The refraction render pass

Refraction is very similar to reflection, except that you only need to preserve the part of the scene where the Y coordinate is negative.

In **Renderer.swift**, add this new property to `Renderer`:

```
let refractionRenderPass: RenderPass
```

In `init(metalView:)`, initialize `refractionRenderPass` as a new render pass, just as you did for the reflection render pass:

```
refractionRenderPass = RenderPass(name: "refraction",
                                  size: metalView.drawableSize)
```

Update the size of these textures on resize of the view. In `mtkView(_:drawableSizeWillChange:)`, add:

```
refractionRenderPass.updateTextures(size: size)
```

In `draw(in:)` add this code before `// Main render`:

```
// 1
clipPlane = float4(0, -1, 0, 0.1)
uniforms.clipPlane = clipPlane
uniforms.viewMatrix = camera.viewMatrix
// 2
let refractEncoder =
    commandBuffer.makeRenderCommandEncoder(
        descriptor: refractionRenderPass.descriptor)!
refractEncoder.setDepthStencilState(depthStencilState)
renderHouse(renderEncoder: refractEncoder)
renderTerrain(renderEncoder: refractEncoder)
renderSkybox(renderEncoder: refractEncoder)
refractEncoder.endEncoding()
```

Going through the code:

1. Set the clip plane back to -1 since the camera is now again up and pointing down towards the water.

2. Create the refraction render encoder and render all the elements of the scene again.

In **RendererDraws.swift**, add this line to `renderWater(renderEncoder:)` before the `for` loop:

```
renderEncoder.setFragmentTexture(refractionRenderPass.texture,
                                 index: 1)
```

In **Water.metal**, add a new parameter to `fragment_water`:

```
texture2d<float> refractionTexture [[texture(1)]]
```

Add this line below the one where you define `reflectionCoords`:

```
    float2 refractionCoords = float2(x, y);
```

Similarly, add this line below the one for reflection:

```
    refractionCoords += ripple;
```

And once more for this line to prevent edge anomalies:

```
    refractionCoords = clamp(refractionCoords, 0.001, 0.999);
```

Finally, replace this line:

```
    float4 color = reflectionTexture.sample(s, reflectionCoords);
```

With this line:

```
    float4 color = refractionTexture.sample(s, refractionCoords);
```

Build and run the project, and you'll see that the reflection on the water surface is gone, and instead, you have refraction through the water.

There's one more visual enhancement you can make to your water to make it more realistic: adding rocks and grime. Fortunately, the project already has a texture that can simulate this.

In **Shaders.metal**, in fragment_terrain, uncomment the section under // uncomment this for pebbles.

Build and run the project, and you'll now see a darker texture underwater.

The holy grail of realistic water, however, is having a Fresnel effect that harmoniously combines reflection and refraction based on the viewing angle.

6. The Fresnel effect

The **Fresnel effect** is a concept you've met with in previous chapters. As you may remember, the viewing angle plays a significant role in the amount of reflection you can see. What's new in this chapter is that the viewing angle also affects refraction but in inverse proportion:

- The steeper the viewing angle is, the weaker the reflection and the stronger the refraction.

- The shallower the viewing angle is, the stronger the reflection and the weaker the refraction.

The Fresnel effect in action:

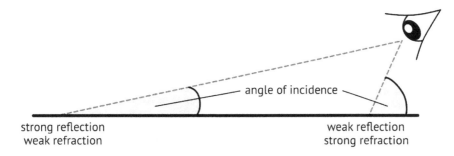

In **Common.h**, add a new member to Uniforms:

```
vector_float3 cameraPosition;
```

In Renderer, add this line to draw(in:) before // Water render:

```
uniforms.cameraPosition = camera.transform.position
```

In **Water.metal**, add two new members to VertexOut:

```
float3 worldPosition;
float3 toCamera;
```

Also, add this code to vertex_water before the return statement:

```
vertex_out.worldPosition =
    (uniforms.modelMatrix * vertex_in.position).xyz;
vertex_out.toCamera = uniforms.cameraPosition -
vertex_out.worldPosition;
```

Replace this line at the end of the fragment shader:

```
float4 color = refractionTexture.sample(s, refractionCoords);
```

With this code:

```
float3 viewVector = normalize(vertex_in.toCamera);
float mixRatio = dot(viewVector, float3(0.0, 1.0, 0.0));
float4 color =
    mix(reflectionTexture.sample(s, reflectionCoords),
        refractionTexture.sample(s, refractionCoords),
        mixRatio);
```

A ratio of 0.5 would mean that reflection and refraction are mixed equally.

Build and run the project.

Move the camera around and notice how reflection predominates for a small viewing angle while refraction predominates when the viewing angle is getting closer to 90 degrees (perpendicular to the water surface).

7. Add smoothness using a depth texture

The light propagation varies for different transparent media, but for water, the colors with longer wavelengths (closer to infrared) quickly fade away as the light ray goes deeper. The bluish colors (closer to ultraviolet) tend to be visible at greater depths because they have shorter wavelengths.

At very shallow depths, however, most light should still be visible. You'll make the water look smoother as depth gets smaller. You can improve the way the water surface blends with the terrain by using a depth map.

In **RendererDraws.swift**, add this code to renderWater(renderEncoder:) before the for loop:

```
renderEncoder.setFragmentTexture(
                refractionRenderPass.depthTexture,
                index: 4)
```

As well as sending the refraction texture from the refraction render pass, you're now sending the depth texture too.

In Renderer, add this code to buildPipelineState() before you create waterPipelineState:

```
guard let attachment = descriptor.colorAttachments[0]
      else { return }
attachment.isBlendingEnabled = true
attachment.rgbBlendOperation = .add
attachment.sourceRGBBlendFactor = .sourceAlpha
attachment.destinationRGBBlendFactor = .oneMinusSourceAlpha
```

Here, you configure the blending options on the color attachment just as you did back in Chapter 10, "Fragment post-processing."

In **Water.metal** add a new parameter to fragment_water:

```
depth2d<float> depthMap [[texture(4)]]
```

Add this code before the ripples code:

```
float proj33 = far / (far - near);
float proj43 = proj33 * -near;
float depth = depthMap.sample(s, refractionCoords);
float floorDistance = proj43 / (depth - proj33);
depth = vertex_in.position.z;
float waterDistance = proj43 / (depth - proj33);
depth = floorDistance - waterDistance;
```

> **Note**: See **references.markdown** for an explanation of converting a non-linear depth buffer value to a linear depth value.

Finally, change the alpha channel so that blending goes into effect. Add this line before the `return` statement:

```
color.a = clamp(depth * 0.75, 0.0, 1.0);
```

Build and run the project, and you'll now see a smoother blending of the water with the terrain.

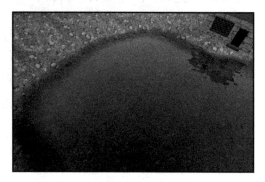

Challenge

Your challenge for this chapter is to use the normal map from the ripples section, this time to add surface lighting.

At the end of this section, you'll render an image like this:

All the work you need to do will be in `fragment_water`. Here are the steps:

1. Get the normal vector as you did for the ripples. In this case, however, you also need to get the B channel, but since that will be the "up" vector, you need to swap G and B so you'll end up with a normal vector of the form RBG.

2. Normalize both the normal and the direction of light before calculating the reflected light using the `reflect` function as you did before.

3. Compute the specular light using the reflected light and the view vector which you used for the Fresnel effect. Apply a higher power until you are pleased with the intensity of the specular light.

4. Add the specular light to the final color.

The completed project is in the **Challenge** folder.

Where to go from here?

You've certainly made a splash with this chapter! If you want to explore more about water rendering, the **references.markdown** file for this chapter contains links to interesting articles and videos.

This concludes the series of chapters using raymarching. But don't worry — rendering is far from over. In the next chapter, "Metal Performance Shaders," you'll get to learn about the newly added feature, Metal for accelerating ray tracing, as well as dip your toes into image processing.

Chapter 21: Metal Performance Shaders

By Marius Horga

In Chapter 11, "Tessellation and Terrains," you had a brief taste of using the Metal Performance Shaders (MPS) framework. MPS consists of low-level, fine-tuned, high-performance kernels that run off the shelf with minimal configuration. In this chapter, you'll dive a bit deeper into the world of MPS.

Overview

The MPS kernels make use of data-parallel primitives that are written in such a way that they can take advantage of each GPU family's characteristics. The developer doesn't have to care about which GPU the code needs to run on, because the MPS kernels have multiple versions of the same kernel written for every GPU you might use. Think of MPS kernels as convenient black boxes that work efficiently and seamlessly with your command buffer. Simply give it the desired effect, a source and destination resource (buffer or texture), and then encode GPU commands on the fly!

The Sobel filter is a great way to detect edges in an image. In the projects folder for this chapter, open and run **sobel.playground** and you'll see such an effect (left: original image, right: Sobel filter applied):

Assuming you already created a device object, a command queue, a command buffer and a texture object for the input image, there are only two more lines of code you need to apply the Sobel filter to your input image:

```
let shader = MPSImageSobel(device: device)
shader.encode(commandBuffer: commandBuffer,
            sourceTexture: inputImage,
            destinationTexture: drawable.texture)
```

MPS kernels are not thread-safe, so it's not recommended to run the same kernel on multiple threads that are all writing to the same command buffer concurrently.

Moreover, you should always allocate your kernel to only one device, because the kernel's init(device:) method could allocate resources that are held by the current device and might not be available to another device.

> **Note:** MPS kernels provide a copy(with:device:) method that allows them to be copied to another device.

The MPS framework serves a variety of purposes beyond image filters. One of those areas is Neural Networks, which is not covered in this book. Instead, you'll stay focused on:

1. Image processing

2. Matrix/vector mathematics

3. Ray tracing

Image processing

There are a few dozen MPS image filters, among the most common being:

• Morphological (area min, area max, dilate, erode).

• Convolution (median, box, tent, Gaussian blur, Sobel, Laplacian, and so on).

• Histogram (histogram, histogram equalization, histogram specification).

• Threshold (binary, binary inverse, to zero, to zero inverse, and so on).

• Manipulation (conversion, Lanczos scale, bilinear scale, transpose).

> **Note:** For a complete list of MPS kernels, consult Apple's official page at https://developer.apple.com/documentation/metalperformanceshaders/image_filters. If you want to implement your own filters, you can get inspired from Gimp's list at https://docs.gimp.org/en/filters.html.

An RGB image is nothing but a matrix with numbers between 0 and 255 (when using 8-bit color channels). A greyscale image only has one such matrix because it only has one channel. For color images, there are three separate RGB channels (red, green, blue) so consequently three matrices, one for each channel.

One of the most important operations in image processing is **convolution** which is an operation consisting of applying a much smaller matrix, often called the kernel, to the original image and obtaining the desired effect as a result.

As an example, this matrix is used for obtaining Gaussian blur:

$$\begin{bmatrix} 1 & 2 & 1 \\ 2 & 4 & 2 \\ 1 & 2 & 1 \end{bmatrix}$$

> **Note:** You can find a list of common kernels at https://en.wikipedia.org/wiki/Kernel_(image_processing)

Here's a diagram showing how the kernel is applied to two pixels:

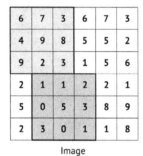 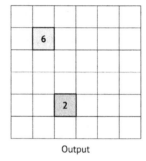

Image   Kernel   Output

And here's how the result shown in green was calculated:

```
(6 * 1  +  7 * 2  +  3 * 1  +
 4 * 2  +  9 * 4  +  8 * 2  +
 9 * 1  +  2 * 2  +  3 * 1) / 16 = 6
```

In this example, 16 represents the weight, and it's not a randomly chosen number — it's the sum of the numbers from the convolution kernel matrix.

When you need to apply convolution to the border pixels, you can apply padding to the input matrix. For example, when the center of a 3×3 convolution kernel overlaps with the image element at position (0, 0), the image matrix needs to be padded with an extra row and extra column of zeros. However, if the bottom rightmost element of the convolution kernel overlaps with the image element at position (0, 0), the image matrix needs to be padded with two extra rows and two extra columns of zeros.

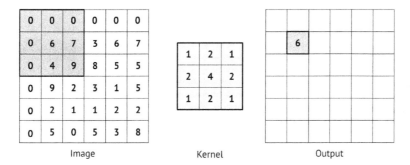

Image   Kernel   Output

Applying the convolution kernel to an image matrix padded with an extra row, and extra column of zeros, gives you this calculation for a 3×3 kernel:

```
(0 * 1  +  0 * 2  +  0 * 1  +
 0 * 2  +  6 * 4  +  7 * 2  +
 0 * 1  +  4 * 2  +  9 * 1) / 9 = 6
```

In this case, the weight, 9, is the sum of the numbers from the convolution kernel matrix that are affecting only the non-zero numbers from the image matrix (4 + 2 + 2 + 1).

Something like this is straightforward, but when you need to work with larger kernels and multiple images that need convolution, this task might become non-trivial.

You know how to calculate by hand and apply convolution to an image — and at the very beginning of the chapter you saw an MPS filter on an image too — but how about using MPS in your engine?

What if you were to implement **bloom** in your engine?

Guess what? You are going to do just that next!

Bloom

The bloom effect is quite a spectacular one. It amplifies the brightness of objects in the scene and makes them look luminous as if they're emitting light themselves.

Below is a diagram that gives you an overview of how to achieve bloom:

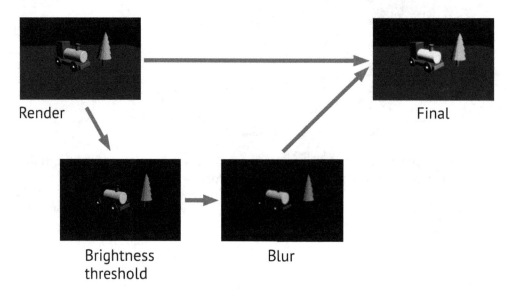

Here are the steps you're going to take:

- Render the entire scene to a texture.

- Apply a threshold filter to this texture. This will amplify the lighter parts of the image, making them brighter.

- Apply a blur filter to the threshold texture from the previous step.

- Combine this texture with the initial scene for the final image.

The project

In the starter folder, open the **Bloom** project. Build and run, and you'll see a familiar scene from previous chapters.

The project currently renders to the view's drawable texture. Instead of sending this texture straight to the screen, you'll intercept and use the drawable texture as input to the threshold filter.

First, import the MPS framework at the top of **Renderer.swift**:

```
import MetalPerformanceShaders
```

Define two textures at the top of Renderer:

```
var outputTexture: MTLTexture!
var finalTexture: MTLTexture!
```

outputTexture will hold the blurred threshold texture, and finalTexture will hold this texture combined with the initial render.

Add this to the end of mtkView(_:drawableSizeWillChange:). Remember, you call this method at the end of init(metalView), and every time the window resizes:

```
outputTexture =
    createTexture(pixelFormat: view.colorPixelFormat,
                  size: size)
finalTexture =
    createTexture(pixelFormat: view.colorPixelFormat,
                  size: size)
```

You create the MTLTextures using a helper method. You'll be able to read, write and render to these textures.

Image Threshold To Zero

Using the following test, MPSImageThresholdToZero is a filter that returns either the original value for each pixel having a value greater than a specified brightness threshold or 0:

```
destinationColor = sourceColor > thresholdValue
                   ? sourceColor : 0
```

This filter has the effect of making darker areas black, while the lighter areas retain their original color value.

In draw(in:), look for // MPS brightness filter, and below that line, add the following:

```
let brightness =
```

```
    MPSImageThresholdToZero(device: Renderer.device,
                           thresholdValue: 0.2,
                           linearGrayColorTransform: nil)
  brightness.label = "MPS brightness"
  brightness.encode(commandBuffer: commandBuffer,
                    sourceTexture: drawable.texture,
                    destinationTexture: outputTexture)
```

Here, you create an MPS kernel to create a threshold texture with a custom brightness threshold set to 0.2 — where all pixels with less than a color value of 0.2 will be turned to black. The input texture is the drawable texture, which contains the current rendered scene. The result of the filter will go into outputTexture.

Internally, the MPS kernel samples from drawable.texture, so you have to set the drawable to be used for read/write operations. Add this to the top of init(metalView:):

```
  metalView.framebufferOnly = false
```

Metal optimizes drawable as much as possible, so setting framebufferOnly to false will affect performance slightly.

To be able to see the result of this filter, you'll blit outputTexture back into drawable.texture. You should be familiar with the blit encoder from Chapter 14, "Multipass & Deferred Rendering."

Locate // blit encoder in draw(in:), and add this afterward:

```
  finalTexture = outputTexture
  guard let blitEncoder = commandBuffer.makeBlitCommandEncoder()
        else { return }
  let origin = MTLOriginMake(0, 0, 0)
  let size = MTLSizeMake(drawable.texture.width,
                         drawable.texture.height,
                         1)
  blitEncoder.copy(from: finalTexture, sourceSlice: 0,
                   sourceLevel: 0,
                   sourceOrigin: origin, sourceSize: size,
                   to: drawable.texture, destinationSlice: 0,
                   destinationLevel: 0, destinationOrigin: origin)
  blitEncoder.endEncoding()
```

This copies the output of the previous filter into the drawable texture.

Build and run the project, and you'll see the brightness texture.

Notice how only half of the tree and part of the train were bright enough to make it to this texture. These white areas are all you need to create the bloom effect.

Before using this texture, you need to add a little fuzziness to it which will make the model edges appear to glow. You can accomplish this with another MPS kernel — the Gaussian blur.

Gaussian blur

MPSImageGaussianBlur is a filter that convolves an image with a Gaussian blur with a given sigma value (the amount of blur) in both the X and Y directions.

In **Renderer.swift**, in draw(in:), locate MPS blur filter, and add this code:

```
let blur = MPSImageGaussianBlur(device: Renderer.device,
                                sigma: 9.0)
blur.label = "MPS blur"
blur.encode(commandBuffer: commandBuffer,
            inPlaceTexture: &outputTexture,
            fallbackCopyAllocator: nil)
```

In-place encoding is a special type of encoding where, behind the curtains, the input texture is processed, stored to a temporary texture and finally written back to the input texture without the need for you to designate an output texture.

The fallbackCopyAllocator argument allows you to provide a closure where you can specify what will happen to the input image should the in-place normal encoding fail.

Build and run the project, and you'll see the result of this blur.

Image add

The final part of creating the bloom effect is to add the pixels of this blurred image to the pixels of the original render.

MPSImageArithmetic, as its name suggests, performs arithmetic on image pixels. Subclasses of this include MPSImageAdd, MPSImageSubtract, MPSImageMultiply and MPSImageDivide.

Adding the rendered scene pixels to the lighter blurred pixels will brighten up those parts of the scene. In contrast, adding them to the black pixels will leave them unchanged.

Just before // blit encoder, add this:

```
let add = MPSImageAdd(device: Renderer.device)
add.encode(commandBuffer: commandBuffer,
          primaryTexture: drawable.texture,
          secondaryTexture: outputTexture,
          destinationTexture: finalTexture)
```

This adds the drawable texture to outputTexture and places the result in finalTexture.

Since you're now creating finalTexture by combining two other textures, remove the line:

```
finalTexture = outputTexture
```

Build and run the project, and you'll see this:

Notice how the tree, train tank and wheel caps appear to glow more? Awesome bloom!

Matrix/vector mathematics

You learned in the previous section how you could quickly apply a series of MPS filters that are provided by the framework. But what if you wanted to make your own filters?

You can create your own filter functions and calculate convolutions yourself, however, when working with large matrices and vectors, the amount of math involved might get overwhelming.

The MPS framework not only provides image processing capability, but it also provides functionality for decomposition and factorizing matrices, solving systems of equation and multiplying matrices and/or vectors on the GPU in a fast, highly parallelized fashion. You're going to look at matrix multiplication next.

Create a new empty playground for macOS, named **matrix.playground**, and add the following code to it:

```
import MetalPerformanceShaders

guard let device = MTLCreateSystemDefaultDevice(),
      let commandQueue = device.makeCommandQueue()
else { fatalError() }

let size = 4
let count = size * size

guard let commandBuffer = commandQueue.makeCommandBuffer()
else { fatalError() }
```

```
commandBuffer.commit()
commandBuffer.waitUntilCompleted()
```

This creates a Metal device, command queue, command buffer and adds a couple of constants you'll need later.

Above the line where you create the command buffer, add a new method that lets you create MPS matrices:

```
func createMPSMatrix(withRepeatingValue: Float) -> MPSMatrix {
  // 1
  let rowBytes = MPSMatrixDescriptor.rowBytes(
                            forColumns: size,
                            dataType: .float32)
  // 2
  let array = [Float](repeating: withRepeatingValue,
                 count: count)
  // 3
  guard let buffer = device.makeBuffer(bytes: array,
                            length: size * rowBytes,
                            options: [])
  else { fatalError() }
  // 4
  let matrixDescriptor = MPSMatrixDescriptor(
                            rows: size,
                            columns: size,
                            rowBytes: rowBytes,
                            dataType: .float32)

  return MPSMatrix(buffer: buffer, descriptor: matrixDescriptor)
}
```

Going through the code:

1. Retrieve the optimal number of bytes between one row and the next. Whereas simd matrices expect column-major order, MPSMatrix uses row-major order.

2. Create a new array and populate it with the value provided as an argument to this method.

3. Create a new buffer with the data from this array.

4. Create a matrix descriptor; then create the MPS matrix using this descriptor and return it.

Use this new method to create and populate three matrices. You'll multiply A and B together and place the result in C. Add this just before creating the command buffer:

```
let A = createMPSMatrix(withRepeatingValue: 3)
```

```
let B = createMPSMatrix(withRepeatingValue: 2)
let C = createMPSMatrix(withRepeatingValue: 1)
```

Add this to create a MPS matrix multiplication kernel:

```
let multiplicationKernel = MPSMatrixMultiplication(
                          device: device,
                          transposeLeft: false,
                          transposeRight: false,
                          resultRows: size,
                          resultColumns: size,
                          interiorColumns: size,
                          alpha: 1.0,
                          beta: 0.0)
```

Below the line where you create the command buffer, add this code to encode the kernel:

```
multiplicationKernel.encode(commandBuffer:commandBuffer,
                          leftMatrix: A,
                          rightMatrix: B,
                          resultMatrix: C)
```

You multiply A and B together and the result is placed in C. At the very end of the playground add this code to read C:

```
// 1
let contents = C.data.contents()
let pointer = contents.bindMemory(to: Float.self,
                                  capacity: count)
// 2
(0..<count).map {
  pointer.advanced(by: $0).pointee
}
```

Going through the code:

1. Read the result back from the matrix C into a buffer typed to `Float`, and set a pointer to read through the buffer.

2. Create an array filled with the values from the buffer.

Run the playground; click **Show Result** on the last line; right-click on the graph of the results, and then choose "Value History."

You'll see that the array contains 16 values, all of which are the number 24.0. That's because the matrix is of size 4×4, and multiplying one row of A with one column of B results in the value 24.0, which is 2×3 added four times.

This is only a small matrix, but you can change the size of the matrix in the `size` variable at the top of the playground, and the matrix multiplication will still be blisteringly fast.

Ray tracing

In Chapter 18, "Rendering with Rays," you looked briefly at ray tracing and path tracing. In this section of the chapter, you're going to implement an MPS-accelerated raytracer, which is, in fact, a path tracer variant using the **Monte Carlo** integration.

> **Note:** You'll create a scene using an adaptation of Apple's sample app https://developer.apple.com/documentation/metalperformanceshaders/metal_for_accelerating_ray_tracing which is translated to Swift, modified to work with .obj files for scene objects and simplified for better understanding.

Remember that with the Monte Carlo integration you shoot primary rays for each pixel, and when there's a hit in the scene, you shoot one more secondary ray in a random direction for each primary ray shot.

Ray tracing and path tracing are known for photorealistic rendering and accurate shadows, reflection, refraction, ambient occlusion, area lights, depth of field, and so on.

The path tracing algorithm looks like this:

```
For each pixel on the screen:
  Reset the pixel color C.
```

```
    For each sample (random direction):
      Shoot a ray and trace its path.
      C += incoming radiance from ray.
  C /= number of samples
```

The outline of this section is as follows:

1. Primary rays

2. Shadow rays

3. Secondary rays

All right, that's a plan. Ready, set, go!

1. Primary rays

Primary rays render the equivalent of a rasterized scene, but the most expensive part of ray tracing is finding all of the intersections between rays and triangles in the scene.

The MPS framework provides a high performance **MPSRayIntersector** class specifically created to accelerate ray-triangle intersection tests on the GPU.

The `MPSRayIntersector` object uses two inputs: a ray buffer and an acceleration structure. It outputs into another buffer all the intersections it finds for each ray cast.

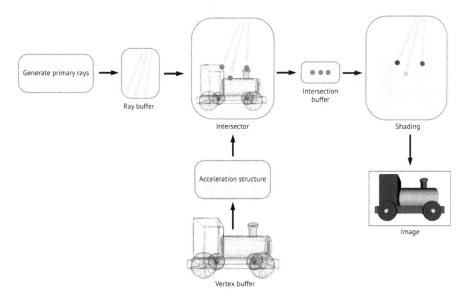

MPSTriangleAccelerationStructure is the class used to build the acceleration structure from vertices that describe the triangles in a scene. You pass the structure on to the intersector.

1.0 The starter app

Time for some coding! Open the starter project named **Raytracing**, build and run it. Although you won't see anything but a dull solid color, the starter project contains much of the setup needed.

In **RendererExtension.swift**, `loadAsset(name:position:scale)` is the method that loads object positions, normals and colors into separate arrays. Call this method with OBJ files to add objects to the scene.

In `Renderer`:

- `createScene()` loads a default scene.

- `createBuffers()` creates buffers from the OBJ file arrays, sets up the uniforms buffer, and creates a random buffer that will contain random numbers.

- `update()` gets called every frame. It updates the uniforms and then generates 256 random numbers between 0 and 1. You'll use these random numbers for antialiasing, choosing a random point on the light source and bouncing secondary rays randomly.

- `draw(in:)` has sections that you'll fill out for the ray tracing, and it renders a simple quad at the end of the method. It's this quad that's currently colored turquoise in the fragment shader.

1.1 Create the render target

As you go through the various passes, you'll write to a render target texture. You'll accumulate values, and this will be the texture you render onto the screen quad.

In **Renderer.swift**, at the top of `Renderer`, add the render target property:

```
var renderTarget: MTLTexture!
```

In `mtkView(_:drawableSizeWillChange:)` create the texture by adding this to the end of the method:

```
let renderTargetDescriptor = MTLTextureDescriptor()
renderTargetDescriptor.pixelFormat = .rgba32Float
```

```
renderTargetDescriptor.textureType = .type2D
renderTargetDescriptor.width = Int(size.width)
renderTargetDescriptor.height = Int(size.height)
renderTargetDescriptor.storageMode = .private
renderTargetDescriptor.usage = [.shaderRead, .shaderWrite]
renderTarget = device.makeTexture(descriptor:
renderTargetDescriptor)
```

This sets up the texture with a descriptor that defines it for both read and write operations on the GPU.

1.2 Create the Ray Intersector

When you generate the primary rays in a kernel, you send the results to a Ray struct array of a particular format. The ray intersector decides this format.

In **Renderer.swift**, at the top of the class, declare the ray intersector object:

```
var intersector: MPSRayIntersector!
let rayStride =
MemoryLayout<MPSRayOriginMinDistanceDirectionMaxDistance>.stride
    + MemoryLayout<float3>.stride
```

rayStride specifies how large the Ray struct will be. It also allows for holding custom fields in the struct. As well as holding origin, minimum distance, direction and maximum distance, you'll also hold a custom float3 color field.

Add a new method to Renderer to create the intersector:

```
func buildIntersector() {
  intersector = MPSRayIntersector(device: device)
  intersector?.rayDataType
      = .originMinDistanceDirectionMaxDistance
  intersector?.rayStride = rayStride
}
```

rayDataType matches the stride you just set up and determines what fields the ray buffer structure should contain. Add a call to this method at the end of init(metalView:):

```
buildIntersector()
```

1.3 Generate primary rays

Before you can generate the primary rays, you need to create a new compute pipeline state and a buffer to hold the generated rays. At the top of Renderer, add this code:

```
var rayPipeline: MTLComputePipelineState!
var rayBuffer: MTLBuffer!
var shadowRayBuffer: MTLBuffer!
```

At the same time as you create and manage the ray buffer, you'll also set up the shadow ray architecture — which is similar to the ray architecture — but you'll handle the shadow calculations later.

Add this to the end of mtkView(_:drawableSizeWillChange:):

```
let rayCount = Int(size.width * size.height)
rayBuffer = device.makeBuffer(length: rayStride * rayCount,
                              options: .storageModePrivate)
shadowRayBuffer =
    device.makeBuffer(length: rayStride * rayCount,
                      options: .storageModePrivate)
```

This creates the ray and shadow buffers large enough to accommodate one ray for each pixel of the rendered image.

In buildPipelines(view:), add this code before the do statement:

```
let computeDescriptor = MTLComputePipelineDescriptor()
computeDescriptor.threadGroupSizeIsMultipleOfThreadExecutionWidt
h
    = true
```

You set threadGroupSizeIsMultipleOfThreadExecutionWidth to true to tell the compiler to optimize the compute kernel. For that to work, you need to also set the thread group size to be a multiple of threadExecutionWidth when you dispatch threads to do work.

Inside the do statement, add this code:

```
computeDescriptor.computeFunction = library.makeFunction(
                                        name: "primaryRays")
rayPipeline = try device.makeComputePipelineState(
                                descriptor: computeDescriptor,
                                options: [],
                                reflection: nil)
```

Here, you set up the pipeline for the generate primary rays compute kernel.

In draw(in:), add this code right below // MARK: generate rays:

```
// 1
let width = Int(size.width)
let height = Int(size.height)
let threadsPerGroup = MTLSizeMake(8, 8, 1)
let threadGroups =
    MTLSizeMake((width + threadsPerGroup.width - 1)
                                / threadsPerGroup.width,
                (height + threadsPerGroup.height - 1)
                                / threadsPerGroup.height,
                1)
// 2
var computeEncoder = commandBuffer.makeComputeCommandEncoder()
computeEncoder?.label = "Generate Rays"
computeEncoder?.setBuffer(uniformBuffer,
                          offset: uniformBufferOffset,
                          index: 0)
computeEncoder?.setBuffer(rayBuffer, offset: 0, index: 1)
computeEncoder?.setBuffer(randomBuffer,
                          offset: randomBufferOffset,
                          index: 2)
computeEncoder?.setTexture(renderTarget, index: 0)
computeEncoder?.setComputePipelineState(rayPipeline)
computeEncoder?.dispatchThreadgroups(threadGroups,
   threadsPerThreadgroup: threadsPerGroup)
computeEncoder?.endEncoding()
```

Going through the code:

1. Configure the number of threads per group and the number of thread groups that will run on the GPU.

2. Create a compute encoder for the ray pipeline, send the texture and buffers to the GPU and dispatch the threads to execute the kernel function on the GPU.

To generate primary rays, you launch a 2D grid of threads, one per render target pixel. Each thread will write a Ray struct to the ray buffer in the kernel. The intersector will read this array of Rays.

Open **Raytracing.metal**. It contains a few helper functions that you'll need later. At the top of the file, after // add structs here, add this:

```
struct Ray {
  packed_float3 origin;
  float minDistance;
  packed_float3 direction;
  float maxDistance;
  float3 color;
};
```

The intersector's `rayDataType` specifies that the struct should be of type `.originMinDistanceDirectionMaxDistance`, so you define the struct according to that type. You also define the extra custom field `color` which will later hold the scene objects' color.

Each primary ray starts at the camera position (`origin`) and passes through a pixel on the image plane resulting in one primary ray per pixel.

Add this kernel function below `Ray`:

```
kernel void
    primaryRays(constant Uniforms & uniforms [[buffer(0)]],
            device Ray *rays [[buffer(1)]],
            device float2 *random [[buffer(2)]],
            texture2d<float, access::write> t [[texture(0)]],
            uint2 tid [[thread_position_in_grid]]) {
    // 1
    if (tid.x < uniforms.width && tid.y < uniforms.height) {
        // 2
        float2 pixel = (float2)tid;
        float2 r = random[(tid.y % 16) * 16 + (tid.x % 16)];
        pixel += r;
        float2 uv =
            (float2)pixel / float2(uniforms.width, uniforms.height);
        uv = uv * 2.0 - 1.0;
        // 3
        constant Camera & camera = uniforms.camera;
        unsigned int rayIdx = tid.y * uniforms.width + tid.x;
        device Ray & ray = rays[rayIdx];
        ray.origin = camera.position;
        ray.direction =
            normalize(uv.x * camera.right + uv.y * camera.up
                        + camera.forward);
        ray.minDistance = 0;
        ray.maxDistance = INFINITY;
        ray.color = float3(1.0);
        // 4
        t.write(float4(0.0), tid);
    }
}
```

Going through the code:

1. Check to make sure you're not using threads outside of the pixel grid.

2. Assign one thread to each pixel on the UV plane. Randomize the pixel slightly to prevent aliasing.

3. Create a Ray for each thread, and fill out the Ray struct. Set the ray's origin to the camera position, calculate the ray direction, set the min/max distance the ray

could extend to, and finally, give the ray a white color.

4. Reset the render target texture to a black image. You'll add color later.

At this point, you could use a refreshment!

1.4 Accumulation

You're writing to the render target texture that you'll combine with the other textures; you'll create these other textures later for shadows and secondary rays, and then render to the background quad. You'll set this render up now so that you can see your progress.

First, set up the pipeline state and final render target texture. In **Renderer.swift**, add this code at the top of `Renderer`:

```
var accumulatePipeline: MTLComputePipelineState!
var accumulationTarget: MTLTexture!
```

In `buildPipelines(view:)`, inside the do statement create the pipeline state:

```
computeDescriptor.computeFunction = library.makeFunction(
  name: "accumulateKernel")
accumulatePipeline = try device.makeComputePipelineState(
  descriptor: computeDescriptor, options: [], reflection: nil)
```

In `mtkView(_:drawableSizeWillChange:)`, add this code at the end of the method to create the texture:

```
accumulationTarget = device.makeTexture(
  descriptor: renderTargetDescriptor)
```

In draw(in:), locate // MARK: accumulation, and add this code right below it:

```
computeEncoder = commandBuffer.makeComputeCommandEncoder()
computeEncoder?.label = "Accumulation"
computeEncoder?.setBuffer(uniformBuffer,
                          offset: uniformBufferOffset,
                          index: 0)
computeEncoder?.setTexture(renderTarget, index: 0)
computeEncoder?.setTexture(accumulationTarget, index: 1)
computeEncoder?.setComputePipelineState(accumulatePipeline)
computeEncoder?.dispatchThreadgroups(threadGroups,
  threadsPerThreadgroup: threadsPerGroup)
computeEncoder?.endEncoding()
```

Here, you call the accumulation kernel which writes from renderTarget to accumulationTarget.

A little further down in draw(in:), add this line before the draw call:

```
renderEncoder.setFragmentTexture(accumulationTarget, index: 0)
```

This sends the texture to the fragment shader for the final draw.

In **Shaders.metal**, add this kernel function:

```
kernel void accumulateKernel(constant Uniforms & uniforms,
                  texture2d<float> renderTex,
                  texture2d<float, access::read_write> t,
                  uint2 tid [[thread_position_in_grid]])
{
  if (tid.x < uniforms.width && tid.y < uniforms.height) {
    // 1
    float3 color = renderTex.read(tid).xyz;
    if (uniforms.frameIndex > 0) {
      // 2
      float3 prevColor = t.read(tid).xyz;
      prevColor *= uniforms.frameIndex;
      color += prevColor;
      color /= (uniforms.frameIndex + 1);
    }
    t.write(float4(color, 1.0), tid);
  }
}
```

Here, you're outputting an average of the input texture over the previous frames.

Going through the code:

1. Read the color value at each pixel from the current render target texture, and if the frame index is 0, simply return the same color and store it into the accumulation texture.

2. If the frame index is not 0, add the current color to the color value from the current render target texture and store it into the accumulation texture.

In `fragmentShader`, replace the return line with this code:

```
constexpr sampler s(min_filter::nearest,
                    mag_filter::nearest,
                    mip_filter::none);
float3 color = tex.sample(s, in.uv).xyz;
return float4(color, 1.0);
```

Instead of returning turquoise, you sample the color from the accumulation texture and return that color as the current pixel color.

Build and run the app, and you'll get a black screen. Remember, you set the render target texture to black during the ray generation kernel.

You've now generated random rays and set up the interceptor. The other part of interception is the **acceleration structure** created from the model vertices.

1.5 Create the acceleration structure

In **Renderer.swift**, at the top of the class, declare the acceleration structure object:

```
var accelerationStructure: MPSTriangleAccelerationStructure!
```

Add a new method to create the structure:

```
func buildAccelerationStructure() {
  accelerationStructure =
    MPSTriangleAccelerationStructure(device: device)
  accelerationStructure?.vertexBuffer = vertexPositionBuffer
  accelerationStructure?.triangleCount = vertices.count / 3
  accelerationStructure?.rebuild()
}
```

This creates the acceleration structure from the provided vertex buffer. `loadAsset(name:position:scale:)` loads up all of the vertices for the models into the vertex position buffer, so the number of triangles in the acceleration structure is the number of vertices divided by 3.

Add a call to this method to the end of `init(metalView:)`:

```
buildAccelerationStructure()
```

1.6 Intersect Rays with the Scene

The next stage is to take the generated rays, and the acceleration structure, and use the intersector to combine them into an intersection buffer that contains all of the hits where a ray coincides with a triangle.

First, you need a new buffer to store the intersections. In **Renderer.swift**, add this to the top of Renderer:

```
var intersectionBuffer: MTLBuffer!
let intersectionStride =
MemoryLayout<MPSIntersectionDistancePrimitiveIndexCoordinates>.s
tride
```

Similar to setting up the Ray struct that contains the generated rays, you'll define an Intersection struct to hold the generated intersections. intersectionStride defines the stride of this struct.

In mtkView(_:drawableSizeWillChange:), add this code at the end to set up the buffer:

```
intersectionBuffer = device.makeBuffer(
    length: intersectionStride * rayCount,
    options: .storageModePrivate)
```

In draw(in:), add this code right below // MARK: generate intersections between rays and model triangles:

```
intersector?.intersectionDataType
= .distancePrimitiveIndexCoordinates
intersector?.encodeIntersection(
    commandBuffer: commandBuffer,
    intersectionType: .nearest,
    rayBuffer: rayBuffer,
    rayBufferOffset: 0,
    intersectionBuffer: intersectionBuffer,
    intersectionBufferOffset: 0,
    rayCount: width * height,
    accelerationStructure: accelerationStructure)
```

You specify the data type to match the stride. Your intersection struct for the kernel will contain distance, primitive indices and coordinates.

The intersector's encodeIntersection method computes intersections and encodes its results to a Metal command buffer.

For primary rays, you set the intersection type to `MPSIntersectionType.nearest` so that the intersector returns the intersections that are closest to the camera. Then, you send the intersector the generated rays, the acceleration structure and the intersection buffer to receive the intersection results.

1.7 Use intersections for shading

The last step in casting primary rays is shading. This depends on intersection points and vertex attributes, so yet another compute kernel applies the lighting based on this information. At the top of `Renderer`, add a new pipeline for this new kernel:

```
var shadePipelineState: MTLComputePipelineState!
```

In `buildPipelines(view:)`, inside the do statement, create the pipeline state:

```
computeDescriptor.computeFunction = library.makeFunction(
  name: "shadeKernel")
shadePipelineState = try device.makeComputePipelineState(
  descriptor: computeDescriptor,options: [], reflection: nil)
```

In `draw(in:)`, under `// MARK: shading`, add this code for the shading compute encoder:

```
computeEncoder = commandBuffer.makeComputeCommandEncoder()
computeEncoder?.label = "Shading"
computeEncoder?.setBuffer(uniformBuffer,
                          offset: uniformBufferOffset,
                          index: 0)
computeEncoder?.setBuffer(rayBuffer, offset: 0, index: 1)
computeEncoder?.setBuffer(shadowRayBuffer, offset: 0, index: 2)
computeEncoder?.setBuffer(intersectionBuffer, offset: 0,
                          index: 3)
computeEncoder?.setBuffer(vertexColorBuffer, offset: 0,
                          index: 4)
computeEncoder?.setBuffer(vertexNormalBuffer, offset: 0,
                          index: 5)
computeEncoder?.setBuffer(randomBuffer,
                          offset: randomBufferOffset,
                          index: 6)
computeEncoder?.setTexture(renderTarget, index: 0)
computeEncoder?.setComputePipelineState(shadePipelineState!)
computeEncoder?.dispatchThreadgroups(threadGroups,
  threadsPerThreadgroup: threadsPerGroup)
computeEncoder?.endEncoding()
```

Compared to the first compute encoder, you're now also sending to the GPU: the shadow ray buffer, the intersection buffer, the vertex color buffer and the vertex normal buffer. You also switched to using the shadePipeline state.

In **Raytracing.metal**, add this struct after Ray:

```
struct Intersection {
  float distance;
  int primitiveIndex;
  float2 coordinates;
};
```

The contents of this struct depend upon the intersectionDataType that you specified in the intersector.

As you can see, intersections depend on the distance between the intersecting ray origin and the geometry, the primitive index, and the **barycentric coordinates** of the intersection on the triangle.

The shading kernel runs one thread per pixel and has the same effect as a fragment shader; however, you'll have to do the interpolation of vertex attributes yourself.

In **Raytracing.metal**, uncomment the function interpolateVertexAttribute. This helper function performs the color and normal interpolations that the rasterizer would normally do for you.

```
template<typename T>
inline T interpolateVertexAttribute(device T *attributes,
                    Intersection intersection) {
  // 1
  float3 uvw;
  uvw.xy = intersection.coordinates;
  uvw.z = 1.0 - uvw.x - uvw.y;
  // 2
  unsigned int triangleIndex = intersection.primitiveIndex;
  T T0 = attributes[triangleIndex * 3 + 0];
  T T1 = attributes[triangleIndex * 3 + 1];
  T T2 = attributes[triangleIndex * 3 + 2];
  return uvw.x * T0 + uvw.y * T1 + uvw.z * T2;
}
```

Going through the code:

1. Get the first two barycentric coordinates from the intersection buffer and compute the third one.

2. Get the vertex attributes from the vertex attribute buffer using primitive index offsets, and then return the interpolated vertex attribute.

The shading kernel itself is pretty hefty, but you'll create it gradually. Add the new kernel at the end of **Raytracing.metal**:

```
kernel void shadeKernel(uint2 tid [[thread_position_in_grid]],
                        constant Uniforms & uniforms,
                        device Ray *rays,
                        device Ray *shadowRays,
                        device Intersection *intersections,
                        device float3 *vertexColors,
                        device float3 *vertexNormals,
                        device float2 *random,
                        texture2d<float, access::write>
  renderTarget)
{
    if (tid.x < uniforms.width && tid.y < uniforms.height) {

    }
}
```

- rays holds a ray color for every sample.

- You'll use shadowRays shortly to calculate the shadow.

- intersections holds the array of intersections in the form of the intersection data type struct Intersection.

From these, you'll be able to work out the intersection point for the thread, so you also pass vertex normals and vertex colors. You'll interpolate the intersection result to get the correct normal and color for the thread.

- The texture renderTarget is unnecessary for the generation of rays, but you'll temporarily write the result of this shading kernel to it so you can see what's happening.

Add this inside the if statement:

```
unsigned int rayIdx = tid.y * uniforms.width + tid.x;
device Ray & ray = rays[rayIdx];
device Ray & shadowRay = shadowRays[rayIdx];
device Intersection & intersection = intersections[rayIdx];
float3 color = ray.color;
```

This extracts the primary ray, shadow ray and intersection per thread/pixel and gets the primary ray color. On the first run, this will be white, which you initially set in primaryRays.

Continue adding after the previous code:

```
// 1
if (ray.maxDistance >= 0.0 && intersection.distance >= 0.0) {
  float3 intersectionPoint = ray.origin + ray.direction
                             * intersection.distance;
  float3 surfaceNormal =
      interpolateVertexAttribute(vertexNormals,
                                 intersection);
  surfaceNormal = normalize(surfaceNormal);
  // 2
  float2 r = random[(tid.y % 16) * 16 + (tid.x % 16)];
  float3 lightDirection;
  float3 lightColor;
  float lightDistance;
  sampleAreaLight(uniforms.light, r, intersectionPoint,
                  lightDirection, lightColor, lightDistance);
  // 3
  lightColor *= saturate(dot(surfaceNormal, lightDirection));
  color *= interpolateVertexAttribute(vertexColors,
                                      intersection);
}
else {
  ray.maxDistance = -1.0;
}
// 4
renderTarget.write(float4(color, 1.0), tid);
```

Going through the code:

1. If both the ray maximum distance and the intersection distance are non-negative, calculate the intersection point and the surface normal using the interpolateVertexAttribute function with the vertex normal buffer.

2. Use another utility function named sampleAreaLight that takes in a light object, a random direction and an intersection point, and returns the light direction, color and distance.

3. Adjust the light color using the surface normal and light direction from the previous steps. Also, adjust the pixel color by using the `interpolateVertexAttribute` function again, but this time, with the vertex color buffer.

4. Write the calculated color for the pixel to the render target texture.

Build and run the project, and you'll see the results of your hard work so far. Instead of using the rasterizer to render your objects, you created the scene with rays and testing vertex intersections.

So far you're not calculating shadows, but it's a start.

Important! Remove this from the end of `shadeKernel`:

```
renderTarget.write(float4(color, 1.0), tid);
```

That line was just for visualization, and you shouldn't write to the render target until you've also calculated the shadow rays.

2. Shadow rays

As well as calculating the color of the pixel in the final texture, you'll need to check if the point is in shadow.

You'll cast a ray from the point to the light source and check whether the shadow ray reaches the light. If it doesn't, then the point is in the shadow.

In the previous kernel, you sent a buffer named `shadowRays` which you're currently not using. You'll write the shadow result into this buffer.

In **Raytracing.metal**, in shadeKernel, locate color *=
interpolateVertexAttribute(vertexColors, intersection);. Add this
afterwards:

```
shadowRay.origin = intersectionPoint + surfaceNormal * 1e-3;
shadowRay.direction = lightDirection;
shadowRay.maxDistance = lightDistance - 1e-3;
shadowRay.color = lightColor * color;
```

This saves the origin of the point, the direction from the point to the light and the
current color. You'll use these values in the next kernel.

In the else part of the same conditional, reset the maximum distance when both the
ray maximum distance and the intersection distance are non-negative:

```
shadowRay.maxDistance = -1.0;
```

The following diagram illustrates the similarity to the primary rays step. You cast
shadow rays from the intersection points to the light source.

If the ray does not reach the light source, it will be in the shadow:

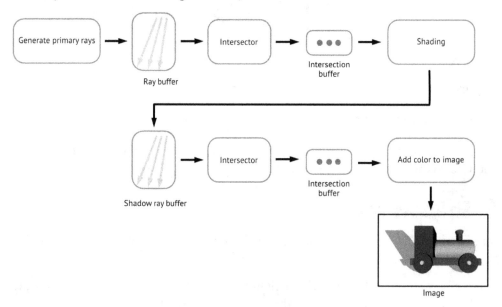

In **Renderer.swift**, add a new pipeline state for the new kernel. Add this code at the top of Renderer:

```
var shadowPipeline: MTLComputePipelineState!
```

In buildPipelines(view:), inside the do statement add this code:

```
computeDescriptor.computeFunction = library.makeFunction(
                                        name: "shadowKernel")
shadowPipeline =
    try device.makeComputePipelineState(
                descriptor: computeDescriptor,
                options: [],
                reflection: nil)
```

This creates the pipeline for the upcoming shadow kernel.

Shadow rays need a maximum distance so they don't go beyond the light source origin. Primary rays don't need that, but they do need the triangle index or barycentric coordinates, neither of which are needed anymore here. Shadow rays carry the color from the shading kernel to the final kernel.

You can reuse the intersector and acceleration structure that you used for primary rays to compute shadow ray intersections, but you'll need to configure it to use a ray data type that supports shadow rays based on the differences listed earlier.

In draw(in:), locate // MARK: shadows, and add this code right below:

```
intersector?.label = "Shadows Intersector"
intersector?.intersectionDataType = .distance
intersector?.encodeIntersection(
            commandBuffer: commandBuffer,
            intersectionType: .any,
            rayBuffer: shadowRayBuffer,
            rayBufferOffset: 0,
            intersectionBuffer: intersectionBuffer!,
            intersectionBufferOffset: 0,
            rayCount: width * height,
            accelerationStructure: accelerationStructure!)
```

Note that you're now using shadowRayBuffer for the intersection generation. Because shadows don't require the triangle index and coordinates anymore, you set the intersection data type to MPSIntersectionDataType.distance. You can still use the same Intersection struct in the kernel, but the other fields will be ignored by the MPSRayIntersector.

For primary ray intersections you had to know the nearest surface to the camera that intersects the ray, but now it doesn't matter which surface intersects a shadow ray. If any triangles exist between the primary intersection and the light source, the primary intersection is shadowed so when computing shadow ray intersections set the intersector's intersection type to .any.

Under the previous code, add the compute encoder for the shadow kernel:

```
computeEncoder = commandBuffer.makeComputeCommandEncoder()
computeEncoder?.label = "Shadows"
computeEncoder?.setBuffer(uniformBuffer,
                          offset: uniformBufferOffset,
                          index: 0)
computeEncoder?.setBuffer(shadowRayBuffer, offset: 0, index: 1)
computeEncoder?.setBuffer(intersectionBuffer, offset: 0,
                          index: 2)
computeEncoder?.setTexture(renderTarget, index: 0)
computeEncoder?.setComputePipelineState(shadowPipeline!)
computeEncoder?.dispatchThreadgroups(
                threadGroups,
                threadsPerThreadgroup: threadsPerGroup)
computeEncoder?.endEncoding()
```

Add this new kernel to the end of **Raytracing.metal**:

```
kernel void shadowKernel(uint2 tid [[thread_position_in_grid]],
             constant Uniforms & uniforms,
             device Ray *shadowRays,
             device float *intersections,
             texture2d<float, access::read_write> renderTarget)
{
  if (tid.x < uniforms.width && tid.y < uniforms.height) {
    // 1
    unsigned int rayIdx = tid.y * uniforms.width + tid.x;
    device Ray & shadowRay = shadowRays[rayIdx];
    float intersectionDistance = intersections[rayIdx];
    // 2
    if (shadowRay.maxDistance >= 0.0
        && intersectionDistance < 0.0) {
      float3 color = shadowRay.color;
      color += renderTarget.read(tid).xyz;
      renderTarget.write(float4(color, 1.0), tid);
    }
  }
}
```

Going through the code:

1. Get the current thread index and create both a shadow ray and intersection distance at the current pixel.

2. If the shadow ray's maximum distance is non-negative, but the distance to the intersection point is negative, add the shadow color to the current color from the render target texture, and save it back to the render target texture. If the shadow ray's intersection distance is negative, it means the intersection point wasn't in shadow because it reached the light source.

Build and run the project, and you'll finally see a shaded scene.

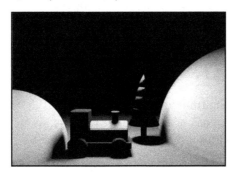

3. Secondary rays

This scene looks quite dark because you're not bouncing any light around. In the real world, light bounces off all surfaces in all directions.

To reproduce this effect, you'll iterate over the central kernels several times. Each time, you'll send the secondary rays in a random direction; this adds diffuse reflected light to areas in shadow.

In Renderer, in draw(in:), extend a for loop from // generate intersections between rays and model triangles to just above // accumulation:

```
for _ in 0..<3 {
    // MARK: generate intersections between rays and model
triangles
    // MARK: shading
    // MARK: shadows
}
// MARK: accumulation
```

This repeats the kernels three times. The more iterations you have, the clearer and more vibrant the image becomes over time, however, the final render will take much longer to complete.

On the first iteration, the ray direction is taken from the initial `primaryRays` kernel; but for secondary rays, the ray direction, or bounce, should be random.

In **Raytracing.metal**, update the secondary rays by giving them a random direction.

In `shadeKernel`, locate where you calculated `shadowRay` in the `if` statement, and add the following code afterward:

```
float3 sampleDirection = sampleCosineWeightedHemisphere(r);
sampleDirection = alignHemisphereWithNormal(sampleDirection,
                                            surfaceNormal);
ray.origin = intersectionPoint + surfaceNormal * 1e-3f;
ray.direction = sampleDirection;
ray.color = color;
```

The project already has the functions `sampleCosineWeightedHemisphere` and `alignHemisphereWithNormal` added. They're responsible for the random direction of the secondary rays and for reducing the amount of noise from the rendered image.

Build and run the project. You should see this image:

Where to go from here?

What a great journey this has been. In this chapter, you were able to use the MPS framework to:

• Add Bloom effect to the scene.

• Write a matrix multiplication basic playground.

- Create an entirely ray-traced scene.

Apple documentation for the MPS frameworks is still being written, but one particular section to pay attention to is the *Tuning Hints* at https://developer.apple.com/documentation/metalperformanceshaders/tuning_hints.

Also, for more information about using the MPS framework for image processing, matrix multiplication and raytracing, you can read **references.markdown** included with this chapter.

Chapter 22: Integrating SpriteKit & SceneKit

By Caroline Begbie & Marius Horga

Now that you have mastery over rendering, you can put your knowledge to use in other APIs.

SceneKit, SpriteKit and Core Image all have some integration with Metal shaders and Metal rendering.

There may be times when you don't want to write a full-blown 3D Metal app, but you want to take advantage of SceneKit. Or perhaps all you want is a 2D layer in your Metal app — for that, you can use SpriteKit. And even though you have less control over your final output with SceneKit and SpriteKit, you can still incorporate shaders to give your games a unique look.

In this chapter, you'll have a look at a collection of APIs that integrate with Metal. You'll first create a toon outline and cel shader for the jet in Apple's SceneKit template.

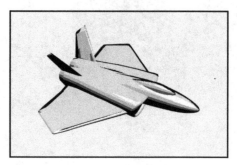

After that, you'll open a scene similar to the game scene from Chapter 9, "Scene Graph." and add to it a 2D overlay that feeds information to the player.

By creating this overlay, you'll learn how to render a SpriteKit scene during each Metal frame rendering.

Finally, you'll create a Core Image Metal kernel to do the blending of the SpriteKit overlay and the 3D rendered scene.

SceneKit starter project

Before creating the toon shader, you'll first learn how to create your own custom shaders in SceneKit, and then find out how to pass data to the shaders.

Create a new project using the macOS Game template (or you can choose the iOS Game template if you prefer). Use the Product Name of **Toon-SceneKit** and make sure that **SceneKit** is specified in the Game Technology dropdown.

> **Note**: Alternatively, you can choose to open the starter project for this chapter instead.

Build and run, and you'll see Apple's default game template jet animating on the screen. You can turn the jet by dragging.

This chapter assumes you have some familiarity with SceneKit, but if not, you can get the general idea of how SceneKit works by reading through **GameViewController.swift**, which has extensive comments.

Just like the game engine you've worked on throughout this book, each element is a node. You have geometry nodes such as the jet, light nodes and a camera node. These nodes are placed into a scene, and you attach the scene to a view. To animate the nodes, you run actions on them.

Open **GameViewController.swift**, and in `viewDidLoad()`, replace the rotation animation:

```
// animate the 3d object
ship.runAction(
  SCNAction.repeatForever(SCNAction.rotateBy(x: 0, y: 2, z: 0,
                        duration: 1)))
```

With:

```
ship.eulerAngles = SCNVector3(1, 0.7, 0.9)
```

This gives you a better angle to see your toon shading.

Next, configure a different background color. Change:

```
scnView.backgroundColor = NSColor.black
```

To:

```
scene.background.contents = nil
scnView.backgroundColor = NSColor(calibratedWhite: 0.9,
                                  alpha: 1.0)
```

This removes the procedural sky that ship.scn created, and replaces it with a light gray background.

SceneKit shaders

To run a Metal shader on a node, you create an SCNProgram object and attach it to the node.

Once you do this, you are fully responsible for transforming vertices, lighting and other shading and, even if you only want to change the fragment color, you have to create **both** a vertex shader and a fragment shader. However, to make it easier, SCNProgram will create uniform values, such as the model matrix or camera position, that you can access in your shaders.

> **Note**: If you're only performing a simple shader operation, such as changing the fragment color, look at SCNShadable where you can provide short strings of shader code instead of taking control of transformations and lighting. The downside is that these compile at run-time, so your app will load slower, and you won't have the benefit of seeing compiler errors if you make a syntax error.

In viewDidLoad(), just after configuring ship.eulerAngles, add this:

```
let program = SCNProgram()
program.vertexFunctionName = "shipVertex"
program.fragmentFunctionName = "shipFragment"
```

This creates a program and tells it what the shader names will be.

Shaders go with materials so that you can render each of your model's materials differently. The jet only has one material, so add this to set the program on the jet's first material:

```
if let material = ship.childNodes[0].geometry?.firstMaterial {
  material.program = program
}
```

For your first SceneKit shader, you'll create the most basic shader possible and render the jet in red. Create a new Metal file named **Shaders.metal**.

Add this to the bottom of your new file:

```
#include <SceneKit/scn_metal>
```

This lets you access the SceneKit buffers and uniforms.

Vertex attributes are available to the vertex shader using a struct. Add this:

```
struct VertexIn {
   float4 position [[attribute(SCNVertexSemanticPosition)]];
};
```

This creates a struct to access vertex position, but you can also access normals, uvs, tangents and skeletal joint and weight information too.

> **Note:** You can see a full list of all the vertex attributes, as well as all the other SceneKit data available to you, in the Apple documentation: https://developer.apple.com/documentation/scenekit/scnprogram.

Your vertex shader has to multiply the vertex by the current model-view-projection matrix. You can access this and other transform data by declaring a struct and binding it to `[[buffer(1)]]`.

Add this new struct:

```
struct Uniforms {
   float4x4 modelViewProjectionTransform;
};
```

Now add the struct containing the data that you'll output from the vertex shader and input to the fragment shader:

```
struct VertexOut {
```

```
    float4 position [[position]];
};
```

Add the vertex function:

```
vertex VertexOut shipVertex(VertexIn in [[stage_in]],
                    constant Uniforms& uniforms [[buffer(1)]]) {
  VertexOut out;
  out.position =
      uniforms.modelViewProjectionTransform * in.position;
  return out;
}
```

The hard-coded property name modelViewProjectionTransform is where the model-view-projection matrix is held. As you'll see, there are various other properties available too.

Once you've worked out how to access the SceneKit data, all of the Metal Shading Language code should be familiar to you.

Add the fragment function:

```
fragment half4 shipFragment(VertexOut in [[stage_in]]) {
  return half4(1, 0, 0, 1);
}
```

Build and run, and you get a plain gray window.

Match SceneKit names

When you're using Metal with SceneKit, you'll find that parameter names must match what SceneKit is expecting. Here, in the vertex function, SceneKit expects the Uniforms buffer to be named scn_node. When you give a parameter the name scn_node, you can name the struct Uniforms any name, and give the buffer index any index, and SceneKit will recognize the buffer as being the uniform values.

Replace uniforms with scn_node in two places, build and run, and you'll see the jet rendered in red.

You just learned the basics of how to integrate SceneKit with Metal shaders, but there are a couple of tricks to send textures and constants to the shaders.

Send a texture to the fragment shader

In **Shaders.metal**, add these attributes to `VertexIn`:

```
float3 normal [[attribute(SCNVertexSemanticNormal)]];
float2 uv [[attribute(SCNVertexSemanticTexcoord0)]];
```

These properties will allow you to access normals and uv coordinates.

Add the uv to `VertexOut`:

```
float2 uv;
```

At the end of `shipVertex`, before `return`, to send the uv coordinates to the fragment shader, add:

```
out.uv = in.uv;
```

Add the texture as a parameter to the fragment function:

```
texture2d<float> baseColorTexture [[texture(0)]]
```

Replace the contents of the fragment function with:

```
constexpr sampler s(filter::linear);
float4 baseColor = baseColorTexture.sample(s, in.uv);
return half4(baseColor);
```

Here, you sample the texture based on the uv coordinates and return the sampled color. If you run the app now, you'll see a white jet. You have to set up the texture in the jet's materials.

In **GameViewController.swift**, in `viewDidLoad()`, locate:

```
material.program = program
```

Add this just afterward, but still inside the conditional block:

```
if let url =
    Bundle.main.url(forResource: "art.scnassets/texture",
                    withExtension: "png") {
  if let texture = NSImage(contentsOf: url) {
    material.setValue(SCNMaterialProperty(contents: texture),
                                  forKey: "baseColorTexture")
  }
}
```

This locates the texture within the scene assets folder and loads it into the material. Note that `baseColorTexture` must be the exact name that you used as the texture parameter in the Metal fragment function.

> **Note:** If your texture is outside of the scene assets folder, you can load it with `NSImage(named: "texture")`.

Build and run to see your textured jet:

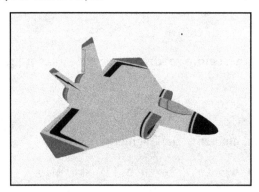

Sending constant data to shaders

You've rendered a textured, unlit model, but if you want to do lighting, then you have to set it up yourself, with the usual light positions, model normals and lighting calculations.

Although SceneKit keeps uniform values for the transformation matrices, you'll have to send lighting constants to the shaders by setting a value on the material.

In **GameViewController.swift**, in the conditional block where you set up the material, add this:

```
let lightPosition = lightNode.position
material.setValue(lightPosition, forKey: "lightPosition")
```

`lightNode.position` is of type `SCNVector3`. SceneKit will convert this to a Metal `float3`. If you need to send other data types, you can convert them to a `Data` type and pass that.

Previously in the book, you have done lighting in world space, but as long as you do calculations on light positions and normals in the same space, it doesn't matter which space it is. With the matrices provided by SceneKit, it's easier to do the lighting calculation in camera space. You'll need both the light position in camera space, as well as the vertex position in camera space without the projection applied. You'll do these calculations in the vertex function.

In **Shaders.metal**, add these fields to `Uniforms`:

```
float4x4 normalTransform;
float4x4 modelViewTransform;
```

SceneKit provides you with the inverse transpose of the model-view matrix to place the normals into camera space, and the model / view matrix to place the position into camera space.

Add these parameters to `shipVertex`:

```
constant SCNSceneBuffer& scn_frame [[buffer(0)]],
constant float3& lightPosition [[buffer(2)]]
```

Whereas `Uniforms` contains per-node data, `SCNSceneBuffer` contains frame data, and you'll be able to access the camera transformation matrix in `scn_frame.viewTransform`.

Add these three variables to `VertexOut`:

```
float3 normal;
float4 viewLightPosition;
float4 viewPosition;
```

These will hold the normal, the light position and the vertex position in camera space to pass along to the fragment function.

Add this to `shipVertex` before the return:

```
out.normal =
    (scn_node.normalTransform * float4(in.normal, 0)).xyz;
out.viewLightPosition =
    scn_frame.viewTransform * float4(lightPosition, 1);
out.viewPosition = scn_node.modelViewTransform * in.position;
```

In `shipFragment`, add this before the `return` line:

```
float3 lightDirection =
    (normalize(in.viewLightPosition - in.viewPosition)).xyz;
float diffuseIntensity =
    saturate(dot(normalize(in.normal), lightDirection));
baseColor *= diffuseIntensity;
```

Build and run, and your jet is now shaded.

Obviously, you didn't go through all of this work to only reproduce what the SceneKit renderer does, but now you can send constants, textures, and do anything in the shader that you care to, like what you're about to see.

Toon shading

A full toon shader consists of an edge detection algorithm and a cel shader where you reduce the color palette. Generally, shading is a gradient from light to dark, but the shading in this rocket demonstrates cel shading where abrupt steps in the gradient occur:

Edge detection is difficult. One way of creating a solid outline is to render the model twice, one larger than the other. Render the larger one in black (or the outline color) behind the smaller model. That will give a solid outline around the model, but it won't take into account curves within the outline.

In Chapter 11, "Tessellation and Terrains", you used the Sobel filter on a height map to find out the difference in slope. If you render the entire screen to a texture, you could run a Sobel filter which convolutes the image and locates edges, but during a fragment shader, so far, you've only been able to access the current rendered fragment, and you have no idea whether that fragment is an edge.

The fwidth function

In fragment shaders, you have access to the current fragment, but you also have access to the change in slope of the fragment from neighboring fragments. Fragments pass through the rasterizer in a 2 x 2 arrangement, and the partial derivatives of each fragment can be derived from the other fragment in the group of four.

`dfdx()` and `dfdy()` return the horizontal and vertical changes in slope, and `fwidth()` gives you the absolute derivative of the combined `dfdx()` and `dfdy()`.

To quickly see how this can be of use in edge detection, replace the entire contents of `shipFragment` with this:

```
float3 v = normalize(float3(0, 0, 10)); // camera position
float3 n = normalize(in.normal);
return fwidth(dot(v, n));
```

Here, you take the dot product of a constant camera position and the fragment's normal and run it through `fwidth()`.

Build and run to see the effect.

You're seeing the slope of the dot product. White is a steep slope, where the fragment normal is at almost 90° to the camera, and black is front on to the camera with no slope at all. Reverse the color, and widen the line.

Replace the `return` with:

```
float edge = step(fwidth(dot(v, n)) * 10.0, 0.4);
return edge;
```

Here, you take the slope of the dot product, multiply it by 10 to increase it, and, if the slope is greater than a threshold of 0.4, return a black line. Otherwise, return white.

The `step` function returns 0.0 when the first argument value is greater than the second and 1.0 if the first argument value is less than the second.

Build and run to see the effect:

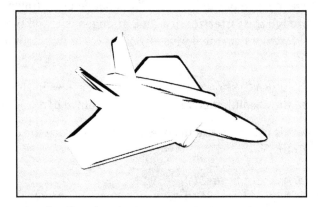

This is not a smooth edge line, but it gives an artistic touch to a toon.

Cel shading

When you render non-photorealistic toons, you generally use a minimal color range. Instead of having a smooth gradient for shading, you use a stepped flat color gradient.

In `shipFragment`, replace the `return` statement with the following:

```
if (edge < 1.0) {
  return edge;
}
float3 l =
    (normalize(in.viewLightPosition - in.viewPosition)).xyz;
float diffuseIntensity = saturate(dot(n, l));
float i = diffuseIntensity * 10.0;
i = floor(i) - fmod(floor(i), 2);
i *= 0.1;
half4 color = half4(0, 1, 1, 1);
```

```
return color * i;
```

If you're not on an edge, calculate the lighting. Generally, you'd use `diffuseIntensity` for the shading, but by flooring the value and subtracting the remainder, you can manipulate the gradient value to be stepped.

Build and run, and you'll see the gradient shading on the sides of the jet.

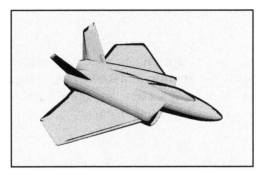

You can spread out the color variation by replacing the `return` with:

```
return color * pow(i, 4) * 4;
```

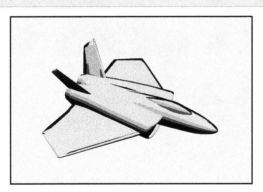

The last thing to add is a specular highlight. Before `return`, add this:

```
float specular = pow(max(0.0, dot(reflect(-l, n), v)), 5.0);
if (specular > 0.5) {
  return 1.0;
}
```

Build and run, and you'll see your final cel shaded jet.

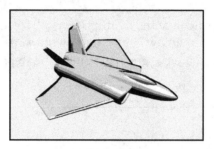

Toon shading is just one of many non-photorealistic techniques. The field is called **NPAR: Non-Photorealistic Animation and Rendering**. You can find further reading on drawing toon lines and other non-photorealism in **references.markdown** accompanying this chapter.

> **Note:** You can also use shaders with SpriteKit nodes. However, you write these in GLSL, as SpriteKit doesn't support shaders written in the Metal Shading Language.

SpriteKit rendering in Metal

> **Note:** As of the time of writing, CIContext.render hangs the app when using Xcode 11 or macOS Catalina 10.15. However, you can still do the rest of this chapter using Xcode 10 on macOS Mojave 10.14.

Apple's WWDC 2017 video, "Going beyond 2D with SpriteKit" shows an example of a 3D rendered video game machine showing a playable 2D SpriteKit scene on the machine's screen.

Another example of why you might want to use a SpriteKit scene rendered in Metal is a **HUD** — that's a **head-up display**. A HUD is an overlay that shows scores or other 2D information you might want to show the player. This term originated from wartime military aviation, where the flight data was projected onto the airplane's windshield. This meant that the pilot didn't have to look away from the action to read the instruments.

SpriteKit is an excellent solution for a HUD because you can put it together quickly with very little code, and render the SpriteKit scene to a texture that you overlay on your 3D Metal scene.

Open the starter project **CarGame**. This a similar project to the one at the end of Chapter 9, "Scene Graph". Relevant changes are:

- Renderer holds the current command buffer as a class property.
- Scene maintains the complete node tree in a flattened array called allNodes.
- RenderPass allows you to hold separate render passes.

The main scene is **GameScene.swift**, which is where you set up the trees and oilcans and perform the game logic, such as collision testing. Build and run to remind yourself what the scene does. Use the keyboard controls W and S for forward and back and QR for rotate (or left and right arrow).

The aim is to collect all of the oilcans while avoiding trees.

You'll create a simple HUD that counts the number of oilcans you collect while driving the car.

Create the HUD in SpriteKit

Create a new SpriteKit scene using the **SpriteKit Scene** template, and name it **Hud.sks**.

Choose **View ▸ Show Library** (or press **Cmd Shift L** to show the library) and drag two Labels onto the Scene. These are SKLabelNodes, and you'll position them in code, so it doesn't matter where they are in the scene. Open the **Attributes inspector**, and enter these values for the two labels:

- **Name:** label
- **Label Text:** Oil cans remaining:

- **Name:** count

- **Label Text:** 100

Choose any font and color you'd like for the two labels. The sample project uses **Avenir Heavy 32.0** and the color yellow.

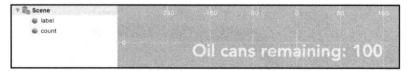

Click on the background of the scene to select the scene node. In the **Custom Class inspector,** name the custom class **Hud**. This is an important step that connects the .sks file with the Hud class you're about to create.

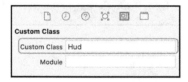

Create a new Swift file named **Hud**. This will hold the class that controls the SpriteKit scene.

Add the code to initialize the new class:

```
import SpriteKit

class Hud: SKScene {
  private var labelCount: SKLabelNode?
  private var label: SKLabelNode?

  override func sceneDidLoad() {
    label = childNode(withName: "//label") as? SKLabelNode
    labelCount = childNode(withName: "//count") as? SKLabelNode
```

```
    }
  }
```

This connects the two label SKNodes with their class properties.

Override the SpriteKit update method:

```
override func update(_ currentTime: TimeInterval) {
  print("updating HUD")
}
```

When you update the scene, you'll print out a message to the debug console. Later, you'll use this method to update the HUD.

Override size to position the two nodes when the scene size changes:

```
override var size: CGSize {
  didSet {
    guard let label = label,
      let labelCount = labelCount else { return }
    label.horizontalAlignmentMode = .left
    labelCount.horizontalAlignmentMode = .left
    let topLeft =
        CGPoint(x: -size.width * 0.5, y: size.height * 0.5)
    let margin: CGFloat = 10
    label.position.x = topLeft.x + margin
    label.position.y = topLeft.y - label.frame.height - margin
    labelCount.position = label.position
    labelCount.position.x += label.frame.width + margin
  }
}
```

This positions the two label nodes at the top left.

You now have a SpriteKit scene and a controlling class. You'll create a subclass of Node so that you can add it to your game scene.

Create a new Swift file named **HudNode.swift**. Add this initialization code to the file:

```
import SpriteKit

class HudNode: Node {
  let skScene: Hud

  init(name: String, size: CGSize) {
    guard let skScene = SKScene(fileNamed: name) as? Hud
      else {
        fatalError("No scene found")
```

```
    }
    self.skScene = skScene
    super.init()
    sceneSizeWillChange(to: size)
    self.name = name
  }

  func sceneSizeWillChange(to size: CGSize) {
    skScene.isPaused = false
    skScene.size = size
  }
}
```

This node subclass holds a reference to the SpriteKit scene and unpauses the scene when it loads. You separate out any initialization so that you can call this method when the user resizes the scene or rotates a device. On a change of size, the SpriteKit scene lays itself out.

In **GameScene.swift**, add the new HUD node. Add this new property:

```
var hud: HudNode!
```

In `setupScene()`, add the node to the scene:

```
hud = HudNode(name: "Hud", size: sceneSize)
add(node: hud, render: false)
```

Your HUD will be a non-rendering node. To be able to render the SpriteKit scene, you'll render it to a separate texture. You then have the choice of rendering the texture on to a quad, or, as you'll do in this chapter, blend the SpriteKit scene texture with the view's current drawable texture.

In `sceneSizeWillChange(to:)`, add the following line:

```
hud.sceneSizeWillChange(to: size)
```

The HUD now updates the label positions when the screen size changes.

SKRenderer

Generally, when you create a SpriteKit app, you hook up the SKScene with an SKView. The SKView takes care of all the rendering and places the scene onto the view. SKRenderer takes the place of SKView, allowing you to control updating and rendering of your SpriteKit scene.

Instead of allowing the view's current drawable to render straight to the scene, you'll intercept the render to blend the SpriteKit scene texture with the drawable in a post-processing stage.

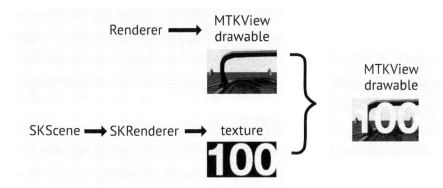

To refresh how this will work in your engine, at each frame, Renderer currently calls update on the current scene. The current scene then updates all nodes. Renderer then renders all the nodes that conform to Renderable.

You'll insert a post-processing stage into Renderer after the render encoder completes, and post process all the nodes that conform to a new PostProcess protocol.

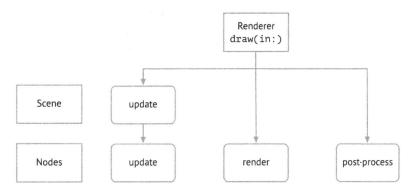

In **HudNode.swift**, add two new properties to HudNode:

```
let skRenderer: SKRenderer
let renderPass: RenderPass
```

The first is the SpriteKit renderer, and the second is a render pass that will contain the rendered SpriteKit scene texture. RenderPass is the same class as you used when rendering the various water passes in Chapter 20, "Advanced Lighting".

In init(name:size:), initialize these before calling super.init():

```
skRenderer = SKRenderer(device: Renderer.device)
skRenderer.scene = skScene
renderPass = RenderPass(name: name, size: size)
```

renderPass contains the HUD texture, so to update the size of it every time the scene size changes, add this to sceneSizeWillChange(to:):

```
renderPass.updateTextures(size: size)
```

To render the SpriteKit scene, override update(deltatime:):

```
override func update(deltaTime: Float) {
  skRenderer.update(atTime: CACurrentMediaTime())
  guard let commandBuffer = Renderer.commandBuffer else {
    return
  }
  let viewPort = CGRect(origin: .zero, size: skScene.size)
  skRenderer.render(withViewport: viewPort,
              commandBuffer: commandBuffer,
              renderPassDescriptor: renderPass.descriptor)
}
```

During each frame, Renderer asks the scene to update its nodes before doing the rendering. By overriding update(deltaTime:), you can update and render the SpriteKit HUD and hold the resulting texture until the post-processing stage. First, you tell skRenderer to update the SpriteKit scene. This will call Hud's update(_:) which currently prints out "updating HUD" to the debug console.

You then render the scene using Renderer's current command buffer. skRenderer will write the SpriteKit scene to the texture held in renderPass.

Build and run the app. Aside from the debug console message which assures you that the SpriteKit scene is updating, you won't see any difference. Click the **Capture GPU Frame** icon to see what's happening behind the scenes.

The frame's command buffer holds the **SKRenderer Pass**. The purple exclamation point warns you that this pass has an unused texture - i.e., you're rendering the texture but not using it yet.

Select **CommandBuffer** to see what textures have rendered during the frame:

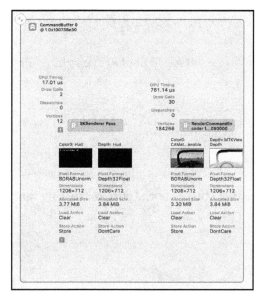

If you look closely, the black texture on the left shows your SpriteKit label nodes. All you have to do now is combine these textures in a post-processing stage.

Post-processing

Create a new Swift file named **PostProcess.swift**, and replace the code with:

```
import MetalKit

protocol PostProcess {
  func postProcess(inputTexture: MTLTexture)
}
```

Each node that conforms to PostProcess will take the view's drawable texture as a parameter.

In **Scene.swift**, add this computed property:

```
var postProcessNodes: [PostProcess] {
  return allNodes.compactMap { $0 as? PostProcess }
}
```

This will extract the PostProcess nodes from the flattened node hierarchy.

In **Renderer.swift**, toward the end of draw(in:), before commandBuffer.present(drawable) process each node:

```
scene.postProcessNodes.forEach { node in
  node.postProcess(inputTexture: drawable.texture)
}
```

In **HudNode.swift**, conform HudNode to PostProcess by adding this after the class definition:

```
extension HudNode: PostProcess {
  func postProcess(inputTexture: MTLTexture) {
    print("post processing")
  }
}
```

Build and run to ensure that you see both "post-processing" and "updating HUD" in the debug console.

Core Image

So far in this chapter, you've used Metal with SpriteKit and SceneKit. There's one other framework whose shaders you can replace with your own custom Metal shaders: Core Image.

It would be more efficient to render a quad onto the screen and do the blending during the quad's fragment shader. However, Core Image, with its huge number of filters, gives you great flexibility in how your final scene looks. These Core Image filters use Metal Performance Shaders under the hood, so they are blazingly fast.

> **Note:** The Core Image Filter reference lists all the available filters: https://developer.apple.com/library/mac/documentation/GraphicsImaging/Reference/CoreImageFilterReference/index.html. Each of the filters shows the parameters you can use with the filter.

First, you'll see how easy it is to render your scene as a cartoon in real time.

In **HudNode.swift**, in postProcess(inputTexture:), replace print with:

```
guard let commandBuffer = Renderer.commandBuffer else { return }
```

```
let drawableImage = CIImage(mtlTexture: inputTexture)!
```

Add the Core Image filter you want to use.

```
let filter = CIFilter(name: "CIComicEffect")!
filter.setValue(drawableImage, forKey: kCIInputImageKey)
let outputImage = filter.outputImage!
```

`CIComicEffect` will detect edges and render a half-tone effect. There's only one input parameter for `CIComicEffect`: the input image. Set the input image on the filter and extract the output image.

`outputImage` is of type `CIImage`, so you need to render it to a new `MTLTexture` before you can use it in your render.

So that you don't have the overhead of creating a new `MTLTexture` every frame, create a new property in `HudNode` for this new texture:

```
var outputTexture: MTLTexture
```

In `init(name:size:)`, before calling `super.init()`, use `RenderPass`'s type method to create the new texture:

```
outputTexture = RenderPass.buildTexture(size: size,
  label: "output texture",
  pixelFormat: renderPass.texture.pixelFormat,
  usage: [.shaderWrite])
```

At the top of `postProcess(inputTexture:)`, add this code:

```
if inputTexture.width != outputTexture.width ||
  inputTexture.height != outputTexture.height {
  let size = CGSize(width: inputTexture.width,
                    height: inputTexture.height)
  outputTexture = RenderPass.buildTexture(size: size,
                    label: "output texture",
                    pixelFormat: renderPass.texture.pixelFormat,
                    usage: [.shaderWrite])
}
```

This will ensure that the output texture has the same size as the input (drawable) texture.

At the end of `postProcess(inputTexture:)`, add this code:

```
let context = CIContext(mtlDevice: Renderer.device)
let colorSpace = CGColorSpaceCreateDeviceRGB()
```

```
context.render(outputImage, to: outputTexture,
            commandBuffer: commandBuffer,
            bounds: outputImage.extent,
            colorSpace: colorSpace)
```

This will create a new `CIContext` and render `outputImage` to your new `outputTexture`. If you specify `nil` for the `commandBuffer`, the context will create its own command buffer. In this situation, you're in the middle of a frame render, so ensure that you use the current command buffer in `Renderer`.

To see `outputTexture` on the screen, blit the texture to the view's current drawable. Add this to the end of `postProcess(inputTexture:)`:

```
let blitEncoder = commandBuffer.makeBlitCommandEncoder()!
let origin = MTLOrigin(x: 0, y: 0, z: 0)
let size = MTLSize(width: inputTexture.width,
                   height: inputTexture.height,
                   depth: 1)
blitEncoder.copy(from: outputTexture, sourceSlice: 0,
            sourceLevel: 0,
            sourceOrigin: origin, sourceSize: size,
            to: inputTexture, destinationSlice: 0,
            destinationLevel: 0, destinationOrigin: origin)
blitEncoder.endEncoding()
```

You've created a few blit encoders along the way, and there's nothing new here. You blit `outputTexture` to `inputTexture`.

Build and run, and you'll get a runtime error:

```
frameBufferOnly texture not supported for compute
```

This means that you haven't set the view's current drawable texture to be writable. For efficiency, Metal sets up the drawable as read-only by default. However, if you're really sure you want to write to the drawable, even though it will slow things down, then you can.

In **Renderer.swift**, in `init(metalView:)`, add this:

```
metalView.framebufferOnly = false
```

Now build and run again to see your real-time comic book effect rendering.

You've now seen how easy it is to apply whole screen effects to your render using Core Image.

Returning to the aim of this section, which is to layer the SpriteKit HUD on top of the rendered scene, you could use a Core Image composite operation using this code:

```
let hudImage = CIImage(mtlTexture: renderPass.texture)!
let drawableImage = CIImage(mtlTexture: inputTexture)!

let filter = CIFilter(name: "CISourceOverCompositing")!
filter.setValue(drawableImage, forKey:
kCIInputBackgroundImageKey)
filter.setValue(hudImage, forKey: kCIInputImageKey)
```

However, all of these operations take place in sRGB space, and your render expects linear space. If you try out the above code, the final image will appear washed out and pale.

This is an excellent excuse to try out a Core Image kernel written in Metal.

You'll take in the two images into the kernel and return the correct pixel from each, at the same time converting the sRGB value to linear.

Core Image Metal kernels

There are a few pre-defined kernel types you can use with Core Image:

- **CIKernel:** a general custom filter.

- **CIColorKernel:** process color information.

- **CIWarpKernel:** process geometry (pixel position) information.

- **CIBlendKernel:** blend two images.

Each of these expects a different data type in the function arguments. It's the last of these that you'll use: CIBlendKernel. This takes two inputs of type sample_t for each of the images.

Create a Metal library for Core Image

Create a new file using the Metal template named **CIBlend.metal**. Include the Core Image headers:

```
#include <CoreImage/CoreImage.h>
```

To access the Core Image types, wrap your functions inside the coreimage namespace:

```
extern "C" { namespace coreimage {

}}
```

Pre-multiplied alpha blending

In this example, the HUD texture has anti-aliasing, where the texture is partially transparent around the edge of the letters:

Aliased   Anti-aliased

Checking the HUD texture in the GPU debugger, you can see that the anti-aliased texture has been pre-multiplied with the alpha value:

In this image, where the solid yellow value in BGRA format is (2, 254, 251, 255), when the anti-aliasing alpha becomes 174, then the multiplied BGR is (1, 173, 171).

When you blend with a pre-multiplied color, the blend formula is:

```
destination.rgb =
    source.rgb + (destination.rgb * (1 - source.a))
```

Inside the `coreimage` namespace, add the new blending function:

```
float4 hudBlend(sample_t hudTexture, sample_t drawableTexture) {
  float4 color =
    (1 - hudTexture.a) * drawableTexture + hudTexture;
  color = float4(srgb_to_linear(color.rgb), 1);
  return color;
}
```

This function takes in the two images and performs pre-multiplied alpha blending. You also convert this pixel from sRGB to linear and return it.

> **Note**: Core Image has its own Kernel Language reference at https://developer.apple.com/metal/CoreImageKernelLanguageReference11.pdf. `srgb_to_linear()` is an example of one of the color functions included in the Core Image Kernel Language.

Compiling and linking a Core Image kernel

You can build the kernel to check that it has no syntactical errors, however, because it's wrapped up in the Core Image namespace, it won't be available at runtime from your default Metal library.

As a rule, when you compile and link your Metal shaders, internally, the Xcode compiler builds to a **.air** file. The linker then links this .air file to a **.metallib** file and includes it with the app resources. The default library with all the Metal shader functions is called **default.metallib**.

> **Note:** To view your default library in Finder, build your project, and under the **Products** group Ctrl-click **CarGame-macOS.app**. Choose **Show In Finder**. Ctrl-click the app file in Finder and choose **Show Package Contents**. Under **Contents ▸ Resources**, you'll find the Metal library with compiled shaders **default.metallib**.

Core Image kernels require extra flags when compiling and linking. If you create a project that doesn't already use Metal, you can set these flags in the Target Build Settings, however, in this project, those Build Settings would conflict with your existing Metal shaders.

The answer is to compile and link the kernel through the command line in Terminal.

Open a terminal window and navigate to the directory that contains **CIBlend.metal**.

Run these two commands to compile and link the Core Image kernel file:

```
xcrun -sdk macosx metal -c -fcikernel CIBlend.metal -o
CIBlend.air
xcrun -sdk macosx metallib -cikernel CIBlend.air -o
CIBlend.metallib
```

Alternatively, for iOS:

```
xcrun -sdk iphoneos metal -c -fcikernel CIBlend.metal -o
CIBlend.air
xcrun -sdk iphoneos metallib -cikernel CIBlend.air -o
CIBlend.metallib
```

> **Note:** You may have to set the path correctly for the Command Line Tools to work. Go to **Xcode ▸ Preferences**, select the **Locations** tab and make sure the **Command Line Tools** dropdown is set appropriately.

```
Betas-iMac:Metal Shaders beta$
Betas-iMac:Metal Shaders beta$ xcrun metal -c -fcikernel CIBlend.metal -o CIBlend.air
Betas-iMac:Metal Shaders beta$ xcrun metallib -cikernel CIBlend.air -o CIBlend.metallib
Betas-iMac:Metal Shaders beta$ ls -l
total 64
-rw-r--r--  1 beta   staff   3312 16 Sep 15:55 CIBlend.air
-rw-r--r--@ 1 beta   staff   1980 16 Sep 15:35 CIBlend.metal
-rw-r--r--  1 beta   staff   3594 16 Sep 15:55 CIBlend.metallib
-rw-r--r--@ 1 beta   staff   3545 14 Jun 15:29 CharacterShaders.metal
-rw-r--r--@ 1 beta   staff   3015 14 Jun 15:29 Common.h
-rw-r--r--@ 1 beta   staff   2775 14 Sep 15:07 HUD.metal
-rw-r--r--@ 1 beta   staff   6858 14 Jun 15:29 Shaders.metal
Betas-iMac:Metal Shaders beta$
```

Two new files will appear in the directory: **CIBlend.air** and **CIBlend.metallib**.

Add **CIBlend.metallib** to your project, checking only the target, either macOS or iOS, that you compiled for. Whenever you change the Core Image kernel, you'll have to recompile and relink this **.metallib** file.

Make sure that you move the compiled .metallib file to the correct CarGame-macOS or CarGame-iOS group. You can delete the .air file.

You can now use the compiled kernel in your app.

In **HudNode.swift**, create a new property for the kernel:

```
let kernel: CIBlendKernel
```

In `init(name:size:)`, before calling `super.init()`, initialize `kernel`:

```
// 1
let url = Bundle.main.url(forResource: "CIBlend",
                          withExtension: "metallib")!
do {
  // 2
  let data = try Data(contentsOf: url)
  // 3
  kernel = try CIBlendKernel(functionName: "hudBlend",
                             fromMetalLibraryData: data)
} catch {
  fatalError("Kernel not found")
}
```

With this code, you:

1. Get the URL for the **.metallib** resource.

2. Load the library data.

3. Get the kernel from the library.

In postProcess(inputTexture:), remove the lines that initialize filter, and replace:

```
let outputImage = filter.outputImage!
```

With:

```
let hudImage = CIImage(mtlTexture: renderPass.texture)!
let extent = hudImage.extent
let arguments = [hudImage, drawableImage]
let outputImage = kernel.apply(extent: extent,
                               arguments: arguments)!
```

Here's the breakdown:

• extent is a CGRect that provides the size of the image.

• arguments match the two arguments that you set up in hudBlend:

```
float4 hudBlend(sample_t hudTexture, sample_t drawableTexture)
```

Build and run, and you'll see your HUD overlaying your rendered scene:

Challenge

Currently, you're printing out "updating HUD" in the debug console. This `print` comes from `update(_:)` in the SpriteKit scene class `Hud`. Your challenge is to update the HUD, keeping track of the oil cans that the player has collected. To achieve this, in `GameScene`, on colliding with an oil can, you'll tell `HudNode` to update `Hud` using `oilcanCount`. As always, you'll find a solution in the challenge directory for this project.

Where to go from here?

In this chapter, you created two simple examples that you can experiment with further. Fragment shaders, and to a lesser extent vertex shaders, are endlessly fascinating.

Examine contributions for each shader type at:

• **Fragment shader**: https://www.shadertoy.com

• **Vertex shader**: https://www.vertexshaderart.com

After looking things over, try to express the shader in the Metal Shading Language.

For Core Image filters, the go-to (free for now) book is Core Image for Swift by Simon Gladman available at https://itunes.apple.com/us/book/core-image-for-swift/id1073029980?mt=13. You will learn how to chain filters together and explore your creativity.

Finally, in **references.markdown** for this chapter there are some interesting links for Non-Photorealistic Rendering.

Chapter 23: Debugging & Profiling

By Marius Horga

Debugging and **Profiling** are must-have skills for optimizing the performance of your projects, and Apple has provided developers with several fantastic optimization tools to achieve this. In this chapter, you'll look at:

1. **Debugging:** Locate hard-to-find bugs using the GPU debugger.

2. **Profiling:** Monitor your app's performance with Instruments and other tools.

Time to go on a bug hunt!

Debugging

Rather than trying to guess the truth, it's always more useful to capture a GPU frame and examine it for clues.

The aim of this section is to render a scene similar to this:

In the **starter** folder, open the **Debugging** project. Build and run, and you'll notice the rocks and grass are missing from the scene.

You'll look into potential causes for why that happened, shortly.

Launch the **Capture GPU Frame** tool by clicking the camera button in the debug bar.

Debug navigator

After Xcode finishes capturing the GPU frame, it displays the debugger windows.

On the left side, you'll see a GPU trace in the Debug navigator. The debugger always stops at the last encoder the command buffer commits, so select RenderCommandEncoder.

This is where you'll see the command encoders within each command buffer.

Press **Cmd Shift T** or **File ▸ New ▸ Window** to open up a new window. In this new window, open **Renderer.swift** and locate draw(in:). With side-by-side windows, you can compare the code in draw(in:) with the commands listed in the debugger.

In this frame, you have one render command encoder that renders all of the elements of the scene, and one compute command encoder that doesn't do anything yet. The debugger lists each command in the command encoder, such as setFragmentBytes and setComputePipeline.

It's a good idea, as draw(in:) currently does, to surround each draw command with a debug group with renderEncoder.pushDebugGroup(renderable.name) as it gives a friendly name to each draw call, and you can easily see what items are rendering. In the debugger, you can see debug groups with ground.obj, grass and Rocks.

Close the new window when you have finished comparing the command list.

Central pane

The top middle area of the captured frame has the central pane that normally opens
to the **Dependency Viewer** — a nice summary of the current command buffer.

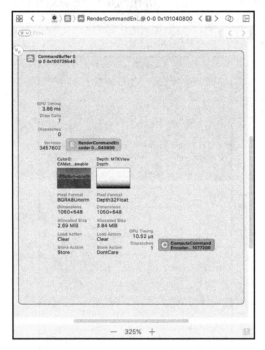

On the right side, the assistant editor lists attachments and the **Debug** and **Inspect
Pixels** buttons.

Attachments are the resources held by color and depth attachments.

> **Note:** To see the attachments, you may have to choose **Attachments** from the top jump bar.

Debug area

The bottom area is the **Debug area**, and it has two larger areas — **GPU States** and **Console** — as well as the debug bar that hosts the **Debug Shader** and the **Reload Shader** buttons; You'll use these a lot in your debugging career.

All right, time for debugging!

In the **Debug navigator**, open the `Rocks` group, and select `drawIndexedPrimitives`.

Bound Resources should automatically display in the central pane, and Attachments in the assistant editor pane, but you can also select these from the jump bars.

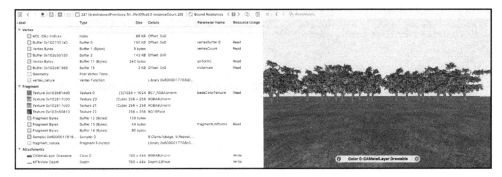

You can see in the Debug navigator that both `Grass` and `Rocks` are listed, and both of them have draw calls. This means that these models are rendered, but for some reason, they don't appear on the screen. A logical next step is to look at how vertices are rendered.

The geometry viewer

While still having `drawIndexedPrimitives` for the `Rocks` group selected, click the **Debug Shader** icon on the debug bar, and select the Vertex pane. This is the **Geometry Viewer** tool.

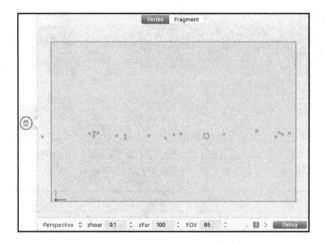

> **Note**: The shader debugger magically "knows" if you're debugging a render encoder or a compute encoder and adapts its contents accordingly. For vertex shaders, it opens the Geometry Viewer. You can learn more about it on the Apple documentation web page at https://developer.apple.com/documentation/metal/vertex_data/inspecting_vertices_with_the_geometry_viewer.

Notice how the frustum only has a few vertices rendered for Rocks, and most of them are being skipped. A next logical step is to look at the shader code. There are two ways to go to your shader code:

- Double-click vertex_nature in the central pane to open the vertex shader in place (in the central pane).

- While in a shader debugger session, clicking Debug takes you to the shader code.

> **Note**: When entering the shader debugger in your own Metal projects, you may get an error. To see the debugging information, you have to compile with shader source code included. You can do this in your project's build settings. Under **Produce Debugging Information**, on the **Debug** option, switch to **Yes, include source code**. On the **Release** option, verify it's set to **No**. Production apps are not allowed to contain debug information, so you wouldn't want to leave your app with such info when publishing it later to the App Store.

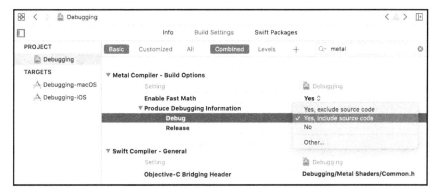

Examining the code in the vertex shader, you realize that with this line:

```
VertexIn vertexIn = in[offset];
```

You're reading only one vertex per offset value. What you should be doing is offsetting the vertex buffer index instead. Change the previous line to this:

```
VertexIn vertexIn = in[vertexID + offset];
```

On the debug bar, click **Reload Shaders** next to Debug Shader.

All of the vertices are now showing in the shader debugger.

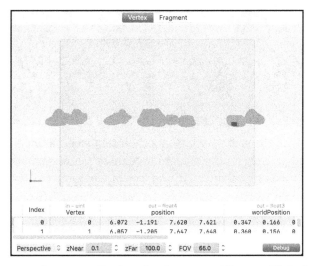

You can use the central pane to display the Geometry Viewer. Click the Rocks group to expand it, and then select the draw call for the rocks. In the central pane, double-click **Geometry** and you'll see a much more useful screen for exploring geometry.

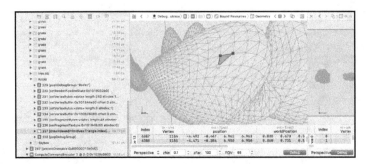

You can drag to rotate, use the mouse scroll wheel, or pinch gestures for zooming, and use the mouse middle button for panning. You can also right click to show/hide other viewing options such as wireframe. You also get a bottom pane containing all of the relevant primitive's vertex values. You can click any of the vertices to display it in the viewer.

The Geometry Viewer is handy for analyzing triangles. Are they visibly rendered incorrectly? Are they missing? Are they outside of the viewing frustum? And so on.

In the main app window, notice that you now have both the grass and the rocks showing in the scene.

That's great! However, the rocks are missing their textures. Taking a quick look at the vertex structs, again in the vertex shader, notice there's a uv member that's not being passed through in the vertex shader. So, add this line before `return`:

```
out.uv = vertexIn.uv;
```

Click **Reload Shaders** again, and you'll see that the rocks now have their textures.

The rocks look better now, but there's something off about the lighting in the scene. The next logical step is to move to the fragment shader and investigate how the light is calculated.

> **Note:** Changing shader functions in the shader debugger, as of the time of writing, does not update the functions in your code. They will revert to the original code after you finish running the app. Remember what you have changed to make your functions work, and re-enter the code in the shader functions when you have completed your debugging.

The pixel inspector

With the draw call in the Rocks group still selected, click **Debug Shader** again. This time, you'll use the Inspect Pixels tool to look at the scene. You can, once again, confirm with the magnifier that the textures are indeed applied to rocks, because you can see other colors as well besides shades of grey.

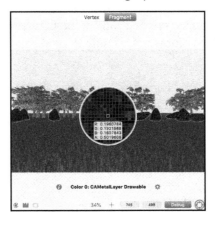

The shader debugger

There are two ways to navigate to the fragment shader code. With the magnifier placed on an active fragment — i.e., one that is in the group currently being drawn — either:

- In the assistant editor pane, click Debug next to the Inspect Pixels tool. If the Debug button is grayed out, it means that the magnifier is not over one of the fragments currently being drawn. Drag the magnifier over a rock.

- In debug shader, click Debug, which takes you to the fragment shader code.

Just like a playground, the shader debugger shows you a snapshot of the calculations that make up the final fragment. When the fragment shader opens in the shader debugger, click the little square next to the line where `diffuseIntensity` is defined. This little square turns blue and opens a preview pane for the selected variable:

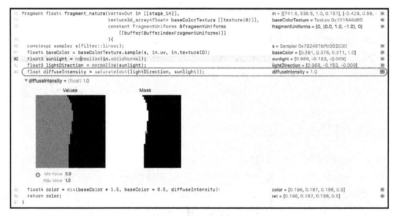

You immediately notice that the result of this calculation is incorrect because the value of this and surrounding pixels is a solid color. Diffuse intensity should be a value between 0 and 1. The color is red, as only the red channel is being used here, so 1.0 results in a solid red.

You also know from Chapter 5, "Lighting Fundamentals," that to calculate diffuse light, you need to take the dot product of two vectors: the direction of light and the surface normal. If that did not make you say "A-ha!" then take another look at this line:

```
float3 sunlight = normalize(in.worldNormal);
```

All you need to do here is normalize the surface normal but a mistake must have been made in calling this variable `sunlight` when it should be named `normal` or something similar. It may have been confused with the constant vector named sunlight, which you use for `lightDirection`.

Change the previous line to:

```
float3 normal = normalize(in.worldNormal);
```

Then, update this line:

```
float diffuseIntensity = saturate(dot(lightDirection,
                                      sunlight));
```

To use the proper normal vector:

```
float diffuseIntensity = saturate(dot(lightDirection, normal));
```

Click **Reload Shaders** on the debug bar and review the result:

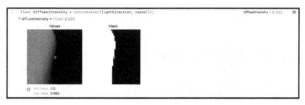

The diffuse intensity is now properly calculated and contributing to the light in the scene. Look at the main app window to see:

As you look closely at it, you notice that the light is now so intense that it looks almost fluorescent. A next logical step is to examine how `diffuseIntensity` is being factored into the color calculation:

```
float4 color = mix(baseColor * 1.5, baseColor * 0.5,
                   diffuseIntensity);
```

Looking at the line above, notice how the start and end values of the range in which to interpolate baseColor are reversed. Swap the two values:

```
float4 color = mix(baseColor * 0.5, baseColor * 1.5,
                   diffuseIntensity);
```

Once again, click **Reload Shaders**.

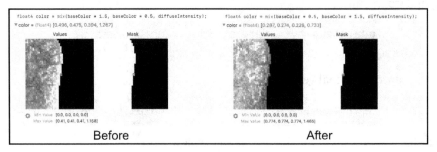

Notice how the values changed in the preview pane for color.

You can also see that your final image now almost matches the one from the beginning of the chapter; almost, because the grass, rocks and trees are randomly positioned at every run. The skybox currently isn't rendered in your app window either, because it renders after the rocks.

> **Note:** Remember to update both vertex_nature and fragment_nature in **Nature.metal** with the changes you just made, once you stop the app.

GPU frame capture

There's one more debugging feature that you'll love and use a lot. You can trigger the GPU Capture Frame tool to start at a breakpoint!

As you know, you can't put breakpoints inside shaders, but you can put them after the line where the CPU sends work to the GPU.

In **Renderer.swift**, in draw(in:), look for //compute debugging. You're going to debug a compute pipeline this time so you can see how the shader debugger tool looks for compute too.

Place a new breakpoint after the command encoder ends encoding. Right-click the breakpoint and choose **Edit Breakpoint**. Click the **Add Action** button next to **Action** and from the Action drop-down, choose **Capture GPU Frame**.

Build and run the project. The breakpoint automatically starts a GPU frame capture. In the Debug navigator, with dispatchThreadgroups selected under the computer command encoder, click **Debug Shader**.

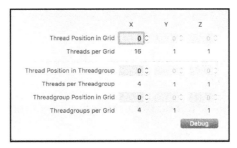

This shows you the most important variables you need: the number of threads per grid, the number of threads per threadgroup and the number of threadgroups per grid.

Select any thread id, and then click **Debug** to jump right to it in the shader debugger. Click on the little square next to the selected line of code to, once again, make use of the handy preview panes:

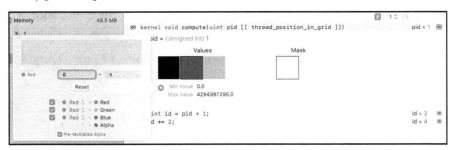

As you can see, you can follow each thread in real time and see how its values change throughout the kernel function. As in this example, clicking the third thread automatically selects it on the next two preview panes and updates the corresponding values on each of the affected lines.

The `pid` before any line executes has the value 1 for that thread, `id` gets updated to 2 on the first line, and finally, `id` gets updated again to 4 on the next line where it's being multiplied.

By the way, you can also capture a GPU frame programmatically by using a **MTLCaptureDescriptor** object and setting its destination to either **.developerTools** if you want the capture to live inside Xcode, or **.gpuTraceDocument** if you want to write capture data to a file on disk.

Debugging is great for finding anomalies or missing content. However, what makes your app run even more content, and faster too, is profiling! You'll be working on that next.

Remove the breakpoint from your app before continuing.

Profiling

Always profile early and do it often.

There are a few ways to monitor and tweak your app's performance. You'll be looking at each of these next.

GPU history

GPU history is a tool provided by the macOS operating system via its Activity Monitor app, so it is not inside Xcode. It shows basic GPU activity in real time for all of your GPUs. If you're using eGPUs, it'll show activity in there too.

Open **Activity Monitor**, and from the Window menu, choose GPU History; a window will pop up containing separate graphs for each GPU, showing the GPU usage in real time.

You can change how often the graph is updated from the View ▸ Update Frequency menu. The graph moves right-to-left at the frequency rate you set.

Here's a screenshot taken from a MacBook Pro that has a discrete GPU — AMD Radeon Pro 450 — and an integrated one — Intel HD Graphics 530:

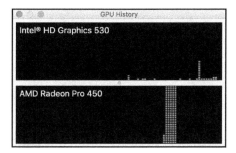

The system is using the integrated Intel GPU for regular tasks, and it switches to the discrete AMD GPU when running a graphics-intensive task such as this Xcode project you're working on.

The GPU History tool offers a quick way to see overall GPU usage, but it's not helpful with showing GPU usage for individual running apps and processes.

The GPU report

Build and run your app again, then capture a GPU frame. On the Debug navigator, click FPS gauge on the left side.

The GPU report shows in the central pane and contains three major GPU metrics.

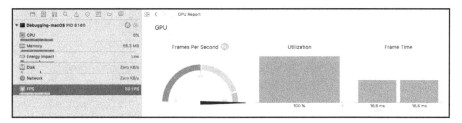

The first GPU report metric is Frames Per Second and represents the current frame rate of your app. Your target should always be 60 FPS or better.

The second GPU report metric is Utilization which shows how busy your GPU is doing useful work. A healthy app will have the GPU always utilized to some extent. Having it sit idle might be an indication that the CPU has not given it enough work to do.

698 Metal by Tutorials

On iOS and tvOS devices, the GPU utilization is separated into geometry processing (tiler) and pixel processing (renderer). The third column includes both utilization values.

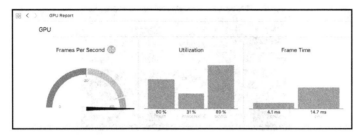

The third GPU report metric is `Frame Time` and represents the actual time spent processing the current frame on the CPU and the GPU. What's most important here is that the frame does not take longer than 16.6ms which corresponds to 60 FPS.

Your app is running at 60 FPS (16.6ms), and the GPU is not sitting idle. So far so good!

The shader profiler

This is perhaps the most useful profiling tool for the shader code you are writing. It has nothing to do with the rendering code the CPU is setting up, or the passes you run or the resources you're sending to the GPU. This tool tells you how your MSL code is performing line-by-line and how long it took to finish.

Unfortunately, the shader profiler shows you the individual line execution times (per-line cost) on iOS devices only.

Build and run the project on an iOS device this time, then capture a new GPU frame. In the Debug navigator, switch to **View Frame By Performance** using the **View frame in different ways** icon. You can now see how much time each pipeline took during the frame.

> **Note**: Your times and percentages will vary depending on your iOS device, Xcode and iOS version.

The entire pipeline took 5.63ms to complete. That time consists of 2.04ms for the vertex shader and 3.59ms for the fragment shader.

Drilling down the cost tree, most of the fragment shader execution time is taken by the sample() function (1.86ms) and the normalize() function (1.34ms).

As soon as you select the pipeline, the central pane updates to show the shaders, and more importantly, a convenient column with times and percentages for the code lines that affect the cost the most.

The total time that the shader takes to complete shows on the function header line. Inside the shader for each impactful line, you'll see the percentage the line took out of that total time. In the case of the sample() function on line 81, that 1.86ms correspond to 36.25% of the 3.24ms total shader time.

On iOS devices from the **family 4** (iPhone X) or later, the shader profiler will even show you a pie chart with activities displayed as slices representing the total time an activity took to complete.

Hover over the colored dot to disclose the pie chart.

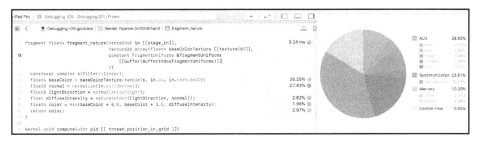

Analyze the percentages for each GPU activity. A high number might indicate an opportunity for performance optimization.

Looking at the various GPU activities and their percentages, notice how the ALU took 31.99% of the total shader time processing the various data types and calculations involving them.

Here's the first opportunity for optimization using shader profiling. Notice that processing floats seems to take more time than processing other types. As you might know, a half is, well, half the size of a float, so you can optimize this one spot.

Change all of the `floats` to `halfs` everywhere in the fragment shader, as well as in the `sunlight` definition line above the fragment shader.

When done, click **Reload Shaders**. The pie chart will also update in real time, as well as the Attachments contents if you also have the assistant editor open.

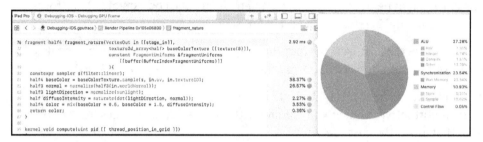

> **Note:** Reloading the shader might not save your changes so make sure to take a note of what you changed and later update **Nature.metal** manually.

Well, look at that! Not only did you eliminate the cost of processing `Floats`, but you also reduced the shader execution time from 8.17ms to only 7.35ms (almost 1ms gain). Great job for such a minor effort. Other ALU optimizations you can do includes replacing `ints` with `shorts`, simplifying complex instructions such as trigonometry functions (sin, cos, etc.) and other arithmetic calculations.

Next, you can look into Synchronization issues. The biggest concern here is the Wait Memory time which is taking almost a quarter of all the shader time (23.54%). This is happening because some instructions are waiting for dependent memory accesses that took place in previous instructions. The `sample()` function is a good candidate for this bottleneck because the `mix()` function heavily depends on it. You'll deal with synchronization in the next chapter.

The next part, Memory, took 11% of the shader execution time. This represents the time `sample()` spent waiting for access to the texture memory. You can shorten this time by down-sampling the textures.

The final category, Control Flow, did not take any time all because you did not use conditionals, increments or branching instructions.

GPU Counters and Memory

The **GPU Counters** information panel is another profiling tool you can use for optimizing the performance of your command encoders.

To access the GPU Counters, capture a new GPU frame. In the Debug navigator, click the Counters gauge.

This automatically displays the Pipeline Activity Bar Chart in the center pane, while the assistant editor should update to show the Performance view. Choose **Performance** from the assistant editor jump bar, if it does not update. If the center pane has Encoder selected at the top, switch to Draw view:

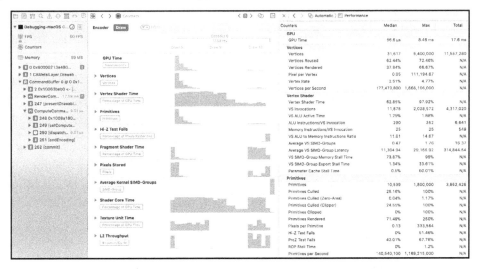

These are general statistics broken down by render command encoders shown next to each other. You only have one render command encoder in this app. If you right click anywhere on the bar chart you get the option to Export GPU Counters as a CSV file to disk.

In the Debug navigator, select the draw call with the highest cost and expand it. Then, select Performance from the list. In the Counters column, observe the GPU counters for the encoder that contains the selected draw call.

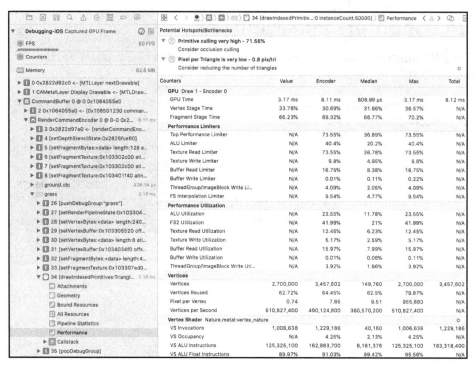

Each of the columns gives you useful information about your draw calls. The total column values refer to all of the draws for the selected command encoder. The other values are per selected draw call. You can also get this data programmatically on macOS by calling the encoder's `sampleCounters` method and by using a **MTLCounterSampleBuffer** object to store the counter data to.

In the Potential Hotspots/Bottlenecks section you'll see optimization recommendations for the selected draw call based on the GPU Counters data.

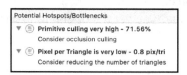

One of the recommendations is **Occlusion culling**. Currently you're rendering everything, no matter whether the camera can see it or not. If a rock is completely behind another rock, but is rendered first, then rendering that rock may be a waste of resources. One technique is to render objects forward to backward, as the rasterizer will automatically cull objects that have a greater z depth than previous objects. Another technique performs a separate render pass, checking bounding boxes and visibility.

Finally, click the Memory tool (below Counters) to see the total memory used and how the various resources are allocated in memory:

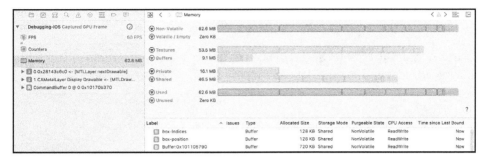

Pipeline statistics

Pipeline statistics is yet another profiling tool that tells you the number of instructions each of the GPU activities of your draw call is using.

Capture another GPU frame. In the Debug navigator, select the draw call with the highest cost and expand it, then select Pipeline Statistics from the list.

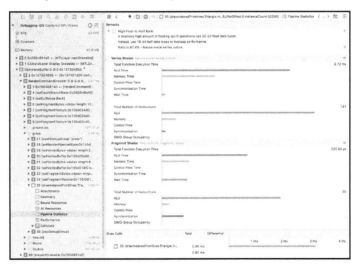

That opens the pipeline statistics informational panel in the central pane, containing Remarks at the top, graph bars for shader metrics in the center and related draw calls at the bottom.

Earlier, you replaced the `fragment_nature()` floats with `half`, but the profiler informs you that you will increase performance if you repeat that for the vertex function too.

Dependency viewer

The **Dependency Viewer** is one of the new tools introduced at WWDC 2018, along with the Shader Debugger and the Geometry Viewer.

Capture another GPU frame. In the Debug navigator, select your command buffer or a command encoder and see the dependency viewer in the central pane.

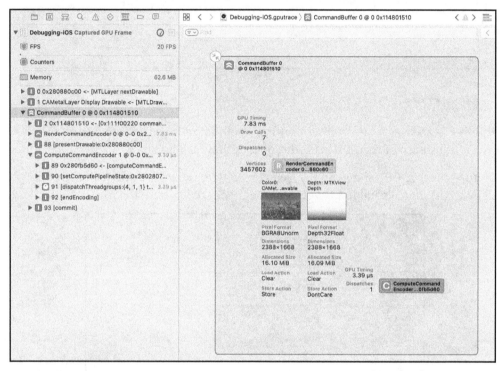

You can see the render and compute command encoders as a hierarchical flowchart. It's easier to see multiple dependencies in this view than looking at the call list in the Debug navigator. The dependencies can quickly get crowded, however.

This is the dependency chart for the final project from Chapter 14, "Multipass & Deferred Rendering."

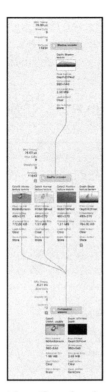

Using its visual layout, it's easy to identify redundant command encoders or passes that you could have missed in the code or in the draw calls list.

For each command encoder in the graph, you'll see the execution time, the number of draw calls, the bound resources and, based on the type of the encoder, either the number of vertices processed or the number of thread dispatches. A line going to another command encoder indicates dependency for it.

Metal System Trace

The last and most essential profiling tool is the **Metal System Trace** (MST) which is a specialized Instruments template for Metal. There are two ways of launching an MST session:

- Build and run your app in Xcode. Launch the Instruments app and from the profiling templates window, choose **Metal System Trace**. In the Instruments window, from the devices list, choose your Mac and then your running app you want to profile.

- While in Xcode, instead of building and running your app, choose **Product ▸ Profile**. This will open Instruments. Choose the **Metal System Trace** template or the **Game Performance** template and then Instruments will auto-select your running app.

Either way you choose, the next step applies to both approaches. Click the big red dot on the top left side of Instruments.

This starts recording your app running in windowed mode. After about 10 seconds or so, stop the recording and review the results.

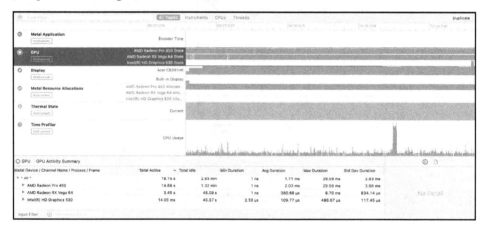

In the bottom pane, if you select the GPU instrument, you can see which GPU was used more than the others (AMD Radeon Pro 450 here).

Using the Option key, and your mouse or pinch gesture, you can zoom in and out of areas of interest.

Close the Instruments window without saving it, and open **GrassScene.swift**. You'll stress the app by increasing the number of grass blades rendered. Change:

```
setupGrass(instanceCount: 50000, width: 10, depth: 10)
```

To:

```
setupGrass(instanceCount: 400000, width: 10, depth: 10)
```

Run the app, and check the frames per second on the Debug navigator. You're looking for around 50-55 fps. Change `instanceCount` to suit your device. You may need to increase or decrease it to get similar results.

Now stop the app, and choose **Product ▸ Profile** to run Instruments. Choose **Metal System Trace** and press the Record button at the top left. Press the right arrow to rotate in a full circle, then stop the profiling using the Stop button at the top left.

At the top left of the Detail area, click **Metal Encoder Hierarchy** and change it to **Observations**.

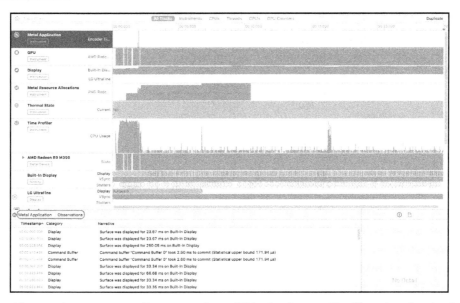

The Observations category lists a number of Display issues. You'll notice that in the **Built-in Display** trace (or if you're running several monitors, then whichever monitor holds the app), there are a lot of exclamation marks in circles in the **Stutters** row. These correspond to the Display issues listed in the Observations:

```
Surface was displayed for 33.33ms on Display.
```

This message means the drawable is being held for longer than desired (16.66ms). One indication might be the fact that the drawable was acquired too quickly by the command buffer.

On the console list, you can click any entry, and it takes you to that frame on the graph bars.

Your app is currently trying to achieve 60 frames per second. When you run the app at 50 fps, you'll get stutters as indicated in this Metal System Trace. If you can't improve your frames per second, a last resort method is to lower the expected fps from 60 to a number that you can achieve every single frame. This will mean a lower fps, but the visuals will be smoother.

Open **Renderer.swift**, and in init(metalView:), immediately after the guard statement, and before assigning the static variables, add this:

```
metalView.preferredFramesPerSecond = 30
```

Profile the app with instruments again, and turn a complete circle using the right arrow key. You may notice that the action is smoother.

When you profile the app, many of the Display observations will have disappeared. You'll still have stuttering on loading the app, but once it's fully loaded, the game should run smoothly.

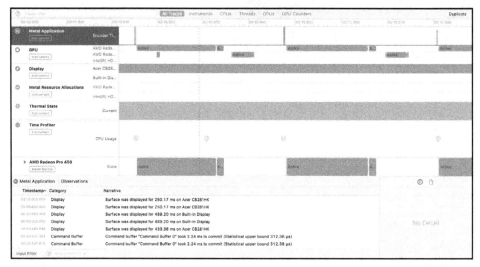

The largest gaps are between two consecutive frames. You can see on the Metal Application graphs bars that the render encoder finishes its work before the frame ends.

You can take at least two actions here. First, you should synchronize the CPU and GPU shared access to resources. Second, you should run your encoders on multiple threads.

In the next chapter, you'll be working on taking your project to a highly parallelized state.

Where to go from here?

The path to optimal performance is not trivial, and it's going to be a journey full of trial and error experiments. Where debugging is a science, profiling is a work of art. Experiment, take a step back, look at it, go back and tweak some more. In the end, it's all going to be worth the effort.

In the next chapter, you will learn how to optimize the performance of your application, taking your project to a highly parallelized state, and always staying on top of the Metal best practices.

Chapter 24: Performance Optimization

By Marius Horga

In the previous chapter, you took a first stab at optimizing your app by profiling your shaders and using Instruments to find even more bottlenecks to get rid of. In this chapter, you'll look at:

1. **CPU-GPU Synchronization**

2. **Multithreading**

3. **GPU Families**

4. **Memory Management**

5. **Best Practices**

CPU-GPU synchronization

Always aim to minimize the idle time between frames.

Managing dynamic data can be a little tricky. Take the case of Uniforms. You're changing them usually once per frame on the CPU. That means that the GPU has to wait until the CPU has finished writing the buffer before it can read the buffer. Instead, you can simply have a pool of reusable buffers.

Triple buffering is a well-known technique in the realm of synchronization. The idea is to use three buffers at a time. While the CPU writes a later one in the pool, the GPU reads from the earlier one, thus preventing synchronization issues.

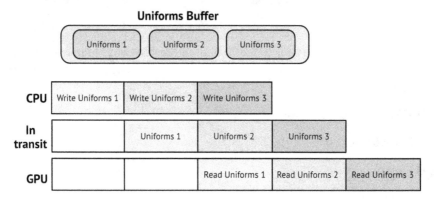

You might ask, why three and not just two or a dozen? With only two buffers, there's a high risk that the CPU will try to write the first buffer again before the GPU finished reading it even once. With too many buffers, there's a high risk of performance issues.

Before you implement the triple buffering, use Instruments to run a Metal System Trace (MST) session and get a baseline level of the CPU activity:

Notice that most tasks peak at about 10% and this is fine, assuming that the GPU has enough work to do on its own without waiting for more work from the CPU.

All right, time to implement that triple buffering pool like a champ!

Open the starter project that comes with this chapter. In **Scene.swift**, replace this line:

```
var uniforms = Uniforms()
```

With this code:

```
static let buffersInFlight = 3
var uniforms = [Uniforms](repeating: Uniforms(),
                          count: buffersInFlight)
var currentUniformIndex = 0
```

Here, you replaced the uniforms variable with an array of three buffers and defined an index to keep track of the current buffer in use.

In `update(deltaTime:)`, replace this code:

```
uniforms.projectionMatrix = camera.projectionMatrix
uniforms.viewMatrix = camera.viewMatrix
```

With this:

```
uniforms[currentUniformIndex].projectionMatrix =
    camera.projectionMatrix
uniforms[currentUniformIndex].viewMatrix = camera.viewMatrix
currentUniformIndex =
    (currentUniformIndex + 1) % Scene.buffersInFlight
```

Here, you adapted the update method to include the new uniforms array and created a way to have the index loop around always taking the values 0, 1 and 2.

Back in **Renderer.swift**, add this line to `draw(in:)`, before the renderables loop:

```
let uniforms = scene.uniforms[scene.currentUniformIndex]
```

Replace `scene.uniforms` with `uniforms` in the two places Xcode complains about.

Build and run the project. It'll show the same scene as before. Run another MST session and notice that now the CPU activity has increased.

This is both good news and bad news. It's good news because that means the GPU is not getting more work to do. The bad news is that now the CPU and the GPU will spar over using the same resources.

This is known as **resource contention** and involves conflicts, called race conditions, over accessing shared resources by both the CPU and GPU. They're trying to read/write the same uniform, causing unexpected results.

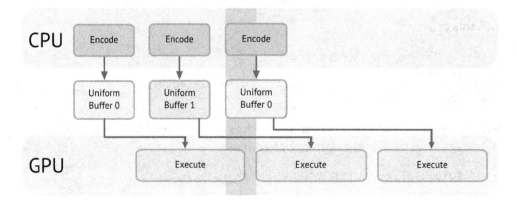

In the image below, the CPU is ready to start writing the third buffer again. However, that would require the GPU to have finished reading it, which is not the case here.

What you need here is a way to delay the CPU writing until the GPU has finished reading it.

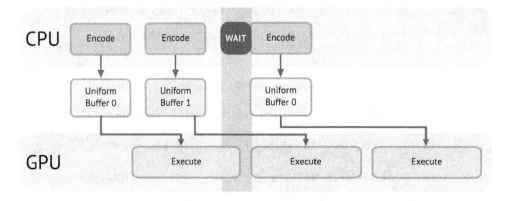

In Chapter 8, "Character Animation," you solved this synchronization issue in a naive way by using `waitUntilCompleted()` on your command buffer. A more performant way, however, is the use of a synchronization primitive called a **semaphore**, which is a convenient way of keeping count of the available resources — your triple buffer in this case.

Here's how a a semaphore works:

- Initialize it to a maximum value that represents the number of resources in your pool (3 buffers here).

- Inside the draw call the thread tells the CPU to wait until a resource is available and if one is, it takes it and decrements the semaphore value by one.

- If there are no more available resources, the current thread is blocked until the semaphore has at least one resource available.

- When a thread finishes using the resource, it'll signal the semaphore by increasing its value and by releasing the hold on the resource.

Time to put this theory into practice.

At the top of Renderer, add this new property:

```
var semaphore: DispatchSemaphore
```

In init(metalView:), add this line before super.init():

```
semaphore = DispatchSemaphore(value: Scene.buffersInFlight)
```

Add this line at the top of draw(in:):

```
_ = semaphore.wait(timeout: .distantFuture)
```

At the end of draw(in:), but before committing the command buffer, add this:

```
commandBuffer.addCompletedHandler { _ in
  self.semaphore.signal()
}
```

At the end of draw(in:), remove:

```
commandBuffer.waitUntilCompleted()
```

Build and run the project again, making sure everything still renders fine as before.

Run another MST session and compare the performance metrics with the previous ones.

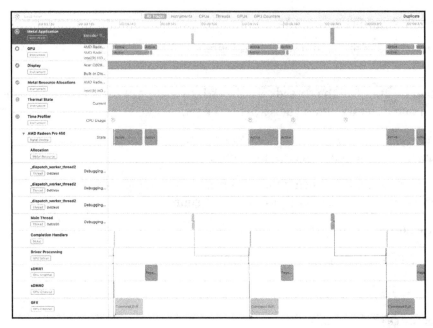

If you look at the GFX bar under your specific graphics processor, the gaps are all narrower now because the GPU is not sitting idle as much as it was sitting before. You can intensify the rendering workload by increasing the number of trees, rocks or grass blades, and then the gaps might be completely gone. Those "Thread blocked waiting for next drawable" messages are also gone.

Notice an old issue you did not fix yet. Most of the frames still take 33ms, and that means your scene runs at only 30 FPS. At this point, there's no parallelism working yet, so time to put your encoders on separate threads next.

Multithreading

Build all known pipelines up front and asynchronously.

When balancing workloads you can find yourself in one of these two extremes: the CPU is giving the GPU too much work to do (your app is GPU-bound), or the CPU is working too much and the GPU is sitting idle (your app is CPU-bound). You will work on managing the CPU workload next.

The biggest performance gain will come from running different command buffers on different threads. You can even split one encoder into new smaller encoders and run them on multiple threads using `MTLParallelRenderEncoder`.

Assume that in your project you have grass that takes 10ms to render; you have trees that take another 7ms to render; and you have rocks + skybox + ground that all take 5ms to render.

Instead of having an encoder that takes 22ms to finish, you could split the encoder into three smaller new encoders and run them in parallel on an MTLParallelRenderEncoder that would have all three threads finish by the time the longer running thread finishes (10ms).

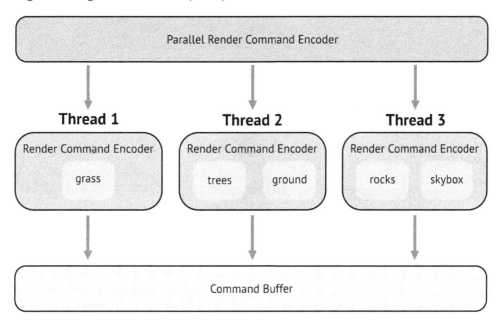

You don't have to type the code for building a parallel render command encoder, but it would look similar to this:

```
let commandBuffer = Renderer.commandQueue.makeCommandBuffer()
let descriptor = MTLRenderPassDescriptor()
let parallelEncoder =
commandBuffer.makeParallelRenderCommandEncoder(
                                    descriptor: descriptor)
let encoder1 = parallelEncoder.makeRenderCommandEncoder()
// ... encoder1.draw() ...
encoder1.endEncoding()
let encoder2 = parallelEncoder.makeRenderCommandEncoder()
// ... encoder2.draw() ...
encoder2.endEncoding()
parallelEncoder.endEncoding()
commandBuffer.commit()
```

You're going to implement multithreaded command buffers where each command buffer has its own encoder, and they're running on separate threads:

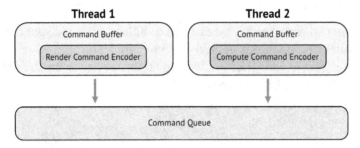

At the top of `Renderer`, add this new property:

```
let dispatchQueue = DispatchQueue(label: "Queue",
                                  attributes: .concurrent)
```

In `draw(in:)`, locate `// compute debugging`, and create a second command buffer for the compute command encoder by replacing this line:

```
guard let computeEncoder =
    commandBuffer.makeComputeCommandEncoder()
else {
```

With this code:

```
guard let computeCommandBuffer =
        Renderer.commandQueue.makeCommandBuffer(),
      let computeEncoder =
        computeCommandBuffer.makeComputeCommandEncoder() else {
```

At the end of `draw(in:)`, replace this code:

```
commandBuffer.addCompletedHandler { _ in
  self.semaphore.signal()
}
commandBuffer.commit()
```

With this:

```
// 1
commandBuffer.enqueue()
computeCommandBuffer.enqueue()
// 2
dispatchQueue.async(execute: commandBuffer.commit)
weak var sem = semaphore
dispatchQueue.async {
```

```
    computeCommandBuffer.addCompletedHandler { _ in
      sem?.signal()
    }
    computeCommandBuffer.commit()
  }
  // 3
  __dispatch_barrier_sync(dispatchQueue) {}
```

Going through everything:

1. Use the enqueue() function, which is the explicit way to guarantee buffer execution order.

2. Dispatch each buffer in parallel, asynchronously, and then commit the work for each buffer.

3. Use a barrier to block the threads until all of them finish.

Run a new MST session, and compare the metrics with previous traces.

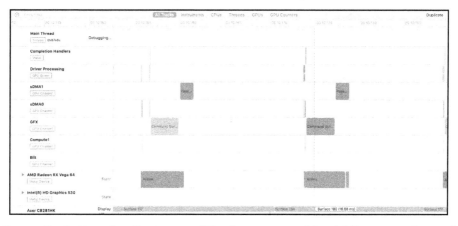

Notice on the bottom bar that some of the frames are taking 16.7ms to render again. This is a great start, but your work is not done yet. You should lower instanceCount to see if that helps get your project back to a stable 60 FPS status.

Also, notice the command encoders are now rendered on separate threads which is what you set out to achieve in this part of the chapter.

You should be proud of what you've achieved in this chapter so far. Keep tweaking your project like a pro until you're pleased with the performance.

GPU families

GPU families are classes of GPUs categorized by device and/or build target type. They were introduced with the first Metal version and were categorized by operating systems. At WWDC 2019 Apple repurposed and renamed them as follows:

1. **Apple Families**: Refers to GPUs manufactured by Apple for iOS and tvOS devices:

- Apple 1 - the A7 GPU.

- Apple 2 - the A8 GPU.

- Apple 3 - the A9 and A10 GPUs.

- Apple 4 - the A11 GPU.

- Apple 5 - the A12 GPU.

- Apple 6 - the A13 GPU.

2. **Mac Families**: Refers to GPUs manufactured by Intel, Nvidia and AMD for Macs:

- Mac 1 - the Intel HD Graphics 4000, Intel Iris, Intel Iris Pro, Intel Iris Graphics 6100, and all the Nvidia GeForce GT GPUs.

- Mac 2 - the Intel HD Graphics 5xx, Intel Iris Plus Graphics 6xx, AMD Radeon, AMD Radeon Pro, and AMD FirePro GPUs.

3. **Common Families**: Refers to Metal features that are available to all GPU families.

- Common 1 - all the universally supported features.

- Common 2 - Indirect Draw/Dispatch, Counting Occlusion Queries, Tessellation, Read/Write Buffer Arguments, Arrays of Textures/Samplers, Compressed Volume Textures, Metal Performance Shaders, and more.

- Common 3 - Stencil Feedback, MSAA Depth/Stencil Resolve, Programmable Sample Positions, Invariant Vertex Position, Indirect Stage-In, Indirect Command Buffers, Quad-scoped Shuffle/Broadcast, Cube Texture Arrays, Read/Write Texture Arguments, Attachment-less Render Passes, Layered Rendering, Multi-Viewport Rendering, Argument Buffers, Pipelined Compute, Indirect Tessellation, Heap Placement, Texture Swizzle, and more.

4. **iOSMac Families**: Refers to Metal features for Mac Family GPUs running iPad apps ported to macOS via Catalyst.

• iOSMac 1 - features from the Common 2 family, plus BC Pixel Formats, Managed Textures, Cube Texture Arrays, Read/Write Textures Tier 1, Layered Rendering, Multiple Viewports/Scissors and Indirect Tessellation.

• iOSMac 2 - features from the Common 3 family, plus BC Pixel Formats and Managed Textures.

> **Note:** A GPU can be a member of more than one family so it supports one of the Common families and one or more of the other families. For a complete list of supported features, consult Apple's webpage at https://developer.apple.com/metal/Metal-Feature-Set-Tables.pdf

You can test what GPU Families your devices have by using an #available clause. Add this code at the end of init(metalView:) in **Renderer.swift**:

```
let devices = MTLCopyAllDevices()
for device in devices {
  if #available(macOS 10.15, *) {
    if device.supportsFamily(.mac2) {
      print("\(device.name) is a Mac 2 family gpu running on macOS Catalina.")
    }
    else {
      print("\(device.name) is a Mac 1 family gpu running on macOS Catalina.")
    }
  }
  else {
    if device.supportsFeatureSet(.macOS_GPUFamily2_v1) {
      print("You are using a recent GPU with an older version of macOS.")
    }
    else {
      print("You are using an older GPU with an older version of macOS.")
    }
  }
}
```

Build and run. The output in the debug console will look something like this:

```
AMD Radeon RX Vega 64 is a Mac 2 family gpu running on macOS
Catalina.
```

```
Intel(R) HD Graphics 530 is a Mac 2 family gpu running on macOS
Catalina.
AMD Radeon Pro 450 is a Mac 2 family gpu running on macOS
Catalina.
```

Memory management

Whenever you create a buffer or a texture, you should consider how to configure it for fast memory access and driver performance optimizations. Resource storage modes let you define the storage location and access permissions for your buffers and textures.

All iOS and tvOS devices support a unified memory model where both the CPU and the GPU share the system memory, while macOS devices support a discrete memory model where the GPU has its own memory. In iOS and tvOS, the Shared mode (MTLStorageModeShared) defines system memory accessible to both CPU and GPU, while Private mode (MTLStorageModePrivate) defines system memory accessible only to the GPU. The Shared mode is the default storage mode on all three operating systems.

macOS also has a Managed mode (MTLStorageModeManaged) that defines a synchronized memory pair for a resource, with one copy in system memory and another in video memory for faster CPU and GPU local accesses.

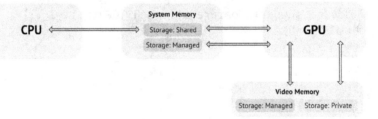

There are basically only four main rules to keep in mind, one for each of the storage modes:

- **Shared**: Default on macOS buffers, iOS/tvOS resources; not available on macOS textures.

- **Private**: Mostly use when data is only accessed by GPU.

- **Memoryless**: Only for iOS/tvOS on-chip temporary render targets (textures).

- **Managed**: Default mode for macOS textures; not available on iOS/tvOS resources.

For a better big picture, here is the full cheat sheet in case you might find it easier to use than remembering the rules above:

	Shared	Private	Memoryless	Managed
iOS/tvOS buffers	default mode	- use when data is only accessed by GPU	N/A	N/A
iOS/tvOS textures	default mode	- use when data is only accessed by GPU	- only for on-chip temporary render targets	N/A
macOS buffers	- use when data is only accessed by CPU, or - use when data is accessed by both CPU/GPU when data is small/dirty and updated every frame	- use when data is only accessed by GPU, or - use when data is accessed by both CPU/GPU when data is large/clean and only updated once	N/A	- use when data is accessed by both CPU/GPU when data is medium-sized, partially dirty and it changes infrequently (every few frames)
macOS textures	N/A	- use when data is only accessed by GPU	N/A	default mode

The most complicated case is when working with macOS buffers and when the data needs to be accessed by both the CPU and the GPU. You should choose the storage mode based on whether one or more of the following conditions are true:

- **Private**: For large-sized data that changes at most once, so it is not "dirty" at all. Create a source buffer with a Shared mode and then blit its data into a destination buffer with a Private mode. Resource coherency is not necessary in this case as the data is only accessed by the GPU. This operation is the least expensive (a one-time cost).

- **Managed**: or medium-sized data that changes infrequently (every few frames), so it is partially "dirty". One copy of the data is stored in system memory for the CPU and another copy is stored in GPU memory. Resource coherency is explicitly managed by synchronizing the two copies.

- **Shared**: For small-sized data that is updated every frame, so it is fully dirty. Data resides in the system memory and is visible and modifiable by both the CPU and the GPU. Resource coherency is only guaranteed within command buffer boundaries.

How do you make sure coherency is guaranteed? First, make sure that all the modifications done by the CPU are finished before the command buffer is committed (check if the command buffer status property is `MTLCommandBufferStatusCommitted`). After the GPU finishes executing the command buffer, the CPU should only start making modifications again only after the GPU is signaling the CPU that the command buffer finished executing (check if the command buffer status property is `MTLCommandBufferStatusCompleted`).

Finally, how is synchronization done for macOS resources?

- **For buffers**: After a CPU write, use `didModifyRange` to inform the GPU of the changes so Metal can update that data region only; after a GPU write use `synchronize(resource:)` within a blit operation, to refresh the caches so the CPU can access the updated data.

- **For textures**: After a CPU write, use one of the two **replace** region functions to inform the GPU of the changes so Metal can update that data region only; after a GPU write use one of the two **synchronize** functions within a blit operation to allow Metal to update the system memory copy after the GPU finished modifying the data.

Now, look at what happens on the GPU when you send it data buffers. Here is a typical vertex shader example:

```
vertex Vertices vertex_func(
    const device Vertices *vertices [[buffer(0)]],
    constant Uniforms &uniforms [[buffer(1)]],
    uint vid [[vertex_id]]) {}
```

The Metal Shading Language implements address space qualifiers to specify the region of memory where a function variable or argument is allocated:

- **device**: Refers to buffer memory objects allocated from the device memory pool that are both readable and writeable unless the keyword const precedes it in which case the objects are only readable.

- **constant**: Refers to buffer memory objects allocated from the device memory pool but that are read-only. Variables in program scope must be declared in the constant address space and initialized during the declaration statement. The constant address space is optimized for multiple instances executing a graphics or kernel function accessing the same location in the buffer.

- **threadgroup**: Used to allocate variables used by kernel functions only and they are allocated for each threadgroup executing the kernel, are shared by all threads in a threadgroup and exist only for the lifetime of the threadgroup that is executing the kernel.

- **thread**: Refers to the per-thread memory address space. Variables allocated in this address space are not visible to other threads. Variables declared inside a graphics or kernel function are allocated in the thread address space.

Starting with macOS Catalina some Mac systems directly connect GPUs to each other (they are said to be in the same *peer group*), allowing you to quickly transfer data between them. These connections are not only faster, but they also avoid using the memory bus between the CPU and GPUs, leaving it available for other tasks. If your app uses multiple GPUs, test to see if they're connected (if `device.peerGroupID` returns a non-zero value), and when they are, you can use a blit command encoder to transfer data. You can read more on Apple's webpage at https://developer.apple.com/documentation/metal/transferring_data_between_connected_gpus

Best practices

When you are after squeezing the very last ounce of performance from your app, you should always remember to follow a golden set of best practices. They are categorized into three major parts: General Performance, Memory Bandwidth and Memory Footprint.

General performance best practices

The next five best practices are general and apply to the entire pipeline.

1. **Choose the right resolution**.

The game or app UI should be at native or close to native resolution so that the UI will always look crisp no matter the display size. Also, it is recommended (albeit, not mandatory) that all resources have the same resolution. You can check the resolutions in the GPU Debugger, on the Dependency Viewer. Below is the multi-pass render from Chapter 14, "Multipass & Deferred Rendering":

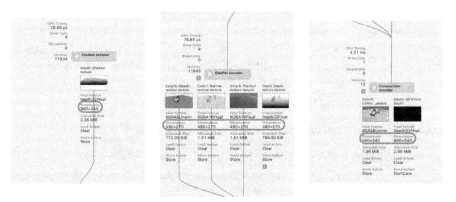

Notice here that the G-Buffer pass uses render targets that have a different resolution than the shadow and composition passes. You should consider the performance trade-offs of each image resolution and carefully choose the scenario that best fits your app needs.

2. **Minimize non-opaque overdraw**.

Ideally, you'll want to only draw each pixel once. That means you will want only one fragment shader process per pixel. You can check the status of that in the Metal Frame Debugger, by clicking the Counters gauge. In the right side pane at the bottom there is a filter bar. In there type `FS Invocations` followed by pressing the Enter key and then type again `Pixels Stored` followed by pressing the Enter key again:

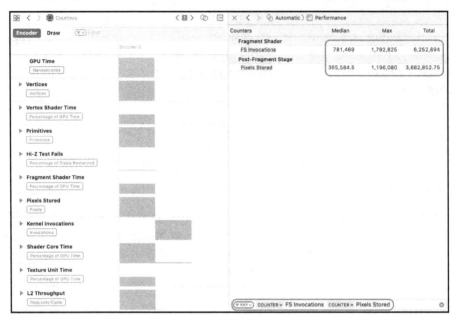

Overdraw would be if the number of shader invocations would be much larger than the number of pixels stored. In your case, they seem to all match which means it is an opaque scene. The best practice is to render opaque meshes first followed by translucent meshes. If they are fully transparent that means they are invisible so they should never be rendered.

3. **Submit GPU work early**.

You can reduce latency and improve the responsiveness of your renderer by making sure all the off-screen GPU work is done early and is not waiting for the on-screen part to start.

You can do that by using two or more command buffers per frame:

```
create off-screen command buffer
encode work for the GPU
commit off-screen command buffer
...
get the drawable
create on-screen command buffer
encode work for the GPU
present the drawable
commit on-screen command buffer
```

Create the off-screen command buffer(s) and commit the work to the GPU as early as possible. Get the drawable as late as possible in the frame and then have a final command buffer that only contains the on-screen work.

4. **Stream resources efficiently**.

All resources should be allocated at launch time if they are available because that will take time and will prevent render stalls later. If you need to allocate resources at runtime because the renderer streams them, you should make sure you do that from a dedicated thread. You can see the resource allocations in the Metal System Trace, under the Allocation track:

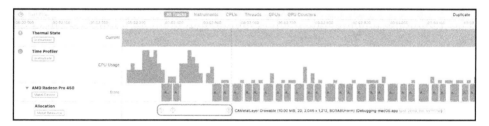

You can see here that there are a few allocations, but all at lunch time. If there were allocations at runtime you would notice them later on that track and identify potential stalls because of them.

5. **Design for sustained performance**.

You should test your renderer under serious thermal state. This can improve the overall thermals of the device as well as the stability and responsiveness of your renderer.

Xcode now lets you see and change the thermal state in the Devices window from **Window ▸ Devices and Simulators**:

You can also use Xcode's Energy Gauge to verify the thermal state that the device is running at:

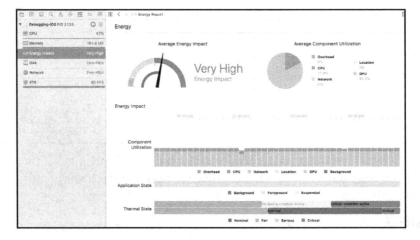

Memory Bandwidth best practices

Since memory transfers for render targets and textures are costly, the next six best practices are targeted to memory bandwidth and how to use shared and tiled memory more efficiently.

6. **Compress texture assets**.

Compressing textures is very important because sampling large textures may be inefficient. For that reason, you should generate mipmaps for textures that can be minified. You should also compress large textures to accommodate the memory bandwidth needs. There are various compression formats available. For example, for older devices you could use PVRTC and for newer devices you could use ASTC. Review Chapter 6, "Textures," for how to create mipmaps and change texture formats in the asset catalog.

With the frame captured, you can use the Metal Memory Viewer to verify compression format, mipmap status and size. You can change which columns are displayed, by right clicking the column heading:

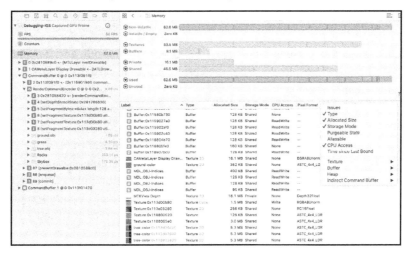

Some textures, such as render targets, cannot be compressed ahead of time so you will have to do it at runtime instead. The good news is, the A12 GPU and newer supports lossless texture compression which allows the GPU to compress textures for faster access.

7. **Optimize for faster GPU access**.

You should configure your textures correctly to use the appropriate storage mode depending on the use case. Use the private storage mode so only the GPU has access to the texture data, allowing optimization of the contents:

```
textureDescriptor.storageMode = .private
textureDescriptor.usage = [ .shaderRead, .renderTarget ]
let texture = device.makeTexture(descriptor: textureDescriptor)
```

You shouldn't set any unnecessary usage flags such as unknown, shaderWrite or pixelView, since they may disable compression.

Shared textures that can be accessed by the CPU as well as the GPU, should explicitly be optimized after any CPU update on their data:

```
textureDescriptor.storageMode = .shared
textureDescriptor.usage = .shaderRead
let texture = device.makeTexture(descriptor: textureDescriptor)
// update texture data
texture.replace(region: region, mipmapLevel: 0,
                withBytes: bytes,
                bytesPerRow: bytesPerRow)
let blitCommandEncoder = commandBuffer.makeBlitCommandEncoder()
blitCommandEncoder.optimizeContentsForGPUAccess(
                          texture: texture)
blitCommandEncoder.endEncoding()
```

Again, the Metal Memory Viewer will show you the storage mode and usage flag for all textures, along with noticing which ones are compressed textures already, as in the previous image.

8. Choose the right pixel format.

Choosing the correct pixel format is crucial. Not only will larger pixel formats use more bandwidth, but the sampling rate also depends on the pixel format. You should try to avoid using pixel formats with unnecessary channels and also try to lower precision whenever possible. You've generally been using the RGBA8Unorm pixel format in this book, however, when you needed greater accuracy for the G-Buffer in Chapter 14, "Multipass & Deferred Rendering," you used a 16-bit pixel format. Again, you can use the Metal Memory Viewer to see the pixel formats for textures.

9. Optimize load and store actions.

Load and store actions for render targets can also affect bandwidth. If you have a suboptimal configuration of your pipelines caused by unnecessary load/store actions, you might create false dependencies. An example of optimized configuration would be this:

```
renderPassDescriptor.colorAttachments[0].loadAction = .clear
renderPassDescriptor.colorAttachments[0].storeAction = .dontCare
```

In this case, you're configuring a color attachment to be transient which means you do not want to load or store anything from it. You can verify the current actions set on render targets in the Dependency Viewer.

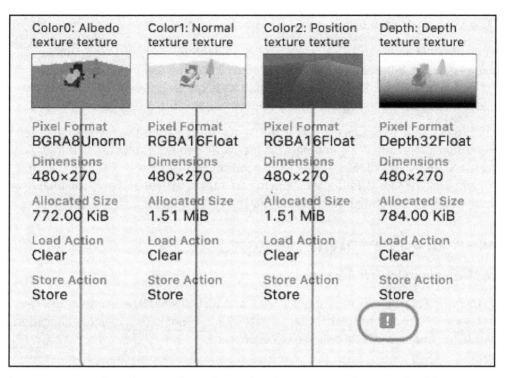

As you can see, there is an exclamation point that suggests that you should not store the last render target.

10. **Optimize multi-sampled textures**.

iOS devices have very fast multi-sampled render targets (MSAA) because they resolve from Tile Memory so it is best practice to consider MSAA over native resolution. Also, make sure not to load or store the MSAA texture and set its storage mode to `memoryless`:

```
textureDescriptor.textureType = .type2DMultisample
textureDescriptor.sampleCount = 4
textureDescriptor.storageMode = .memoryless
let msaaTexture =
    device.makeTexture(descriptor: textureDescriptor)
renderPassDesc.colorAttachments[0].texture = msaaTexture
renderPassDesc.colorAttachments[0].loadAction = .clear
renderPassDesc.colorAttachments[0].storeAction = .
    multisampleResolve
```

Dependency Viewer will again help you see the current status set for load/store actions.

11. **Leverage tile memory**.

Metal provides access to Tile Memory for several features such as programmable blending, image blocks and tile shaders. Deferred shading requires storing the G-Buffer in a first pass, and then sampling from its textures in the second lighting pass where the final color accumulates into a render target. This is very bandwidth-heavy.

iOS allows fragment shaders to access pixel data directly from Tile Memory in order to leverage programmable blending. This means that you can store the G-Buffer data on Tile Memory and all the light accumulation shaders can access it within the same render pass. The four G-Buffer attachments are fully transient and only the final color and depth are stored, so it's very efficient.

Memory Footprint best practices

12. **Use memoryless render targets**.

As mentioned previously in best practices 9 and 10, you should be using `memoryless` storage mode for all transient render targets which do not need a memory allocation, that is, are not loaded from or stored to memory:

```
textureDescriptor.storageMode = .memoryless
textureDescriptor.usage = [ .shaderRead, .renderTarget ]
// for each G-Buffer texture
textureDescriptor.pixelFormat = gBufferPixelFormats[i]
gBufferTextures[i] =
    device.makeTexture(descriptor: textureDescriptor)
renderPassDescriptor.colorAttachments[i].texture =
    gBufferTextures[i]
renderPassDescriptor.colorAttachments[i].loadAction = .clear
renderPassDescriptor.colorAttachments[i].storeAction = .dontCare
```

You'll be able to see the change immediately in the Dependency Viewer.

13. **Avoid loading unused assets**.

Loading all the assets into memory will increase the memory footprint so you should consider the memory and performance trade-off and only load all the assets that you know will be used. The GPU frame capture Memory Viewer will show you any unused resources:

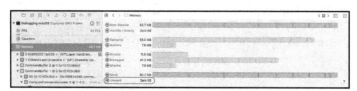

Fortunately, your app correctly uses all its textures.

14. **Use smaller assets**.

You should only make the assets as large as necessary and consider again the image quality and memory trade-off of your asset sizes. Make sure that both textures and meshes are compressed. You may want to only load the smaller mipmap levels of your textures, or use lower level of detail meshes for distant objects.

15. **Simplify memory-intensive effects**.

Some effects may require large off-screen buffers, such as Shadow Maps and Screen Space Ambient Occlusion so you should consider the image quality and memory trade-off of all of those effects, potentially lower the resolution of all these large off-screen buffers and even disable the memory-intensive effects altogether when you are memory constrained.

16. **Use Metal resource heaps**.

Rendering a frame may require a lot of intermediate memory especially if your game becomes more complex in the post-process pipeline so it is very important to use Metal Resource Heaps for those effects and alias as much of that memory as possible. For example, you may want to reutilize the memory for resources which have no dependencies such as those for Depth of Field or Screen Space Ambient Occlusion.

Another advanced concept is that of purgeable memory. Purgeable memory has three states: non-volatile (when data should not be discarded), volatile (data can be discarded even when the resource may be needed) and empty (data has been discarded). Volatile and empty allocations do not count towards the application memory footprint because the system can either reclaim that memory at some point or has already reclaimed it in the past.

17. **Mark resources as volatile**.

Temporary resources may become a large part of the memory footprint and Metal will allow you to set the purgeable state of all the resources explicitly. You will want to focus on your caches that hold mostly idle memory and carefully manage their purgeable state, like in this example:

```
// for each texture in the cache
texturePool[i].setPurgeableState(.volatile)
// later on...
if (texturePool[i].setPurgeableState(.nonVolatile) == .empty) {
  // regenerate texture
}
```

18. **Manage the Metal PSOs**.

Pipeline State Objects (PSOs) encapsulate most of the Metal render state. You create them using a descriptor which contains vertex and fragment functions as well as other state descriptors. All of these will get compiled into the final Metal PSO.

Metal allows your application to load most of the rendering state up front, improving the performance over OpenGL. However, if you have limited memory make sure to not hold on to PSO references that you don't need anymore. Also don't hold on to Metal function references after you have created the PSO cache because they are not needed to render, they are only needed to create new PSOs.

> **Note**: Apple have written a Metal Best Practices guide that provides great advice for optimizing your app: https://developer.apple.com/library/archive/documentation/3DDrawing/Conceptual/MTLBestPracticesGuide/index.html.

Where to go from here?

Getting the last ounce of performance out of your app is paramount. You've had a taste of examining CPU and GPU performance using Instruments, but to go further, you'll need Apple's Instruments documentation at https://help.apple.com/instruments/mac/10.0/.

Over the years, at every WWDC since Metal was introduced, Apple have produced some excellent WWDC videos describing Metal best practices and optimization techniques. Go to https://developer.apple.com/videos/graphics-and-games/metal/ and watch as many as you can, as often as you can.

Congratulations on completing the book! The world of Computer Graphics is vast and as complex as you want to make it. But now that you have the basics of Metal learned, even though current internet resources are few, you should be able to learn techniques described with other APIs such as OpenGL, Vulkan and DirectX. If you're keen to learn more, look at the books suggested in **references.markdown**.

Conclusion

Thank you again for purchasing *Metal by Tutorials*. If you have any questions or comments as you continue to develop for Metal, please stop by our forums at http://forums.raywenderlich.com.

Your continued support is what makes the tutorials, books, videos and other things we do at raywenderlich.com possible. We truly appreciate it.

Best of luck in all your development and game-making adventures,

– Caroline Begbie (Author), Marius Horga (Author), Adrian Strahan (Tech Editor) and Tammy Coron (FPE).

The *Metal by Tutorials* team

CPSIA information can be obtained
at www.ICGtesting.com
Printed in the USA
LVHW101652210521
688148LV00013B/535